Leisure and Tourism Policy and Planning

Leisure and Tourism Policy and Planning

Second Edition

A.J. Veal

CABI *Publishing*

CABI *Publishing* **is a division of CAB** *International*

CABI Publishing
CAB International
Wallingford
Oxon OX10 8DE
UK

Tel: +44 (0)1491 832111
Fax: +44 (0)1491 833508
E-mail: cabi@cabi.org
Web site: www.cabi-publishing.org

CABI Publishing
10 E 40th Street
Suite 3203
New York, NY 10016
USA

Tel: +1 212 481 7018
Fax: +1 212 686 7993
E-mail: cabi-nao@cabi.org

A catalogue record for this book is available from the British Library, London, UK.

Library of Congress Cataloging-in-Publication Data
Veal, Anthony James.
   Leisure and tourism policy and planning / A.J. Veal.--2nd ed.
      p. cm.
Includes bibliographical references (p.   ).
      ISBN 0-85199-546-2 (alk. paper)
      1. Leisure--Government policy--Great Britain. 2. Tourism--Government policy--Great Britain. 3. Recreation--Great Britain--Planning. I.
Title.
   GV75 .V399 2002
   790'.941--dc21   2002004506

ISBN 0 85199 546 2

Typeset in Palatino by Columns Design Ltd, Reading
Printed and bound in the UK by Biddles Ltd, Guildford and King's Lynn.

Contents

List of Tables

List of Figures

Preface

This book is the second edition of *Leisure Policy and Planning*, published in 1994 by Longman. As well as being updated, it has also been considerably expanded. Tourism has been included more explicitly, as reflected in the change in the title, and a number of topics have been developed in more depth, including human rights, the local state, best value and other aspects of evaluation, and demand-change factors. Much has changed in the public sector environment since the mid-1990s, including changes in party political power in many Western countries, the emergence of new political alignments, intensification of globalization trends and the playing out of a number of experiments in privatization. I have attempted to reflect these changes in the book.

One of the aims of the book is to bridge the gap between theory and practice. This gap has developed in the leisure and tourism studies areas as a result of the necessary growth of academic teaching and research, resulting in increased specialization among researchers. Thus, for example, there are specialists – and associated books and journals – in critical theory and others in planning and marketing. It is my belief that students should be familiar with as wide a range of social and political theory as possible, but should also be able to reconcile that knowledge and awareness with their own current and future roles as competent practising professionals, deploying practical, constructive, analytical skills. So the book includes theoretical and critical material as well as detailed how-to-do-it sections. The aim is therefore to contribute in a modest way to the development of a critically aware and technically competent leisure and tourism management profession.

The book arises from my teaching of public policy at Birmingham University, the Polytechnic (now University) of North London and the University of Technology, Sydney (UTS). Thus, while the intention is for much of the book to be general in nature, it relates particularly to the institutional setting and experiences of Britain and Australia.

I am grateful to the many cohorts of students who have inspired me to develop this text. I would like to acknowledge the contribution of my colleague at UTS, Simon Darcy, who, as my partner in teaching and developing the unit 'Leisure and Public Policy' over a number of years, has provided much encouragement and many valuable insights. I am grateful to Geoff Nichols of the University of Sheffield for helpful and constructive comments on a draft of the book and Ian Cooper for guidance on the UK best-value programme. Finally, I would like to thank Tim Hardwick of CABI *Publishing* for showing faith in the book and nursing it to fruition.

Questions and exercises have been provided at the ends of the chapters. The first few questions are of a revision nature, to check whether the reader has understood and/or retained key ideas from the chapter. Later questions are more in the nature of exercises, requiring further reading and research. A web-site has been established for the book, which contains downloadable versions of some of the graphics and tables, including dollar versions, and, in due course, will contain updates, further reading material and data for exercises. Where statistical information is presented in the book, it generally relates to Great Britain; in some instances, equivalent data for Australia are provided on the web-site. The web-site can be found at: www.business.uts.edu.au/leisure/students/books.html.

Tony Veal
Sydney, January 2002

1

Introduction

Introduction

This book is concerned with the activities of policy-making and planning as carried out by governments and associated agencies in the field of leisure and tourism. Governments are distinguished from the private/commercial and voluntary/not-for-profit sectors, in that they are generally democratically elected and therefore accountable to the public at large and exercise considerable power over citizens and other institutions, albeit within a framework of law. Government, together with a plethora of appointed and elected agencies and an independent judiciary, is referred to as the state or the public sector. The distinction between the public and non-public sectors has, however, become less clear in many fields in recent years as more services traditionally provided by public bodies have been leased and contracted out to private and not-for-profit operators. Such arrangements have, however, been commonplace in the field of leisure and tourism for many years. Public-sector leisure and tourism services have often been provided in whole or in part through contract arrangements or through partnerships in which public bodies have leased buildings or provided grant aid to other organizations. It is hard to think of any type of leisure facility or service which is not provided by public, commercial *and* not-for-profit organizations. For example, golf-courses are provided by local authorities, by commercial companies and by not-for-profit clubs. Theatres are similarly owned and operated by governments at all levels, by com-mercial organizations and by not-for-profit trusts. Tourist attractions, such as heritage sites, are owned and managed by all three sectors. Contracting out of services such as catering and retail outlets and leasing of buildings such as theatres and seasonal swimming-pools to commercial bodies and sporting facilities and heritage sites to the voluntary sector are traditional ways of doing things. There has always been a mixed economy of leisure and tourism. But the scale of change in the last years of the 20th century was substantial, bringing a marked shift away from direct public-sector management and giving rise to much soul-searching as to the appropriate role of the public and private sectors, in leisure and tourism, as in many other sectors.

Governments and Leisure and Tourism

Substantial parts of the leisure industries nevertheless continue to lie within the public domain, including urban and national parks, many sports facilities and events, arts facilities and organizations, public broadcasting, natural and cultural heritage and tourism promotion. Even when private- or voluntary-sector management is involved, public agencies generally retain overall responsibility or provide operating funds and/or land and capital. Local authorities in particular have a wide-ranging responsibility and concern for the economic vitality of the local economy and for the overall quality of life of the community. This involves a broad concern for the level and quality of available leisure services and facilities and for tourism as a sector of economic activity.

In addition, a great deal of leisure and tourism activity is regulated and/or heavily taxed by the local or national state, including entertainment and gambling, the consumption of alcohol and the operation of hotels, restaurants and transport. In Western countries, governments at various levels spend substantial sums each year on leisure and tourism services and also garner substantial sums in the form of duties and taxes on leisure and tourism services. Table 1.1 provides some indication of the economic scale of this activity.

In a primarily capitalist society what is the role of the state in the field of leisure and tourism? Is there a rationale for the particular patterns of state involvement which have evolved? What are the competing philosophies concerning the appropriate role of the state? Why do some fields of leisure apparently merit state involvement while others do not? Who benefits and who loses from the institutions and practices that have

Table 1.1. Government expenditure on leisure.

England and Wales, 2001–2002	*£m*
Arts	1100
Libraries	873
Heritage	145
Broadcasting[†]	105
Parks	590
Sport	660
Tourism promotion	130
Other	155
Total England and Wales (population: 50 million)	3758
Australia, 1999–2000	*A$m**
Libraries and archives	835
Museums	370
Art galleries	156
Cultural venues	184
Cultural heritage	143
Performing arts	178
Broadcasting and film[†]	835
Public halls and civic centres	158
National parks and wildlife services	752
Urban parks, outdoor recreation and sport[‡]	4900
Tourism promotion[§]	480
Other	242
Total Australia (population: 19 million)	9233

Sources: Australian data: Australian Bureau of Statistics: Cultural Funding in Australia, 1999–2000 (cat. no. 4183.0).
* A$1 = £0.38
† Broadcasting: in Australia the cost of the Australian Broadcasting Commission is met from taxation, included here; in the UK the cost of the British Broadcasting Corporation (BBC) is met from license fees, not included here.
‡ 1999 data on urban parks, botanic gardens and sport.
§ Estimate based on Veal and Lynch (2001: 178). England and Wales data are author's own estimate based on: Department for Culture, Media and Sport annual report expenditure plans; Chartered Institute of Public Finance and Accounting Leisure and Recreation Statistics Estimates; and Henry (2001: 75, 97) re Lottery expenditure; and Library and Information Statistics Unit (LISU), Loughborough University re library expenditure.

emerged? Why should the community as a whole, the ratepayers and taxpayers, provide for and subsidize some leisure-time activities but not others? Why should taxpayers pay for the promotion and market-research costs of a largely privately owned industry like tourism? If such state activity is justified, on what scale should it be conducted and what is the appropriate distribution of subsidies, facilities and services? How are decisions made on these matters?

The role of governments in leisure and tourism, as in other fields, has evolved over time, and continues to evolve. Sometimes change comes about gradually, for example by means of Acts of Parliament authorizing additional government expenditure or establishing a new government agency. At other times change is cataclysmic, as in Russia, in 1917, when the Communist revolution resulted in the wholesale takeover of economic activity by the workers' state, and the almost equally cataclysmic return to a mixed economy in 1989/90. But, even when change is gradual, it is rarely achieved without controversy. Some groups gain desired services while others lose, because they are required to pay additional rates or taxes for services from which they feel they do not benefit. Some see particular instances of change as the fulfilment of political promises, others as a betrayal.

The role of governments in general in Western societies is particularly contentious and their role in relation to leisure and tourism is not immune to this contention. Philosophy, political ideology and group interests come into play in the debate, as well as technical arguments about what the market and governments are and are not capable of doing. These philosophical, political and technical issues are addressed in this book.

Leisure and Tourism

This book deals with leisure and tourism, sometimes referring to them separately and sometimes together. Leisure can be defined as 'relatively freely undertaken non-work activity' (Roberts, 1978: 3), while tourism is the 'temporary movement of people to desti-

nations outside their normal places of work and residence' (Mathieson and Wall, 1982: 1). Thus the two phenomena overlap: tourism can be seen as a form of leisure that takes place away from home. However, travel for non-leisure purposes is also often included in tourism, for example business and conference travel – but even these travellers generally make use of leisure facilities at their destination, often mixing business and pleasure. Planning for tourism and research on tourism include consideration of transport and hospitality industries, which are given relatively little consideration in leisure planning and research. While leisure facilities are generally planned primarily to meet the needs of the residents of the local communities in which they are located, many cater both for tourists and for locals. Thus the patrons of a restaurant or the visitors to a museum or beach are likely to be a mixture of local residents and tourists. The overlap can also be seen in the phenomenon of the day-tripper or excursionist who does not stay overnight in a destination and is therefore excluded from many definitions of tourism, but who clearly acts like, and has many of the same demands as, the tourist. The overlaps and relationships are illustrated in Fig. 1.1. Thus, while much of the discussion in the book is equally applicable to leisure and tourism, occasionally a distinction is made between the two phenomena.

There are substantial differences between leisure studies and tourism studies. In general the discourse of tourism studies sees the phenomenon as an industry and holiday-makers as customers. In contrast, much discussion of leisure as a whole sees leisure services as a social service and leisure participants as clients or citizens. While it is recognized that the bulk of leisure services are provided by the private sector, the emphasis on the public sector remains strong in leisure studies. The consequence of these differing traditions, which have resulted in separate public institutions, separate professions and often separate university departments and courses, is that the holiday and tourism have generally been ignored by leisure scholars and tourism scholars have not actively pursued the link between tourism and leisure. This partial divorce

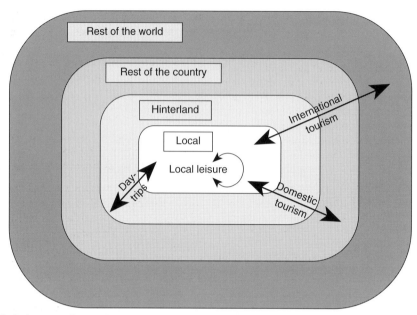

Fig. 1.1. Leisure, tourism and geography.

between the two areas of study has persisted, resulting in curious gaps in research in the two fields. Thus holidays, whether involving travel or not, are the most significant blocks of leisure time enjoyed by the individual but they are generally ignored by leisure scholars, even though inequality, a significant theme in leisure research, is a highly salient issue as far as access to holidays is concerned. Many tourist attractions are in fact leisure facilities or services serving primarily host-community residents, but the significance of this is generally ignored (Crompton, 2000). Much of the research on what has traditionally been referred to as outdoor recreation is in fact concerned with tourist trips, but this is generally downplayed (Veal, 1997: 21). Because of these differing traditions, tourism and leisure are often referred to in this book, as elsewhere in the literature, as separate phenomena.

Policy-making and Planning

An overall framework for viewing the leisure and tourism service delivery system is presented in Fig. 1.2. The framework consists of five elements:

1. People – individuals/households/communities.
2. Organizations – public- and private-sector organizations involved in the provision of leisure and tourism facilities and services, including voluntary organizations, commercial companies and governments and their agencies, including elected and appointed members and senior and strategic management personnel.
3. Leisure and tourism services/facilities – including their complement of line managers and 'front-line' staff.
4. The environment – the natural and built physical environment.
5. The processes – which link these various elements, including planning, marketing, political processes and the use, purchase and consumption of services, and which take place along the three links labelled Sociopolitical, Managerial and Socio-economic.

The essence of the framework is the linkages between the elements. Between any two elements there is a two-way flow of influence and activity. The nature of the processes, or at least their names, varies, depending on whether they relate to the public or private sector:

1. Socio-political link, between the public and organizations. The flows are as follows:

- Commercial sector: from the organization to the public: commercial organizations engage in the processes of market research, gathering information about markets, and public relations, designed to influence the public's views about the firm; from the public to organizations: the provision of market research information about preferences and, in some cases, campaigning against commercial activities.
- Public sector: the political process, including political campaigning, voting, lobbying and public participation in decision-making.
- Non-profit sector: combines features of commercial and public sectors.

2. Managerial link, between organizations and the leisure facilities/services. The flows are as follows:

- From organizations to leisure facilities/services: the processes of planning, developing and managing.
- To organizations from leisure facilities/services: income and profits (or losses).

3. Socio-economic link, between the public and leisure facilities/services:

- Here the process of selling and promotion takes place and the process of using or not using the facility or service provided.

The (physical) environment is represented as a background, but all-pervasive, element of the system and includes the urban, rural and natural environment. It is there as an entity in its own right; it is the object of policy, a constraint on activity and a resource which is used for leisure and tourism. When a part of the environment gets taken over and managed for leisure or tourism it becomes part of the facilities/services element.

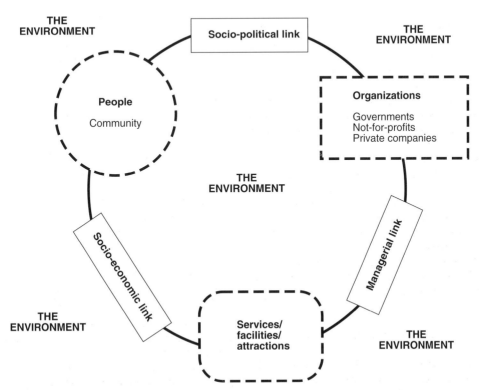

Fig. 1.2. A social, political, economic and managerial framework for viewing leisure and tourism service delivery processes.

The framework demonstrates that leisure and tourism facilities and services are not just there – they arise as a result of interaction between the public, as users and as political/social groups, and organizations and their activities. The framework also illustrates the idea that both public- and private-sector provision exists within the same basic framework, although the relationships between the elements vary. Finally, the framework shows the interconnectedness of the elements in the system and places various processes – politics, planning, design, marketing, market research, management – in context.

The emphasis of the book is therefore on the socio-political link, where the activities of policy-making and planning are mostly to be found. However, much of the book is concerned with generating and analysing information from the other links, concerning people's needs and behaviour, and management practices.

In this context, therefore, policy is concerned with the ongoing principles and broad goals that guide the actions of a government body. Thus a government might have policies concerning equity among social groups, or a policy to support mass participation in sport rather than élite sports, or to promote long-stay visitors rather than day-trippers. Planning, while, in practice, overlapping considerably with policy-making, is seen here as the process by which decisions are made as to the optimum way to implement policies and achieve goals. The term planning is used in a wide range of day-to-day contexts, but here it is intended to refer to a formal activity. Henry Mintzberg (1994: 12) defines such planning as 'a formalised procedure to produce an articulated result, in the form of an integrated system of decisions'. By articulated he means that the results of the exercise must be communicated to interested parties – generally in the form of a written report. An 'integrated system of decisions' indicates that we are dealing with complex matters, usually involving a number of stakeholders and contingent decisions and action.

Government Roles

In Western-style liberal democracies, governments provide and administer the law, which controls, or places limits on, individual and collective behaviour, but are also involved in the economic activity of delivering goods and services. While most economic activity takes place in the market or non-government sector, typically about 30% is accounted for by government activity. The rationale for this activity, particularly as it applies to leisure and tourism, is discussed in some detail in Chapter 4; here we consider the range and types of government activity in general terms. The types of involvement of governments in leisure and tourism activities are indicated in Table 1.2. At one extreme this involves promotion of certain activities, such as sport and the arts, via subsidy or direct provision of facilities. At the other extreme some activities are prohibited, such as the use of certain recreational drugs and cruel sports. In between, legislation and taxation can be used to support or regulate leisure activities in a variety of ways.

Perspective

The framework outlined above is functionalist in nature; in an informal way it uses the metaphor of a biological system or machine to represent society and suggests that society can function smoothly when the various interacting elements behave in certain ways – although it does not imply that this is guaranteed or automatic, the system will malfunction if the various elements fail to interact in certain ways. Chronic malfunctioning of the system results in unsustainability, an issue that has become particularly prominent in discussion of tourism in recent years. It should, however, be stressed that the framework is just a metaphor, an aid to thinking. It is illustrative of certain features of society only: it clearly cannot represent all aspects of society and its operation. Such a functionalist approach has been unfashionable among some theorists and commentators in the field of leisure studies in recent

Table. 1.2. The range of government involvement in leisure and tourism.

Sectors	Types of government involvement			
	Promotion /provision	Support	Regulation/control	Prohibition
Sport	Subsidy/funding to sporting bodies Direct provision of sport facilities/ services (usually subsidized)		Sports drug-testing Animal treatment regulations	Cruel sports Prohibited performance-enhancing drugs
Outdoor/environment/ heritage	Provision of parks Ownership and conservation of natural and historic assets	Protective legislation		Protection of rare species Export bans on species/ heritage
Arts/broadcasting	Subsidy/funding to arts bodies Direct provision of cultural facilities and services (usually subsidized)		Censorship	Export bans on art heritage
Social activities	Some direct provision (e.g. sea fronts, community centres)		Alcohol licensing/taxation Gambling licensing/taxation Prostitution/brothels control	Recreational drugs
Tourism	Funding of tourism promotion agencies Ownership/conservation/provision/ marketing of natural, heritage, arts facilities/services	Trade missions/embassies	Airline/air-traffic regulation Immigration/passports	
All sectors		Training/education Research funding Charitable status Enabling legislation for local authorities	Safety regulations – individual/crowd/venues Noise regulations Town/country planning	

years and is roundly condemned in a number of texts (e.g. Jarvie and Maguire, 1994: 5–28; Wearing, 1998: 1–21). A number of theoretical positions in the social sciences see contemporary society as being chronically dysfunctional and rife with conflict and division. This view reflects emancipatory philosophies, such as Marxism and some radical forms of feminism, which call for radical changes in the way society is organized – in particular, the wholesale replacement of capitalism by some form of socialism. Such perspectives see little point in the development of practices that seek to improve the operation of a fundamentally flawed system.

It is a premise of this book, however, that contemporary Western society is, on balance, more functional than dysfunctional. Clearly it does not function anywhere near perfectly and does not function automatically, but only as a result of the considerable efforts of many people and organizations. It must also be recognized that the system involves a number of tensions and mixed blessings. For example, the extraordinary productive power of capitalism produces considerable threats to the environment; and the very basis of the system – private investment, risk and reward – produces great disparities in income and wealth, which welfare and income-redistribution policies only go some way towards ameliorating. A functional world is therefore not the same as a perfect world. In this book, it is assumed that governments have a legitimate role in seeking to improve an imperfect system and that part of that role involves a concern for the provision of leisure and tourism services and the provision of a regulatory framework for the delivery of many of these services.

Another theoretical perspective that would raise doubts about the value of many of the practices advocated in this book is postmodernism, a view of contemporary society that rejects the idea of social progress. In this book, it is assumed that society can indeed progress and improve through incremental change and that existing institutional structures, while far from perfect, are capable of achieving and accommodating such change or can be reformed to do so. Any

other position would, arguably, be hypocritical, since there would be no point in developing public policy and planning procedures for a society that required to be radically and fundamentally changed or where the ideas of progress or improvement were meaningless. This stance should not, however, be interpreted as being complacent or simply supportive of the status quo. There is a continuum between, at one extreme, a conservatism that sees no need for change of any sort and, at the other extreme, a radicalism that wishes to see the system completely replaced. This book occupies the middle ground; it presents analytical tools designed to achieve improvement in the well-being of communities, in terms of supporting human rights, improving health and achieving greater equity as well as efficiency.

In Chapter 3, a wide range of differing views is explored concerning the appropriate role of the state, from complete state control to a minimalist, roll back the state, view. This book is predicated on a middle-road perspective. While not necessarily accepting the rhetoric of recent third-way politics (Giddens, 1998), the stance is broadly consistent with traditional social democratic ideals, on which third-way ideas are a variation (Veal, 1998). The environment in which leisure professionals in the Western world work is a basically capitalist one, but a strong and essential role is played by the state; and part of that role is legitimately concerned with the provision of leisure and tourism services. That role can be enhanced, and society benefited, by the exercise of certain analytical skills that are directed at a better understanding of community leisure and tourism needs and demands and their more effective and efficient satisfaction.

The development of the public sector of leisure and tourism has not been the result only of the actions of elected governments. Professionals involved directly in the area have also been influential. Professionals work as public servants at national, regional and local level – sometimes referred to as the state bureaucracy – and for the private and not-for-profit sectors, and in academe. They conduct the research and establish the terms of discourse in the field and they produce the reports and policy recommendations that are often the basis of political decisions. Then they are responsible for implementing the decisions and managing the facilities and services, or imposing the regulations, which ensue. Considerable power is therefore exercised by such professionals (Coalter, 1988: 177–180; Bacon, 1989; Henry, 1993: 110–137). This text is concerned with the skills that such professionals bring to their tasks. A number of texts exist that are concerned with leisure management, where the emphasis is primarily on the efficient and effective operation of facilities and services once they are established; this text is concerned with the prior stage of formulating policies and plans, and evaluating their implementation as an input to further policy and plan formulation.

Content and Structure of the Book

Two topics of importance to public policy are not covered in this book, partly for reasons of space and partly because they are adequately covered elsewhere. The first of these is the question of history. There is no doubt that the current patterns of public and non-profit leisure and tourism services and the values and practices that surround them are the result of certain patterns of historical evolution, particularly dating from the industrial revolution. This history has been well documented in a number of texts, including those by Bailey (1979), Cunningham (1980), Coalter (1988) and Henry (1993, 2001). The historical perspective alerts us to the fact that public policy has been as much about controlling leisure and tourism, through laws and regulation, as it has been about providing facilities and services, and that decisions on what to provide and what not to provide, and what to regulate and what not to regulate, reflect the relative power of various interests and classes in the political decision-making process. This historical legacy has on-going consequences in terms of which groups have access to facilities and services of their choice and which do not.

Secondly, the book does not consider political behaviour in any detail. While political ideology, and the role of urban-growth regimes, public participation and community consultation are considered, the role of pressure groups and parties, the relative powers of national, regional and local government and the processes by which political decisions are made are acknowledged but not analysed in detail. For coverage of these important topics, the reader is referred to other sources, including Limb (1986), Coalter (1988), Bramham *et al.* (1993) and Henry (1993, 2001).

Among the most widely accepted roles of governments is the duty to uphold and protect human rights and to ensure that the basic needs of their citizens are met. In Chapter 2, therefore, the status of leisure as a right and a need is examined. In Chapter 3 competing ideas about the right and proper role of the state in society, and in relation to leisure in particular, are examined from the point of view of various political ideologies. In Chapter 4 the ideas of mainstream economics are examined, since they underpin much of the thinking of the centre to right of political thought and provide the basis for economics-based analysis of state activities. Chapter 5 provides an introduction to government processes and public decision-making processes. Chapter 6 examines guidelines for the leisure and tourism planning process, and outlines the rational-comprehensive decision-making process as a framework for planning and policy-making. Chapter 7 considers a range of specific techniques and approaches that can be utilized in preparing leisure and tourism plans. Chapter 8 is concerned with leisure-demand estimation and forecasting techniques. Chapter 9 presents an introduction to two economics-based techniques used in leisure and tourism planning and decision-making, namely cost–benefit analysis and economic impact analysis. Chapter 10, on performance appraisal, is concerned with evaluation of policies and plans once implemented, and how the information generated from such a process is utilized in further rounds of policy formulation and plan-making. Throughout the book there is a tendency to deal with leisure as a whole and with the public or the community as a whole, whereas, in fact, leisure consists of a number of very different activities and sectors and the community consists of numerous groups, with differing resource needs and tastes. The final chapter gives specific attention to these sectors and groups.

Summary

- In this chapter, it is noted that, while tourism can be seen conceptually as primarily a form of leisure, there are significant differences between leisure and tourism and between leisure studies and tourism studies.
- While marked changes took place in the balance between the public and private sectors in the last couple of decades of the 20th century, the public sector remains a significant force in the planning and provision of leisure and tourism services in most Western countries.
- A framework is presented for viewing government activity in a systems context, involving: the public as consumers, clients and members of the political system; public-, commercial- and non-profit-sector organizations; and facilities and services planned and managed by organizations.
- While recognizing the need for critical analysis of the rationale for government activity, the book is premised on the belief that public-sector activity to ensure certain leisure and tourism services in the context of a market economy is legitimate.

2

Leisure and Tourism: Rights, Needs and Citizenship

Introduction

It can be argued that, philosophically, the reason why governments should be involved in leisure and tourism is that leisure and travel are rights or needs and it is the job of governments to protect the rights of its citizens and to ensure that their needs are satisfied. If leisure and travel are seen as human rights and as important human needs, it might be thought that this would provide powerful support for government involvement to ensure adequate levels of provision and minimization of constraints. As indicated in the rest of the book, however, public policy-making is generally a very pragmatic matter, influenced by practical politics, power relationships, availability of resources and technical considerations. But this does not mean that principles and values are irrelevant or should be ignored: hence the discussion of the two concepts of rights and needs in this chapter and of political ideology in the next chapter. In this chapter we examine the concepts of human rights, citizen rights and human need, their complex and contested nature and their implications for public policy, particularly governments' leisure and tourism policies.

Human Rights

Definitions

The *Shorter Oxford English Dictionary* defines a right as a 'justifiable claim, on legal or moral grounds, to have or obtain something, or to act in a certain way'. Thus a right is seen as something which must be claimed by an individual or group and, in turn, be recognized by others as legitimate. Human rights are those rights which all human beings are deemed to be entitled to on the basis of their humanity alone (Donnelly, 1989: 12). Statements of human rights are statements of belief or commitment; they are therefore political and moral in nature. In the 20th century a range of human rights came to be widely recognized, particularly by governments, through various national and international legal instruments.

History

An early exemplification of the idea that people might have rights in the area of leisure can be seen in 16th-century England. Queen Elizabeth I, while a Protestant, did not approve of the extreme Protestants, later known as Puritans, who attempted, through their influence on city councils and the Parliament, to restrict public leisure activity according to the puritan moral code. In 1585 the Queen:

> quashed a Puritan Bill aimed at banning all sports and entertainments on Sundays. The Queen felt that her people had a right to spend their only day of rest enjoying themselves as they pleased, without interference from killjoys … The Puritan authorities in several cities, especially London, held the theatre in special odium, and made strenuous efforts to suppress play-going, as it drew people away from the churches. The Queen sympathised with the theatre-goers … When, in 1575, she discovered

that the renowned Coventry cycle of mystery plays had been banned by the Puritan authorities in that city, she ordered them to be restored. The Puritans in London then began complaining that theatre-goers in the City helped spread the plague that was endemic each summer. In 1583, the Corporation of London closed the theatres on the Surrey shore, but Elizabeth retaliated by forming her own company of players, who became known as The Queen's Men. The civic authorities backed down, but in 1597 they eventually persuaded the Council to agree to close down the theatres on the grounds that they were hotbeds of subversive propaganda against the government. When Elizabeth heard, she was furious, and the Council hastily rescinded the order. There were no further threats to the theatre in her reign.

(Weir, 1999: 56–57)

These 16th-century events can be interpreted as involving a conflict between the supporters of the idea of people's leisure rights as opposed to the morally based views and interests of particular groups. The view of history that has become part of the leisure-studies tradition has tended to see the battles over curtailment of many forms of leisure in 18th- and 19th-century England as a conflict between the undisciplined traditions and natural proclivities of the working class, on the one hand, and the requirements of capital for a disciplined, sober workforce, on the other (Bailey, 1979). Such an interpretation of events has been largely unquestioned in the field of leisure studies for a couple of decades, but it does not explain, for example, why employers appeared to have led the way in granting holidays with pay (Pimlott, 1976: 156–157). Neither does it fully explain the history of the opposition to drink, which came from middle-class, religiously motivated, reform groups and from working-class groups (Harrison, 1967), rather than from capitalists, for whom the sale of alcohol was a growing source of profit. And it does not explain why conflict over undesirable leisure activities, such as gambling and recreational drug use, continues to this day, when the establishment of a disciplined industrial workforce has long been achieved. These conflicts can also be viewed, then, at least in part, as a struggle between groups with differing views of human rights and freedoms.

The clash between capital and labour can, however, be seen in the campaigns for shorter working hours (first for a 10-hour working day, then for an 8-hour day) which arose in Europe in the 19th-century in response to the inordinately long working hours demanded by factory owners. While health, self-improvement and family life, rather than leisure *per se*, were often advanced as justification for reductions in working hours, eventually, Gary Cross (1990: 83) notes: 'workers no longer felt the need to justify their leisure on family or moral grounds. The American slogan "Eight Hours for What We Will" expressed this attitude clearly. Leisure was a right that required no rationale.' He further notes that 'short-hour activists' often linked their demands to the 'rights of "free born Englishmen"' and to the proposition that "all citizens had an equal right to personal liberty"' (Cross, 1990: 77). In a pamphlet entitled *The Right to be Lazy*, originally published in France in 1848, Paul Lafargue stated:

> If … the working class were to rise up in its terrible strength, not to demand the Rights of Man, which are but the rights of capitalist exploitation, not to demand the Right to Work, which is but the right to misery, but to forge a brazen law forbidding any man to work more than three hours a day, the earth, the old earth, trembling with joy would feel a new universe leaping within her.
>
> (Lafargue, 1958: 114)

These examples demonstrate that the idea of rights associated with leisure has certain historical roots, albeit of an ad hoc nature. But they can be seen as reflections of a wider development of the modern idea of human rights as a philosophical principle, which emerged from 17th-century Europe as a reaction against the arbitrary exercise of power by rulers and as an element of liberal thinking (Donnelly, 1989: 89).

One of the most famous declarations of human rights was contained in the 1776 American Declaration of Independence, which stated:

> We hold these truths to be self-evident: that all men are created equal; that they are endowed by their Creator with certain inalienable rights; that among these are life, liberty and the pursuit of happiness.

The reference to the 'pursuit of happiness' is one of earliest indications of a formal recognition of leisure as a human right, although, of course, leisure is only one means by which people might pursue happiness. In the intervening years, further declarations have located leisure and travel more firmly in the context of human rights.

Human rights declarations

The contemporary successor to the ideals of the American Declaration of Independence is the Universal Declaration of Human Rights, adopted by the United Nations (UN) in 1948. Leisure received explicit recognition in Articles 24 and 27 of the Declaration and the right to travel was recognized in Article 13. The 1966 International Covenant on Economic, Social and Cultural Rights made specific reference to holidays with pay and the 1989 UN Convention of the Rights of the Child specifically recognized children's right to play. These references are presented in Box 2.1. Since all the members of the UN are signatories to these declarations, it might reasonably be assumed that all national governments recognize leisure, travel and play as rights and accept a responsibility to uphold those rights. However, as Donnelly (1989: 42) states, 'The sad fact is that in the contemporary world virtually all internationally recognised human rights are regularly and systematically violated.'

Article 24 is one of a group of four in the Universal Declaration which deal with economic rights, including social security, the right to work and acceptable conditions of work, to equal pay for equal work and 'just and favourable remuneration' and to a decent standard of living, including 'food, clothing, housing and medical care and necessary social services, and the right to security in the event of unemployment, sickness, disability, widowhood, old age or other lack of livelihood'. In considering this group of declared rights in contrast to the more familiar political and civil rights, David Harvey comments as follows.

> What is striking about these articles … is the degree to which hardly any attention has been paid over the last fifty years to their implementation or application and how almost all countries that were signatories to the Universal Declaration are in gross violation of these articles. Strict enforcement of such rights would entail massive and in some senses revolutionary transformations in the political-economy of capitalism. Neoliberalism could easily be cast, for example, as a gross violation of human rights.
>
> (Harvey, 2000: 89–90)

This conclusion is perhaps ironic given the origins of the idea of human rights in Western liberal philosophy, as mentioned above.

Cranston (1973: 5) argues that rights can be divided into positive rights, which are enshrined in national law, and moral rights, which are not so enshrined. He uses the example of Article 13 of the Universal Declaration, relating to freedom of travel, which was consistently violated by the USA and the then Soviet Union during the Cold War and by South Africa during the apartheid era, to make the distinction.

> Clearly, therefore, the right to leave any country, which the United Nations Declaration says 'everyone' has, is not a positive right. The intention of the sponsors of that declaration was to specify something that everyone *ought* to have. In other words the rights they named were moral rights.
>
> (Cranston, 1973: 6)

The declarations on leisure and culture could similarly be termed moral rights, since they do not specify the amount of leisure time that is considered acceptable, or what constitutes reasonable limitation of working hours, or the amount of paid holidays or public holidays. Only some of these matters are codified in the laws of some countries and the details vary from country to country. Indeed, some critics have suggested that such declarations are not in fact universal in application, but relate primarily to developed countries with the resources to implement them.

Leisure rights

More detailed declarations exist in relation to leisure and in relation to different aspects of

Box 2.1. UN Declarations on Human Rights and Leisure
Source: www.un.org/rights/.

1948: The Universal Declaration of Human Rights

Article 24:   Everyone has the right to rest and leisure, including reasonable limitation of working hours and periodic holidays with pay.

Article 27:   Everyone has the right freely to participate in the cultural life of the community, to enjoy the arts and to share in scientific advancement and its benefits.

1966: International Covenant on Economic, Social and Cultural Rights

Article 7:   The 'right of everyone to the enjoyment of just and favourable conditions of work', includes the right to: 'Rest, leisure, reasonable limitation of working hours and periodic holidays with pay, as well as remuneration for public holidays.'

1975: Declaration on the Rights of Disabled Persons

Article 3:   Disabled persons have the inherent right to respect for their human dignity. Disabled persons, whatever the origin, nature and seriousness of their handicaps and disabilities, have the same fundamental rights as their fellow-citizens of the same age, which implies first and foremost the right to enjoy a decent life, as normal and full as possible.

Article 8:   Disabled persons are entitled to have their special needs taken into consideration at all stages of economic and social planning.

1979: Convention on the Elimination of All Forms of Discrimination against Women

Article 3:   States Parties shall take in all fields, in particular in the political, social, economic and cultural fields, all appropriate measures, including legislation, to ensure the full development and advancement of women, for the purpose of guaranteeing them the exercise and enjoyment of human rights and fundamental freedoms on a basis of equality with men.

Article 5:   States Parties shall take all appropriate measures ... to modify the social and cultural patterns of conduct of men and women, with a view to achieving the elimination of prejudices and customary and all other practices which are based on the idea of the inferiority or the superiority of either of the sexes or on stereotyped roles for men and women.

Article 10: States Parties shall take all appropriate measures to eliminate discrimination against women in order to ensure to them equal rights with men in the field of education and in particular to ensure, on a basis of equality of men and women ... the same opportunities to participate actively in sports and physical education.

Article 13: States Parties shall take all appropriate measures to eliminate discrimination against women in other areas of economic and social life in order to ensure, on a basis of equality of men and women, the same rights, in particular ... (c) The right to participate in recreational activities, sports and all aspects of cultural life.

Continued

Box 2.1 continued

1989: Convention on the Rights of the Child

Article 31:   1. States Parties recognize the right of the child to rest and leisure, to engage in play and recreational activities appropriate to the age of the child and to participate freely in cultural life and the arts.
2. States Parties shall respect and promote the right of the child to participate fully in cultural and artistic life and shall encourage the provision of appropriate and equal opportunities for cultural, artistic, recreational and leisure activity.

1989: Convention Concerning Indigenous and Tribal Peoples in Independent Countries

Article 2:   1. Governments shall have the responsibility for developing, with the participation of the peoples concerned, co-ordinated and systematic action to protect the rights of these peoples and to guarantee respect for their integrity.
2. Such action shall include measures for:
a. ensuring that members of these peoples benefit on an equal footing from the rights and opportunities which national laws and regulations grant to other members of the population;
b. promoting the full realisation of the social, economic and cultural rights of these peoples with respect for their social and cultural identity, their customs and traditions and their institutions;

Article 5:   In applying the provisions of this Convention:
a. the social, cultural, religious and spiritual values and practices of these peoples shall be recognised and protected, and due account shall be taken of the nature of the problems which face them both as groups and as individuals;
b. the integrity of the values, practices and institutions of these peoples shall be respected.

1999: Declaration on the Rights of Persons Belonging to National or Ethnic, Religious or Linguistic Minorities

Article 2:   1. Persons belonging to national or ethnic, religious and linguistic minorities (hereinafter referred to as persons belonging to minorities) have the right to enjoy their own culture, to profess and practise their own religion, and to use their own language, in private and in public, freely and without interference or any form of discrimination.
2. Persons belonging to minorities have the right to participate effectively in cultural, religious, social, economic and public life.

Article 4:   Persons belonging to minorities have the right to establish and maintain their own associations.

leisure. The *Charter for Leisure* (Box 2.2), drawn up by the international organization World Leisure in 1970 and revised in 2000, declares leisure to be a right, extols the virtues of leisure and exhorts governments to make provision for leisure as a social service, but it stops short of declaring access to leisure facilities and services as a right.

Sporting rights

Various bodies have declared the practice of sport to be a right (see Box 2.3), including the International Olympic Committee, the UN Educational, Scientific and Cultural Organization (UNESCO) and the Council of Europe. As with the World Leisure charter,

Box 2.2. World Leisure: *Charter for Leisure*

Approved by the World Leisure Board of Directors, July 2000. The original version was adopted by the International Recreation Association in 1970, and subsequently revised by its successor, the World Leisure and Recreation Association in 1979. See: www.worldleisure.org

Introduction

Consistent with the Universal Declaration of Human Rights (Article 27), all cultures and societies recognise to some extent the right to rest and leisure. Here, because personal freedom and choice are central elements of leisure, individuals can freely choose their activities and experiences, many of them leading to substantial benefits for person and community.

Articles

1. All people have a basic human right to leisure activities that are in harmony with the norms and social values of their compatriots. All governments are obliged to recognise and protect this right of its citizens.
2. Provisions for leisure for the quality of life are as important as those for health and education. Governments should ensure their citizens a variety of accessible leisure and recreational opportunities of the highest quality.
3. The individual is his/her best leisure and recreational resource. Thus, governments should ensure the means for acquiring those skills and understandings necessary to optimize leisure experiences.
4. Individuals can use leisure opportunities for self-fulfilment, developing personal relationships, improving social integration, developing communities and cultural identity as well as promoting international understanding and co-operation and enhancing quality of life.
5. Governments should ensure the future availability of fulfilling leisure experiences by maintaining the quality of their country's physical, social and cultural environment.
6. Governments should ensure the training of professionals to help individuals acquire personal skills, discover and develop their talents and to broaden their range of leisure and recreational opportunities.
7. Citizens must have access to all forms of leisure information about the nature of leisure and its opportunities, using it to enhance their knowledge and inform decisions on local and national policy.
8. Educational institutions must make every effort to teach the nature and importance of leisure and how to integrate this knowledge into personal lifestyle.

these declarations envisage a major role for governments in coordinating, planning and providing for sport. The *Sport for All Charter* has received the formal endorsement of the member governments of the Council of Europe and individual member countries have generally adopted Sport for All policies, which the Council of Europe monitors through a permanent committee. The idea of the general right to participate in sport has not been the subject of much attention in the scholarly literature: attention in the area of sport and human rights has been concentrated on racial, ethnic and gender discrimi-

nation, primarily in relation to élite-level sport (Taylor, 2000). However, if denial of access to sporting opportunity for particular social groups is considered an infringement of human rights, this implies the acceptance of a general right to participate.

Artistic and cultural rights

The arts are explicitly recognized in Article 27 of the Universal Declaration in the reference to the right to 'participation in the cultural life of the community' and to 'enjoy

Box 2.3. Declarations on the Right to Sport

Sources: UN: www.un.org/rights; *Sport for All Charter* (Council of Europe, 1978); Council of Europe: www.coe.int

The Olympic Charter

Article 1:   The practice of sport is a human right. Every individual must have the possibility of practising sport in accordance with his or her needs (International Olympic Committee, 1995: 1, and at: www.olympic.org)

1978: UNESCO International Charter of Physical Education and Sport

Article 1:   The practice of physical education and sport is a fundamental right for all.
Article 2:   Physical education and sport form an essential element of lifelong education in the overall education system.
Article 3:   Physical education and sport programmes must meet individual and social needs.
Article 4:   Teaching, coaching and administration of physical education and sport should be performed by qualified personnel.
Article 5:   Adequate facilities and equipment are essential to physical education and sport.
Article 6:   Research and evaluation are indispensable components of the development of physical education and sport.
Article 7:   Information and documentation help to promote physical education and sport.
Article 8:   The mass media should exert a positive influence on physical education and sport.
Article 9:   National institutions play a major role in physical education and sport.
Article 10:   International cooperation is a prerequisite for the universal and well-balanced promotion of physical education and sport.
Source: UNESCO (1982)

1976: European Sport for All Charter

Article I: Every individual shall have the right to participate in sport.

1992: European Sports Charter

Article 1:   *Aim of the Charter*
Governments, with a view to the promotion of sport as an important factor in human development, shall take the steps necessary to apply the provisions of this charter in accordance with the principles set out in the Code of Sports Ethics in order:
1. To enable every individual to participate in sport and notably:
   a. to ensure that all young people should have the opportunity to receive physical education instruction and the opportunity to acquire basic sports skills;
   b. to ensure that everyone should have the opportunity to take part in sport and physical recreation in a safe and healthy environment; and, in co-operation with the appropriate sports organizations:
   c. to ensure that everyone with the interest and ability should have the opportunity to improve their standard of performance in sport and reach levels of personal achievement and/or publicly recognised levels of excellence;
2. To protect and develop the moral and ethical bases of sport, and the human dignity and safety of those involved in sport, by safeguarding sport, sportsmen and women from exploitation from political, commercial and financial gain, and from practices that are abusive or debasing, including the abuse of drugs.

Continued

Box 2.3 continued

Article 3:   The Sports Movement
1. The role of the public authorities is primarily complementary to the action of the sports movement. Therefore, close co-operation with non-governmental sports organizations is essential in order to ensure the fulfilment of the aims of this Charter, including where necessary the establishment of machinery for the development and co-ordination of sport.
2. The development of the voluntary ethos and movement in sport shall be encouraged, particularly through support for the work of voluntary sports organizations.
3. Voluntary sports organizations have the right to establish autonomous decision-making processes within the law. Both governments and sports organizations shall recognise the need for a mutual respect of their decisions.
4. The implementation of some of the provisions of this Charter may be entrusted to governmental or non-governmental sports authorities or sports organizations.
5. Sports organizations should be encouraged to establish mutually beneficial arrangements with each other and with potential partners, such as the commercial sector, the media, etc, while ensuring that exploitation of sport or sports people is avoided.

Article 4:   Facilities and Activities
1. No discrimination on the grounds of sex, race, colour, language, religion, political or other opinion, national or social origin, association with a national minority, property, birth or other status, shall be permitted in the access to sports facilities or to sports activities.
2. Measures shall be taken to ensure that all citizens have opportunities to take part in sport and, where necessary, additional measures shall be taken aimed at enabling both young gifted people, but also disadvantaged or disabled individuals or groups to be able to exercise such opportunities effectively.
3. Since the scale of participation in sport is dependent in part on the extent, the variety and the accessibility of facilities, their overall planning shall be accepted as a matter for public authorities. The range of facilities to be provided shall take account of public, private, commercial and other facilities which are available. Those responsible shall take account of national, regional and local requirements, and incorporate measures designed to ensure good management and their safe and full use.
4. Appropriate steps should be taken by the owners of sports facilities to enable disadvantaged persons including those with physical or mental disabilities to have access to such facilities.

Article 5:   Building the Foundation
Appropriate steps shall be taken to develop physical fitness and the acquisition of basic sports skills and to encourage the practice of sport by young people, notably:
1. by ensuring that programmes of and facilities for sport, recreation and physical education are made available to all pupils and that appropriate time is set aside for this;
2. by ensuring the training of qualified teachers in this area at all schools;
3. by ensuring that appropriate opportunities exist for continuing the practice of sport after compulsory education.

Article 6:   Developing Participation
1. The practice of sport, whether it be for the purpose of leisure and recreation, of health promotion, or of improving performance, shall be promoted for all parts of the population through the provision of appropriate facilities and programmes of all kinds and of qualified instructors, leaders or 'animateurs'.

the arts'. Donald Horne, in *The Public Culture* (1986: 232–237), produced a 'declaration of "cultural rights"', consisting of rights to access to the human cultural heritage, rights to new art and rights to community art participation. Statements about the right to participate 'freely in the cultural life of the community' and the right to 'enjoy the arts' are even more vague than those relating to leisure. If culture includes popular culture, then the statement is hardly worth making since popular culture is, by definition, enjoyed by the mass of the population. If culture and the arts refer to high culture, then, as Harvey (2000: 89–90) suggests, most countries could be said to violate these rights on a wide scale, since such participation and enjoyment are generally highly skewed in favour of the better-off groups in society. Most governments would point to programmes of subsidy and free services, such as public broadcasting, but the result is often still a pattern of minority participation and enjoyment. As user-pays policies are pursued in public services, this becomes more and more pronounced. Again, such situations are never spoken of in terms of violation of human rights.

Tourism and travel rights

In the area of tourism, the right to holidays with pay and the right to freedom of travel, for any purpose, are enshrined in the Universal Declaration and reiterated in a number of subsequent declarations, as indicated in Box 2.4. Of particular note is the *Global Code of Ethics for Tourism* promulgated by the World Tourism Organization in 1998, which extends the idea of rights in this area to 'the discovery and enjoyment of the planet's resources', to conditions of work in the tourism industry and to the right of host communities not to be exploited by tourism.

The right to holidays with pay illustrates the moral rights/positive rights distinction. Even among the most highly developed economies, holiday entitlements vary substantially – workers in the USA and Japan,

for example, enjoy only about half the entitlements of workers in Europe. But there are no claims that American and Japanese workers' human rights are therefore being violated. As noted in Chapter 1, the study of tourism has been less public-sector-orientated than the study of leisure, so the idea of the holiday as a right, which might parallel the idea of leisure services as a right, is not a significant feature of debates in the tourism literature. An exception among tourism researchers is Krippendorf, who states:

> What our society offers routine-weary people is tourism, a variety of holidays outside the everyday world, extolling them as escape-aids, problem-solvers, suppliers of strength, energy, new lifeblood and happiness. The get-away offer should be accessible to everyone. After the 'right to holidays', the 'right to holiday travel' has now become a socio-political issue: tourism for all social classes.
> (Krippendorf, 1987: 17)

He does not, however, indicate where or with whom these matters have become a 'socio-political issue'.

A further exception to the rule is the idea of social tourism. While the term is occasionally used in a different sense, here it refers to the practice of social-security organizations providing for people in various disadvantaged situations to take a holiday away from home (Finch, 1975). This practice, less common than it once was, can be seen as extending the right to a holiday to those who would otherwise be denied. It merits a passing mention in the *Global Code of Ethics for Tourism*, but only as something which 'should be developed'. The concept is discussed further in Chapter 11.

Group rights

Campaigns for equal or special rights have been mounted by or on behalf of numerous social groups with varying degrees of success, a number having been the subject of UN declarations, as shown in Box 2.1. In this section we consider rights as they relate to children, women, people with disabilities and ethnic minorities and indigenous peoples.

Box 2.4. Declarations on Rights to Travel, Holidays and Tourism
Source: World Tourism Organization, at: www.world-tourism.org

1948: The Universal Declaration of Human Rights

Article 13: Everyone has the right to leave any country, including his own, and to return to his country.
Article 24: Everyone has the right to rest and leisure, including reasonable limitation of working hours and periodic holidays with pay.

1998: Global Code of Ethics for Tourism

We, members of the World Tourism Organization (WTO) representatives of the world tourism industry, delegates of States, territories, enterprises, institutions and bodies that are gathered for the General Assembly at Santiago, Chile on this first day of October 1999 … affirm the right to tourism and the freedom of tourist movements …

Article 7: *Right to tourism*
1. The prospect of direct and personal access to the discovery and enjoyment of the planet's resources constitutes a right equally open to all the world's inhabitants; the increasingly extensive participation in national and international tourism should be regarded as one of the best possible expressions of the sustained growth of free time, and obstacles should not be placed in its way.
2. The universal right to tourism must be regarded as the corollary of the right to rest and leisure, including reasonable limitation of working hours and periodic holidays with pay, guaranteed by Article 24 of the Universal Declaration of Human Rights and Article 7.d of the International Covenant on Economic, Social and Cultural Rights.
3. Social tourism, and in particular associative tourism, which facilitates widespread access to leisure, travel and holidays, should be developed with the support of the public authorities.
4. Family, youth, student and senior tourism and tourism for people with disabilities should be encouraged and facilitated.

Article 8: *Liberty of tourist movements*
1. Tourists and visitors should benefit, in compliance with international law and national legislation, from the liberty to move within their countries and from one State to another, in accordance with Article 13 of the Universal Declaration of Human Rights; they should have access to places of transit and stay and to tourism and cultural sites without being subject to excessive formalities or discrimination.
2. Tourists and visitors should have access to all available forms of communication, internal or external; they should benefit from prompt and easy access to local administrative, legal and health services; they should be free to contact the consular representatives of their countries of origin in compliance with the diplomatic conventions in force.
3. Tourists and visitors should benefit from the same rights as the citizens of the country visited concerning the confidentiality of the personal data and information concerning them, especially when these are stored electronically.
4. Administrative procedures relating to border crossings, whether they fall within the competence of States or result from international agreements, such as visas or health and customs formalities, should be adapted, so far as possible, so as to facilitate to the maximum freedom of travel and widespread access to international tourism; agreements between groups of countries to harmonize and simplify these procedures should be encouraged; specific taxes and levies penalizing the tourism industry and undermining its competitiveness should be gradually phased out or corrected.

Continued

Box 2.4 continued

      5. So far as the economic situation of the countries from which they come permits, travellers should have access to allowances of convertible currencies needed for their travels;

Article 9:   *Rights of the workers and entrepreneurs in the tourism industry*

      1. The fundamental rights of salaried and self-employed workers in the tourism industry and related activities, should be guaranteed under the supervision of the national and local administrations, both of their States of origin and of the host countries with particular care, given the specific constraints linked in particular to the seasonality of their activity, the global dimension of their industry and the flexibility often required of them by the nature of their work.

      2. Salaried and self-employed workers in the tourism industry and related activities have the right and the duty to acquire appropriate initial and continuous training; they should be given adequate social protection; job insecurity should be limited so far as possible; and a specific status, with particular regard to their social welfare, should be offered to seasonal workers in the sector.

      3. Any natural or legal person, provided he, she or it has the necessary abilities and skills, should be entitled to develop a professional activity in the field of tourism under existing national laws; entrepreneurs and investors – especially in the area of small and medium-sized enterprises – should be entitled to free access to the tourism sector with a minimum of legal or administrative restrictions …

      4. As an irreplaceable factor of solidarity in the development and dynamic growth of international exchanges, multinational enterprises of the tourism industry should not exploit the dominant positions they sometimes occupy; they should avoid becoming the vehicles of cultural and social models artificially imposed on the host communities; in exchange for their freedom to invest and trade which should be fully recognized, they should involve themselves in local development, avoiding, by the excessive repatriation of their profits or their induced imports, a reduction of their contribution to the economies in which they are established.

The 19th-century campaigns for reduced working hours, discussed above, initially related to children and women and such campaigns continue today in relation to certain Third World countries that exploit child labour. Others who have sought to assert their rights include the aged, people with disabilities and ethnic minorities and indigenous people. Planning for leisure in general for these various groups is discussed in Chapter 10; here the question of leisure rights in relation to each group is briefly discussed.

The rights of disabled persons were the subject of a 1975 UN declaration, but it makes no specific reference to the leisure of disabled people, just to the right to 'enjoy a decent life' and for disabled people to have their needs taken into account in social planning. In many countries these rights have been enshrined in legislation but, as Darcy (1998) points out, declarations of rights, and even legislation, do not ensure suitable provision; this requires a change in the mind-set of the community and decision-makers.

The statements in regard to children's cultural rights and the right to play suffer from many of the same defects of vagueness as the general statements of the Universal Declaration. However, they do assert that governments should 'encourage the provision of appropriate and equal opportunities'. Again, the term 'appropriate' is undefined and it is certainly arguable that these rights are being widely violated. Among the most graphic examples of such rights being violated were the scenes of gross neglect of orphans in Rumania, revealed with the fall of the Communist regime in 1990. The effects of the denial of any opportunity for play and exercise, along with denial of education and human affection, were all too plain to see on television screens throughout the world. But the perpetrators of such human rights violations were not apparently pursued and brought to justice by the international community. Similarly, campaigns against child labour, which is widespread in many countries, are generally conducted by voluntary/charitable bodies rather than by governments.

Campaigns for the rights of women are part of the platform of feminist movements, discussed in Chapter 3. As Box 2.1 indicates, the 1979 *Convention on the Elimination of All Forms of Discrimination Against Women* contains references to 'recreational activities, sports and all aspects of cultural life'. In the feminist leisure-studies literature, however, there is little mention of the idea of rights – the exception being a brief reference by Horna (1994: 25) to a report of Lenskyj (1991) on Canadian women's use of human rights legislation in the area of sport. It is notable that Article 24 of the Universal Declaration, which is concerned with hours of work and holidays with pay, is entirely addressed to those in paid employment and, in reality, those in full-time paid employment. Thus there is an implicit bias towards men since, certainly in 1948 when the Universal Declaration was drawn up, only a minority of women were in full-time paid employment. The idea that people not in paid employment might also have leisure rights is thus ignored. It is curious that this has not been taken up in discussion of women's rights to leisure.

The rights of ethnic minorities and indigenous peoples have been the subject of more recent UN declarations. Here, as well as issues of discrimination and access to mainstream activities, there is an emphasis on cultural pluralism, with the declarations asserting the rights of minority groups to practise their own culture. This has implications for planning and provision, which are discussed in Chapter 7.

Meaningfulness of rights declarations

Are these declarations of rights of assistance in determining the appropriate role of governments in relation to leisure? Yes and no. An analysis of the UN statements raises some doubts about the nature, scope and meaningfulness of the declared rights. Article 24 of the Universal Declaration refers to the right to 'rest and leisure', but these concepts are not defined, let alone quantified. Rest and leisure are, however, said to include 'reasonable limitation of working hours and periodic holidays with pay'. As moral statements, the declarations of human rights indicate a broad consensus that governments should be concerned about leisure but, with many more pressing matters engaging governments in the international arena, such statements about leisure rarely translate into positive rights. They therefore provide little guidance on the nature or extent of government involvement necessary to secure such rights.

Rights and freedoms

The upholding of some rights involves the denial of others, giving rise to dilemmas for defenders of civil rights and often to much political conflict. For example, upholding the right of people not to be abused on racial grounds involves denial of some people's right to freedom of expression, but where such discrimination has been outlawed it is generally accepted that the former right is more important. In the area of leisure and tourism, examples of curtailment of freedom can be seen in relation to taxation, in relation to direct controls over activities with moral implications and in the area of national sovereignty.

Taxation

Where rights involve the provision of goods or services – for example, education or housing – any public provision must generally be funded from taxation. The compulsory nature of taxation can be seen as an infringement of individuals' right to spend their money as they please. Thus those on the right of the political spectrum, as discussed in Chapter 3, often oppose increased levels of public service provision, even if based on a reasonable claim of rights, because they see this leading to increased levels of taxation and hence to increased infringement of individual financial rights. For some right-wing political adherents, the accumulation of public expenditure and the extension of legal controls on all sorts of activity have given rise to *big government*, which, of its very nature, is seen as a threat to human rights and freedoms.

Moral concerns

There are many instances where leisure activities are strictly controlled, are subject to punitive levels of taxation or are outlawed, for moral or health reasons – a phenomenon that has been termed 'morality policy' (Mooney, 1999). Such controls are often opposed, by individuals or organized groups. Regardless of the motive for the controls, they can be seen as an infringement of the rights of the individuals involved. Examples generally fall into the category of activity traditionally known as *vices*, including gambling, prostitution and taking recreational drugs, including alcohol. In some cases controls or outright prohibition can be seen as the imposition of one group's moral or religious values on others and hence the denial of the latter's rights. An example is the period of alcohol prohibition in the USA in the 1920s. In tourism the process may involve a culture clash between visitors' and residents' values and norms of behaviour. It is not possible to pursue this complex area of public policy further here, but it is a subject that merits further research attention. Only limited attention has been given to these contentious issues in the research literature, including, for example, the area of gambling (Dombrink, 1996; Veal and Lynch, 1998). The outlawing of leisure activities involving cruelty to animals, as discussed below, is another case where rights of some individuals are claimed to be infringed.

National sovereignty

Declarations of rights are often international in nature. Individual nations sign agreements or treaties that commit them to upholding the declarations – they become, in effect, international law. In some cases there are enforce-ment mechanisms, or at least monitoring systems, for example the International Court of Human Rights in The Hague. In signing treaties and accepting the jurisdiction of such entities, nations surrender a part of their sovereignty, which can be seen as a loss of freedom. This loss of sovereignty provides political ammunition for those opposed to the treaties in the first place.

Other rights

A number of ideas about rights have developed in recent years, some of which have implications for leisure and tourism, including the idea of the rights of future generations and the rights of animals.

Future generations

Sustainable development has become a significant theme in tourism following the publication in 1987 of the report of the World Commission on Environment and Development (WCED), *Our Common Future* (the Brundtland Report). Sustainable development was defined in the report as: 'development that meets the needs of the present without compromising the ability of future generations to meet their own needs' (WCED, 1990: 43). Thus the principle was established that development should respect the rights of future generations. It is not proposed to explore this issue in detail here: suffice it to say that it introduces a whole new dimension to the discussion of rights and imposes potentially highly significant constraints on development.

Animal rights

Another type of right that has been increasingly recognized and has had implications for leisure and tourism is animal rights. In the Colosseum in ancient Rome animals were slaughtered by the thousand for public entertainment. Part of the history of leisure in many countries has been the gradual outlawing of leisure activities involving cruelty to animals, including bear-baiting, cock-fighting and many forms of hunting, although they continue in many parts of the world. Bull-fighting in Spain and fox-hunting in Britain are examples of the violation of animal rights for leisure and tourism purposes which continue today, although the latter is currently the subject of legislation. The banning of these forms of activity can, of course, be seen as an infringement of the rights of those who wish to participate, and such arguments are used by participants when the activity is threatened. The resolution of the conflict of interest between defenders of the right, for example, to hunt and the defenders of the rights of the animal to live, or at least to be killed humanely, becomes a matter of politics, a matter of which group has more political power. Less extreme examples include performing animals in circuses, unsuitable caging of animals in zoos and often illegal capture of wild and endangered species for pets.

The Rights of the Citizen

Human rights, as discussed above, are intended to be universal in nature, which perhaps makes the link with leisure and tourism provision somewhat tenuous for most people. The idea of rights arising from citizenship is arguably more tangible, since citizenship applies to a particular country with a responsible government. Citizenship has been defined as:

> a bundle of entitlements and obligations which
> constitute individuals as fully fledged
> members of a socio-political community,
> providing them with access to scarce resources.
> (Turner, 1994: xv)

The idea of citizenship has a long history, stretching back at least to the ancient Greek and Roman civilizations, but its modern form has developed over the last 300 years. In work originally published in the 1950s and 1960s, T.H. Marshall (1994) divided the rights of the citizen into three groups: civil, political and social:

- Civil, or legal, rights concern the 'liberty of the person, freedom of speech, thought and faith, the right to own property and to conclude valid contracts and the right to justice'.

- Political rights concern the right to take part in the democratic process of electing governments.
- Social rights include the right to 'a modicum of economic welfare and security … the right to share to the full in the social heritage and to live the life of a civilized being according to the standards prevailing in that society' (Marshall, 1994: 9).

The last of these categories, social rights, is the most controversial because of its link with the welfare state. Critics from the radical left have attacked the idea because of the claim that equality of social rights can overcome or ameliorate class-based inequality (Hindess, 1993). The guarantee of a minimum income or a minimum level of provision of certain services may, if effectively administered, eliminate the worst excesses of inequality but, it is argued, this does not eliminate inequality. The idea of citizenship has traditionally been defended by those on the right of the political spectrum, since it appears to accommodate the principles of the free individual and a compassionate market system (Saunders, 1993). However, the 20th-century rise of social rights in the form of the welfare state has been the focus of criticism from the political New Right, which has wished to see a rolling back of the welfare state.

Citizenship implies not only rights but also duties or obligations. In earlier eras, obligations were often numerous – for example, duties owed to the local church or to the lord of the manor or, less formally, to neighbours. As the rights of citizenship became formalized, so did the obligations. In the civil/legal area citizens are expected to observe the law and, for example, to pay taxes, to serve on juries and, if called upon, to bear arms to defend the state. In the political arena, citizens are expected to take part in the democratic process by voting, a duty enforced by law in a few countries – for example, Australia. In the social area, the right to education is matched by the legal obligation of parents to send children to school. The right to social security is matched by the obligation to work when work is available. The right to a retirement pension is linked with the expectation of having worked for a living. Unemployment benefit is matched by an expectation that the unemployed will actively search for paid work and undertake required training. However, as Roche (1992: 159) argues, there is also an expectation of a right to work and high levels of unemployment undermine this social contract. In general, however, as the idea of social rights developed during the 20th century, there was no commensurate increase in citizen obligations, except the obligation to continue to pay taxes to meet the increasing cost of the welfare state.

While rights to leisure time, including holidays with pay, can be said to arise from civil rights, any rights to leisure services arise as a social right. The idea is implicit in the concept of standards of provision, as discussed in Chapter 7. This principle, applied in areas such as education, housing and public health as well as in leisure services, suggests that people have a right to expect a certain minimum standard of public services regardless of where they live in a country, and that government should ensure that right. This is not an uncontested view: a free-market perspective would be that people who are not satisfied with services in one area should simply move to an area where the combination of service level and taxation suits their needs and that those (local government) areas that wish to attract and retain residents should ensure that they maintain an appropriate level of services. For basic services the standards approach is probably more widely accepted – but the question arises as to whether leisure services are included among those basic services that are seen as social rights.

In a number of contributions, Fred Coalter (1988: 31–32; 1998) has critically discussed the relationship between citizens' (social) rights and leisure services. His concern is primarily with the way interest in this nexus has exerted an undue influence on the theoretical study of leisure, resulting in an overemphasis on the role of public-sector provision. The bulk of leisure services in Western countries is provided by the market, which is therefore likely to be satisfying some citizens' rights in regard to leisure provision. It is therefore not necessarily the case that only publicly provided leisure services are capable of contributing to the satisfaction of social rights.

Coalter suggests that the idea of 'citizens' rights' was an accepted basis of government policy in Britain, at least until the 1970s. In fact, the evidence for this is quite thin; his sources are primarily other academics who hold similar views. Wilson (1988: 10) makes a similar claim, that 'the right to leisure' is included among the social rights of citizenship, but without providing any evidence that this is in fact recognized by governments. In the 1970s the British Labour government of the day produced a White Paper on *Sport and Recreation* (Department of the Environment, 1975), which accepted the view of an earlier parliamentary inquiry that recreation should be regarded as part of the 'general fabric of the social services'. Coalter states merely that this implies that leisure services had been recognized as rights of citizenship. The Marshallian schema outlined above would lead to the conclusion that something which is declared to be part of the social services must therefore be regarded as a social right of citizenship, but it is notable that the final step, of explicitly declaring leisure provision as a right, has never been taken by a British government. It is notable that, even with a Labour government in power, the 1975 White Paper was not followed by an Act of Parliament. And it is notable that a government which, in the international sphere, endorsed the Council of Europe's 'Sport for All' policy and the accompanying charter did not explicitly declare sport, or access to sport facilities, as a right of citizenship. It had long been the wish of the leisure-management profession in Britain that a statutory obligation be placed on local government to provide leisure facilities, but such provision has remained discretionary – hardly a ringing endorsement of a right of citizenship.

A similar reticence has existed in Australia, where a 1985 Labor government policy document on recreation spoke of the valuable contribution that various forms of leisure activity could make to a 'healthy lifestyle' (Brown, 1985), but stopped short of declaring any right of access to leisure services. In a more recent policy statement on culture, again from a Labor government, the recommendation of a panel of experts that the Australian government commit itself to a 'Charter of Cultural Rights' is reproduced as a Preamble to the policy document, but ignored in the main body of the document (Commonwealth of Australia, 1994).

In Britain, the philosophy of the Conservative government that came to power in 1979 under Margaret Thatcher was to roll back the welfare state rather than extend it, so earlier talk of leisure as a social service was soon abandoned. In the early 1990s, however, under the leadership of John Major, the Conservative government enshrined the idea of citizenship in the *Citizen's Charter* (Prime Minister, 1991). The charter, however, involved a quite limited conceptualization of 'the citizen' as a consumer of public services, although principles were set out for areas such as health services, transport, social services, the police and postal services. With its emphasis on delivery of public services, the charter was more of a 'political administrative initiative' than a 'full rights-orientated constitutional approach' (Doern, 1993). With its emphasis on choice and value for money, it could be seen as a stalking-horse for privatization of public services that failed to measure up to expectations. The opening paragraphs of the charter state:

> Choice can ... be extended within the public sector. When the public sector remains responsible for a function it can introduce competition and pressure for efficiency by contracting with the private sector for its provision. ... choice can be restored by alternative forms of provision, and creating a wider range of options wherever that is cost-effective ... Through the Citizen's Charter the Government is now determined to drive reforms further into the core of the public services, extending the benefits of choice, competition, and commitment to service more widely.
>
> (Major, 1991: 4)

Thus the *Citizen's Charter* could be said to be focused more on the right of individuals as customers than their rights as citizens.

Local authorities' responses to the charter in a range of service areas were assessed through performance indicators developed by the Audit Commission. As Lentell (1996) points out, the limited attempts of the Audit Commission to achieve this in relation to leisure services raised as many questions as they answered.

With another change of government, to New Labour in 1997, this particular approach was not abandoned, but modified. Charters have mushroomed under Labour: a total of 30 from different government agencies are listed on the Cabinet Office (2001) *Service First* web-site. However, as with the former Conservative government's initiative, the rights enshrined in these charters are consumer rights: they are concerned with the efficient and fair administration of services rather than with consideration of the overall range and quantum of services to which the individual might be entitled.

With the change of government to New Labour came the 'third way' in politics, as discussed in Chapter 3. Third-way politics, as outlined by Anthony Giddens, involves a re-examination of the relationship between rights and obligations:

> Having abandoned collectivism, third way politics looks for a new relationship between the individual and the community, a redefinition of rights and obligations. One might suggest as a prime motto for the new politics, *no rights without responsibilities.* Government has a whole cluster of responsibilities for its citizens and others, including the protection of the vulnerable. Old-style social democracy, however, was inclined to treat rights as unconditional claims. With expanding individualism should come an extension of individual obligations. Unemployment benefits, for example, should carry the obligation to actively look for work, and it is up to governments to ensure that welfare systems do not discourage active search. As an ethical principle, 'no rights without responsibilities' must apply not only to welfare recipients, but to everyone. It is highly important for social democrats to stress this, because otherwise the precept can be held to apply only to the poor or to the needy – as tends to be the case with the political right.
>
> (Giddens, 1998: 65)

The nature of the obligations of non-welfare recipients are not, however, spelled out. It is a sign of the confusing politics of our times that, while these principles are being expounded by a Labour government in Britain, on the other side of the world, in Australia, a right-wing conservative government, under John Howard, is expounding a similar principle, using the term 'mutual obligation', under which unemployed people can be required to 'work for dole' and can lose benefits if they fail to fill a prescribed quota of job interviews.

While informal leisure-related obligations exist for the citizen – for example, to support various charitable fund-raising efforts, to serve on committees or act as sports officials, to attend social functions and, in smaller communities, to turn out for sporting or celebratory events – obligations in regard to state-provided services have traditionally been virtually non-existent. The nearest to an obligation is the notion of 'user pays', in whole or part. This increasingly common feature of public leisure services reflects the idea that the state should not bear the full cost of leisure services, but just that proportion which produces social benefits for the community, while the individual bears the cost of the private benefits (see Chapter 4).

Social rights arising from the idea of citizenship may be seen as more meaningful and practical and less contentious than the idea of human rights, but along with the possibility of implementation goes political dispute and uncertainty. Despite the rhetoric, it would seem that government practice implicitly reflects the view of Roberts, that leisure demands are so numerous, diverse and 'capable of indefinite extension' that servicing them 'cannot be made into a right of citizenship' (Roberts, 1978: 155).

Needs

Providing a link between the UN's concern with rights and the concept of need, in 1987 the then Secretary-General of the United Nations declared:

> One of the primary needs of the human person is leisure and such use of it as will provide psychological strength and refreshment.
> (Perez de Cuellar, 1987)

Such a statement is, however, unusual since, unlike discussions of rights, much of the literature on need, including that relating to leisure and tourism, has sought to establish an objective or scientific basis for needs assessment as an underpinning for leisure and tourism studies and particularly for leisure-service provision.

The idea of need occupies an important place in the lexicon of leisure studies and leisure-service provision. Iso-Ahola has said:

> In a way, the future of the entire field of leisure studies as well as the recreation profession depends on the construct of leisure need. That is, if it could not be shown that people have a need for leisure and recreation, professionals and practitioners might as well give up and begin searching for new jobs.
> (Iso-Ahola, 1980: 227)

As discussed above, the British Labour government of the 1970s adopted a welfare approach to leisure services, exemplified in the 1975 White Paper and its statement that 'recreation should be regarded as "one of the community's everyday needs"'. It also funded a major study entitled *Leisure Provision and People's Needs*, which sought to achieve a 'sharpened understanding of people's needs and of the relevance of leisure to them' (Dower *et al.*, 1981: 2). The Chairmen's Policy Group, the committee of chairmen (*sic*) of a number of British leisure quangos, stated, in a 1982 report:

> Leisure provision has become accepted as a major element of social policy, aiming at enhancement of the quality of life of all citizens. This calls for a change of emphasis, away from catering simply for leisure demands, to understanding and meeting of leisure needs.
> (Chairmen's Policy Group, 1982: 61)

These statements are not merely saying, in effect, 'people desire leisure'. If something is a need, in the sense used in these statements, then there is an implied imperative: the implication is that society as a whole, and particularly government, has an obligation to ensure that something which is a need is provided for all. Societies or social systems are condemned as inadequate if they are unable to meet these sorts of need. The terminology of the Chairmen's Policy Group suggests that this obligation should be fulfilled by the state, since demand is seen to be something dealt with by the market. However, none of these sources deals explicitly with the question: what is a need? To explore this issue, we examine a number of perspectives on the concept of need which have been put forward in the literature. This literature is considered in six sections: Taylor's typology; the Bradshaw/Mercer typology; Maslow's hierarchy of needs; motivation theory; neo-Marxist views; and the work of Doyal and Gough on universal needs.

Taylor – uses of the word 'need'

A major problem in discussing need is that the word is used in a number of different ways. In large supermarkets there is usually a section labelled 'party needs' - clearly such needs are of a different order from the idea of the needs of people for food or shelter or of children for love and affection. Taylor identified four different uses of the term, as follows.

> (1) To indicate something needed to satisfy a rule or law; e.g. 'I need a sticker to park here'.
> (2) To indicate means to an end (either specified or implied); e.g. 'I need a watch (in order to tell the time)'; 'He needs a doctor (in order to get well)'.
> (3) To describe motivations, conscious or unconscious, in the sense of wants, drives, desires, and so on. So we speak of people having a need for achievement, the need to atone for guilt, needs for status, security, etc. Needs in this sense constitute conative dispositions.
> (4) To make recommendations or normative evaluations. These are sometimes difficult to distinguish from (3) which are intended as purely descriptive statements. So, for instance, it is asserted that men have needs for affection, identity, self-esteem, the esteem of others, etc. But what is meant by such claims when they fall into this category is that men have these needs, whether or not they actually feel them, or whether or not they in fact count them as needs. This category also covers those more obvious kinds of recommendations such as 'what this country needs is good fighting men', or 'people need freedom', etc.
>
> (Taylor, 1959: 107)

Only in the fourth, normative sense does the concept of need give rise to a collective or public policy response. Needs of types (1), (2) and (3) are technically and empirically derived; there is no implication that society has an obligation to satisfy them. It is only when some external, collective evaluation of needs takes place that a collective, government response may be called for. The question arises as to which needs are subject to such collective evaluations and why, and in particular whether leisure time, leisure activities or leisure or tourism services can be so classified. The literature that is commonly referred to in discussions of leisure and need tends to avoid this question, concentrating instead on various ways of assessing type (3) needs.

Bradshaw/Mercer typology of need

The typology of social need put forward by David Mercer (1975) was based on the work of Bradshaw (1972) relating to welfare services. It consists of four categories: felt need, expressed need, comparative need and normative need. Felt needs are those which individuals are aware of but which are not formally expressed in any explicit or active way and are generally unmet. Expressed needs are those which individuals demonstrate by some action – for example, people indicate an expressed need for a service by using it or by joining a waiting-list to receive it. Comparative needs arise when individuals or groups of individuals compare themselves with others – when people develop a desire to have a similar range of goods and services to those of others and feel deprived if they do not. Normative need involves external assessments or judgements made, in Mercer's view, by experts.

In Bradshaw's schema, assessments of need for policy purposes should involve the use of measures related to all four categories and policy should be based on evaluation of all four measures. The latter evaluation process, though only briefly explicated by Mercer, seems to involve taking action in areas where the various measures of need are in agreement, but provides no solution in situations where the various measures are not in agreement.

Of the four Mercer/Bradshaw categories, only normative needs correspond to Taylor's category (4) needs, the others being versions of category (3). But normative need assessments in recreation are viewed with suspicion by Mercer, because the experts who make them are seen to be generally a 'small elite group in our society – the well-educated, well-to-do planners, politicians, engineers and academics' (Mercer, 1975: 41) – who are unlikely to truly understand the needs of ordinary people. But, in his conclusions, Mercer suggests that:

> it would be of considerable value to focus much greater research attention on the *normative* aspects of need; more specifically, on the decision-making processes associated with the formulation of normative standards and measures of adequacy.
>
> (Mercer, 1975: 46)

The Bradshaw/Mercer typology does not therefore provide an answer to the question of how or why particular needs – including leisure – might come to be classified as normative needs requiring government action. This can be illustrated by example. It is widely accepted among experts that people need a certain amount of exercise to stay healthy and that, if such exercise is not obtained during paid or unpaid work time, people should take it during their leisure time. Thus a normative need to take exercise during leisure time is accepted by experts and most governments. In most Western countries many people fail to follow such advice – they appear to have no expressed need for exercise. This may be because people do not personally feel a desire to take exercise (no sense of felt need) and/or because they live in a milieu where their contemporaries or role models do not do so (no sense of comparative need). The assessment of normative need is at variance with the other three types of need. Knowing this may help the experts to target their message and explore other ways of overcoming people's resistance, but it has no bearing on whether the normative assessment is appropriate or inappropriate; the normative assessment is based on other criteria, but the typology itself does not provide any insight as to the nature or validity of those criteria.

Maslow's hierarchy of need

Maslow's well-known hierarchy of need is even more widely referred to in the leisure- and tourism-studies literature than the Bradshaw/Mercer typology. As usually presented, Maslow's theory posits that human needs are arranged in a hierarchy. The lowest level of the hierarchy involves physical needs for food, drink and shelter; higher levels involve needs for safety/security, love/affiliation, social esteem and self-esteem needs and, at the highest level, self-actualization (Maslow, 1954). As needs lower down the hierarchy are satisfied, the theory states, so the higher needs become relevant and the individual is motivated to satisfy them.

The hierarchy has often been used to argue that leisure and tourism are capable of satisfying a wide range of needs (e.g. Ravenscroft, 1993; Ryan, 1995: 52; Kraus, 1998: 72). For example: rest, relaxation, going on holiday and exercise can be seen as physical needs; friendship groups and youth subcultures, based largely around leisure activities, are said to reflect the need for safety and security; much family leisure, leisure activities related to sexual partnering and team sports can be said to relate to the need for love and affiliation; the exercise of skills in sport and cultural activities is believed to reflect the need for esteem as can the taking of holidays in certain locations; and it is claimed that many of those same activities, engaged in for their own sake, provide for self-actualization. Since leisure is involved at all levels of the hierarchy, the argument goes, all forms of leisure are needs, or need satisfiers, in the Maslow sense.

But it would be absurd to conclude from this analysis that all leisure desires are needs in the normative sense and should therefore be a collective responsibility. As presented here, the Maslow hierarchy refers only to Taylor's type (3) needs, equivalent to the Bradshaw/Mercer felt needs. For example, holding a party could be related to three levels of the hierarchy: rest and relaxation, affiliation (getting to know people) and esteem (being thought well of by your friends) – but the provision of parties is not usually seen as something for which there should be a collective concern and government responsibility. The Maslow hierarchy, as generally presented, therefore does nothing to help in deciding what leisure or tourism desires are needs in the normative sense.

However, one aspect of Maslow's theory that is often omitted in popular summaries is the fact that the hierarchy does not apply to all needs but only to what Maslow calls *basically important needs*. Basically important needs are defined as those desires which, if not satisfied, would produce psychopathological consequences.

> Thwarting of unimportant desires produces no psycho-pathological results: thwarting of basically important needs does produce such results.
>
> (Maslow, 1970: 57)

So 'basically important needs' are those whose denial produces psychopathological consequences: the rest are 'unimportant desires'. Most would accept that there should be a collective concern to prevent psychopathological conditions. Thus, in order to decide when collective or government involvement is justified, it would simply be a matter of agreeing on a definition of psychopathological and identifying those needs/desires the denial of which would produce psychopathological results. Measures should clearly be taken to prevent such results; and such measures could well include leisure-service provision. This seems to imply that society might be able to avoid difficult normative decisions about which needs it should and should not meet collectively. It implies that needs can be read off from empirical facts: that, if people are likely to behave psychopathologically if they are denied certain things, then such things can be defined as basically important needs and must be met, by the state if necessary.

However, if this approach to providing state services were accepted without qualification, society would be hostage not only to potentially unlimited calls on its resources (Chapelle, 1973) but also to all sorts of potentially socially unacceptable behaviour. Thus people who are liable to become neurotic unless they can engage in behaviour that humiliates or annoys others (perhaps to satisfy their need for esteem) would have to be humoured. There would be no control on drug use or firearms if these were required to satisfy some people's 'basically important needs' for self-actualization. Thus it is impossible to exclude a normative dimension, particularly in relation to higher-level Maslovian needs such as self-actualization. Here society must make choices between those needs it is prepared to meet and those it is not. It cannot be assumed that society must satisfy particular self-actualization needs simply because they exist in an empirical sense. As Fitzgerald puts it:

> Human selves have many potentialities … If by 'self-actualisation' is meant *whatever* the individual can be motivated to act out or express, it provides us with no standard whatsoever for distinguishing between desirable (or appropriate) forms of self-expression and undesirable (or inappropriate) forms. This, of course, Maslow and those theorists using his scheme do not intend. Manifestly the murderer, sadist, fascist, rapist, incendiarist or machete man do not fit in with Maslow's notion of a person developing his potentialities or expressing 'what he has in him' … 'Self-actualisation' cannot be rendered empirical. Maslow must, and by implication does, set up standards of what the individual in his freedom ought to become or express, and what he ought not to become or express.
>
> (Fitzgerald, 1977: 49)

Clearly every society has moral codes that override any simplistic, mechanical approach to need satisfaction. Indeed, religion, moral codes, ideology, education, the whole panoply of civilization can be said to be aimed at providing a system of rules and codes of behaviour about how and to what extent needs should be satisfied. In a more positive sense, these codes are devised to socialize individuals into not seeking to satisfy their needs in socially or personally destructive ways. But these codes vary and are adopted as a matter of faith, conviction or socialization: they cannot be proved. It follows that views on acceptable ways of satisfying needs will vary, depending on the moral code adhered to. It therefore follows that needs-based public policy must be based on such codes and cannot be based on value-free needs assessments of the sort which the Maslow hierarchy or the Mercer/Bradshaw typology appears to offer.

This re-examination of Maslow's analysis of needs leads to the conclusion that, for the purposes of public policy, the hierarchy, far from being the most useful feature of the theory, is, in fact, its least relevant feature. The most useful feature of the theory is the idea that needs must be examined in terms of the consequences of their denial. But such an examination is only part of the process of arriving at a decision on what leisure and tourism needs have implications for public policy: it is also necessary to assess leisure and tourism activities from the point of view of moral and/or political values. Hence, like rights, public policy decisions concerning leisure needs and tourism will inevitably be political.

Motivation theory and need

Iso-Ahola has provided the most comprehensive expositions of psychological motivation theories of need, including Maslow's. Among these approaches is the idea of the need for 'optimal arousal and incongruity', which suggests that 'too little or too much stimulation is damaging to the individual, both physiologically and psychologically' (Iso-Ahola, 1980: 229). This type of need therefore has much the same basis as Maslow's conception – the idea that the denial of the need would be damaging to the individual. But the same cautionary arguments apply as regards their relationship to public policy: the means of satisfying the need for optimal arousal and incongruity cannot be accepted without reference to sets of values. This much Iso-Ahola recognizes when he concludes that the 'social nature of leisure motivation is also manifested in behavior prompted by normative and comparative recreation needs' (Iso-Ahola 1980: 249).

Iso-Ahola also explores the idea of intrinsic and extrinsic motivations for participation in leisure activities and leisure-needs studies, such as those by London *et al.* (1977) and Tinsley *et al.* (1977), which seek to analyse the satisfaction reportedly gained by participants in various leisure activities. Here needs are seen to be merely the corollary of satisfactions. By definition, these theories relate to Taylor's type (3) conception of need, or even

type (2). The fact that leisure activities provide satisfactions does not justify their designation as type (4), normative, needs.

Marxist and neo-Marxist views on needs

The idea of human need is at the core of Marxist thought, which sees the failure of capitalism as its inability to meet human needs, while a socialist or communist society would be based on the principle: 'from each according to his or her abilities, to each according to his or her needs'. Under capitalism, however, the Marxist view is that needs are corrupted by the economic and social relationships which the system engenders – giving rise to false needs (Heller, 1976; Springborg, 1981). Marx argued that, while capitalism has demonstrated that human needs are not static, but develop in accordance with the technological and economic capabilities of a society, at the same time it has demonstrated that the very nature of that society shapes people's needs. Thus, under capitalism, people develop false needs for money and for the commodities that capitalism delivers.

Marx himself envisaged that under capitalism even the basic needs of the masses would eventually be denied to them, causing the downfall of the capitalist system. Since this has not come about, neo-Marxists have developed the idea of the generation and continued satisfaction of false needs to explain the longevity of capitalism. Marcuse defines false needs as:

> those which are superimposed upon the individual by particular social interests in his repression: the needs which perpetuate toil, aggressiveness, misery, and injustice … Most of the prevailing needs to relax, to have fun, to behave and consume in accordance with the advertisements, to love and hate what others love and hate, belong in this category of false needs.
>
> (Marcuse, 1964: 5)

According to Marcuse, under the conditions of capitalism, it is impossible to discover which needs are true and which are false. True needs will only emerge when society is transformed.

In the last analysis, the question of what are true and false needs must be answered by the individuals themselves, but only in the last analysis; that is, if and when they are free to give their own answer. As long as they are … indoctrinated and manipulated their answer to this question cannot be taken as their own. By the same token, however, no tribunal can justly arrogate to itself the right to decide which needs should be developed and satisfied.

(Marcuse, 1964: 6)

Under capitalism therefore, in this view, human agency is denied: human beings are passive objects, their (false) needs being entirely manipulated and determined by the system. We have to take it on trust that true needs will become apparent under socialism, once social conditions are transformed. But the socialist or communist society would not escape the problem of defining need any more than can the state within a capitalist society. Such decisions require, as Soper puts it:

a criterion of needs, a concept of value, and thus, in turn, political decisions about what is 'good' for society and its individuals to consume, and therefore what it is *worth* it producing.

(Soper, 1981: 208)

This was indeed seen in practice in the East European Communist regimes of the post-Second World War era, when, as working hours fell and leisure time increased, research was conducted on what constituted a socialist lifestyle and therefore what leisure activities should be provided for (Filipcova, 1972).

Doyal and Gough and universal needs

Doyal and Gough (1991), in a major study of human needs, refer to relativist theories of need, which state that only individuals or particular groups of individuals can know their own needs and that, since needs vary across individuals, groups and cultures, no universal needs can be identified. The Bradshaw/Mercer typology, although it raises questions about real needs, can be classified as relativist in the reliance it places on individual statements of need and the

suspicion of normative assessments. Similarly, the Maslow hierarchy and other psychological motivation theories, in their reliance on individuals alone and denial of the collective, normative dimension, can be termed relativist. They are relativist in a very extreme way, in that they imply that only individuals can assess their own needs.

The criticisms of existing needs theories advanced above suggest that, to make Taylor's type (4) statements, reference must be made to sets of values/beliefs – a view of the good or moral life which may be threatened by the denial of certain requirements, which can then be termed needs. However, such a position can itself be seen as relativist, in that it suggests that all value systems have equal weight in assessing needs – for example, the Hitler Youth were provided with a comprehensive set of values to establish the 'need' to persecute Jews.

Doyal and Gough (1991) point to other forms of relativism. The acceptance of the liberal tenet that individuals are the best judges of their own interests has led to the rise of New Right policies that have given more emphasis to the market and have rolled back the state, resulting in reductions in public services. The trend has been accelerated by relativists of the left, including, for example, anti-racist and feminist activists, who argue that only ethnic groups themselves or only women themselves can know and judge their own needs.

Doyal and Gough set out to develop a theory of universal human need to rebut existing relativist theories. They argue that, without some normative idea of universal needs that are common to all, we are in no position to judge the success of any social or political organization, since the main criterion for such judgements must be their success in meeting people's needs. Their approach is to start with values as the basis for the establishment of a theory of human needs, rather than starting from the biological, as is the case with the psychological approaches discussed above.

Beginning with the minimal moral propositions that any human society at least has the obligation to prevent serious harm to its members and to optimize its members' ability to operate effectively as members of it, Doyal and Gough argue that universal needs consist of health and personal autonomy. Health refers to physical health and therefore coincides with the lower orders of Maslow's hierarchy – but it is based on the idea of the individual's right to health rather than just the desire for it. Autonomy goes further; it means that the individual, to be human, has to be able to be a competent and dignified participant in society. This entails being educated to at least the minimum level required for the society concerned, being mentally healthy (as per Maslow) and being accorded and able to exercise certain civil and political rights. This set of needs is values-based rather than biologically based; as such it can be accepted or rejected by individuals, groups or organizations but, if accepted, is universal in application.

Doyal and Gough's resultant list of needs and their designation as universal, can be seen as closely aligned with the concept of rights discussed in the first half of this chapter. Through consideration of international data, they, in effect, seek to develop the case for converting moral rights to positive rights in the social and economic area.

While Doyal and Gough do not include leisure or tourism explicitly in their detailed lists of needs, it could be argued that adequate leisure time and the resources to facilitate physical and cultural leisure activity are an indispensable part of the conditions necessary to ensure human health and personal autonomy – that is, they are needs satisfiers in Doyal and Gough's universal sense.

Summary: Rights, Needs and Public Policy

- Declarations of human rights and of citizens' rights, including certain rights in the area of leisure and tourism, while they may have a philosophical or biological basis, are clearly political in nature. Declarations of rights are not scientific statements; they are values-based and reflect political commitment. Thus international rights declarations and covenants achieve legitimacy only when

they have been formally ratified by governments. Once ratified, the declarations have a status similar to an international treaty and become part of international law. Subsequent failure of governments to observe such statements becomes the focus of political protest and/or legal proceedings. In contrast, attempts have been made, particularly in the leisure studies literature, to imbue statements of need with a scientific status.

- The discussion in this chapter leads to the conclusion that, if they are to form the basis for public policy, statements of need must also be seen as values-based and political in nature. Thus rights and needs, in this context, are one and the same thing. It follows that public policy must inevitably be about values and politics. This leads logically to the discussion of ideology in the next chapter.

Further Reading

- Human rights: Cranston (1973); Kamenka and Tay (1978); MacFarlane (1985); Brownlie (1992); Donnelly (1989); Villiers (2001).
- Human rights and tourism: Edgell (1990) reproduces a number of international agreements and declarations as appendices.
- Human rights and sport: Kidd and Donnelly (2000).
- Citizenship: Roche (1992); Doern (1993); Saunders (1993); Turner and Hamilton (1994); Lentell (1996); Coalter (1998); Houlihan (2001).
- The concept of need: Maslow (1954); Taylor (1959); Bradshaw (1972); Chappelle (1973); Mercer (1975); Heller (1976); Fitzgerald (1977); Dower *et al.* (1981); Soper (1981); Springborg (1981); Paddick (1982); Coalter (1988); Iso-Ahola (1989); Doyal and Gough (1991).

Questions/Exercises

1. What is the difference between a right and a need?
2. In what ways are the right to (a) travel, (b) leisure infringed by governments?
3. Marshall outlines three types of rights of the citizen: what are they and how is each defined?
4. If individuals have obligations as well as rights, what obligations are there in (a) leisure, (b) tourism?

5. In what way can declarations of needs and rights be seen as potential threats to freedom?

6. Examine any one of the declarations in Boxes 2.1–2.4 and discuss the implications for public leisure and tourism policy at (a) national level, (b) local level.

7. Provide leisure or tourism examples to illustrate each of Taylor's senses of the word 'need'.

8. Why is the idea of need political?

9. Examine three examples of a public leisure/tourism service and suggest in what way, if at all, the service can be said to be meeting a need.

10. Rank the leisure activities you have engaged in over the last month (or ask a willing subject to do so) and rank them in order of importance. Draw a line dividing the activities into 'needs' and 'others' and explain the rationale for this.

3

Political Ideologies and the Role of the State

Introduction: the Role of Ideology

It is argued in Chapter 2 that a concept of need, as a basis for public policy, cannot be adequately formulated without reference to some set of values. Values can be based on philosophical, religious or political systems of thought. While philosophical and religious dimensions are not unimportant, they are beyond the scope of this text, but references to writings on those themes are given in the list of Further Reading at the end of the chapter. The aim here is to outline some major political ideological perspectives and discuss their implications for public policy in relation to leisure and tourism in Western capitalist societies. First the nature of ideology is discussed and this is followed by outlines of the basic ideas involved in eight ideological positions and their implications for the role of the state and for leisure and tourism policy.

The *Shorter Oxford English Dictionary* defines ideology as: 'A system of ideas concerning phenomena, especially those of social life; the manner of thinking of a class or an individual.' Generally then, political ideology consists of sets of political ideas – ideas about how society should be run. People may agree with or support an ideology because of intellectual conviction or self-interest or a combination of both. Self-interest arises when individuals believe that the achievement of the sort of society envisaged by the ideology would be to their benefit. Since people in similar social or economic situations – classes – are likely to have similar views on which ideologies best serve their interests, ideologies are often class-based, as suggested in the definition.

The fact that ideology is concerned with how society should be run means that ideology is involved with the political process. People act in the political arena to achieve a society run along the lines of their preferred ideology. Such action invariably involves like-minded groups of individuals organized into political parties. Hence political parties are generally associated with particular ideologies and/or group interests. The party which gains power attempts to mould society to operate in accordance with its ideology and in the interests of its supporters.

It can be argued that ideology is less relevant to the real world of contemporary politics than it was even a decade ago. One explanation for this is that it is part of the shift from a modern to a postmodern society. Pre-modern societies are guided primarily by religious values and goals, often in the context of hereditary class and status systems with an aristocracy and monarchy. Modern societies, as seen since about the 18th century in the West, while not abandoning religion and hereditary class systems, have been ostensibly guided by humanitarian values and ideals and the ideas of human progress towards a better society – hence political ideologies. Such all-encompassing ideologies are sometimes referred to in modern/postmodern discourse as 'grand narratives'. The collapse of Communism in the former Soviet Union and Eastern Europe in the late 1980s is believed to have heralded the demise of such grand narratives of both the left and the right.

The other explanation for the reduced relevance of political ideology is more prosaic: as Western societies have become more affluent, with higher levels of education and a growing preponderance of services and white-collar occupations, the old class divides have become blurred – politically, there has been a shift to the middle ground. To gain power political parties must capture the support of 'floating voters' with no particular allegiance to class-based parties. In order to do this, parties have abandoned long-held policies and beliefs if they were seen to be unattractive to voters. Thus ideology has been abandoned in favour of pragmatic seeking after power. Since all major parties are competing for the same middle ground and are subject to the same national and international political, social and economic pressures, they often tend to adopt remarkably similar platforms – as instanced by the *Citizen's Charter* discussed in Chapter 2. Thus it has been suggested that the political process is from time to time overlain with particular political rationalities that transcend ideology. For example, 'economic rationalism' has been pursued by both right-wing and centre-left governments in recent years.

While these arguments are plausible, it is too early to ignore ideology – for at least two reasons. First, while certain ideological creeds are fading – for example, socialism – others can be growing in influence – for example New Right liberalism, feminism and green politics. Secondly, many of the debates in contemporary politics – for example, third-way politics or 'compassionate conservatism' – involve reshaping of traditional political parties and their philosophies, often amid considerable controversy. It is necessary to be informed about the traditional political ideologies in order to understand the debates about their reform or abandonment – to understand what all the fuss is about.

Hall and Jenkins (1995: 33–46), in discussing the relationship between politics, policy-making and planning in the context of tourism, choose to focus on values rather than ideologies, while admitting that the concept of values is 'closely related to that of ideology' (p. 35). However, while stressing the importance of values and ideology, they do not outline specific sets of values and how they impinge on tourism.

Ideology might be seen as the way in which disembodied values are assembled into coherent, internally consistent sets. For example, it is difficult to reconcile the value of favouring social equality with that of favouring individual enterprise, since giving full reign to the latter inevitably results in inequality of outcomes. So it would not make much sense for one person or organization to espouse both those values at the same time. Thus one type of ideology, such as socialism, 'bundles' a set of values around the idea of equality, while another, such as liberalism, bundles a set of ideas around the idea of individual enterprise. Thus, in this chapter, the aim is to examine specific sets, or bundles, of values, namely ideologies, and to explore their implications for leisure and tourism policy-making.

There is a tendency to think that many of the elements of leisure – sport, recreation, the arts, tourism – are above politics and that they are not a factor in competing ideologies and are not, or should not be, affected by party politics. This is far from true, as this chapter seeks to demonstrate.

In one short chapter it is not, of course, possible to provide a definitive analysis of even the leading political ideologies, but an attempt is made to outline key features of five major ideological positions: (i) conservatism; (ii) liberalism; (iii) Marxism; (iv) democratic socialism; and (v) social democracy and third-way politics. Conservatism and liberalism are on the right of politics, while the others are generally considered to be on the left, as illustrated in Fig. 3.1. The left/right designation reflects where politicians sit in elected parliaments, based on a tradition dating back to the French Revolution in the late 18th century. In most Western democracies, conservatism, liberalism, social democracy and democratic socialism compete for power.

In addition to the mainstream ideologies, the chapter also includes consideration of three ideological movements that do not nec-

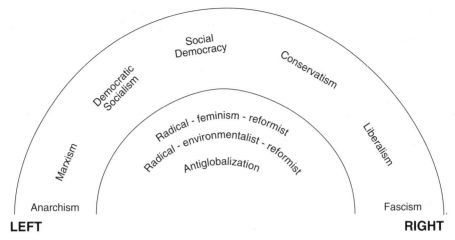

Fig. 3.1. The political spectrum.

essarily fit neatly into the left–right spectrum of politics, although they each have radical, left-leaning, wings and reformist, right-leaning, wings; these are: (vi) feminism; (vii) environmentalism; and (viii) antiglobalization. Other ideologies, such as fascism on the extreme right and anarchism on the extreme left, are not considered here because of lack of space (but see Further Reading for sources).

In the discussion that follows, the broad principles of the ideology are outlined and this is followed by examination of how these relate to particular political parties and recent national governments in Britain and Australia and how the ideas relate, in broad terms, to leisure and tourism policy. Table 3.1 provides a summary of the political parties and governments referred to, while Table 3.2, at the end of the chapter, provides a synopsis of the various ideologies discussed.

Conservatism

Conservatism, as its name implies, is an ideology in which emphasis is placed on conserving what exists – that is, in not changing things – in contrast to all the other ideologies outlined below, which stand for social and economic change in one form or another. The roots of conservatism predate the period of industrial revolution in Europe, but it emerged as a political force in the 18th and

19th century in opposition to the rise of liberalism and socialism, which sought to radically change society. At that time, conservatives represented the landed classes, rural interests and old money, and they defended the right of the monarchy and the aristocracy to rule and resisted the democratic demands and the rising power of industrialists and professions and, later, the labour movement. While modern conservative parties maintain their traditional links with landed and rural interests, and sometimes with conservative religions, in contemporary political life they draw political support from conservative sentiment across a wide spectrum of society.

An important feature of conservatism, which distinguishes it from leftist ideologies, is the defence of inequality in society: the belief that inequality is part of the natural order of things and that, for example, wealth is part of the reward system that maintains society as we know it. Generally the conservative outlook favours élitism as a concept, but in the guise of such concepts as quality and excellence. As well as being conservative in economic and political matters, conservative doctrine also applies to social matters, such as defence of the family, traditional religion and traditional values; and it also tends to favour higher levels of expenditure on defence and a tough approach to crime and punishment.

Table 3.1. Parties, governments and ideologies.

Ideology	Britain			Australia		
	Party	Government/ Prime Minister	Dates	Party	Government/ Prime Minister	Dates
Conservatism	Conservative Party	Harold Macmillan Edward Heath	1957–1964 1970–1974	Liberal Party	Robert Menzies Malcolm Fraser	1949–1961 1975–1983
				National Party	Junior coalition partner with Liberals	
Liberalism	Conservative Party	Margaret Thatcher John Major	1979–1993 1993–1997	Liberal Party	John Howard	1996–
Marxism/communism	Communist Party	No government	–	Communist Party	No government	–
Democratic socialism	Labour Party	Clement Atlee	1945–1951	Australian Labor Party	Gough Whitlam	1972–1975
Social Democracy/ third way	Labour Party	Harold Wilson James Callaghan Tony Blair	1964–1970, 1974–1976 1976–1979 1996–	Australian Labor Party	Bob Hawke Paul Keating	1983–1991 1991–1996
Environmentalism	Social Democrats Social Democrats	No government No government	– –	Australian Democrats Greens	No government No government	– –

Conservatism is, however, nothing if not pragmatic, so that, over the years, the status quo which it has sought to defend has changed. For example, when they have regained power after a period of socialist or social democratic rule, conservatives have not necessarily dismantled the welfare state, reduced levels of personal taxation or privatized government-owned industries. They have been in favour of stability and not rocking the boat. They defend capitalism, but not with the ideological fervour of liberals. Their attitude can often be viewed as paternalistic towards the working classes rather than confrontational – evoking the idea that 'we know best how to look after the country and will take care of you – trust us'.

In party terms, the Conservative Party in Britain was basically conservative in nature before the rise of the New Right/liberal thinkers under Margaret Thatcher in the 1980s. The left wing of the Conservative Party – the 'wets' in Mrs Thatcher's terms – remain the flag carriers for conservatism in Britain but are viewed as somewhat old-fashioned by the New Right. In Australia, the National Party, previously called the Country Party, is the main conservative force, along with the left wing of the Liberal Party, the party with which it operates in coalition. In the USA, the Republican Party is the more conservative of the two major parties, but it also incorporates much New Right liberal philosophy, as discussed below. In Europe, conservative parties are often associated with the Catholic Church, using the label Christian Democrat.

Conservatives can be expected to support those public services which are seen to have worked well in the past, and to seek to strengthen services which uphold traditional values and élitism. On the other hand, they would be reluctant to see the state take on new areas of public responsibility unless seen as necessary in relation to its traditional values, such as defence, rural interests and so on. In relation to leisure and the role of the state, therefore, the use of public funds to support élite activity and excellence presents no problem to conservatives. Indeed, the provision of high-profile, prestige facilities and the fostering of winning national ath-

letes and teams is consistent with the paternalistic approach to government. Similarly support for excellence and prestigious organizations in the arts is consistent with conservative values, with preference being given to artistic activities that are themselves conservative. The gradual growth of public spending to provide community leisure facilities is also consistent with the paternalistic dimension of conservatism, but support for voluntary-sector activity would be favoured. Because conservatives do not adopt a hard ideological line on market economics, they frequently find themselves supporting government aid to industry, such as tourism. As far as environmental issues are concerned, however, conservatives are likely to be on the side of the exploiters of the environment rather than the conservationists, even though their links with the land lead them to see themselves as custodians of rural values.

Liberalism

The word liberalism shares the same Latin root as liberation and liberty: hence its basic tenet is the idea of freedom – of the individual. Its origins lie in the late 18th and the 19th centuries in Europe among the newly emerging capitalist and middle-class interests who were trying to throw off the shackles of feudalism – the system under which monarchs ruled by divine right, hand in hand with the entrenched privileges of the aristocracy, the landed classes and the church, and everyone from monarch to peasant knew his/her place. Liberals, building on the ideas of philosophers such as Adam Smith, believed in the power of the emerging market system and so wanted restraints on trade, investment and commerce removed. Government control, linked as it then was to tradition and privilege, was to be dismantled and economic success was to be achieved by hard work, industry and trade. The cry of the French Revolution was 'liberty, equality and fraternity' – the liberals placed the emphasis on liberty. As with conservatives, inequality was not seen in a bad light. But, whereas conservative inequality was based on class privilege and heredity, liberal inequality was seen as a positive and dynamic force for change in society, providing incentives and rewards for effort.

In its modern guise, liberalism has re-emerged in the form of the New Right of the British Conservative Party (Thatcherism) and the Australian Liberal Party of John Howard. Rather than accepting, and even encouraging, the growth of the state, as previous Labour and Conservative governments had done during the 1960s and 1970s, they have sought to reverse the tide of 'creeping socialism' and give free rein to the market. Since much of the distinctiveness of the ideology is focused on economic policy, it is often referred to as *economic rationalism* – a link with economic theory that is explored in Chapter 4. The policies advocated by economic rationalists involve the following:

1. Reductions in personal and corporate taxation, since taxation is seen as a disincentive to work and an infringement of the freedom of individuals to spend their money as they see fit.
2. Reductions in industry protection, such as tariffs and subsidies, to encourage efficiency, competition and international competitiveness.
3. Privatization of state assets, because it is believed that they will be more efficiently run by private enterprise.
4. Reduction of welfare spending, because of its cost and because it is seen to encourage a hand-out mentality among recipients.
5. Reduction of government spending generally, to enable taxes to be reduced and to shift economic resources away from the public sector, which is regarded as inefficient and bureaucratic, to the private sector, which is regarded as efficient and more responsive to people's needs.

The public sector is generally seen by liberals as being less efficient than the private sector (costing more) and less effective (failing to deliver what people want). These failings arise because public services are often monopolies (with no competitors seeking to provide better services or lower prices) and they do not have the incentive of profit and reward for good performance or the discipline of losses or going out of business if performance is poor. Generally, therefore, the liberal philosophy espouses a private-enterprise solution to leisure and tourism services. Even where it is accepted that government should be involved in leisure provision – for example, in the case of urban parks – the liberal approach is for such services, while being financed by government, to be provided where possible by private enterprise. Indeed, the flexibility and responsiveness of the market are seen as making it an ideal mechanism for providing for people's leisure demands (Roberts, 1978: 155–164): hence the extensive programme of privatization of public services under New Right/liberal governments in recent years. The liberal perspective tends to see leisure and tourism as industries. While this is unexceptionable in the case of tourism, which is largely a private-sector phenomenon, it marks a break with tradition for areas such as parks, sport and the arts, which, from a public policy perspective, have been seen as non-profit community services. One of the early statements of the liberal principles in this area, from the British Conservative Party, asserted:

> new jobs can be created by the commercial provision of pleasure and recreation to foreign tourists and Britons in their leisure time. The key is to understand the need for commercial provision. Too often, people expect their leisure to be subsidized. There are no jobs to be had there – only higher taxes. When people pay for their own pleasure they create a job for someone else.
>
> (Banks, 1985: 1)

Similarly, a recent policy document on sport from the Australian Liberal–National coalition government stated:

> Australia's reputation as an active nation and its record of high performance in sporting arenas around the world will be supported by a sport and recreation industry known for its:
> ● innovation in design and intellectual property;
> ● quality of sporting goods and services;
> ● ability to anticipate and lead the markets of the world;
> ● brand and design presence throughout the world;
> ● skill in adding value to our sporting and recreational resources;
> ● use of technology to achieve a competitive edge; and
> ● quality and range of sports tourism products.
>
> (Department of Industry, Science and Resources, 1999: 5)

The purist liberal sees no need for organizations that assist or usurp private-enterprise roles, such as government-funded tourism-promotion agencies or government-owned airlines or airports. This is in contrast to some of their supporters, including voters in electorates affected by government enterprises, those with a more conservative philosophy and even industry itself, which is often happy to see governments provide subsidized infrastructure to ensure the viability of related private-sector enterprises. The purist liberal, however, believes that many services which have traditionally been publicly provided can, in fact, be operated more efficiently and effectively on a commercial, 'user pays' basis. Hence, recent years have seen the privatization of, for example, substantial parts of the transport industry, including airports, docks, railways and airlines – all key elements of the tourism-industry infrastructure. Whether privatization in these and other industry sectors can be judged a success is a matter for debate (Hodge, 2000).

In Britain in the 1980s and early 1990s, the New Right government under Margaret Thatcher and John Major sought to impose privatization and the discipline of the market on local government, including leisure services, by introducing compulsory competitive tendering (CCT), by which certain management contracts – for example, parks maintenance, leisure-centre management – had to be put up for public tender, with the possibility that the contract would be won by a commercial company. Similar measures were taken in Australia in the early 1990s by the Liberal government of Victoria under Jeff Kennet. The CCT phenomenon is discussed in more detail in Chapter 4.

In the interests of smaller government, liberals also encourage involvement of the voluntary sector in leisure provision. As with the conservatives, the support for excellence and élitism – for instance, in sport or the arts – is to be welcomed but, even here, the preference is for private-sector sponsorship. It might be argued from a liberal perspective that the very idea of leisure as freedom of choice is reflected in the free play of market forces, which seek to meet the expressed demands of the consumer. Some liberal

groups, following the logic of their basic philosophy, have advocated the legalization of recreational drugs, a cause usually associated with the left, but on the grounds of the upholding of individual freedom of choice.

It is worth noting that, for historical and electoral reasons, the use and meaning of political labels change over time and can vary between countries. This can lead to some confusion, both in terms of party labels and in the use of the word to describe a political philosophy. Thus, for example, the Liberal Party in Britain had its origins in the 19th century as a radical opposition to the conservative Tories, espousing free trade and the interests of commerce – thus it was originally liberal in philosophy, as discussed above. Later, with the rise of the Labour Party on the left, it came to occupy the middle ground in British politics, espousing largely social democratic policies (see below); this was confirmed when it combined with a dissident wing of the Labour Party, the Social Democrats, to form the Liberal Democrats in the 1980s. In the USA the term 'liberal' is often used to refer to left-wing rather than right-wing political positions. This can be seen as partly a reflection of history, when liberals were the champions of change based on ideas of personal freedom, partly a reflection of the fact that the American political spectrum is considerably to the right of that of European countries and partly a genuinely different use of the word.

Marxism

Marxism, might also be termed revolutionary socialism, scientific socialism (Henry, 1984b) or communism. The ideology is based on the ideas of Karl Marx, who, with his collaborator Friedrich Engels, set out his ideas in a number of key works published in the middle and second half of the 19th century, notably *The Communist Manifesto* and *Capital*.

Marx's thesis can be summarized very briefly as follows. Capitalist society is characterized by the irreconcilable clash of interests between the capitalists (or bourgeoisie), who own the means of production, and the workers (or proletariat), who own nothing but their labour power. The relationship between capitalists and workers is an exploitative one – capitalists minimizing the wages they pay and retaining maximum profits for themselves. The state in capitalist countries merely plays the role of propping up this exploitative system by curbing and regulating some of the worst excesses of capitalism and providing it with a human face. Because opportunities for further investment will eventually be exhausted and maintenance of profit levels will only be achievable by increased levels of exploitation and immiseration of the workers, capitalism will eventually collapse under the stress of its own internal contradictions. The workers should hasten this process by combining to overthrow capitalism (revolution) and transform society into a socialist state controlled by a working-class party (dictatorship of the proletariat). In the final stage of transformation – the Communist society – the state would no longer be required.

With the Communist revolution in Russia in 1917 and wars and depression in the West, followed by the triumph of Communism in Eastern Europe and China in the 1940s, it appeared that Marx's predictions were coming true. But capitalism survived, and later Marxist theorists, referred to as neo-Marxists, sought to explain its continued existence in a number of ways. For example, the institution of colonialism, or imperialism, provided expanded, international, scope for capitalist investment and exploitation, thus delaying the fall in the return on capital that Marx had predicted. Later, neocolonialism, in which capitalism extended its global reach via economic means, without the aid of colonial armies (e.g. the Coca-colonization of the world), was seen to achieve the same economic effects as colonialism. It was further argued that the capitalist ruling class achieved *hegemony*, a sort of control over the generally accepted view of the world achieved through the engendering of false consciousness and false needs by such means as control over the media and advertising, thus subliminally persuading society at large, and the workers in particular, that life under capitalism is the norm, that there is no realistic alternative, that they need the products

and service which capitalism has to offer and must work to obtain them. A third approach has been to analyse the adaptability and longevity of the capitalist system by a historical analysis of accumulation regimes – that is, the particular forms of arrangement between the state and capital or forms of regulation (regimes) that have emerged to ensure the continued survival and growth (accumulation) of capital at particular times. Thus the social democratic consensus supported by Keynesian economic management, which held sway in the West in the 1950s and 1960s, is seen as one accumulation regime, which, when it was no longer successful, was replaced by the Thatcherist New Right era of the 1980s, which, in turn has been replaced by a 'flexible' regime of accumulation, consistent with the move to a post-Fordist environment (Allen, 1992: 194; Henry, 2001: 199ff.).

Under the Marxist or Communist regimes in the Soviet Union and Eastern bloc, all industrial and economic power was vested in the state and the Communist Parties instituted one-party states. International politics was dominated by the cold war between the Communist East and the capitalist West from the 1950s to the end of the1980s and the collapse of the Communist system in the Soviet Union and Eastern Europe. While Marxism was clearly a force to be reckoned with internationally, its political influence within the Western democracies during this period was, with a few exceptions (e.g. Italy), minimal, being largely confined to some left-leaning trade unions and the left wings of democratic socialist parties. Its influence was, however, quite marked in some academic disciplines, notably sociology and cultural studies. The demise of the Soviet Union and the Eastern bloc Communist states, symbolized by the fall of the Berlin Wall in 1989, produced a crisis of confidence in Western Marxists. David Harvey refers to the collapse of the Wall as:

> the last nail in the coffin of any sort of Marxist credibility … To pretend there was anything interesting about Marx after 1989 was to sound more and more like an all-but extinct dinosaur whimpering its own last rites. Free-market capitalism rode triumphantly across the globe, slaying all such old dinosaurs in its path. 'Marx talk' was increasingly confined to what might

best be described as an increasingly geriatric 'New left' … By the early 1990s the intellectual heft of Marxian theory seemed to be terminally in decline'.

(Harvey, 2000: 5)

Admitting that Marx's ideas were difficult to relate to everyday life in the 1970s and 1980s, he argues that, with the changed international economic environment of the 1990s and beyond, Marx's writing 'teems with ideas as to how to explain our current state', but that it remains unfashionable among social scientists. Cassidy (1997) notes that even some business people in the West are beginning to suggest that Marx's portrayal of capitalism is surprisingly relevant to the current globalized system, with its massive international flows of speculative money, substantial and disruptive changes affecting ordinary people's lives and huge fortunes won and lost on the stock exchanges of the world.

The relevance of Marxism to the study of leisure and leisure policy lies not so much in the proposals for leisure provision in a future communist society, but in its critical analysis of contemporary capitalist societies. The idea of false needs is particularly pertinent to leisure, since many of the goods and services that people in Western societies seek, once basic necessities have been acquired, are leisure goods and services, including such consumer goods and services as home-entertainment equipment, leisure footwear and clothing, photographic and video equipment, swimming-pools and boats, and such services as restaurant meals, concerts and holidays. Marxist analysis would suggest that it is the clever marketing activity of capitalism that keeps people on the materialist treadmill, working and striving to achieve these products of the market system and thereby perpetuating the capitalist system. One view is that modern technology could release the masses from the burden of constant labour if capitalism were replaced by a socialist society (Harrington, 1974; Gorz, 1980a). Leisure is also seen as a means of *resistance* to the forces of capitalism: youth groups and subcultures, certain art and music forms, the historical struggle for reduced working hours, the phenomenon of 'dropping out', and institutions such as workers' clubs (Alt, 1979) are all means by which ordinary people are seen to attempt to 'do their own thing' rather than conform to the dictates of the capitalist system.

The Marxist critique also applies to the role of the state in leisure provision. It argues that by providing those leisure services which the market is incapable of delivering – such as parks, sports facilities, children's play facilities, quality arts output and conservation of the natural and historic heritage – the state provides capitalism with a civilized face. Left to the market system, the leisure scene would be bleak indeed, and people might begin to question the efficacy of the market as a system for meeting needs. Not only does the state provide capitalism with a human face, but, the argument goes, it provides a basic infrastructure at the public expense upon which the private sector builds profitable enterprises – for example, the public underpinning of sport enables the private sector to profit from the sale of sporting equipment and clothing and the subsidized arts underpin profits in the music, film and television industry.

Additional Marxist analysis would point to the divisiveness, élitism and competitiveness of leisure institutions, particularly in sport, which perpetuate and reinforce the class divisions in society (see Clarke and Critcher, 1985: 147–150; McKay, 1986, 1991).

Democratic Socialism

Democratic socialism or, as Henry (2001: 49) terms it, Utopian or reformist socialism, can trace its roots back to before the industrial revolution in Europe, in the form of various workers' and peasant protest and reform movements. However, it emerged as a reformist political movement under 19th-century capitalism, reflecting the interests of the working classes as against the liberal industrialists and middle classes and the conservative aristocracy.

The essential tenets of democratic socialism are an emphasis on equality and fraternity rather than liberty; defence of the interests of the working class as against those of the middle and ruling classes; belief in the power of the state to control capitalism through state ownership and control of key industries; belief in the power of the state to create more equality and provide welfare for the community through progressive taxation and the establishment of a welfare state; belief that change can be brought about by democratic means, via parliamentary methods; and a belief that capitalism can be tamed and controlled and perhaps gradually replaced by socialism and does not have to be overthrown by force.

Social democracy is a related ideology which does not envisage the replacement of capitalism by socialism, but accepts the continued existence of capitalism alongside a strong welfare state. There is, therefore, considerable overlap between the ideas of democratic socialism and those of social democracy. The latter segment of the political spectrum is discussed separately below. The major state organizations, such as the institutions of the welfare state, public health-care systems and state utilities and enterprises, have generally been established by democratic socialist or social democratic governments.

Traditionally in Britain, the Labour Party, the political arm of the labour/trade union movement, has been sometimes a democratic socialist party, sometimes a social democratic party and often an amalgam of the two. However, in its struggle to gain electoral support, it has faced a great deal of soul-searching over which of its long-standing socialist tenets to retain and which to abandon.

In the case of the democratic socialist therefore, capitalism is tolerated, at least in the medium term. A socialist society is a long-term aim. Meanwhile the state is embraced as the main vehicle for achievement of goals – which is the exact opposite of the liberal position, which is to tolerate the state and embrace the market. These beliefs translate into a very active role for the state in leisure provision in all its forms. Mainstream-economics arguments about market failure, as discussed in Chapter 4, are accepted and used to support and justify state activity where necessary, but concerns

for equality and democracy are probably the stronger motivators. Thus democratic socialists see a major role for governments to play in supporting sport, the arts and community and outdoor recreation. While excellence and élitism are viewed with suspicion by some democratic socialists, for others they are supported as a celebration of the success of state activity. However, at the same time, access, mass participation and democratization of institutions are stressed. At the local level, access to leisure facilities is seen as a right and the provision of such services as a part of social welfare, a means by which the standard of living and quality of life of disadvantaged groups can be improved. Even though tourism is a largely private-sector industry, democratic socialists generally have no qualms about using government funds to promote tourism or to finance tourism enterprises – since they believe in government involvement in economic development and in the efficacy of state enterprise.

As with each of the political philosophies discussed in this chapter, democratic socialism embraces a range of beliefs. The left wing are happy to embrace much of Marxism, seeking fundamental change to the capitalist system, but via democratic reforms. Right-wing democratic socialists, however, would reject most of Marx, would be happier to call themselves social democrats and may be indistinguishable from some members on the left of conservatism.

Social Democracy and Third-way Politics

As indicated above, social democracy is a left-leaning philosophy that supports the welfare state and public services and greater social equality. But it differs from democratic socialism in being generally more tolerant of private enterprise, believing that capitalism, suitably regulated, is here to stay; it does not therefore envisage, even in the long term, a transformation into a socialist society (Veal, 1998). In practice, therefore, attitudes towards leisure and policies for leisure tend to be almost identical to those of democratic socialists.

In Britain, social democrats have tradition-ally been the middle to right wing of the Labour Party, with the centre–left of the party consisting of democratic socialists. In the 1980s, a dissident group of social democrats broke away from the Labour Party to form the Social Democratic Party, but it gained lit-tle electoral support. During the latter half of the 20th century the Liberal Party had, con-fusingly, become a social democratic party and, in the late 1980s, they joined together with the Social Democrats to form the Liberal Democrats. A similar pattern occurred in Australia, but in a different time frame, with the Australian Democrats being formed by a breakaway group of the Australian Labor Party in the 1960s. In the USA the Democratic Party is generally seen as being social democ-ratic in philosophy, although a more right-wing electorate prevents the development of the sorts of welfare state developed under other social democratic parties. In Europe social democratic parties occupy a similar position to the Labour Party in Britain, with the Scandinavian parties being particularly strong and electorally successful.

Social democracy was given a new spin in the second half of the 1990s by the Blair Labour government in Britain, using the terms New Labour and third-way politics, and by the Clinton government in the USA, using the terms new progressivism, New Democrats and later third way. Anthony Giddens, a soci-ologist adviser to Tony Blair, who has written extensively on third-way politics, states that it is 'above all an endeavour to respond to change' (Giddens, 2000: 27), the major changes being: globalization; the declining relevance of class conflict; and the growing importance of the information/knowledge economy. He identifies the main principles of third-way pol-itics as follows:

1. A focus on the 'centre' of politics rather than a class-based left/right divide.
2. Keeping a balance between government, the market and 'civil society'.
3. Adopting the principle of 'no rights with-out responsibilities' as a feature of citizen-ship.
4. Fostering a 'diversified society based on egalitarian principles' – equality of opportu-nity rather than equality of outcomes.

5. Taking 'globalization seriously' – exploit-ing the opportunities it offers rather than opposing it (summary of Giddens, 2000: 50–54).

Third-way politics has been subject to widespread criticism, from both left and right (Giddens, 2000: 1–26). For some, it is just a mishmash of policies designed to appeal to the middle ground and get the Labour Party elected to government in Britain and there-fore, in practice, regardless of the rhetoric, it adopts the policies of many of its liberal/New Right opponents. Thus the first of Giddens principles above could be seen as a desertion of Labour's working-class roots; the second and fifth principles downplay the role of the state and embrace the market as enthusiastically as the Conservatives; the third policy can be seen as abandoning the principles of the welfare state; and the fourth principle can be seen as basically abandoning the quest for equality as too hard and adopt-ing the same supposed level-playing-field philosophy as the Conservatives.

The reference to civil society should be noted. Recent talk of civil society is an attempt to give emphasis to non-economic features of public life. Many believe that technological, economic and social change during much of the 20th century resulted in a loss of community. For a range of reasons, people have become more self-centred or inward-looking, to the family unit and immediate acquaintances: there is less neigh-bourliness and increasing alienation from the wider society. This results in rising levels of such social ills as crime, family breakdown and suicide. An emphasis on civil society is intended to counter these trends: the idea is to take account of *social capital* as well as eco-nomic capital (Cox, 1995). This is clearly rele-vant to leisure, since many leisure-based organizations can be seen as part of a soci-ety's social capital. However, apart from an increased role for the voluntary sector, it is not clear exactly how this is to come about.

Third-way principles are official policy for the Labour Party in Britain. In the USA, with the end of the Clinton administration, it remains to be seen whether the Democratic Party will continue to promote third-way ideas. In Europe, the situation is mixed, with some Labour parties adopting third-way ideas, some being opposed and some claiming to have been practising them for years (Giddens, 2000: 14–21). It is arguable that third way policies were followed by the Australian Hawke/Keating Labor governments of 1982–1996, without the terminology. As right-wing Labor administrations, they adopted many of the policies that later came to be called third-way. In opposition, however, the Australian Labor Party under Kim Beazley has not nailed its colours explicitly to the third-way mast, with avowedly third-way advocates, such as MP Mark Latham (1998), somewhat sidelined.

Given that third-way politics represents a shift to the centre, it can be expected that leisure and tourism policies would move away from heavy state involvement and towards a greater involvement of the private sector. In fact, probably because leisure is rarely a high priority for governments, particularly in a first term, there is little sign of this happening with the Blair government in Britain. The CCT of local government services introduced by the Conservatives has ended, although the emphasis on efficiency and cost-cutting remains, through such programmes as best value and customer service charters, as discussed in Chapters 10 and 2, respectively. Although it was not labelled as third-way, an example of third-way thinking from a social democratic party was the 1994 Australian Labor government's policy on the arts, *Creative Nation* (Commonwealth of Australia, 1994). Reflecting Giddens's fourth principle of third-way politics – embracing globalization – the policy laid great emphasis on new communications technology and allocated substantial funds for initiatives involving the Internet and CD-ROM-based materials. While support for traditional art forms was reaffirmed, it was clear that the excitement lay with the new technology and global thinking.

Feminism

While the struggle for women's rights dates back at least to the campaigns for women's voting rights in the early part of the 20th cen-

tury, modern feminism dates from the 1960s. Whether feminism can be described as a political ideology or a movement or pressure group is open to debate. A number of writers point out that feminism is not a single ideology, but exists in various forms, reflecting the mainstream ideologies discussed above. In party terms, feminists have generally aligned themselves with the forces of the left; in general there have not been separate feminist political parties.

At the core of most feminist analyses of society is the idea of patriarchy – that is, that men organize and control society in their own interests, to the exclusion and disadvantage of women. Essentially the argument is that men wield excessive power in society and that, historically, institutions and customs have developed to perpetuate this situation. Where various feminists disagree is over what should be done about it.

Reformist feminists believe that, through campaigns within the mainstream political process, a range of reforms, such as equal pay, antidiscrimination legislation and improvements in child-care provision, can be instituted, which will eventually achieve equality between men and women in society. Marxist, or radical, feminists, on the other hand, argue that patriarchy is as fundamental to capitalism as the struggle between the classes; the exploitation of women as a group is as endemic to the system as the exploitation of workers as a group. So the only solution is a socialist revolution. Under a socialist or communist society, the conditions for the domination and exploitation of women would be removed.

There is a substantial literature relating feminist ideas and analysis to leisure (e.g. Deem, 1986a; Wimbush and Talbot, 1988; Henderson *et al.*, 1989; Green, E. *et al.*, 1990; Wearing, 1998). This literature points out that, because they continue to bear the bulk of child- and home-care responsibilities, women have much less leisure time than men, and their leisure is often subservient to the leisure of others – for example, in entertaining at home, going out on a family picnic or a self-catering holiday, or in accompanying children or partners to their sporting or other leisure events. Social customs, frequently reinforced by commercial media and marketing, limit the range of activities considered to be suitable for women. The institutions and infrastructure of leisure – especially sport – are dominated by men and orientated to men's needs and ways of doing things (Mowbray, 1992, 1993). Thus the whole pattern of leisure reinforces the patriarchal system of society. As with the Marxist critique, however, it has also been pointed out that such leisure as they enjoy can be used by women as a medium for resistance to the patriarchal forces in society (Wearing, 1990).

In so far as state provision has supported the development of the current institutions (e.g. grants to men-only or male-dominated sports clubs), it has reinforced and perpetuated the inequality of women. The reformist feminist solution as far as leisure provision is concerned, is to use the state to right the balance by, for example, greatly increasing child-care provision at leisure venues and providing more support for traditional women's activities, such as women's sports, and paying attention to such issues as transport access to leisure venues and safety.

Environmentalism

As with feminism, the status of the environmental, or green, movement as a political ideology alongside the mainstream ideologies discussed above is open to debate, given that, as with feminism, there are a variety of green perspectives, often reflecting the mainstream political ideologies. The green movement has been divided on whether it should campaign independently as a pressure group to bring about change, whether it should seek to infiltrate and change mainstream party policies or whether it should form green parties to operate independently. All three solutions continue to be pursued.

The fundamental environmentalist argument is that, while the mainstream political ideologies differ on how society should be organized and which interest groups should dominate, in fact they all share the same, misguided aim, which is the pursuit of materialist economic growth. The greens argue

that this should not be the goal of society because unlimited economic growth, of a conventional kind, is incompatible with the continued survival of planet earth. Existing damage to the environment, in terms of pollution and excessive exploitation of non-renewable natural resources, such as old-growth forests, demonstrates the long-term unsustainability of current practices (Porritt, 1984).

As with feminism, there are leftist and rightist sets of green solutions. Greens of a right-wing or centrist tendency would argue that capitalist industry and commerce can and must be controlled and reformed through legislation requiring it to reduce pollution and environmentally exploitative practices, and that private citizens must be encouraged and required by the state to recycle waste and change consumption patterns. More radical greens would argue that the inexorable search for profit by capitalism makes attempts at such reforms futile and therefore the only way to save the environment is to bring about a fundamental change through the replacement of capitalism altogether. As André Gorz puts it:

> the ecological movement is not an end in itself, but a stage in the larger struggle ... what are we really after? A capitalism adapted to ecological constraints; or a social, economic, and cultural revolution that abolishes the constraints of capitalism and, in so doing, establishes a new relationship between the individual and society and between people and nature? Reform or revolution?
>
> (Gorz, 1980b: 4)

The environmental argument relates to leisure in a fundamental way. Leisure can be seen as a major offender in the consumer society: in so far as people want more, it is often leisure goods and services which they want more of. Of course, it could be argued that not all leisure depends on material props – much of leisure activity involves simple social interaction or the consumption of services, such as going to a show or a sports match or to a restaurant, which are relatively undemanding on material resources. Further, it could be argued that more leisure time means less work, which means less material production. However, many leisure services do involve the use of material resources, such as fuel to travel (particularly air travel) and the range of leisure hardware, on which consumers spend billions of pounds a year. Thus, in most capitalist societies, in practice, more leisure entails more material consumption.

Much leisure and tourism activity makes direct use of the natural environment. If it is not conserved, then it will not be available for the enjoyment of current or future generations. Conservation is generally achieved through the intervention of the state, either directly, through such mechanisms as the designation of national parks and wilderness areas, or indirectly, through planning and pollution controls.

The idea of sustainability has become the catchword of the environmental movement in recent years, as a result, in particular, of the publication of the 1990 report of the World Commission on Environment and Development, *Our Common Future* (The 'Brundtland Report', WCED, 1990) and the publication in 1992 of an action plan, 'Agenda 21', following the United Nations 'Earth Summit' in Rio de Janeiro (Robinson, N.A., 1993). As discussed in Chapter 2, sustainable development is development that does not 'compromise the ability of future generations to meet their needs'. Because of its attraction to unspoilt natural environments, this issue has loomed particularly large in relation to tourism development. The forcefulness of the 'Agenda 21' and international debate about such issues as global warming added considerably to the momentum behind the environmental movement in the 1990s. The result is frequent opposition to many tourism developments in natural areas, arising from a consortium of local residents and politically active environmentalists.

Antiglobalism

Whether or not the opposition to globalization that emerged in the 1990s can be called an ideology or just a movement is debatable, but it is discussed here because it has achieved such a high profile, eclipsing

many more traditional political movements, at least in terms of media attention. The reason for the uncertainty is that, not surprisingly, given its relative youth, the ideas and ideals of the movement have not been as fully spelled out or subject to such detailed examination and analysis as longer-established perspectives.

As Zygmunt Bauman (1998: 1) has said: '"Globalization" is on everybody's lips; a fad word fast turning into a shibboleth, a magic incantation, a pass-key meant to unlock the gates to all present and future mysteries.' Particular features of a globalized world are: the international reach of multinational enterprises (MNEs), such as Sony, AOL–Time–Warner, McDonald's, Nike and News Ltd; the speeding up, massively increased capacity and reduced cost of international telecommunications, facilitated by satellite technology; the consequent massive and instantaneous electronic movement of capital funds between the world's financial centres; the spread of the Internet; the world-wide spread of cultural product, such as film, television programmes, music and sporting events and their influence on national cultures; the internationalization of moral–political–lifestyle debates and movements (such as women's movements, environmentalism, birth-control issues – and, indeed, antiglobalism); and the advent of mass tourism.

While undoubtedly developing rapidly in the last two decades, globalization is not a totally new concept. Langhorne (2001) traces the basis of globalization to the speed-up of international communication brought about by steam trains and ships and the electric telegraph in the 19th century, with its full development emerging with the advent of computers, satellite communications and the Internet in the last quarter of the 20th century. However, even ignoring earlier phenomena, such as the Alexandrian, Roman and Mogul empires, the Roman Catholic Church had reached truly global proportions by the 17th century, with a universal product and even a globally recognized logo. The British Empire, 'on which the sun never set', had extended into five continents by the 19th century. Hollywood established its worldwide reach in the 1930s and companies such as Ford, Shell, British Petroleum (BP) and Hoover had developed into multinational companies by the middle of the 20th century.

The focus of the antiglobalization movement has been the activities of multinational or transglobal companies, which have emerged along with the new communications technology and with the deregulation of international trade established through the General Agreement on Tariffs and Trade (GATT) and its successor the World Trade Organization (WTO). As a result of all these changes, and changes in management practices, there has been a shift of jobs in some industries, notably clothing and footwear manufacture and lightweight assembly, such as electronics, from high-wage Western countries to low-wage developing countries in South America and Asia.

The number and sheer size of the MNEs makes them a significant economic force in the world, with the power to locate their activities wherever they wish, in order to minimize wages and taxation and maximize access to markets. This, together with the free-trade protocols put in place under GATT and WTO agreements, is seen as threatening the powers of individual governments – a shift of sovereignty from democratic governments to unaccountable commercial entities. A further criticism of globalization lies in the cultural area: large, multifunctional, predominantly American-based, communications organizations, such as News Ltd and AOL–Time–Warner, are believed to be potentially dangerous for free speech and, together with MNEs involved in areas such as fashion and music, threaten a world-wide homogenization of culture and consequent loss of local culture and diversity (Barnet and Cavanagh, 1996). The MNEs, the WTO and the international financial system, including special international financial agencies such as the International Monetary Fund (IMF) and the World Bank – collectively referred to as 'global capital' – have become the target of attack by a loose collection of groups of activists, largely from Western countries and themselves organized mainly via the Internet. In particular, the movement has targeted high-profile meetings of such bodies, where mass demonstrations have been organized and widely publicized.

One of the most well-known representatives of the movement is Canadian journalist Naomi Klein, who presents the antiglobalization case in her book *No Logo* (Klein, 1999). The book concentrates on the growth of the brand in the North American economy and consumer culture, particularly consumer brands, such as Nike sports footwear, Gap clothing, Marlboro cigarettes and Starbucks coffee. A particular focus is on the trend for clothing companies in particular to downsize their labour forces in Western countries and to contract all or most of their manufacturing to low-wage sweatshops in developing countries. One of the strategies of the various antiglobalization groups that grew up around these issues in the 1990s has been to seek to embarrass companies like Nike by publicizing the sweatshop phenomenon and leading boycotts of their products until they undertake to ensure improved conditions for their contracted workers. But, as Klein points out, this strategy, even if successful, simply sanitizes and reinforces the position of the companies and does not attack the broader agenda of the movement, which is outright opposition to global capital. Klein's solution is a very traditional one – that the answer will only come through a self-directed struggle for rights and decent conditions by the workers in the sweatshops themselves.

As a protest movement, antiglobalism overlaps with other movements, as illustrated by the collection of papers entitled *The Case Against the Global Economy*, published by the California-based environmental organization the Sierra Club (Mander and Goldsmith, 1996) and papers on feminism and globalization in Sassen's *Globalization and its Discontents* (1998).

Opposition to the antiglobalization movement – or defence of globalization – is likely to come primarily from those who subscribe to a liberal ideology. Rugman (2000), for example, argues that globalization trends have been exaggerated and very few companies are genuinely global. He notes that most international trade takes place within regions (the European Union (EU), Asia, the Americas) rather than between them and that most MNEs are regionally focused, and concludes: 'No credible evidence can be found to support the viewpoint that a system of global capitalism exists' (Rugman, 2000: 218).

There are also alternative academic perspectives on some of the globalization themes. For example, it is suggested that alongside, and possibly countering, the cultural homogenization tendency of globalization is a tendency towards cultural diversity and affirmation of national cultural identities (Maguire, 1999: 21). Featherstone (1990) argues that global culture may not involve homogenization or annihilation of national cultures but may represent a separate, additional cultural phenomenon arising from international exchange. There is also the suggestion that, while globalization may tend to marginalize certain disadvantaged groups, it can provide a platform for some groups to internationalize their cause – for example, indigenous land rights. And the fact that centres for international capital must locate somewhere, notably in international cities (New York, Paris, London, Hong Kong, Sydney), provides a network of globalized platforms for political organization and campaigns by disadvantaged groups (Sassen, 1998).

The globalization debate clearly has implications for leisure and tourism. Many of the global products are leisure-related, including sports (Maguire, 1999), music and associated hardware, film, fashion and eating fast food and drinking coffee, beer and spirits. Tourism is quintessentially a global industry, although, while airlines and some hotel groups are among the major multinational corporations, tourism companies are rarely the target of antiglobalist protest. Much tourism research in recent years has focused on the type of tourism that involves seeking out the strange and exotic – hence the use of the term the 'tourist gaze' (Urry, 1990). The threatened homogenization of culture might, therefore, be considered a threat to tourism. In fact, however, this type of tourism is far outweighed in volume by domestic tourism generally, 'non-gazing'

domestic and international tourism, such as the Blackpool/Southend phenomenon in Britain and the Gold Coast in Australia, the European Spanish 'costa' tourism and pilgrimages to the headquarters of world popular culture – Disneyland, Disney World and Hollywood. On this evidence, it would appear that tourism could survive global homogenization.

Summary: Ideologies, Leisure, Tourism and the State

- Ideologies can be characterized by their attitudes towards a range of issues, including: social change; economic growth; social inequality; élitism; the market system; and the role of the state. These characteristics are summarized in Table 3.2.
- Generally only the conservative ideology is not in favour of changing the status quo. This is, however, to some extent a reflection of the particular current situation in the Western democracies. Where non-conservatives hold power for a long period of time, sufficient to bring about radical change, then what were previously conservative forces themselves become supporters of change and the previous radicals become conservative: hence the confusing terminology in the former Communist states of Eastern Europe. But similar confusion could come about in Western countries such as Britain, where the liberal right have held sway for some time: here the conservative 'wets' may in future be seen as the forces of change as they seek to return to a former, less market-dominated society.
- Environmentalism is notable for being the only ideology that has a clearly negative attitude towards conventional economic growth, with antiglobalism somewhat ambivalent on this issue. While some proponents and governments of other ideological persuasions may be more or less green in outlook, in general they seek to show that they have a superior approach to achieving and distributing the product of economic growth.

Table 3.2. Ideologies summarized*

	Change	Economic growth	The capitalist market system	Role of the state	Social equality	Elitism
Conservatism	Against	For	For	Limited	Against	For
Liberalism	For	For	For	Against	Against	For – as symbol of individual success
Marxism/communism	For – by revolution if necessary	For	Against	For – total control	Against	Against (although regimes use it)
Democratic socialism	For – by democratic means	For	For	For – extensive role	For	Against
Social democracy/ third way	For	For	For	For – but limited	For	Ambivalent
Radical feminism	For – by revolution if necessary	For	Against	For	For – between men and women	Against
Reformist feminism	For – by democratic/ legislative means	For	For	Ambivalent	For – between men and women	Ambivalent
Environmentalism	For	Against	For	For – as regulator	Ambivalent	Ambivalent
Antiglobalism	For	Ambivalent	Against	For	Against	Ambivalent

*This table inevitably presents information in highly simplified, 'black and white', form. More details, and qualifications, are provided in the main body of the chapter.

- Attitudes towards the market system vary significantly, with Marxists committed to its abolition and liberals being its main champion, while others wish to see it modified by the activities of the state and voluntary sector. The corollary to this is attitudes towards the role of the state, with liberals being most suspicious and Marxist and democratic socialists most accepting.
- The ideologies differ in their approach to social inequality. Liberals see inequality as the other side of the coin of incentive and freedom – the very mechanism that drives the successful market economy, whereas, at the other extreme, both forms of socialism see the inequalities of the capitalist system as its worst fault, and feminism focuses on the inequality between men and women.
- It cannot be said that leisure is the focus of any of the ideologies discussed above, but it can be shown that they each provides a distinctive perspective for viewing the role of leisure in contemporary society and the role of the state in relation to leisure provision and regulation.

Further Reading

- Philosophical and religious aspects of leisure: Pieper (1965); Dare *et al.* (1987); Fain (1991); Cooper (1999); Sylvester (1999).
- Political ideology and leisure generally: Henry (1984a, b, 1985, 1993, 2001); Bramham and Henry (1985); Coalter (1988, 1990); Wilson (1988); Henry and Spink (1990a).
- Sport and politics: Houlihan (1997).
- Social democracy: Dow (1993); Veal (1998).
- Third-way politics: Giddens (1998, 2000).
- Tourism, politics and the role of government: Hughes (1984); Richter (1989); Jeffries (2001).

- Fascism and anarchism: Wilson (1988); Leach (1993).
- Feminism: Deem (1986a); Wimbush and Talbot (1988); Henderson *et al.* (1989); Green, E. *et al.* (1990); Kenway (1992); Wearing (1998).
- Environmentalism: Gorz (1980b); Porritt (1984); Spretnik and Capra (1985); WCED (1990); Papadakis (1993); Robinson, N.A. (1993); Doyle (2000).
- Antiglobalism: Mander and Goldsmith (1996); Klein (1999); Held and McGrew (2000); Hertz (2001).

Questions/Exercises

1. Consider how the public funding of (a) élite sport, (b) tourism promotion might be viewed from the perspective of each of the political ideologies outlined in this chapter.
2. Why is Marxism relevant today?
3. What are the differences between democratic socialism and social democracy?
4. What are the differences between conservatism and liberalism?
5. Discuss ways in which the leisure and tourism perspectives arising from feminism differ from those from the mainstream political ideologies.
6. Discuss ways in which the leisure and tourism policies arising from environmentalism differ from those from the mainstream political ideologies.
7. What part do leisure and tourism play in globalization and why might these features be subject to criticism by antiglobalists?
8. Examine any national or local-government leisure or tourism policy document and suggest what the implicit political philosophy behind it is.
9. Via the Internet, explore the possibility of discovering the leisure and tourism policies of one of the major political parties.
10. Discuss the place of equality and inequality in leisure and tourism as seen from different political perspectives.

4

The Market versus the State

Introduction

In a book on public policy, it is important to examine, theoretically as well as practically, the role of the state. In the preceding chapter this issue was considered from a number of ideological perspectives. Here the issue is considered using the perspective of academic disciplines, although the two types of perspective cannot always be easily separated. For example, Marxism is both an ideology and a mode of academic analysis. At the other end of the political spectrum, New Right liberalism is generally associated with mainstream economic analysis. The rest of this chapter is divided into four sections: first there is a brief discussion of the current world-wide triumph of capitalism, followed by an outline of the approach of mainstream economics to the role of the state within capitalism, and next a number of further issues concerning the role of the state are discussed, including the question of facilitating versus direct provision and the effects of globalization. The chapter concludes with an outline of recent history in the role of the state, particularly in Britain.

The Triumph of Capitalism

Since the collapse of the Communist regimes in Eastern Europe, most of the world now operates, or is attempting to operate, under a capitalist or market economic system. In this system the process of organizing the production and distribution of goods and services is largely in the hands of a mass of private-enterprise organizations operating through market processes, with governments playing a restricted role. Nevertheless, in most Western capitalist countries, about a third of all economic activity is accounted for by government activities (Hodge, 2000: 3).

The evidence of opinion polls and elections suggests that the majority of people in Western societies, rightly or wrongly, see market capitalism as a basically acceptable system for running economic affairs. Some want to see less state activity and some want to see more, but few seem to wish to see the system changed fundamentally, to the extent that the society would no longer be basically capitalist. At present, capitalism is triumphant around the world – it has its critics (e.g. Korten, 1996) but few, if any, plausible, realistic alternatives. This does not of course mean that the majority are correct and the minority are wrong: it merely indicates the apparent political status quo. We have seen that neo-Marxist theorists have argued that this apparent acceptance of the status quo is achieved only through a massive deception imposed on the Western public by the economic and cultural power of the ruling élites in the capitalist system, who control and manipulate the communication media. The idea of hegemony, by which powerful groups succeed in persuading society at large that current arrangements are the natural order of things, has been put forward as one way of theorizing this process. Others, particularly mainstream economic theorists, provide what they see as a perfectly rational explanation as to why the market should be viewed as an acceptable system for organizing economic activity. Yet others, such as postmodern and post-structuralist theorists, reject both of these grand theories and argue that the socio-cultural system cannot be understood in terms of single grand theories.

However, it is the economic rationalist perspective which holds political sway in most of the world at present. It is therefore important that anyone studying the public policy process should understand its basis, which lies in mainstream economics. What is often neglected by critics of economic rationalism is that mainstream economics, while primarily concerned with market processes, also includes a well-developed theory of the role of the state, which identifies situations in which the state might, and even should, intervene in a basically capitalist/market economy, but which is still consistent with the continuation of the market system – indeed, in some cases is fundamental to its continued viability.

Mainstream Economics

Introduction

The idea that the market mechanism is the norm and government activity is appropriate only in certain specified circumstances is the basis of mainstream economics, the basic approach to economics as taught in business and economics courses in most Western universities. It is referred to here as mainstream economics to distinguish it from various forms of Marxist, socialist or radical economics, which reject the market system on ideological grounds, and from other critics, such as Galbraith (1973) and Hirsch (1977), who have questioned aspects of mainstream economics on more technical grounds (see Stretton, 1999).

Taken as a whole, mainstream economics should perhaps be referred to as political economy, the area of academic thought which spans politics and economics. When interpreted in its most extreme form, this framework is referred to as 'dry' economics or 'economic rationalism'; it takes on ideo-

logical overtones associated with the liberal beliefs outlined in Chapter 3. However, since mainstream economic analysis provides a useful framework for examining the role of the state within the market system, it can and is used by those of more left-leaning political persuasions to successfully justify state activity within a market environment.

The review below includes few references to sources, since what is presented is standard economic theory, widely accepted among economists, but references to texts that outline the theory in more depth are given in the Further Reading section at the end of the chapter. The review is divided into four sections, dealing in turn with: the workings of the market in general; the role of the state; market failure – the main theoretical arguments for state intervention; and social/political arguments for state intervention.

The workings of the market

The free, unregulated market mechanism should, according to mainstream economic theory, be the best means of organizing the delivery of goods and services to meet people's needs. In the market-place people indicate their desires, preferences and priorities for goods and services by their willingness to pay, or not to pay, for the goods and services on offer. Entrepreneurs note this willingness-to-pay and this justifies them in hiring the labour and investing the capital necessary to provide the goods or services in demand. Entrepreneurs bid in the market-place to buy the labour and other resources, such as land and raw materials, which are necessary to produce the goods and services that people demand. Things that people want are successfully sold; things people do not want stay on the supermarket shelves. The entrepreneurs use this information about what people want and are willing and able to pay for, and what they do not want and/or are not willing or unable to pay for, to adjust their production schedules so that supply is brought into line with demand. No central body is needed to organize this – the market mechanism brings the resources, the supplier and the consumer together: the consumer pays and the consumer is believed to be sovereign because he or she decides whether or not to buy. Economic theory is, of course, more complex than this, and includes explanations of how consumers with different tastes and preferences balance their purchases within their income constraints, how firms respond to market information and seek to maximize profits, and how capital and labour markets work. Some economic theory involves the development of mathematical models to replicate these various market processes.

There are some stringent conditions attached to the analysis, the most important of which is that there must be competition among suppliers – monopoly negates much of the analysis.

Therefore, it is argued, in a competitive market situation, state activity should be kept to a minimum, because the state is less effective, efficient and responsive in meeting people's needs than the market, In fact, it is argued, the state, through its coercive powers, such as regulation and taxation, is a potential threat to the freedom of operation of the market. Government activity should therefore be permitted only where it is unavoidable – for example, in providing a framework of law and order and enforceable contracts – and all efforts should be made to keep the activities of government to a minimum.

The role of the state

The economist Milton Friedman, who was a guru of economic rationalists in the 1970s and a staunch advocate of the market system, quotes approvingly the 18th century political economist Adam Smith, who outlined three essential duties of government:

> first, the duty of protecting the society from the violence and invasion of other independent societies; secondly, the duty of protecting, as far as possible, every member of the society from the injustice or oppression of every other member of it, or the duty of establishing an exact administration of justice; and, thirdly, the duty of erecting and maintaining certain public works and certain public institutions, which it

can never be for the interest of any individual, or small number of individuals, to erect and maintain; because the profit could never repay the expense to any individual or small number of individuals, though it may frequently do much more than repay it to a great society.
> (quoted in Friedman and Friedman, 1979: 49)

Thus national defence, maintenance of the rule of law and public works are seen as necessary and legitimate activities for government. Friedman adds a fourth, namely 'the duty to protect members of the community who cannot be regarded as "responsible" individuals' (p. 53). These include children and the mentally ill or handicapped. In the discussion below, Friedman's 'public works' have been subsumed under the category of 'market failure' and his fourth argument is widened somewhat to include other social/political arguments for government activity. Four broad functions of government within a primarily market system can therefore be identified as: (i) national defence; (ii) law and order; (iii) dealing with market failure; and (iv) interventions based on socio/political arguments. Each of these is discussed in turn below.

National defence

Leisure and tourism have some indirect connections with national defence. Certain sporting activities, such as equestrian activities, fencing and archery, have a military history and these and other sports are seen as valuable for training and maintaining fitness of military personnel. Sport has in the past been promoted as a means of maintaining physical fitness for military preparedness for the general (male) population – for example, the 'keep fit' campaign launched in Britain between the two world wars. So, in an indirect way, national defence provides justification for government involvement in sport. The military are also, incidentally, direct providers of leisure and tourism attractions, in the form of military bands and tattoos, air shows, monuments and museums and, in Britain, such rituals as the changing of the guard at Buckingham Palace and the institution of the Yeomen of the Guard at the Tower of London.

National defence also gives rise to government restrictions on leisure activity – for example, the military often occupy substantial areas of land and water that would be ideal for recreation. And international travel restrictions, such as visa requirements, are often, at least partly, related to national security considerations.

Law and order

The impact of the government activity of maintaining law and order on leisure and tourism is largely restrictive. Legal restrictions apply to activities that are seen to have antisocial and/or moral implications, such as gambling, the sale of alcohol and the use of recreational drugs. In some cases government assumes ownership of certain assets and regulates them to prevent a free-for-all - for example, airspace, radio and television broadcast channels and coastal waterways and fisheries. Some regulatory activities are designed to protect economic interests – for example, copyright laws. Others are designed for public safety – for example, fire and safety regulations in places of entertainment or in transport. Gun laws are a particularly controversial area where the recreational activity of hunting is affected by the demands of law and order. In a more positive sense, public leisure provision for young people is often justified on the grounds that, if socially acceptable outlets are not available, then young people are more likely to engage in antisocial, delinquent behaviour (Smith, 1975).

Market failure

Friedman sees the third of these duties as raising the 'most troublesome issue', because it can be 'interpreted to justify unlimited extensions of government power'. In fact, all four categories could be seen as raising troublesome issues: defence expenditure can consume disproportionate amounts of a country's budget and can result in offensive rather than defensive behaviour; law-and-order issues can become highly controversial; and humanitarian measures become politically controversial when they are widened to constitute a welfare state. Much of the economics of the state is aimed at analysing the third, troublesome, option – that is, attempting to analyse those situations where an activity is not profitable for the private sector to undertake, but is beneficial to society at large. In general such situations are referred to as cases of market failure.

Market failure refers to situations where the market mechanism does not work very well or at all. Other situations where the state might become involved in markets are more social and political than economic. Cases of market failure are outlined first and the social and political cases are outlined subsequently. Another term used in this context is inefficiency. Perfectly operating markets can be shown to be an efficient way of distributing goods and services, ensuring maximum output at minimum cost. Market failure is said to produce inefficiencies – the allocation of resources (land, capital, labour) is less than optimal. Measures taken to correct the market failure are therefore said to produce an increase in the *efficiency* of the economy. A number of different types of market failure have been identified by economists; eight of these are discussed in turn in the following section. Subsequently a further four arguments of a more social/political nature are discussed.

Types of Market Failure

A number of different types of market failure are considered in turn below; they are: (i) public goods and services; (ii) externalities/neighbourhood effects; (iii) mixed goods; (iv) merit goods; (v) option demand; (vi) infant industries; (vii) size of project; and (viii) natural monopoly. The ideas have for some time been widely accepted in the economics literature, albeit with slightly varying terminology, interpretation and emphasis. Only minimal reference is therefore made to the literature in the following summaries, but references for further reading are given at the end of the chapter. While each criterion/phenomenon is discussed in turn, it should be noted that more than one criterion usually applies to any particular case of state provision.

Public goods and services

In economic jargon, public goods or services have two characteristics: they are non-excludable and non-rival. Non-excludable means that it is not technically possible to exclude anyone from enjoying the benefits of the good or service. Non-rival means that one person's enjoyment of the good or service does not preclude others from enjoying it also. The classic examples of public goods and services are national defence and the maintenance of law and order – two of Adam Smith's basic functions of government, as discussed above. Another example is the provision of street lighting. These services are non-excludable because people in the areas affected cannot be excluded from benefiting from the service, and they are non-rival because the provision of the service for one person does not affect its provision for others.

In these circumstances the usual market mechanism, where the consumer pays the provider for the service he/she individually receives, cannot function effectively. There is 'market failure'. The market system, left to its own devices, will not, in these circumstances, produce what people want or would benefit from. Government intervention to provide the service and recoup the costs via taxation is therefore seen as a solution.

Examples of public services in this sense in the field of leisure and tourism include: free-to-air broadcasting; public pride in the success of local or national athletes; public displays, such as fireworks or street parades; and major scenic amenities, such as a conserved historic or natural environment. In the case of broadcasting, the product is 'free to air' and is therefore a public good/service – the fact that some governments choose to finance this by means of a licence to operate a television set and some by taxation, and commercial organizations finance it by selling advertising space, does not alter its intrinsic 'public-good' nature.

In some cases the public-good dimension of a facility or service is directly enjoyed by the general public – as in a firework display or broadcasting. In other cases the enjoyment is more indirect – for example, the general satisfaction and pride people might obtain from knowledge that the nation's, or even the world's, natural or cultural heritage is being preserved. People do not need to visit such places as the Tower of London, the Lake District, the Parthenon or the Great Barrier Reef to obtain some satisfaction from the knowledge that they exist and are being protected from damage. This satisfaction is worth something to people who experience it. These non-users or non-visitors are sometimes referred to as 'vicarious' consumers, and their enjoyment is sometimes referred to as 'psychic' benefit, in contrast to financial or material benefit. Governments feel entitled to contribute to the upkeep and preservation of these phenomena on behalf of these vicarious consumers.

The maintenance of law and order and street lighting were mentioned as examples of 'classic' public services, but such services also have important implications specifically for urban leisure and tourism. If city streets are poorly lit and considered unsafe, then certain groups in the community are discriminated against in terms of their access to leisure at night; such groups include particularly the elderly, women and young people and those without access to private transport. In addition, such areas are not attractive to tourists. Law and order and street lighting can therefore be seen as important leisure-related public services.

In the case of the pure public good, it is technically impossible to charge the consumer for the service. In other cases, it is possible to conceive of a charge being made, but the cost of collecting the charge would be likely to exceed the revenue. This situation can apply in the case of public open space, especially when there are many access points. In this case the facility becomes, de facto, a public good.

It could be argued that people could contribute voluntarily for their enjoyment of public goods and services, but this would give rise to the problem of the free-rider – the person who enjoys the good or service in question but does not pay, assuming that others will bear the cost. Contributions via the taxation system are seen as a fair and efficient means of collecting payment. It might be argued that this can result in some people contributing who do not enjoy the goods or services involved, but, in fact, taxation is levied on the basis of ability to pay, rather than services rendered to the individual taxpayer.

Externalities/neighbourhood effects

Externalities, sometimes referred to as 'neighbourhood effects' or 'third-party effects', arise when specific third parties are affected by transactions between providers and consumers, or when society at large might be considered a third party. Externalities can be negative or positive.

The classic example of a negative externality is pollution – for example, smoke pollution from a factory or noise pollution from an airport. The factory or airport is the *first* party and its customers are the *second* party and they are involved in the transaction of producing and buying the products of the factory or airport; the residents adversely affected by pollution are the *third* party; they are affected by negative externalities. There is market failure here because the producers and consumers are not taking account of all the costs involved in producing the product in question; they are ignoring the costs imposed on the third party. This is a distortion of the market. To overcome this market failure, either the producer should be required (by law) to install equipment to eliminate the pollution or the third party should be compensated, by the government making a levy on the factory or airport owners on behalf of the third party or by the third party suing the polluter in court. Either way the costs of the factory or airport would rise (external costs would be internalized); and the prices it would have to charge the users would rise, and so demand/output could fall.

In the extreme case, costs would rise so much that the product would be priced out of the market and the factory or airport would be forced to close down. This would be accepted as right and proper by the econ-

omist. In the initial situation it would be said that the market is distorted because the factory or airport – and the buyers of their services – is not meeting all its costs and, the product or service is artificially cheap. It is said to be overproducing.

This all sounds perfectly rational and reasonable. In practice, of course, such an issue could become very controversial and would focus on what minimal level of pollution is considered acceptable before the polluter is required to do something about it. It should be noted that the offender in situations of externality is not always an organization. It can be an individual. A classic example is road congestion. Every additional car that uses a road increases congestion and imposes a cost on other road users, in terms of delays and increased fuel consumption, not to mention pollution costs imposed on the community at large.

In the leisure and tourism area, examples of negative externalities arise when facilities, such as pubs, nightclubs or resorts, or tourist traffic imposes noise or congestion costs on neighbouring properties.

Positive externalities work in the opposite direction. The third party can gain benefits which he/she does not pay for. In that situation the producer is receiving a lower income than is justified (that is, not getting income from the third-party beneficiaries) and underproduces because the product or service is less remunerative than it should be. In this case, we talk of positive externalities.

An example might be the private golf-course, which preserves pleasant views for surrounding residents. The latter pay in terms of the higher cost of real estate, but not to the golf-course owner. In fact, many resort-style developments attempt to recoup this externality by developing the golf-course and the surrounding homes. When Walt Disney built Disneyland in California in the 1950s, the tourist-generated traffic provided enormous gains for landowners in the area, who sold to hoteliers to service the theme park. When Disneyworld was built in Florida in the 1970s, the Disney organization bought up much of the surrounding land – ensuring that it internalized the externality.

In the case of tourism, the basic attraction of a destination area may be publicly owned – for example, beaches, mountains, lakes or a historic town centre. The whole of the private-sector tourist industry in the area may nevertheless be dependent on this resource. The resources are *de facto* public goods enjoyed by the public, but part of the benefit is gained by the tourism industry and might be termed externalities. Valuing these externalities may become an issue when questions arise as to the cost of maintaining the basic attractions and the contributions which the tourist industry is asked to make. This idea of the tourist industry being dependent on a common public attraction is known as the *asset theory* of tourism (Gray, 1982).

A further example of positive externalities – or the prevention of negative externalities – is the question of provision of leisure facilities for youth. It is widely believed that young people in particular are liable to engage in antisocial activities in their leisure time – that is, activities which impose external cost on others. Such externalities may be short-term and immediate – for example, vandalism and hooliganism – or long-term – for example, becoming involved in criminal subcultures or harmful drugs. The private sector provides some facilities for young people – in fact, it has been claimed that they can do a better job of keeping them off the street than the state (Smith, 1975). But, since the commercial sector gets no financial benefit from the externalities it produces (for example, the reduction in vandalism and hooliganism), which accrue to the wider community, they will tend to underprovide. State provision or subsidy of suitable leisure facilities for young people is therefore seen as justified. In the light of Smith's (1975) comments about the role of the commercial sector, the most effective use of public funds in some cases might well be to provide subsidies for commercial operators to provide the sorts of facilities that young people want. In practice, other objectives come into play in youth policy, resulting in the provision of certain types of youth facility which are not always the most effective in attracting the most at-risk young people.

Mixed goods

The economists Baumol and Bowen (1976) coined the term 'mixed goods' to refer to those goods or services which combine public and private characteristics, applying the idea particularly to the performing arts. For example, when a person attends an arts performance, it is argued, a number of things happen. First, the person gains a personal benefit (the enjoyment of the performance), which he or she might be expected to pay for. Secondly, the person subsequently becomes a conveyor and supporter of culture – a contributor to a more civilized community. Thirdly, a society with viable cultural industries is believed to benefit in many ways, in terms of such things as quality of life, creativity and spin-off in economic areas such as tourism, design, the attraction of industry and commerce and a lively media sector. Finally, arts facilities can be a source of civic pride even to those who do not use them. Therefore it is believed that the state should pay for part of the cost of the public arts performance, in recognition of these wider social benefits, which are partly public goods and partly positive externalities. This is then a justification for a subsidized theatre / opera / concert seat rather than either a totally free one or a fully commercially priced one.

A similar argument could be applied to an urban park. The person entering the park obtains a certain amount of enjoyment, which he or she might be expected to pay for. The park also offers externality benefits to the owners of the buildings that overlook it. These benefits are reflected in the value of the land, which in turn is reflected in the rates levied on the properties, so some payment returns to the public provider of the park – the council – for the benefit received. A further group of beneficiaries of the park are those people who walk or drive past and benefit from viewing a green space rather than a built-up area – the benefit may be very small per person, but many thousands, or even millions, may enjoy this benefit in the course of the year. Finally parks produce a benefit in cities by dispersing pollution and thus contributing to cleaner air. Thus a park produces a mixture of public and private benefits. In practice, as discussed above, few parks charge users for the private element of the visit by means of an entrance fee, because of the likely cost of collecting the fees.

Rural public open space, such as public forests, country parks and national parks, are also mixed goods, in that they are enjoyed by the users directly (private good), in some cases by vicarious users, as discussed above (public good), by owners of property that overlooks the open space (externality) and by the general public who visit or live in the area and benefit from pleasant views (public good). This last phenomenon also occurs in relation to the benefit produced by the exercise of general planning powers by councils to prevent unsightly development in rural or heritage areas: the resultant amenity which people enjoy in their leisure time can be seen as a public good.

Participation in sport or physical recreation can also be viewed as a mixed good. Individuals engaging in physical exercise gain some private benefit from the experience, in the form of increased fitness and enjoyment of the experience. However, if an individual who is inactive, with deteriorating health or poor health prospects, can be persuaded to take exercise, resulting in improved health, other people benefit, including the person's family, his or her employer, and either taxpayers or other payers of health insurance, depending on how the costs of illness are met. Thus, it is argued, the state, on behalf of these beneficiaries (family, employer, taxpayer, health-insurance subscriber), is justified in subsidizing sport and exercise programmes and facilities or providing the individual with the means to buy such services. It might be argued that the direct beneficiaries from a person's good health should pay, rather than the community at large through the state. This is recognized by those employers who provide exercise facilities at the place of work; some even require their employees to take exercise; and health-insurance companies also become involved in sport and fitness in various ways.

However, because the benefits may be spread over a number of beneficiaries, including government organizations, such as the health service, subsidization and promotion of sport and exercise is accepted as an area of legitimate state involvement.

Merit goods

In some cases, society may decide that certain goods or services are highly desirable for the individual but that individuals require time, experience/exposure or even education in order to come to appreciate them; individuals are incapable of immediately appreciating their value. In this case, it is argued, the state is justified in intervening to provide that exposure to the good or service, by making direct provision or subsidizing others to do so. The most common example of a merit good is education; however, as with many merit goods, it is difficult to disengage the merit-good argument from the public-good and externality aspects.

The merit-good argument can be criticized for being élitist or paternalistic. Who is to decide what is meritorious? The idea that the general public is incapable of appreciating the finer things of life unaided and that certain well-informed groups are capable of identifying these oversights and correcting for them can be a difficult proposition to defend. However, the process of deciding on what are and are not merit goods need not be élitist. In the same way that the smoker may agree that he or she should give up and may be happy to see public funds used to conduct antismoking campaigns, so many people might be willing to see public funds devoted to the support of the higher things of life, aware that they themselves might benefit in due course from such a move.

In the leisure area, examples of merit goods include environmentally based outdoor recreation resources, which may be deemed to require education and interpretation to develop public appreciation, and the more demanding art forms. Generally the merit-good argument can be used to justify educationally orientated programmes, for children or adults.

Option demand

Another idea put forward to support public-sector provision is the concept of option demand – sometimes referred to as existence value. This involves the proposition that there may be certain things which groups of individuals do not at present use and may have no specific plans to use, but who may feel that these things should be maintained so that the option to use them is always there, for themselves or for their children or grandchildren. This applies particularly when the loss of the phenomenon in question would be irreversible. In this case people might wish the government to intervene to ensure that those things are maintained so that the option is preserved. The idea is similar to the vicarious consumer in relation to public goods, but in this case the vicarious consumption is something that may happen in the future.

This argument could apply to virtually all leisure facilities and services that individuals do not currently use but of whose existence they approve.

Infant industries

If a country, state or city sets out to establish a new industry where well-established outside competitors already exist, the industry may find that it is unable to become established because operators already established in the market-place will be able to undercut the local product in terms of such things as price, quality, design and delivery. In these instances it is argued that governments may be justified in intervening for a period to protect the new, infant, industry from its competitors until it is well established and can survive without help. Such intervention could include subsidies of various kinds, such as cash grants, tax breaks and low rents, or tariffs or controls placed on the competitors.

This idea, however, is not widely accepted by mainstream economists because it involves governments trying to pick winners – that is, deciding which new industries should be supported and which should not – and governments are thought by many to be very bad at this (although some point out that certain governments, such as that of Japan, appear to have been quite successful at it). It can also be seen as feather-bedding and preventing the new industry from becoming efficient in order to compete in the market-place. It is argued that, if the industry experiences a loss-making period while establishing itself, these losses should be borne by the investor as part of the set-up/investment costs, not by the taxpayer.

The infant industry argument applies particularly to tourism ventures, particularly in developing countries or less developed areas of developed countries. The argument can also be seen applied in modified form in relation to cultural areas, such as film and the local content of television programmes. In these instances, the industry is generally seen as permanently infant, in relation to the size and power of the US industry in particular.

Size of project

It has been argued that certain investment projects are too large and have too long a time-scale to be taken on by the private sector and can only be handled by government. This argument has however now become somewhat outmoded as we see such mammoth projects as Euro-Disney and such projects as the Alaska oil pipeline and the Channel Tunnel being privately financed (although sometimes not without substantial government involvement).

Natural monopoly

The mainstream economic scenario of the market system producing the optimum range of goods and services depends on the market being perfectly competitive – that is, no single or small group of firms being able to dominate a market situation. Once the number of firms becomes small (oligopoly), or even singular (monopoly), excess profits are made and the consumer loses out. Governments in capitalist economies therefore generally have powers to regulate, and even break up, monopolies.

In leisure and tourism, however, there are often natural monopolies. For example, there is only one Tower of London, only one Grand Canyon and only one Great Barrier Reef. Some natural monopolies are social or economic in nature – for example, major transport infrastructure or sewerage systems, where it makes sense to have only one operator. In these instances, the argument goes, government is justified in intervening to prevent private operators exploiting monopolistic advantage, particularly by charging extortionate prices. Such government intervention may take the form of regulation – for example the regulation of air fares – or complete public ownership and/or control, as is the case with the national heritage.

Market failure in summary

A summary of the main features of the above arguments is provided in Table 4.1. Each of the arguments is fairly technical in approach. They attempt to establish that there are things which people want and would probably be prepared to pay for but, for technical reasons, the potential consumers and potential producers are unable to communicate effectively through the normal market mechanisms. Government is therefore seen as the main means of overcoming the problem, by levying taxes and paying for the goods or services to be produced, or by subsidizing their production so that the price is reduced and more are consumed.

The question of how governments assess the extent of the various forms of demand, and how they therefore determine just what scale of public funds to devote to the public provision of leisure and tourism services, is addressed in Chapter 8.

Social/Political Arguments for Government Involvement

While the following arguments for government involvement might, in some circumstances, find favour with mainstream economists, they are in fact less technical in nature and so have been treated separately here. They are: (i) equity/humanitarian; (ii) economic management and development; (iii) incidental enterprise; and (iv) tradition.

Equity/humanitarian

Equity means fairness. It impinges on leisure and tourism because of the belief that certain goods and services – a certain quality of life – should be available to all, regardless of their ability to pay, and that some leisure goods and services are among the minimal package required for a satisfactory quality of life. This is in contrast to all the arguments considered so far, which apply to everyone, regardless of their ability to pay.

The equity argument is the most appealing of arguments because it is not technical in nature; it appeals to people's sense of fairness and everyone likes to think of him/herself as fair (Cushman and Hamilton-Smith, 1980). It is at the heart of the difference between the left and the right in politics, since the right believes that a considerable degree of inequality is equitable, because it reflects the rewards given for effort and risk-taking, whereas the left thinks that the level of inequality we generally see in Western societies is inequitable and therefore unacceptable. The question is very complex, involving consideration of such issues as the distribution of income, payments in cash or in kind and universal versus targeted benefits.

There is nothing in mainstream economics which suggests that everyone, in a market economy, will be able to earn a living wage, since not everyone has skills that command a living wage in the labour marketplace. However, in most developed societies it is accepted that there is a basic minimum subsistence below which no one should be allowed to fall – hence most societies have introduced welfare payments, such as unemployment pay, age and disability pensions and child allowances. There is also progressive taxation, which means that the well-off contribute a greater proportion of their income towards government costs by way of taxes. In short, there is a redistribution of income from rich to poor.

This process, while widely accepted as necessary or desirable, is nevertheless controversial in application. Some argue that taxation of the well-off or rich is too high, resulting in disincentives to work or invest, and that unemployment and pension payments are too high, producing disincentives to seek work. Others argue exactly the opposite. Despite the controversy, the idea of the welfare state is that everyone should have a sufficient minimum income to buy the necessities of life.

If everyone is deemed to have been provided with a minimum income sufficient to provide for the necessities of life, then why are certain additional necessities provided in kind by the state? Why are people not able, with the incomes provided, to pay for their own housing, education, health services – and leisure services?

Suppose that one of the services considered to be a necessity is access to a swimming-pool or some similar form of physical recreation. Suppose that the full-cost recovery price for entry to a public pool is £2 and that the average user might be expected to visit once a week. If swimming is considered a necessity of life, then welfare payments, such as pensions and unemployment benefit, should include £2 per week so that everybody could afford to attend – in the same way that such benefits are designed to cover essentials such as food. Instead, it would appear that we have the situation where, say, £1 is included in the pension for such purposes, but the visit to the pool is subsidized by £1. There are many of these sorts of concessions and subsidies. To gain full benefit from them, a pensioner must go swimming, live in public housing, be ill periodically, attend an adult education course, and so on. Suppose the average pensioner benefits to the extent of £25 a week from such subsidies. One view is that it would be easier, and arguably more respectful of the dignity of the recipient, to increase the benefits by £25 a week and let the pensioner or other beneficiary decide how to spend the money.

One fear might be that the recipients of such a payment might not spend the money on the intended leisure services but might choose to spend it on basics, such as food or clothing. This would imply that the pension or other benefit is not adequate to meet basic needs, and that therefore the provision of certain leisure facilities or services is not a priority. Another possibility is that benefit recipients might not spend the money on approved leisure or on food or clothing but might fritter it away on undesirable items, such as gambling or alcoholic drink. In this case, the argument seems to be: we are entitled to subsidize the swimming-pool – to provide benefits in kind – because we cannot trust poor people to spend money wisely. This, of course, is a paternalistic attitude, which flies in the face of the values held by proponents of the market system, who believe that individuals are the best judges of their own needs, and indeed is at variance with the values of critics of the market, who would advocate self-determination and freedom from bureaucratic regulation.

Thus we can see that the equity-driven 'poor cannot afford to pay' argument can also be seen as an argument that says: 'pay them in kind because you cannot trust them to do the right thing with the money'. Some have advocated a 'voucher' system for leisure, along the lines of the American welfare food stamps (Sears, 1975), but this again implies that people cannot be trusted with money. A substantial proportion of the support for public provision and subsidy of leisure services is probably based on the 'poor cannot afford to pay' argument, but few appear to see that such an argument can also be seen as a form of paternalism reflecting 19th-century attitudes towards the 'undeserving' poor.

One of the reasons for the widespread use of the equity approach is that 'payment in kind' is the only means open for some levels of government to make a contribution to the needs of the less well-off sections of the community. Thus a local council cannot give cash hand-outs to its pensioners – and may be legally constrained over how it levies rates – but it can give concessions at its various facilities. Further, it could be argued that the marginal cost of this sort of assistance is small, so that the payment in kind is a cheaper option for the public sector than the cash-payment option.

Table 4.1. Mainstream economics and the role of the state – summary.

Type of service	Characteristics	Leisure examples
National Defence	Protecting the nation/maintaining peace – a public good (see below)	Some sporting activities promoted to maintain physical fitness for military preparedness (e.g. ancient Greece games and archery in medieval England). In 1930s Australia: a national fitness campaign launched because of concerns about the fitness of men for military service (Hamilton-Smith and Robertson, 1977: 178)
Law and order	Providing a legal framework for society, protection of life and property	Gambling; Sale and consumption of alcohol; Access to radio and television channels; Copyright laws; Fire and safety regulations in places of entertainment
Market failure		
Public goods and services	Non-excludable – not practically possible to exclude anyone from enjoying the good or service – so difficult to charge the user. Non-rival – one person's enjoyment or consumption does not preclude consumption or enjoyment by others – so extra users do not cost more	Parks – amenity enjoyed by passers-by; Pride from national sporting success; Firework displays; Public broadcasting; Public sculpture; Heritage conservation (eg. national parks)
Externalities, neighbourhood or third-party effects	Third parties are affected, positively or negatively, by transactions between providers and consumers – market is distorted by third parties not paying	Negative example: airport noise pollution or pub/club noise disturbance – need for government regulation/rules and/or levy on polluters. Positive example: community health benefits of sport participation – government may therefore subsidize sport facilities/services to encourage participation and produce social benefits
Mixed goods	Both public-good/service and private dimensions (Baumol and Bowen, 1976)	Attendance at an arts event (patrons enjoy personal private benefit; general cultural development of society is a public benefit) – government subsidizes in recognition of public benefit. Urban parks (visitors enjoy personal private benefit; but passers-by and neighbours enjoy neighbourhood benefit)
Merit goods	Goods and services considered beneficial, but with high learning threshold	Subsidy and education for some art forms; Cultural heritage; Environmental/heritage appreciation education
Option demand	Goods and services which people want to maintain in case they or their successors want to use them in future	Significant environmental, cultural and heritage items

Infant industries	Industries where it is difficult for new entrants to get started because of power of existing companies	Local film industry Local publishing industry Airlines
Size of project	Projects too large for private sector to invest	Few examples today – possibly major resort development, Olympic Games
Natural monopoly	Services where only one supplier is technically required	Unique heritage attractions or environmental resources
Socio-political arguments		
Equity or humanitarian measures	Facilities or services considered essential for a minimum standard of living or quality of life so must be provided for all (Cushman and Hamilton-Smith, 1980)	Access to play facilities for all children Access to open space and physical recreation facilities for all – government provision or subsidy
Economic management and development	Development of facilities or programmes that provide jobs and incomes	Tourism developments – e.g. resorts – government may provide land, tax holidays, infrastructure Major sports facilities – e.g. Olympic facilities – government may provide land, funds, infrastructure or direct provision
Incidental enterprise	Trading activities that are incidental to a public facility or service	Restaurants/cafés in museums, leisure centres Gift shops in visitor information centres
Tradition	Facilities/services that are valued because they have been provided for many years	Swimming-pools in areas where population has declined or use patterns have changed

If it is accepted that equity is to be pursued through the provision of benefits in kind, then the question arises as to how this should be done. In the example discussed above, the pensioner was subsidized by means of a concessionary charge. But some argue that such a targeted approach carries a stigma and that therefore the free or reduced charge should be available for everybody – a universal approach. Subsidizing everybody for the sake of a small number of poor users is, however, extremely costly and could be seen as a wasteful and irresponsible use of public funds. In fact, pensioners could be disadvantaged if the subsidized facilities are crowded out with non-pensioners and the facilities are inadequate because of lack of funds from charges.

This does not mean that public leisure facilities should not be subsidized for the general user for market-failure reasons, as discussed above. But, if the aim is to give particular benefits to the poor, then some means of targeting that group should ideally be found.

Children and young people merit a special mention under the heading of equity. It might be argued that children and young people who are still dependent on their parents are the responsibility of their parents and that their parents should therefore provide them with leisure resources. In practice, however, there is a feeling that children and young people should be treated more generously than adults and that children's opportunities should not be entirely dependent on their parents' means. This is shown, for example, in attempts to provide equal educational opportunity, but also extends to leisure – and in some cases to tourism. Here, in the 'cash vs. kind' argument, paternalistic attitudes (ie. not trusting the kids with the money) are probably more justified and there is no problem about stigma in offering concessions to young people. However, the problem still arises that some young people have well-off parents, so targeting is not very precise.

Economic management/development

It is widely accepted that governments have a role in the overall economic management of market economies – although New Right and monetarist theorists claim that the ability of governments to manage the economy is exaggerated and that they often do more harm than good and should do less rather than more in this field. Nevertheless, most governments feel responsible for trying to ensure high levels of material prosperity, high levels of employment, a favourable balance of payments, and so on. To achieve this they often feel justified in intervening directly to assist industries that can provide jobs or income. Such concerns can be felt at national, state or local level, although the lower levels of government have less power in this area.

Tourism is often seen as a suitable industry for such attention, but local leisure industries are also seen to be an increasingly important part of the economic infrastructure. One way in which leisure facilities become involved in this area is when certain facilities – for example, golf-courses or theatres – are seen as key elements in the local quality of life necessary to attract general industrial and commercial investors to an area. Governments at all levels therefore feel justified in providing or subsidizing such facilities for economic-development reasons.

Incidental enterprise

Often governments find themselves involved in certain areas of service provision accidentally, because the provision is incidental to some other activity. For example, government bodies that own theatres also find themselves running bars and restaurants, which happen to be part of the theatre complex. Museums often include restaurants and gift shops. Public broadcasting bodies become publishers of books, records and videos.

The difference between this and other sorts of public service is that there is no reason why they should be run any differently from commercial enterprises: they generally seek to make a profit. In fact, if the government body is competent at running them, they can be used to generate income to cross-subsidize the public activities of the organization.

Sometimes an organization such as a large council or a government agency finds itself running a number of such outlets and sets up an entity – such as a catering section – to run them. In other situations the operation is let out to private operators.

Tradition

It is clear that many publicly provided services are maintained because of tradition; there may have been a rational basis for their provision originally, but not at present. They are maintained, or free or subsidized entry is continued, because it is politically difficult to change.

The reason why it is politically difficult to change such situations is that there is often a lobby or interest group that would be offended by the change. The enjoyment which the members of such groups gain from the continued existence of the public service/facility in question may well be a public good or a mixed good, but, as with all such provisions, there is still the question of balancing the cost of provision with the value of the benefits being received by the users; and over time the benefits may have been eroded – for example, by falling population or use levels – while the costs may have risen. Nevertheless, the service is continued because of political expediency.

Mainstream Economics and Ideology

In this chapter and Chapter 3 we have reviewed a variety of political ideologies and their implications for leisure policy and also the basic tenets of mainstream economics as they apply to the role of the state and the implications for leisure and tourism. While a significant amount of leisure provision is probably made on the basis of pragmatism, tradition and political expediency, it can nevertheless generally be analysed with a certain amount of rationality using one or more of the above frameworks. The various perspectives have implications for later sections of the book. For example, political ideologies must inevitably influence the overall objectives set by public bodies, as discussed in Chapter 5, while the mainstream economics arguments provide a structure for the discussion of cost–benefit analysis in Chapter 9.

The Market versus the State – Issues

Before leaving this discussion of the underlying philosophy of public leisure provision, a number of further issues are discussed below. They are the question of profit-making versus loss-making and the question of government size and government failure.

Profit-making or loss-making?

Various combinations of the above arguments give rise to the provision of a wide range of public-sector leisure and tourism activity. It is clear that most of the arguments show that the costs of making the provision should be borne by the community at large through taxation, rather than by the immediate consumer of the service. This means that such public provision must, by definition, be loss-making, in commercial terms. If this were not the case, then there would be no reason for government to be involved in the first place: if a profit could be made from the service provided at the level required, then a private company could provide it – there would be no market failure. It could therefore be argued that a profit-making public enterprise is a contradiction in terms. Thus criticisms of public services for making a loss are entirely misplaced.

This is not to say that public services cannot often be criticized for being inefficient. It is often possible to run things more cheaply or to obtain a better service from the resources employed. But, if a service can be run profitably and still achieve the social objectives required, then in general there is no need for the state to become involved. The state only becomes involved when a level of service deemed to be necessary cannot be provided by the market – that is, it cannot be provided at a profit.

This does not mean that, if profits can be made from a service, there is no need for any government intervention. For example, if there were no public provision of swimming-pools, some commercial swimming-pool operations would be profitable, but probably only in certain central locations where a sufficient market exists. If it were considered by the appropriate government body – for whatever of the above reasons – that more swimming-pools should be provided so that more people could swim more often, then those additional pools would almost inevitably be loss-making – if they could have been provided profitably, then they would have been provided by the commercial sector. Thus a decision to intervene on the part of the state inevitably costs money.

It should be noted that, in this context, profitability means not just covering running costs but also providing a return on capital investment comparable to expectations in the commercial sector – that is, a rate of return sufficient to attract investment funds, given the level of perceived risk.

Government failure/government size

Many of the arguments advanced above are in the realm of market failure – that is, they recognize the imperfections or failure of the market mechanism and the need to correct this with government intervention.

However, the demands on government are seemingly endless, and all lobby groups can no doubt quote one or more of the above arguments in support of their own particular pet project. This then raises the question of the size of government.

Liberals would argue that the size of government should be limited for two reasons. First government organizations are generally seen as less efficient than private organizations, so the larger the government sector the less efficient the economy is overall (this notion of the generalized inefficiency of the public sector is sometimes referred to as 'X-inefficiency'). Secondly, it is believed that the taxation required to finance government distorts the market, reduces incentives, such as the incentive to work, and reduces personal freedom, particularly people's freedom to spend their income as they wish.

The New Right in particular, believe that government has become too big under post-Second World War Labour and Conservative governments. Others, of course, dispute such a view and argue that state organizations are not necessarily less efficient than private organizations and that a large government is necessary to provide vital services and to preserve a humane and civilized society.

Provider or facilitator?

A key issue is the stance of public bodies towards leisure and tourism provision. As the discussion of ideology and theory in this chapter and Chapter 3 indicates, there is a wide range of views on the appropriate role of public bodies, generally and in relation to leisure and tourism. The explicit desire of national governments, supported at the ballot-box, to roll back the state and move away from high-spending 'big government' in recent years has had a direct impact on patterns of public leisure service provision; in particular, it has undermined the traditional welfare-state approach to provision. While this shift has been seen as wholly negative by some commentators at local level, others have portrayed it in a less explicitly ideological manner, giving it a developmental rationalization or positive spin. Local government, it is often suggested, should now play a facilitating role rather than a direct provision role. Burton and Glover (1999) use the term *enabling state*. While, in practice, most councils will continue to play both direct-provider roles and facilitating/enabling roles, a preference for one or the other would affect strategic direction, in terms of the development of new programmes and facilities.

Facilitating and enabling generally refer to giving assistance and encouragement to the non-profit sector and the commercial sector to provide services and facilities formerly provided by the local council, but the above discussion of the local state and urban-growth regimes raises the issue of just how proactive a local authority should be in facilitating or enabling the activities of the private sector. Related to the idea of visioning, discussed below, Crompton (2000) discusses the issue of the positioning of local-authority leisure services *vis-à-vis* tourism, suggesting that leisure services would gain more support from the local electorate and businesses if they emphasized their role as a key provider in, and engine of, the tourism industry.

The context of globalization

The basic features of globalization and opposition to it are outlined in Chapter 3. Here we are concerned particularly with the implications of the phenomenon for the role of governments. In the same way that 19th-century liberal advocates of the market system promoted free trade and new approaches to national government and economic management, so their 20th- and 21st-century successors have promoted the further freeing up of international restrictions on trade and commerce. Advocates of a truly international, deregulated market system see it delivering rapid growth in international trade and an increase in wealth for all – a win-win situation – pointing to the economic success of the Asian tiger economies and the economic liberalization in China in support of their arguments (Ma, 2001). Opponents see a decline in national sovereignty and many losers left by the wayside, as unaccountable multinational enterprises and international financial and market processes shift resources, investment and jobs around the world to maximize profits, producing instability and suffering. And they point to massive disruption and unemployment in communities in Western industrial countries and exploitative employment practices and undermining of traditional economies in developing countries in evidence, with national governments helpless to intervene because of the commitments to unfettered free trade and competition entered into under the General Agreement on Tariffs and Trade (GATT) and World Trade Organization (WTO) agreements. Questions about the decline of the nation state are further complicated in Europe by the growing influence of the European Union and other multilateral

agreements and the consequent loss of national sovereignty.

These trends can have an impact on policy-making and planning in the field of leisure and tourism in cultural and economic terms.

Global factors clearly have an influence at the cultural level. In particular, the influence of American culture, in film, television, popular music and fashion, is very apparent worldwide and raises questions about national cultural identity. Governments have reacted in various ways; for example, in film, funds to support the maintenance of a local film industry have been established in many countries and many also have regulations concerning local content in television. However there seems to be little or no governmental concern about American domination of youth culture, in music and fashion, although it is curious to note that, while American companies dominate the sport clothing and fashion markets (e.g. Nike, Reebok), the insular nature of sport in the USA has meant that world sport itself has not become dominated by American capital. These global cultural trends, while noticeable at local level, have not generally had much impact on leisure policies and provision by local authorities. It is, however, possible that some of the limited successes of American sports, such as basketball or baseball, can have significant local impacts. For example successfully managed local league can lead to increased local demand for facilities for such sports, even if they are making little impact at national level.

In the arts and cultural area, an exception was the Greater London Council, which, before its abolition in 1986, was actively pursuing programmes to stimulate local cultural industries (Garnham, 1987), and it has been suggested that such programmes will be increasingly necessary in postindustrial cities (Landry and Bianchini, 1995).

Perhaps the more immediate impact of globalization is being felt economically. For example, as manufacturing activity has shifted to other parts of the world, Western countries such as the UK have experienced substantial unemployment in particular communities, resulting from the demise of such industries as steel-making, shipbuilding, coal-mining and now car manufacture. This has resulted in two types of response from national and local governments. First, there has been the attempt to replace old industries with new. Some of the new industries have been leisure-based, including the development of tourism, events, entertainments, arts, sport and exhibition facilities. Secondly, local leisure providers have had to take particular note of the unemployed as a major client group (Glyptis, 1989).

The Market vs. the State: Recent History

In line with liberal principles, as outlined in Chapter 3, the British government under Margaret Thatcher and John Major, in the period 1979–1996, sought to roll back the state and to open up as many sectors of the economy as possible to competitive market forces. This was not a unique situation: in Australia, paradoxically, a Labor government, under Bob Hawke and Paul Keating in the period 1982–1996, went part of the way along this path, but it was a state government, Victoria, under the premiership of Jeff Kennett, which gave full vent to Thatcherism.

The Thatcher/Major governments in Britain introduced full-scale privatization in the case of such services as railways and water-supply, but in local government introduced compulsory competitive tendering (CCT) – the requirement for public services to be put up for tender, so that private firms could compete for the contract to operate them. It was the belief of the government that significant savings would be achieved because private organizations would be more efficient in operating such services, or at least that the threat of competition would force public-sector organizations to become more efficient (Audit Commission, 1989: 17). The government was tackling head-on what it saw as the problem of government failure, as discussed above, and some believed that the long-term aim was also to tackle the perceived problem of big government by fully commercializing many of the leisure services that had traditionally been publicly provided.

Given the political nature of this policy shift and the implied loss of control due to central government telling local government what to do, it is not surprising that there was considerable opposition from local government, particularly from those where political control was in the hands of the Labour Party.

Leisure services were not among the first to be included in the CCT net, but they became involved in the late 1980s. Authorities were required to put up for tender such management tasks as the maintenance of parks and the operation of swimming-pools and leisure centres. A major challenge to local authorities was to specify the brief for inclusion in the tender. This involved making explicit policies and practices which, hitherto, had often been implicit and generally not costed. Thus, for example, the provision of free admission or concessionary admission rates for certain groups in the community or free use of a facility for community events made a difference to the cost of the contract. Authorities intent on saving money by omitting these considerations from the contract experienced a negative community response. In practice, most of the leisure-service contracts were won by the authorities' own labour force (Ravenscroft, 1998: 141), although often only by introducing significant changes to work practices and conditions.

Research was conducted on the outcomes of the experiment (see Centre for Leisure and Tourism Studies, 1993; Coalter, 1995; Nichols and Taylor, 1995; Nichols, 1996; Collins, 1997; Ravenscroft, 1998), noting the deficiencies in the operation of the process and the significant changes in outlook that the experience was bringing about in many local authorities. The research also drew attention to the fact that, in an area where few private operators had the requisite expertise, the bulk of the contracts were awarded to in-house teams. In general, it appeared that the economic savings from CCT in the leisure-services area had been modest and had often been achieved at the cost of valued dimensions of the service. The long-term consequences of a fully-fledged CCT system will, however, never be known, because the new

Labour government, elected in 1996, abolished CCT, replacing it with the best-value system, as a means of seeking to retain some of the efficiency gains of CCT.

Best value implies that all agencies or management units should aim to emulate the value-for-money achievements of the best. This in turn implies that the performance of comparable agencies, facilities and programmes should be measured using common measures – performance indicators – and that such data should be assembled in some central location so that best-value performance can be identified. While the best-value regime represented some shift to the left by the Labour government compared with its predecessor, its managerialist nature suggested a new hard-nosed approach to public services. While such an approach was out of sympathy with some areas of the public services, such as health and education, it had been part of the ethos of much of the recreation management profession in Britain for some years. The operational implications of this shift are discussed in Chapter 10.

Summary

- While mainstream, market economics is not without its critics, in the context of the current triumph of capitalism it seems appropriate to consider the economic arguments for the role of the state in a primarily market economy.
- Four broad functions of government are discussed: national defence; maintenance of law and order; market failure; and social/political arguments. Most of the chapter is devoted to discussing the last two of these.
- Market failure is discussed in terms of: public goods and services; externalities/ neighbourhood effects; mixed goods; merit goods; option demand; infant industries; size of project; and natural monopoly.
- Social and political arguments are discussed under the following headings: equity/humanitarian arguments; economic management/development; incidental enterprise; and tradition.

- A number of further issues on the role of the state are discussed, including the question of profit- and loss-making enterprise; government failure related to government size; the question of whether governments should be providers or facilitators; and the effects of globalization.
- Finally, some recent history on the changing role of the state in Britain is reviewed.
- Many of the principles discussed here are operationalized in the cost–benefit analysis process discussed in Chapter 9.

Further Reading

- For discussion of mainstream economics and its analysis of the role of the state in general: Musgrave and Musgrave (1980);
  - and leisure: Vickerman (1983, 1989); Gratton and Taylor (1985, 1991, 2000);
  - and tourism: Bull (1991);
  - and the arts: Baumol and Bowen (1966; 1976); Throsby and Withers (1979); Hendon *et al.* (1980); Withers (1981); House of Representatives Standing Committee on Expenditure (1986); Bennett (1989); Pearce (1991).
- Changing relationship between the state and the market in leisure: Clarke (1995); Ravenscroft (1996, 1998); Henry (1999); Coalter (2000).
- Globalization generally: Mander and Goldsmith (1996); Bauman (1998); Klein (1999); Beck (2000); Hutton and Giddens (2000); Keller (2000); Langhorne (2001).
- Globalization and culture: Barnet and Cavanagh (1996); Craik *et al.* (2000).
- Globalization and sport: Maguire (1999); Miller *et al.* (2001).
- Privatization/CCT: Ott and Hartley (1991); Coalter (1995); Nichols (1996); Ravenscroft (1998); Hodge (2000).
- Recent history: Henry (2001).

Questions/Exercises

1. Is the 'triumph of capitalism' actually 'mythic', as Korten (1996) suggests?
2. In what ways are leisure and tourism involved in the governmental roles of (a) national defence; (b) maintenance of law and order?
3. What, in general terms, is market failure?
4. What is the difference between the principle of

the public good or service, in the economist's sense, and externalities or neighbourhood effects?

5. Why is the concept of the mixed good particularly associated with the arts?

6. What is the difference between a merit good and option demand?

7. Why is the concept of infant industry particularly relevant to tourism?

8. Why are equity/humanitarian arguments for government activity ideologically controversial?

9. Should publicly owned enterprises make profits?

10. What are the potential problems associated with big government? How can they be overcome?

11. In what ways can globalization be said to be threatening the role of governments? Are there examples in the leisure/tourism sector?

5

Public Policy-making

Introduction

The first four chapters of the book are concerned with theoretical ideas and the social, economic and political context of public policy and planning; in this chapter the variety of ways in which public policy is actually made is considered in more detail. In an increasingly complex world, the question of just how organizations make, or should make, decisions to best fulfil their commitments and meet their objectives has been the subject of much debate among practitioners and theorists. For public bodies there is a formal decision-making mechanism, usually underpinned by a constitution or other legal framework, which indicates how decisions are intended to be made. In the 'real world', however, things rarely work exactly as intended. In this chapter the formal governmental mechanisms that exist in most democratic states are first outlined and this is followed by a discussion of a range of models of and approaches to decision-making that have been put forward by policy theorists. Finally, in recognition that policy often emerges from a political process involving power relationships, rather than from a rational decision-making process, the phenomenon of urban regimes and its application to leisure and tourism is discussed.

Formal Constitutions

In this book we are concerned with policy and planning at the nation-state level and

below. The international dimension is becoming increasingly important, particularly in Europe, as the powers of the European Union increase. The discussion of human rights and of globalization in Chapters 2, 3 and 4 illustrates the growing importance of this dimension. In general, however, international policy-making and planning are still conducted via agreements and treaties that member states become party to if they think it is in their own national interests – although there are stronger and weaker players in the negotiation process and playing by the rules is part of the price to be paid for being allowed to be a member of the club, such as the World Trade Organization. Examples of international policy-making in the area of leisure and tourism are the control of international passenger air routes, telecommunications and intellectual property rights (e.g. for music, film, books) and the designation of World Heritage Areas. Nevertheless, despite supposed threats to national sovereignty, the nation state is still sovereign; thus, for the time being, concentration on national, regional and local government seems justified.

National constitutions can be broadly classified along two dimensions: unitary as opposed to federal and Westminster as opposed to presidential, giving four types in total. Examples of countries with each of these four types of constitution are given in Table 5.1 and the two dimensions are outlined in brief below.

Table 5.1. Examples of countries with different constitutions.

	Westminster	Presidential
Unitary	UK, New Zealand, Holland, Greece, Japan	Italy, Ireland, Korea, Argentina, Kenya
Federal	Canada, Australia, India, Germany	USA, Russia, Brazil, South Africa

Unitary vs. federal systems

In unitary government systems, such as those in France, Italy and the Scandinavian countries, there are two tiers of elected government – central government and local government. In federal systems, as in the USA, Canada, Australia, Germany and India, there are three levels: central or federal government, state or provincial governments and local government. The UK, with its Scottish, Welsh and intermittent Northern Ireland assemblies, now lies between the two systems, since the existence of the assemblies is not protected by a constitution. In both unitary and federal systems, local government, while democratically elected, is very much controlled, in terms of powers and funding, by one or other of the higher tiers.

In Britain in some areas the local-authority system is split into two tiers – county councils and district councils. In large urban areas there is only one tier – city or borough councils. County councils have some similarities to state/provincial governments in federal systems – for example, in running schools, police forces and hospitals. But a fundamental difference is that counties do not have legislative powers – they cannot make laws. They are entirely subject to the national legal system. While leisure and tourism functions are divided in a variety of ways in the two-tier county/district systems, in this book, local government is dealt with as a single level.

Westminster vs. presidential models

Modern governments consist of: a head of state; a head of government and government ministers; and one or more elected assem-blies – usually a lower house with most power and an upper house as a house of review with limited powers. In both unitary and federal systems governments may be of the Westminster type or presidential type. The differences between these two systems are summarised in Table 5.2 and Fig. 5.1.

In the Westminster system, the head of state – a monarch or ceremonial president – is a formal, ceremonial position[1] and the head of government – the prime minister – and the rest of the government are members of the elected assembly or parliament. The government is formed by the party which can command a majority in the elected assembly.

In the presidential system, the roles of head of state and head of government are played by the same person, the elected, executive president. But the president and government are separate from the elected assembly.

In both systems, laws and taxation measures are enacted by the elected assembly. In the Westminster system this process is controlled by the government because the party of government controls the elected assembly, but in the presidential system the political party of the president may or may not enjoy a majority in the assembly, so the process of legislation can involve negotiation between the president and the leaders of the assembly.

In federal systems, the style of government of the national government is replicated at state/provincial level. Thus, in the USA, the states have executive governors separate from their legislative assemblies, whereas, in Australia, the states have a ceremonial governor (nominally representing the Queen) and a premier who is a member of the state parliament. This pattern even flows through to local government, with US cities having directly elected executive mayors, while in British and Australian cities leaders

Table. 5.2. Westminster vs. presidential government: features.

	Westminster	Presidential
Head of state	Ceremonial president or constitutional monarch	Executive president
Head of government	Prime Minister (Germany: 'Chancellor')	Executive president
Government	Ministers drawn from members of Parliament	Ministers appointed by president – not members of Congress
Elected assemblies	Parliament – usually two houses, e.g. House of Commons, House of Lords (UK); House of Representatives, Senate (Australia)	Congress – usually two houses, e.g. House of Representatives, Senate (USA)
Government formed by:	Party which can command a majority in the Parliament	President, elected by the people, who appoints ministers

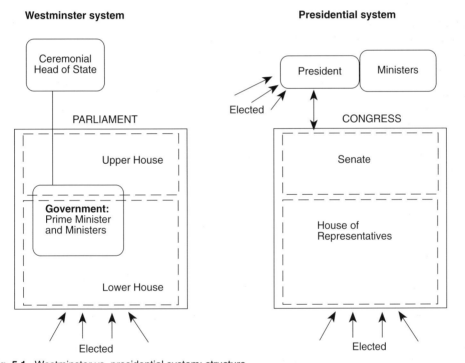

Fig. 5.1. Westminster vs. presidential system: structure.

The location of leisure and tourism

of councils are drawn from among the elected councillors (although Greater London now has a directly elected mayor).

In federal systems the powers of the federal and state/provincial governments are gener-ally laid out in a constitution. Typically, leisure and tourism responsibilities are shared between all levels, as indicated in Table 5.3. In some cases there is a clear demarcation within leisure or tourism – for example, in the case of broadcasting or deal-ing with unequivocally national institutions, such as a National Gallery of National Theatre. In other cases, historical accident has

Table 5.3. Leisure, tourism and levels of government.

	Unitary system		Federal system		
	National government	Local government	National government	State/provincial government	Local government
International tourism promotion	✓		✓	✓	
Air travel	✓		✓		
International travel	✓		✓		
National sport teams	✓		✓		
Broadcasting	✓		✓		
National arts/cultural institutions	✓		✓		
National parks	✓		✓	✓	
Heritage conservation	✓		✓	✓	
Domestic tourism promotion				✓	
Road/rail travel	✓		✓	✓	
Major provincial arts/cultural institutions	✓	✓		✓	
Regional parks	✓	✓		✓	
Major sport stadiums	✓	✓		✓	
Sport development	✓	✓	✓	✓	✓
Urban planning		✓	✓		✓
Beaches		✓			✓
Community sport/arts/recreation facilities/ programmes		✓			✓
Local parks		✓			✓

resulted in all levels of government being involved – for example, in the provision of parks – even if one level is predominant.

Formal decision-making procedures

While principles discussed below apply in a broad sense to both the Westminster and the presidential type of government, for simplicity the Westminster model is assumed.

The formal procedure for democratic governments is for political parties to be formed around an ideology or set of interests, as discussed in Chapter 3. At election time the parties present a manifesto of actions which they would undertake if elected and endorse candidates to stand for election to the Parliament. Following the election, the leader of the party which has a majority of seats in the lower house of the Parliament is called on by the head of state to be Prime Minister and to form a government. If no single party has an absolute majority, the smallest party might be invited to form a minority government, or a coalition of parties might be formed. Subject to the constitutional period for a Parliament (typically 3–5 years), the government will remain in power as long as it continues to command a majority in the Parliament. Laws and taxation measures are enacted by the government to fulfil its election manifesto. This is done by presenting Bills to the Parliament, which, when approved by the Parliament and formally endorsed by the head of state, become Acts of Parliament.

The above outline presents only the very basic characteristics of the political and legislative system. Other procedures and institutions, such as a constitutional court and a judiciary, are also involved, but these are beyond the scope of this book.

Quangos, trusts, the non-profit sector, etc.

Leisure and tourism are, *par excellence*, the field of the 'quango' (quasi-autonomous non-governmental organization). Quangos are organizations established and funded by governments whose board members are appointed by governments but which are seen as, to some extent, separate from and independent of government. One rationale for the use of such an organizational device is referred to, in the arts in particular, as the *arm's-length principle*. This is the idea that government should not be seen to be directly interfering with such matters as the arts or sport or heritage: policy should be in the hands of disinterested experts – government should be at arm's length. An alternative reasoning is that, in these specialized areas, a more flexible organizational structure is required than the traditional, bureaucratic government department; this argument is more likely to be applied in more commercially orientated areas, such as tourism.

Thus, in a number of leisure sectors, the most important single public organization is usually the national quango – the Sports Council, the Arts Council, the Countryside Commission, the Tourism Commission, and so on. Such organizations are extremely important to the field because of the financial resources they command, because of their connection with national government and because of their ability to conduct research, launch campaigns and generally influence the direction of the field. However, it should be borne in mind that quangos, however influential, are only one player in the field. Often the collective importance of other organizations is greater, particularly in the financial sense; thus, for example, local authorities in Britain collectively spend far more money on sport, the arts and the countryside than do the Sports Councils, the Arts Council and the Countryside Commission, respectively, and voluntary organizations are equally important in some areas. Similarly, in sport, tourism and broadcasting, commercial organizations are generally much larger than the public-sector quango.

A major change in Britain in recent years has been the advent of the National Lottery. The profits from the Lottery now provide a substantial proportion of central government funding of leisure, through organizations such as Sport England and the Arts Council (Evans, 1995). This takes some of the sting out of public policy because the funds do not appear to come from taxation. This is, of course, to a large extent an illusion, since the profits are only generated because of the governmental monopoly over this form of gambling – monopolies make excess profits, so the bonanza of the Lottery is, in effect a de facto tax. This is further illustrated by the practice in Australia, where gambling control is a state rather than a federal matter. The six Australian states and two territories, through a mixture of taxation on clubs, casinos, bookmakers and state lotteries, garner sums comparable to those of the British government (A\$4 billion in 1999 – Tasmanian Gaming Commission, 2000). But, regardless of the source of the funds, the task of allocation of funds between competing projects within leisure and tourism and between leisure and tourism and other sectors remains.

Also common in the leisure and tourism field is the phenomenon of the *trust*, which is part of the non-profit or voluntary sector. Trusts and non-profit organizations established as associations or corporate entities frequently play roles that might otherwise be played by governmental bodies, such as quangos or local councils. Trusts may be established under appropriate legislation or, in the UK, under royal warrant and are overseen by a board of trustees. The trust format is common in the arts, where, even though they may be in receipt of substantial government funding, many theatres, museums and galleries operate in this way, partly for historical reasons and partly for taxation reasons – there can, for example be advantages in making bequests to organizations with charitable status. The National Trust is the most well-known example in the heritage area, holding natural and built heritage properties in trust for the nation. In some countries – Germany, for example – voluntary sporting organizations play a wide community role, often underpinned by substantial grants from the state. In the state of New South Wales in Australia, registered clubs related to sport, veterans and ethnic groups play a unique role as community centres and supporters of sport, partly as a result of benefiting from their, until recently, monopoly income from poker machines (Caldwell, 1985).

The International Olympic Committee is high-profile organization in the sporting world, which might be thought to be an intergovernmental organization, particularly in relation to its role in policing illicit drug use in sport, but is in fact part of the third sector (Toohey and Veal, 2000: 38ff.).

In some contexts non-profit organizations can be seen as part of the public sector, in other instances they are closer to the private sector, and this varies from country to country and locally. In this book therefore, no attempt is made to deal systematically with the role of the voluntary or non-profit sector, but its existence should be borne in mind. It should be noted that these organizations are particularly relevant to the pluralist model of government discussed below.

Finally, it should be noted that governments can enter into partnerships and even engage in profit-making enterprises. In tourism, local or regional tourism development organizations often include a mixture of public- and private-sector organizations; the organization may be established as a consultative body, with activities carried out on its behalf by a public body, such as the local council, or it may be established as a corporate entity in its own right, with public- and private-sector shareholders. In some city-centre and harbourside developments, local councils or state governments may enter into a joint venture with private enterprise, setting up a company for the purpose, in which the public body and its private-sector partners have shareholdings, or they may establish trading companies on their own. This sort of device is often used in the 'urban-growth regime' phenomenon, as discussed below.

Models of Decision-making

In practice, the processes by which governmental decisions are made are much more complex than the above outline suggests. In particular, organizations and interests other than the parliament and government are involved to a greater or lesser extent, including business, trade unions, professional bodies, lobby groups, the media, the military, the judiciary, religious groups, public servants, other governments and international organizations. A variety of theories and models have been suggested involving different views on how these various interests interact to influence government decision-making. Parsons (1995) divides such theories and models into five groups, focused respectively on: (i) power; (ii) rationality; (iii) public choice; (iv) institutions; and (v) personality, cognition and information processing. These are discussed in turn below, with the main emphasis being on the first two.

Power-based models

Power-based models concentrate on economic, political, social and military power wielded by various groups in society in addition to elected governments. Parsons (1995: 248ff.) discusses six different forms of power-based model, referred to as élitism, pluralism, Marxism, corporatism, professionalism and technocracy models. These are discussed briefly in turn below. In addition, a model not included in Parsons's list, hallmark decision-making, is also discussed.

Elitism

Elite models hold that power in society is wielded by a relatively small number of people and groups of people who form an élite who have direct contact with ministers and legislators and, often behind closed doors, can influence them to act in their interests rather than in the interests of the wider community. Such groups might include leading business people or media owners, the military-industrial complex involving the leaders of the armed forces and the suppliers of military hardware, religious groups or landed interests. It has been argued that such relationships exist, at least from time to time, in various sections of the leisure industries, such as the arts and sport, thus ensuring continued funding for élite art forms, such as opera and ballet, and for élite sport at the expense of mass participation. In the tourism sector it might be speculated that such phenomena as the continued anticompetitive control of international air routes and the bizarre practice of the duty-free trade may be partly explained by the élite model of government decision-making. An example of the process at work can be found in the following quotation from the memoirs of Hugh Jenkins, a British Labour Minister for the Arts in the 1970s, which outlines the activities of the arts establishment in opposing proposals from the government of the time to introduce a wealth tax, which threatened, among others, wealthy owners of valuable works of art.

> Months before the Green Paper[2] was published the arts plutocrats and their minions sprang into action. The National Arts Collections Fund in the person of Sir Anthony Hornby was quickly off the mark, writing to Denis Healey [Chancellor of the Exchequer] on April 9. Simultaneously, Ernle Money (Tory [Member of Parliament], Ipswich) was asking questions in the House [of Commons] and the Earl of Rosse, Chairman of the Standing Commission on Museums and Galleries was equally active … Lord Perth … [Chairman of the Reviewing Committee on the Export of Works of Art] wrote … to the Chancellor. The Duke of Grafton raised the matter in the [House of] Lords … Letters to the press from Hugh Legatt, a dealer, from George Levy, President of the British Antique Dealers Association, from Denis Mahon, a collector and Trustee of the National Gallery, and from sundry stately home owners continued throughout the summer of '74 and among others I received a *cri-de-coeur* from the Earl of Crawford and Balcarres … I met Sir Geoffrey Agnew at the Hazlitt Gallery and I agreed that he should come in for a talk after the publication of the Green Paper … One must admit that they [the 'plutocrats and their spokesmen'] were remarkably successful in recruiting to their side thousands of people, perhaps millions, who would never pay the tax and who could only benefit from its application to the top group of property owners.
>
> (Jenkins, 1979: 141, 143)

The government eventually withdrew its wealth tax proposals, wealthy art-owners no doubt being just one among many groups which had used their influence to oppose the tax. It is perhaps notable that the British class and honours system provides such convenient labels to identify many members of the élite. Peers and knights of the realm are recruited to membership and to preside over a range of public, voluntary and commercial organizations and are expected to use their status and influence in times like the above. In countries without such titles the membership of the élite is less obvious, but this does not mean that it does not exist.

Pluralism

Pluralist models see political decision-making as involving a much wider range of pressure groups and interest groups, which influence government by use of publicity or by giving financial or political support to or withholding it from individual politicians or political parties. Some groups claim to represent significant numbers of voters – for example, groups representing the retired, farmers or trade unions. Others use research, data and publicity to make their views known in the political arena – for example, groups concerned with welfare or health issues. As indicated in Fig. 5.2 therefore, in this model, political decision-makers, rather than making decisions solely on the basis of their election commitments, technical evaluations of proposals and debate, are believed to base their decisions on an assessment of the competing claims, promises and threats of a range of, possibly opposing, groups and the likely political consequences of favouring one group rather than another. There is a continuum, therefore, between the élite model, which depends on contacts and often on behind-the-scenes influence, and the pluralist model, with its more public political campaigning by known pressure groups.

Political pluralist models have been used particularly to describe the political system in the USA where political lobbying has become an art form, election campaign funds run into billions of dollars and lobby groups can represent millions of votes. One view is that such a pluralist system is democratic in nature because any group can form itself into a lobby group and have its say. But increasingly it has come to be seen as a distortion of democracy, since the system favours the groups with greater financial resources. The arts example given above also illustrates the

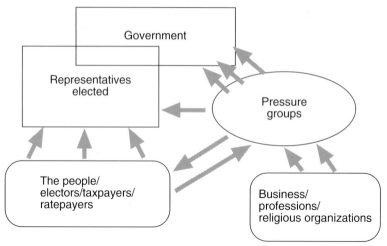

Fig. 5.2. Political pluralism.

pluralist model; while many of the characters involved could be identified as part of the British élite and were able to use their influence behind the scenes, it is clear that representative bodies, such as the British Antique Dealers Association, and public processes, such as writing letters to newspapers, were also utilized in the campaign. It is also clear that those groups which might have supported the wealth-tax proposals were probably less well organized and resourced.

It should be borne in mind that the pluralist model does not apply only to national and state/provincial governments. As the discussion in Chapter 3 suggests, international business interests also bring pressure to bear on governments; some would see organizations such as the World Trade Organization and the International Monetary Fund as the equivalent of pressure groups, although they and individual multinational enterprises also operate in the élite mode, as discussed above, and the corporate mould, as discussed below. At local-government level, pressure groups are often vocal and influential, and are often associated with various forms of leisure, including sporting and arts organizations seeking funding from councils, and environmental groups lobbying for open space and conservation.

Marxism

As discussed in Chapter 3, Marxism sees the contemporary state as propping up the capitalist system. This process must operate in some practical way, and so this Marxist perspective is a particular form of élitist or non-democratic pluralist model, where the interests that influence or control government do so in the interests of capital.

Corporatism

Corporatist models involve governments working very closely with industrial or commercial organizations. They have some similarities with élitist and pluralist models but in this case, rather than being the hapless victim of the elites or lobby groups, the government is an active partner in the process and seeks to control the non-governmental organizations involved. The classic example of the corporatist model in action is the relationship between the Nazi government in Germany in the 1930s and the military-industrial complex. At the urban level a few politicians and commercial interests might be able to, in effect, run the city – such a phenomenon is known as an urban regime and is discussed in more detail later in the chapter.

Professionalism

Long-established and well-organized professional bodies can have an undue influence on government, particularly when they are involved in a major area of public service delivery. Mention has already been made of the military and judiciary, but also of relevance are the education profession and unions and the medical profession, particularly when a socialized health system exists. The humorous British television series *Yes Minister!* and *Yes Prime Minister!* illustrate this thesis in relation to the profession of public servant (Lynn and Jay, 1988, 1999). Such influence can exist at all levels of government. Professions in general have been subject to a considerable critique for using their power to further their own interests at the expense of the wider community – for example, by Ivan Illich *et al.* (1977) in their book *Disabling Professions*.

Many public servants have a personal, even emotional, commitment to the field in which they work and may have strongly held views about particular policies. Such commitment and opinions can be seen as political in nature, especially if the opinions differ from those of the political group in power. Nevertheless, it is widely accepted that, because of their basis in technical expertise and professional knowledge, the work of managers or administrators in the public sector is generally different from the activities of politicians. This expertise is involved in the decision-making processes of public bodies – how influential it may be in those processes varies, according to the political environment, the level of expertise of the manager concerned and the innate nature of the field.

Technocracy

The technocracy model sees decision-making increasingly being taken out of the hands of ordinary people and being usurped by technological experts. This envisages scenarios in which politicians are persuaded that society has no choice but to invest in the form of – usually expensive – technology. In the cold-war period of the 1960s and 1970s the model applied particularly to nuclear power, armaments and space exploration; in recent times it has applied to decisions on such matters as broad-band broadcasting, biotechnology and global warming. While the increasingly significant role of economists in government in recent years might be seen as an example of professional influence, it can also be seen as a form of technocracy, as decisions have been based on increasingly complex economic models.

Hallmark decision-making

The leisure and tourism area is particularly afflicted by a further alternative approach to decision-making, which might be termed hallmark decision-making. The name seems appropriate because it generally arises in relation to what have come to be called hallmark events or projects (Syme *et al.*, 1989; Hall, 1992). Such phenomena include major events, such as the holding of the Olympic Games, and major building and planning projects, such as the building of a national theatre or developments such as the London Docklands or Sydney's Darling Harbour. Because of their high profile such projects usually involve politicians directly, there is a great deal of media attention, and normal planning, decision-making, budgeting and evaluation procedures are often bypassed – for example, by means of special legislation. Cost overruns and controversy tend to be the norm. The decision-making process involved appears to consist of making the decision to go ahead with the project first and then seeking ways of justifying it. While all areas of the public sector are affected by hallmark decision-making, leisure seems to suffer particularly because so many non-experts either consider themselves to be expert in the area or assume that no particular expertise is necessary. One researcher, having analysed the planning of a wide range of hallmark projects (centres for art, culture, exhibitions, sport and conferences) around the world, concluded that:

> decisions to go ahead were most often made before any data collection, analysis, evaluation, or constraint determination. Extra-rational factors such as whim, influence, creativity, intuition, vision and experience played large roles in the planning and/or decision to undertake the project.
>
> (J. Armstrong, quoted in Roche, 2000: 18)

The work of Peter Hall (1980) on *Great Planning Disasters*, Syme *et al.* (1989) on sporting events and Colin Michael Hall (1992: 219) on *Hallmark Tourist Events* represent the beginnings of a literature on this phenomenon. In practice, there is an element of hallmark decision-making in nearly all public investment projects.

Rationality models

That policy decisions should be made on some rational basis is an attractive idea that most people would probably subscribe to. Much of the rest of this book is predicated on the idea that leisure and tourism profession-als should be equipped to contribute to such a rational ideal. The ideal is enshrined in the rational-comprehensive approach to decision-making, which seeks to base decisions on rational evaluation of all available information and all possible courses of action. One representation of such a model is presented in Fig. 5.3. It consists of nine steps or processes, beginning with establishment of the brief or terms of reference for a project, programme or organization and ending (or starting again) with an evaluation or feedback loop. At the heart of the process is the need to consider and evaluate all possible courses of action and choosing that course of action which maximizes the likelihood of the organization achieving its objectives.

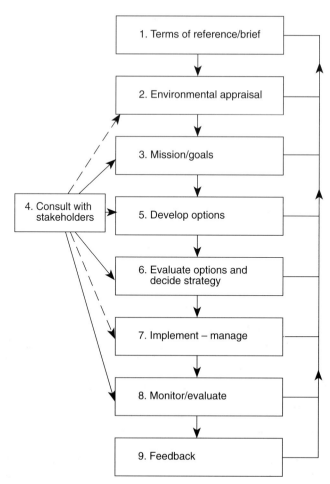

Fig. 5.3. The rational–comprehensive decision-making process.

It is widely believed that this approach, while it remains a model of perfection, is in fact impractical and is rarely implemented in its pure form. The main problem is the time and effort needed to identify and evaluate all possible options, particularly in a large, complex organization. The identification of all possible options is theoretically possible, but not practically. Even consideration of a large number of options is often impossible because of time and resource limitations. In recognition of this, in the 1950s Herbert Simon coined the term *bounded rationality* to describe the more limited scope of most decision-making exercises (Parsons, 1995: 273ff.).

Also in the 1950s, Lindblom (1959) argued that organizations, in practice, do not use the rational-comprehensive approach; they consider only a few alternatives, and often with only limited information to hand, when making decisions and, rather than beginning from scratch with the goals of the organization, they start with consideration of where they are now – current policies, commitments and practices – and generally consider only marginal changes from the status quo situation. This view suggests that only incremental change is considered; alternative courses of action are not identified on a rational–comprehensive basis, but in a somewhat haphazard, or disjointed manner. This style of decision-making Lindblom termed *disjointed incrementalism* or the science of *muddling through*. The advantage of disjointed incrementalism is that it is cheaper and quicker to implement than the ideal rational–comprehensive approach. The latter can involve considerable time and resources in gathering, analysing and evaluating information.

However, while disjointed incrementalism may reflect what goes on in many organizations in practice, it could hardly be recommended as an ideal way to proceed; in particular, it favours the status quo, whether or not that is the best set of policies, and, in failing to consider all alternative courses of action, it is in danger of missing important opportunities for change. Etzioni (1967) proposed, as a compromise, the idea of *mixed scanning*, a two-stage process involving a broad-brush review of all possible courses of action, followed by more detailed evaluation of just a few, selected alternatives.

While the rational-comprehensive model is therefore not without its critics and may have been superseded to some extent in practice, it is widely recognized by managers and still provides a useful framework for discussing the strategic planning process (Mintzberg, 1994: 52). While managers and planners must be aware of the existence of the other models of decision-making discussed, their professional role is generally to contribute inputs to the rational model, with varying degrees of comprehensiveness. Figure 5.3 therefore provides the basis for the discussion of strategic planning in Chapter 6.

Public choice

Public-choice theory draws a parallel between market processes and political processes. In the market process, decisions on what goods and services to produce are made by firms on the basis of how self-interested consumers vote with their money. If more consumers want and are prepared to pay for red apples rather than green apples, then more red apples will be produced and fewer green apples. In the political process, it is argued, voters support, in a self-interested way, political parties that offer them more of what they want. In turn, political parties bid against each other to offer voters more of what they want – a sort of 'bread-and-circuses scenario'. Such a process leads to an expansion of the role of the state as parties seek to meet as many needs of as many groups as possible. Since much of government provision is therefore a quasi-market process, it is argued, why not privatize these services and reduce taxation and the size of government? Thus the public-choice model was used to support the rolling back of the state that took place under New Right governments in the 1980s. Despite the connotations of 'bread and circuses', this model has generally not been pursued in the research literature in the context of leisure and tourism.

Institutional approaches

The decision-making models discussed above concentrate on processes, unlike the formal model of the governmental system initially outlined, which concentrated on institutions (parliament, government, party, etc.). The institutional approach explores this dimension in more detail, examining ways in which the structures and functions of political institutions and the structures and functions of the organizations they relate to (e.g. private-sector firms, trade unions) affect their decision-making practices. The verbal and diagrammatic presentation of formal structures tends to suggest that the system operates smoothly, but this is rarely the case in human affairs. The relationships between tiers of government – national, state/provincial and local – are more often than not in tension, if not open conflict, especially when different political parties control the different tiers.

The institutional model has not been extensively explored in relation to leisure and tourism and so is not pursued in detail here, but reference to general literature on the model can be found in Parsons (1995: 323–326).

Personality, cognition and information processing

Clearly decisions in public organizations are made by people – elected representatives and paid officials. It makes sense, therefore, to explore the characteristics and behaviour of the individuals involved and the processes they use to assess information and arrive at decisions. Again, this is not an area that is pursued in the leisure and tourism research literature and is not discussed further here (see Parsons, 1995: 336–380).

Urban Regimes and the Governance of the Local State

In the discussion of decision-making models above, reference was made to corporatism, in which a close relationship develops between government and business in relation to particular projects or policies. The idea of élites

and their potential to influence government decision-making was also discussed. The idea of urban regimes discussed here relates to both these models.

Much of the policy-making and planning for leisure and tourism with which we are concerned in this book takes place at the local urban or rural level, making the functioning of the *local state* of particular importance. Since the majority of the populations of the developed world live in urban areas, the bulk of the policy-making, planning and provision takes place in towns and cities. Since classical Greek and Roman times and before, cities have been the focus of collective leisure, even when this has been a by-product of other functions, such as commerce (market-day) and government (the activities of the court): cities provided the resources and the people to support collective leisure facilities, including theatres, orchestras, museums and parks and gardens. The industrial revolution transformed cities into centres of industrial production and so research and policy came to be concerned primarily with the city's industrial function and the infrastructure to support it – other aspects of the city were seen as mere appendages to this primary role. Manuel Castells, in his seminal study *The Urban Question* (1977), drew attention to the role of cities as centres for collective consumption – an idea closely allied to the concept of public goods discussed above. Such collective consumption includes transport and other infrastructure and education, health and retail services – and, of course, leisure services and tourist attractions.

In analyses of the local state the term *governance* is often used to refer to the particular combination of formal and informal mechanisms by which local communities are run. These mechanisms involve a number of actors, including elected council members, paid council officials, statutory powers and obligations of the council, financial and administrative controls of national government, local business, voluntary organizations and other pressure groups, electorates or ratepayers and the clients for council services, as represented in Fig. 5.4. Of course, membership of many of these groups overlaps, which gives local governance its particular characteristics.

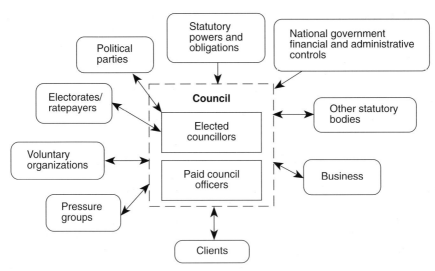

Fig. 5.4. The local state.

As discussed above, the classic view of how government operates is that candidates representing parties with particular political programmes present themselves for election and the successful party or coalition of parties forms the ruling group, which takes control of the government machinery and implements its programme in the interests of the electorate. Because of the role of pressure groups, entrenched interests, personal interests and external constraints, it is doubtful that this pattern ever operates in such a simple way; indeed, Patrick Dunleavy (1980: 135) has argued that such a portrayal is quite misleading. In Britain he notes that the terms of political debate are generally set at national level and that local council elections have generally followed national political swings, suggesting that local policy platforms are largely irrelevant to the political process. At local level parties gain and hold power as a result of national party endorsement rather than as a result of local democratic support for local policy platforms. Decision-making, he argues, does not take place through the formal process of open debate and voting in council chambers, but is controlled by the ruling party's leadership working outside the formal political process, in behind-the-

scenes negotiations with party factions and other interests, with the council chamber acting merely as a rubber stamp. This means that local governmental decision-making, rather than arising from a broadly based democratic process, is often in the hands of a small group of people who do deals with party factions and local interest groups, such as trades unions or business interests. This style of governance has been referred to as an *urban regime* or *urban-growth regime* (Harding, 1994). The ways the various actors and influences interact create a particular style or model of regime focused on achieving, for example, economic growth and development, a reduction in the level of expenditure, privatization of services or a change in a city's image. While this model of local government has found wide acceptance in Europe, doubts have been expressed as to whether it is still relevant in American cities, particularly when focused on growth. Clark (2000: 33–34) suggests that such regimes have been sidelined by the emergence of a 'new political climate', which involves antigrowth sentiments and a displacement of traditional concerns with production and jobs by a greater emphasis on 'consumption, amenity and lifestyle decisions such as the environment'.

The forces of globalization and postindustrialism have, however, made this approach to urban analysis particularly apposite, as leaders in Western cities, faced with deindustrialization, have searched for an understanding of the process of change and the role cities should play. The stage has therefore been set for a rediscovery of leisure and tourism as important functions of cities. Reflecting Castells' ideas on collective consumption (see also Dunleavy, 1980: 42–50), urban regime activity has increasingly turned to leisure- and tourism-related developments, such as retail/leisure complexes (Stevenson, 2000), sport and cultural facilities as a focus for growth strategies (Noll and Zimbalist, 1997; Henry and Paramio Salcines, 1998); tourism (Greenwood, 1992); and major events, such as the Olympic Games (Burbank *et al.*, 2000). Many of these developments have been commercial in nature but Clark, in reviewing a wide range of international research on policy development in cities, detects a shift away from commercial intervention to more traditional public-goods provision:

> Amenities are increasingly recognized as critical … Efforts to improve the 'quality of life', via festivals, bicycle paths, or culture, are recognized as central not just for consumption but for economic development, which is increasingly driven by consumption concerns. How? Amenities are Samuelson-type public goods; they do not disappear like a payment to a firm if the firm goes bankrupt. Amenities benefit all firms as well as citizens in the area. They often enhance the local distinctiveness (of architecture or a waterfront) by improving a locality, rather than just making it cheaper for one business … the focus is less on the firm and its location and more on the citizen as consumer/tourist/workforce member.
>
> (Clark, 2000: 15–16).

Summary

- This chapter has been concerned with the process of decision-making in government. First, the chapter includes brief accounts of some of the formal structures of democratic governments and their for-

mal decision-making processes, including: unitary versus federal systems; Westminster versus presidential models of government; and the roles of quangos, trusts and the non-profit sector.

- Alternative models of decision-making are reviewed, including: power-based models; rationality models; public choice; institutional approaches; and personality, cognition and information processing.

- While the rational–comprehensive model has been criticized as being unrealistic and unworkable in practice, it remains a useful framework for analysing and undertaking planning and policy development; the model presented in Fig. 5.3 is therefore used as a framework for some of the discussion in subsequent chapters in the book.

- Finally, there is a brief introduction to the concept of urban regimes, which are seen as an increasingly common feature of governance of the local state and particularly relevant to leisure and tourism policy-making.

Further Reading

- Policy-making and decision-making generally: Parsons (1995).
- Public-choice theory: Self (1993).
- Interest groups: in tourism: Chapter 4 of Hall and Jenkins (1995).
- Elite theory: Dye (1978: 25–28); Haralambos *et al.* (1996: 110–121).
- The local state: Dunleavy (1980).
- Urban-growth regimes: Harding (1994); Clark (2000). For a leisure-related analysis of an urban-growth regime at work see Henry and Paramio Salcines (1998).

Questions/Exercises

1. What is the difference between a unitary and a federal system of government?

2. What is the difference between a Westminster and a presidential system of government?

3. What is a quango? Name an example in the area of: (a) sport; (b) the arts; (c) tourism.

4. Give examples of where the élitism model of government decision-making might exist in the field of leisure and tourism.

5. Give examples of possible non-governmental participants in the pluralist model of government.

6. What are the characteristics of hallmark decision-making?

7. On what grounds is the rational–comprehensive model of decision-making criticized?

8. What are the main alternatives to the rational–comprehensive model?

9. Examine, using newspaper archives, a recent high-profile leisure/tourism event or planning/development decision and assess to what extent it involved hallmark decision-making and/or the activity of an urban-growth regime.

Notes

[1] In some of the Commonwealth countries, notably the former Dominions (Canada, Australia, New Zealand), the Queen remains formally head of state and is represented by a Governor-General at national levels and by a Governor in the states/provinces.

[2] A Green Paper is a discussion paper outlining government proposals for a new policy and/or legislation. If the proposals survive the public discussion, they are generally presented, possibly modified in light of the discussion, in a White Paper, and eventually, if legislation is involved, in a Bill to Parliament.

6

Leisure and Tourism Plans and Planning

Introduction

In this chapter the overall process of producing a plan is examined, while specific techniques that might be utilized in the process are addressed in Chapter 7. The process of strategic planning is considered initially, followed by a brief examination of some official guidelines for planning recently published in Britain and Australia. The main part of the chapter discusses the overall planning process, in the context of the rational–comprehensive model outlined in Fig. 5.3 (Chapter 5). Finally, the process of land-use planning and its relevance to leisure and tourism are discussed.

The contents of this chapter are addressed primarily to the local-government sector, since local government is the level of government that has a comprehensive range of powers and responsibilities with regard to leisure and tourism services. Much of the book's content is almost equally applicable to specialist agencies, such as tourism-development or national-parks organizations, trusts responsible for single services or facilities, in either the public or non-profit sector and, in federal systems such as Australia and Canada, to state or provincial governments. In what follows reference is made to elected councils as the source of authority and decision-making power, but for other types of agency this role is played by a board or committee or, in the case of state and provincial governments, by state or provincial governments and parliaments.

Strategic Planning

The terms strategic planning and strategic management have been used to refer to an approach to planning and management that seeks to ensure that medium- to long-term goals are given prominence, and day-to-day management is harnessed to the achievement of such goals rather than being distracted by ad hoc, short-term objectives. This approach has its origins in the private sector but, since the 1960s, public bodies have increasingly been required to behave much like private corporations, preparing strategic plans, which are rolled forward annually and which integrate forward planning with budgeting, implementation strategies and performance appraisal (Caret *et al.*, 1992: 5–24). The terms strategic planning and strategic management are used interchangeably by some, but *strategic planning* is seen here as the initial process of preparing a direction and broad programme of activity for the organization, while *strategic management*, on the other hand, is seen as those aspects of management which are concerned with ensuring that the strategic plan is implemented and that the organization does not lose sight of its strategic directions because of day-to-day concerns.

We all make decisions all the time, as individuals and as part of social groupings, such as a household or a group of friends. Some of the decisions are short-term or day-to-day in nature, such as what brand of instant coffee to buy; others are more significant, often with a number of long-lasting

© CAB *International* 2002. *Leisure and Tourism Policy and Planning*, 2nd edn (A.J. Veal)

consequences – for example, buying a house, embarking on an educational course or getting married. These more significant decisions might be called strategic – they imply a strategy for the future with a range of factors and further decisions being dependent on them. More time and care are generally taken over these strategic decisions than over day-to-day decisions; often they involve complete appraisals of our lives, our values and our relationships. Leisure and tourism organizations similarly make day-to-day decisions and strategic decisions. Examples of the range of decision-making, from the minor day-to-day level to the strategic level, in leisure organizations, are given in Table 6.1.

Personal strategic decision-making may be complicated enough, especially when it involves a number of other people, but when an organization makes strategic decisions thousands of people may need to be involved and may be affected by the decisions made. The more strategic the decision the more people are likely to be involved or affected. For example, if a large manufacturing company makes a strategic decision – such as to build a plant to produce a new product or to close down a plant and cease producing a particular product – hundreds or even thousands of staff and their families, local communities and possibly millions of customers may be affected. When an organization makes strategic decisions, therefore, considerable care must be taken both in the process of making the decisions and in considering their effects.

Mintzberg (1994) recorded the rise and fall of strategic planning in 1994, but perusal of library catalogues and relevant web-sites will reveal that strategic plans in the area of leisure and tourism continue to be produced in significant numbers. While strategic planning may change in format and context, it seems to be an unavoidable activity of public leisure and tourism organizations and would appear to be here to stay.

The planning/decision-making process is similar at all levels of a management hierarchy, although it might be expected that the process would be less elaborate at lower levels. A nested planning/decision-making process can therefore be envisaged, in which the basic strategic, rational decision-making process shown in Fig. 5.3 is replicated at lower levels. This is illustrated in Fig. 6.1, in which the overall plan breaks down into four programme areas. Since – in a typical local authority, for example – a programme area might contain a number of subprogrammes or individual facilities, the process could be repeated yet again at a third or fourth tier.

Guidelines

Various official guidelines are produced from time to time to aid local authorities in particular in producing strategic plans for leisure,

Table 6.1. Levels of decision-making.

Level	Leisure centre	Tourist Commission	National Park
▲ Day-to-day	Choose brand of floor cleaner	Decide what information to send to an enquirer	Close park for a day due to flooding
	Decide annual price increases	Commission a market-research project	Appoint one ranger
	Employ new manager	Choose 3-year marketing theme	Designate a new National Park
	Reorganize staff structure	Open offices in target market locations	Adopt user-pays principle
Strategic ▼	Build large extension to centre	Determine target markets for next 5 years	Allow mining in National Parks

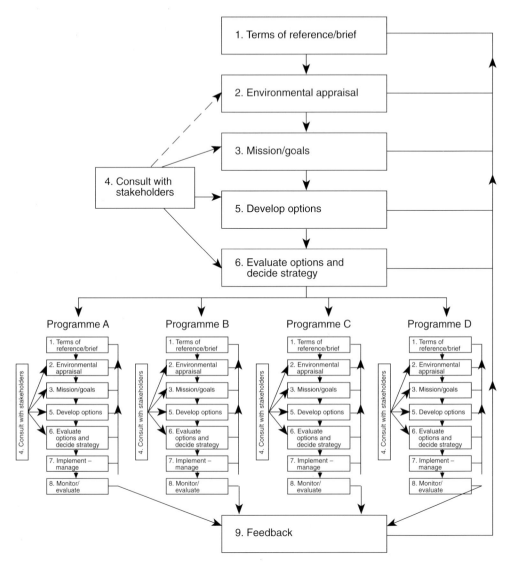

Fig. 6.1. Nested planning decision-making processes.

culture, recreation or tourism. Two examples are summarized below.

Local Cultural Strategies

The guidelines for *Local Cultural Strategies* produced for local authorities in England by the Department for Culture, Media and Sport (1999) 'strongly encourage' local authorities to develop a strategic plan to cover the arts, sports, libraries, museums, children's play, parks, tourism and countryside recreation. The broad content of the guidelines is summarized in Box 6.1. Their main purpose is clearly to encourage local authorities to prepare broadly based strategic plans that are well integrated with the planning activities of other agencies and the authorities' own corporate and other plans and are based on widespread consultation. The guidelines do not, however, constitute a manual on how to

---

Box 6.1. *Local Cultural Strategies* – guidelines summary (from Department for Culture, Media and Sport, 1999).

Principles
- Be based on the 'needs, demands and aspirations of the communities which the local authority serves';
- be guided by a 'vision for the culture' of the area;
- have fair access for all as central;
- adopt a cross-departmental and inter-agency approach;
- involve 'meaningful active consultation' with stakeholders;
- be set in the 'wider central and regional government context';
- contribute to central government's key objectives;
- be strategic, including priorities, forward planning + mechanisms for implementation, monitoring, review.

Preparation Stages
1. Preparation
2. Consultation A
3. Analysis
4. Creation
5. Consultation B
6. Completion
7. Launch

Content
- Advocate the benefits of cultural activities – rationale and contribution to wider social/political objectives
- Set strategic context – links with other plans
- Set local context – data on local population, economy, facilities, participation levels
- Identify key cultural issues – results of consultation
- Establish broad cultural policies
- Action plan – includes performance indicators and links to best-value process

---

prepare a plan. There is an indication that research and analysis are necessary, but no detail is given on this. The implied planning methodology recommended is the approach referred to in Chapter 7 as the issues approach – the proposition that the plan will be based on key issues, which will arise primarily from a process of consultation with stakeholders.

Outdoor Recreation and Open Space

The document *Outdoor Recreation and Open Space: Planning Guidelines for Local Government* was prepared for the New South Wales government by consultants Manidis Roberts (1992). While it is focused on just one sector of leisure, the approach could readily be applied to all sectors. The basic approach of the guidelines is indicated in Fig. 6.2. In this case there is a more explicit demand–supply approach and public consultation is confined to resident surveys and focus groups, but, as with the UK guidelines, the issues approach is still apparent, the link with the authority's corporate plan is made clear and the resultant plan includes performance indicators.

The Strategic Planning Process

The intention here is to consider leisure and tourism plans in a generic sense, rather than the requirements for any particular legal or

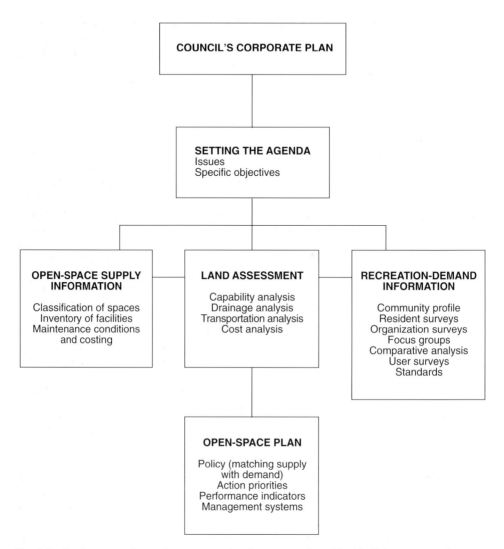

Fig. 6.2. *Outdoor recreation and open space* planning process (from Manidis Roberts, 1992: 4).

institutional context. Plans are produced in differing contexts and for differing purposes, such as an in-house document designed to meet the needs of one organization or an exercise forming part of some wider statutory planning process. In some cases separate plans are produced for leisure and tourism; in other cases they are dealt with together. All such planning exercises have certain principles in common, and it is these principles which are addressed below. The outline that follows is broadly compatible with the guidelines discussed above. The

aim here, however, is to take the process further and, through this and subsequent chapters, to provide a more detailed toolkit for the production of plans and the evaluation of their outcomes. The steps in the discussion below follow the rational–comprehensive model as set out in Fig. 5.3 (page 82).

Step 1. Establish terms of reference/brief

Any task must have a clear brief, or terms of reference, and producing a comprehensive or strategic leisure or tourism plan is no exception. Typically briefs for a team about to embark on such tasks might be:

> *To determine the leisure requirements of the community over the next 10 years and prepare a feasible strategy to address those requirements.*

> *To determine the desirable scale and nature of tourism development and consequent tourism marketing activities for the community over the next 10 years.*

In some strategic planning exercises the terms of reference may relate to the existence of the whole organization and the exercise is aimed at determining the strategic plan for the whole organization. Typically, such whole-of-organization terms of reference are stated in legislation or a charter.

The remaining steps in the process are focused on determining leisure or tourism requirements and developing a feasible strategy. The terms of reference for a strategic plan will generally be determined by the elected council. In some cases the requirement to produce a plan may arise from legislation or central-government guidelines.

Two aspects of the brief need initial consideration, namely time-scale and scope.

Time-scale

The time-scale for a strategy could be longer or shorter than 10 years, depending on the rate of change within the community or the market and, perhaps, the political horizons of the elected authority. Different aspects of the strategy will relate to different time-scales. For example, in step 3, the question of mission, goals and objectives is discussed. The *mission* of an organization does not generally have a time-scale, unless the organization has a specific task, such as the holding of a one-off event. *Goals* tend to be long-term, but may become obsolete or need modification: for example, the goal 'to provide a comprehensive range of leisure facilities in all neighbourhoods' could, once it was judged to have been achieved, be changed to: 'to maintain a comprehensive range of leisure facilities in all neighbourhoods'. *Objectives* tend to be associated with specific times. For example, an objective might be to

'double the number of tourists visiting the city over a 10-year period'. Such an objective may be implemented in stages: for example, each year during the 10 years of the plan, a specific participation target would be set.

Scope

Whether a local authority is left-leaning or right-leaning in its politics or more or less community-orientated in its approach to planning and decision-making, a decision has to be made about the scope of the authority's responsibilities. One approach is a minimalist one, where the authority's activities are determined only by statutory obligations and obvious electoral demands. An alternative approach is to accept a broad-ranging responsibility for enhancement of the quality of life of the community, using statutory powers as tools to achieve this end. It is important, therefore, to clarify the scope of the plan. This has differing implications for leisure and tourism, discussed in turn below.

The question of scope is particularly important in the area of leisure, which means different things to different people. Local government is in the unique position of being able to take a comprehensive view of leisure in the community. In practice, however, this opportunity is rarely grasped. Since, for a variety of reasons, local government is itself involved in direct provision of only a limited range of leisure facilities and services, local-authority leisure plans often deal only with that particular restricted range. Frequently planning documents begin by considering leisure – or recreation – in its entirety, but then proceed to ignore major aspects of leisure, simply because the local council is not directly involved in their provision.

Examples of major aspects of leisure that are usually excluded from local authority plans are: home-based leisure, entertainment, pubs and restaurants, and holidays. Such aspects are ignored presumably because local authorities feel that, since they are not direct providers, they have no powers or rights to engage in planning in these areas. The commercial and the private sector are often deemed to be out of bounds. This logic is, however, not applied in areas such as retailing and industrial and office space, where detailed planning activity is undertaken by councils, despite the fact that these are primarily commercial activities. In the past, the leisure facilities which were 'in' and those which were 'out' of the planning process at least corresponded to broad sectors, but, with increasing levels of private-sector involvement in traditionally public-sector areas, this will no longer be the case: almost all forms of leisure are served by a mixture of public- and private-sector organizations. The fact that the local authority identifies a need and puts forward a plan to meet the need does not necessarily imply that it will be the agency which will be responsible for meeting the need.

Because the inclusion of these particular areas of leisure in the public planning process is so rare, it is perhaps worth considering briefly just how they might be incorporated into plans and what relationship the plan and the local authority might have with them.

Home-based leisure. It is known from leisure surveys that the home is the most important site for leisure for virtually everybody. It is sometimes noted in plans that people living in flats are likely to be in need of more out-of-home leisure provision because of lack of access to gardens, but such observations are rarely followed through into policies. In mainland Europe, allotments often take the form of 'leisure gardens', rather than areas for growing food, but this has not generally happened in Britain. This may be because of differing cultural traditions, but it may also be because local authorities have not considered the question of home-based leisure in their planning, so the provision of leisure gardens has not arisen. It might also be suspected that the somewhat untidy collective appearance of 'leisure gardens', with their summer houses and sheds and varying standards of upkeep, would not conform to the architect-planners' vision of the urban landscape.

Electronic forms of entertainment are generally accepted as being the most significant of the home-based leisure activities. One way in which the public sector has been involved with this area is that public libraries have for many years offered loans of recorded music. However, in considering the quality of leisure in a community, local councils could adopt a position on, for example, local broadcasting or, in contrast, on the need to encourage alternatives to television for young people.

Entertainment, pubs, restaurants. This area of what might be termed *social leisure* could be said to be a major contributor to the quality of life of a community. The contribution that the quantity, quality and distribution of such facilities make to the character of an urban environment is often considered in plans – although not very systematically – in the context of visitors to an area, but rarely in relation to the needs of local residents. There is clearly a difference between a successful leisure precinct in a town centre, whether it has been deliberately planned or not, and an unsuccessful one. In the successful precinct, transport systems, cinemas, bingo halls, theatres, pubs, restaurants, gardens, walking areas and associated retail activity all complement one another, and there is an appropriate ambience, so that the whole is greater than the sum of the parts, business booms and more investment in facilities is attracted. Such a scenario can be facilitated or hindered by planning (Stansfield and Rickert, 1970; Jansen-Verbeke, 1985). Little work has been done on standards of provision for such facilities, but the 'hierarchies' approach discussed in Chapter 7 is one way in which levels of provision might be addressed.

THE SCOPE OF TOURISM PLANS. A more inclusive approach is often taken in planning for tourism because tourism is clearly primarily a private-sector industry, so it would be absurd to ignore the role of the private sector in any plan. Local-government and other public-sector agencies are often responsible for key attractions, such as beaches, waterways, museums and galleries and heritage items, but hotels, restaurants and many attractions are generally commercially operated. Plans therefore often have a town-planning and economic-development perspective, with public- and private-sector development being considered together, often in the context of 'growth-regime' politics, as discussed in Chapter 5. Local government in tourism areas is often also involved in tourism promotion, marketing and information services, usually in collaboration with private-sector organizations and other councils, so forecasting demand and setting targets for visitor numbers also become part of the planning activity.

While the production of development and marketing strategies to attract tourists to their areas is common, local authorities tend not to consider the *holiday needs* of their own residents. And yet a holiday is, arguably, one of the most important forms of leisure to the individual. In the same way that variable, and inequitable, access to sporting facilities is examined in leisure plans, there is no reason why variable and inequitable access to holidays should not also be examined. National tourism organizations tend not to collect data on those who *do* go on holiday, as a group, and are not generally interested in those who do not. The idea of social tourism – helping deprived groups, such as people with disabilities or carers, to take a holiday – is not a new idea (Finch, 1975). In this case, however, social-services organizations are more likely to be involved, and they tend not to be involved in tourism planning.

While the above is a plea for comprehensiveness, particular authorities or agencies may find themselves constrained in what they can include by legislation and/or by the responsibilities and activities of other bodies. For example, while health education might arise naturally in considering a sport and fitness plan, it would be inappropriate for a local authority to attempt to muscle in on the territory of education authorities or health authorities – although working cooperatively with such bodies on joint programmes might well be possible. It would also make sense to take account of the existing plans and current planning activities of such bodies, which might well already include health education programs. Figure 6.3 is based on a diagram presented in the *Local Cultural*

Strategies guidelines discussed above, and shows the relationships between a local cultural plan and strategies and plans by other agencies.

Step 2. Environmental appraisal

Environmental appraisal involves bringing together all the available information relevant to the brief. This sounds simple enough, but can be extremely complex and demanding of resources, especially when being undertaken for the first time and especially in the public sector. For example, one item of information that might be expected to be available for such an appraisal would be trends in output or sales. In the private sector, the output of the organization is sold in the market and paid for by customers, so sales figures are always available; but, in the public sector, information on 'sales' – for example, the number of users of a local authority's parks or the number of tourists visiting an area – is rarely routinely available and must be gathered by means of special research projects.

The environmental appraisal might be expected to include a number of different types of information, as set out in Table 6.2. A complete appraisal of this kind could involve an enormous data-collection exercise, which could take an inordinate amount of time and resources; and the results could be somewhat indigestible. Initially, therefore, judgements would need to be made about the balance between the need for information and the time and cost of collecting it. But, as experience with the strategic planning process develops, so the data base is likely to develop, in terms of its content and its presentation.

Data routinely collected for performance-assessment purposes, as discussed in Chapter 11, is available as an input to this process. Thus the cost of data collection can be seen as shared between the two processes. The third column in Table 6.2 suggests the need for a well-developed management information system (MIS) – that is, procedures that routinely produce information

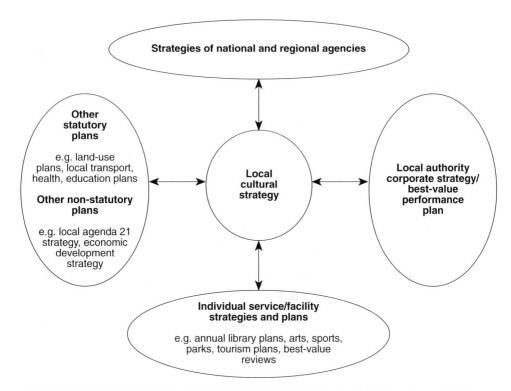

Fig. 6.3. Links between strategies and plans (adapted from Department for Culture, Media and Sport, 1999: 25).

necessary for strategic planning and on-going management. Thus a public leisure-provision agency should, ideally, have available:

- an accurate, detailed and up-to-date inventory of facilities;
- regular reports on usage levels from ticket sales and, where ticket sales are not available, from special counts;
- regular public/customer feedback from user and community surveys;
- in tourist areas: data on regional tourism trends and information on local visitors from periodic visitor surveys;
- regular financial reports on services/facilities.

It has often been the case in the past that planning exercises have been overwhelmed by the data-collection process and, as a result, the analysis of the data has been neglected, so that both planning and data collection have acquired a bad reputation in some circles, due to the poor return on the time and effort invested. It is likely that this situation may now have improved as better MISs have developed. In addition, modern computer-based technology and increasing familiarity with it have made data collection and analysis simpler and cheaper. Thus most public bodies now have a good inventory of their own facilities (although not necessarily of others'); this was not always the case. Similarly, computerized ticketing provides good usage data for many facilities, and user and community surveys are no longer the rarity they once were.

The nine types of data listed in Table 6.2 are discussed in turn below.

Political

Political commitments are generally of more significance at national level than at local level, but commitments made by politicians in manifestos and in speeches and public

Table 6.2. Information for environmental appraisal.

Type	Information items	Sources
A. Political	A1 Policy commitments of ruling party group A2 Higher-tier government policies A3 Community opinion	• Party manifesto, speeches, etc. • Policy documents • Pressure-group activity • Community surveys • Media comment
B. Existing policies	B1 Policy statements B2 Higher-tier government directives	• Policy documents • Council leaders' statements to council/press
C. Legal	C1 Legal obligations/limitations	• Legislation • Leases, covenants, deeds, etc.
D. Existing facilities/services	D1 Inventory – public/private/non-profit – actual and planned D2 Capital value/running costs D3 Age/state of repair of facilities D4 Use levels of facilities D5 User/community satisfaction D6 Performance indicators D7 Coverage – areas of unmet need D8 Programmes/events D9 Grants awarded	• Files/databases/directories • Survey of clubs/firms • Facility physical survey • Ticket sales/counts/bookings • Financial records • User surveys
E. Visitors/tourists	E1 Numbers, origins, activities	• Visitor/tourist surveys
F. Neighbouring areas/regional dimension	F1 Major provision – actual and planned F2 Local use of regional facilities	• Consultation with neighbouring authorities • Special studies
G. Population trends	G1 Future increases/decreases in population G2 Changing age structure	• Planning department
H. Demand/social trends	H1 Activity-demand forecasts H2 Trends in tastes, social values, etc.	• Literature, special studies • Social surveys

statements are usually sacrosanct, despite public cynicism about politicians' broken promises. Such commitments, which are deemed to have been sanctioned by the democratic process, must therefore inevitably be included as part of any plan.

Existing policies

It makes sense to gather together existing policies of the organization and its management units, whether they result from earlier strategic-planning exercises or have developed in an ad hoc manner. Part of the input to the plan will be an evaluation and review of such policies. If monitoring and evaluation procedures have been built into the policies in the past, then this may not be a large task.

A key aspect of existing policies relates to the general planning framework of the organization. The leisure or tourism plan may be part of a wider planning exercise, but, even if it is not, there are likely to be advantages in seeking to complement other planning activity. Complementarity may involve using the same time horizons, so that use can be made of such things as existing population projections. It may also involve utilizing existing planning zones or precincts, which divide the local-authority area into neighbourhoods. Of course, the choice of such zones will also be influenced by the existence of zones for administrative purposes or by research, which may reveal that spatial patterns of leisure or tourism suggest suitable zones or precincts for planning purposes. All aspects of data collection and subsequent analysis and policy formulation will relate to the zones chosen.

This information might initially be assembled as a library of documents, but in due course summaries for analysis and for inclusion in the plan document will have to be prepared.

Legal obligations

Local government in Britain generally possesses *powers* in relation to leisure provision and tourism development, but not *duties* or *obligations*. However, there may be obliga-

tions in relation to conservation of natural or cultural heritage. Government agencies, on the other hand, often have their duties enshrined in legislation or charters and these are often the starting-point for any planning activity.

Existing facilities/services

As discussed above, most local authorities now have comprehensive inventories of their own facilities and services, including detailed descriptions, such as the areas of open space and the facilities they contain. Ideally they should be available in mapped form. The costs of and time taken to gather such information are an example of the problems that strategic planning has faced in the past, but data are now becoming more readily available as a result of developments in performance monitoring and asset management (Premier's Department *et al.*, 1992) and the ready availability of computerized database systems.

Information is generally less complete with regard to facilities and services owned or managed by other organizations. Often information is available on voluntary organizations because authorities often work closely with such organizations, offering grant aid and the use of facilities and compiling documents, such as sports directories. It is in the commercial and social-leisure area where information is often lacking. Information on policies of significant other organizations, such as voluntary sports and social organizations, central-government instrumentalities and major commercial organizations, should be collated, in so far as they are readily available in written form. If they are not readily available then the requisite information might be more suitably collected by special surveys or in the consultation phase (step 4). Competitor analysis has traditionally been seen as more important in the private sector and is therefore particularly important in the case of tourism, but it is increasingly important in leisure, as the public sector is no longer the monopoly provider in many sectors, but is increasingly in competition with private-sector providers, as discussed under 'Scope' above. Such gaps in the information should be remedied, via such sources as *Yellow Pages*, land-use maps and directories, so that a comprehensive picture of leisure and tourism provision is available. Table 6.3 provides an indicative list of the facilities and services that might be included in an inventory.

In addition to an inventory of facilities, information should be collated on current levels of utilization. Levels of utilization and catchment-area information can indicate patterns of undersupply and oversupply of facilities and services. The question of measuring use levels and capacity is discussed in relation to the organic approach to planning discussed in Chapter 7. Ideally, identical information should be collected for both private- and public-sector facilities and services, but, in practice, where facilities and services are run by organizations other than the local authority, it may be difficult or even impossible to gather information directly, but it may be collected via community and visitor surveys, as discussed under 'Demand/social trends'.

Visitors/tourists

Gathering information on visitors is clearly important in tourist areas, but visitors can be of significance even in areas that are not thought of as tourist attractions. Many urban centres attract visitors from beyond the local-authority boundary, for shopping and similar purposes, and the viability of some town-centre amenities, such as pubs, restaurants and entertainment facilities, may be affected by such visitors. Visitors to tourist areas are often treated separately in a tourism strategy rather than a leisure plan. Many of the facilities used by tourists, such as parks, museums, theatres, pubs and restaurants, are in fact community leisure facilities: more often than not, even in recognized tourist areas, locals form the majority of the patrons of such facilities. This is, of course, highly desirable from the tourists' point of view, since most would prefer to mix with the locals rather than visit a tourist 'ghetto'. Generally, the locals also benefit from a higher level of provision and greater variety than would be possible without the visitors. Planning for the leisure of tourists and for the leisure of residents should therefore be complementary. User surveys of such facilities will therefore include tourists as well as local residents.

Some sort of periodic survey is the most effective means of gathering the required data, involving random sampling and interviewing of visitors in areas which they frequent. The aim would be to discover just how many visitors there are, and what facilities they use. Some forecasting of future visitor numbers would also be required (see Chapter 8).

Neighbouring areas/regional dimension

Planning should take account of major facilities, services and resources available and planned in neighbouring areas and/or the wider region. The public is no respecter of administrative boundaries; authorities should be aware of the extent to which catchment areas of their own and neighbouring authorities' facilities overlap. This information may be gathered by routine examination

Table 6.3. Facility/service inventory content.

• Adult education centres	• Public halls
• Amusement arcades	• Public open space
• Bingo halls	Playing pitches/courts
• Bookshops	Parkland
• Cinemas	Beaches
• Clubs	• Other open space
• Education facilities	• Pubs
• Gyms/fitness/squash centres	• Restaurants
• Hobby clubs	• Sport/leisure centres
• Hotels/motels	• Swimming-pools
• Libraries	• Sporting clubs
• Private halls	• Theatres

of written plans of neighbouring authorities or by special surveys.

Population trends

Establishing the socio-demographic characteristics of a community is a relatively simple task making use of the census of population. Problems do arise however, in areas where significant population change is taking place and the census is out of date. Usually in these situations the local planning department is in a position to provide current population estimates.

For the local-authority area as a whole and for each of the selected planning zones, the following data should be collated:

- resident population by: age/sex, occupation, car ownership, housing type
- workforce.

Planning departments are also generally the source of population forecasts. While the population is static or growing very slowly in most areas in Britain, there can be pockets of growth in suburban areas and some country and coastal areas. In other parts of the world rapid population growth is still the norm – Sydney, Australia, for example, is growing at a rate of 500,000 every 10 years. However, it is not just the overall future population size that is important, but also its characteristics. In particular, future age-specific population estimates should be obtained, since the ageing of the population is one of the most significant social changes taking place in the current era, as discussed in Chapter 8.

Demand/social trends

A community survey is the only practical way of obtaining comprehensive information on current patterns of leisure participation in an area. Such a survey can obtain information on:

- levels of participation in a range of leisure activities;
- use of a range of leisure facilities and services;
- resident opinions.

Information on participation is essential if policy is to focus on participation rather than purely on facilities and programmes. There is a reluctance among many authorities to commit themselves to policies related to participation, since this appears to be 'telling people what to do'. The preferred approach is, very often, to express policies in terms of 'providing opportunity'. But it would seem illogical to be concerned with providing opportunity but not with whether or not those opportunities are taken up. At the facility or programme-management level, maximization of participation – or attendances – is the norm. Success is at least partly measured in terms of visits. It is sometimes argued that it is quality that matters rather than quantity; however, the two are not really alternatives but are complementary: since leisure is voluntarily undertaken, maximizing participation must usually be achieved by offering a high-quality product.

A well-designed community leisure-participation survey can form the focus of much of the planning exercise. As discussed in earlier chapters, certain activities, such as sport and the arts, are widely supported by the public sector because of the social benefits they bring. It makes sense for public policy to seek to maximize those social benefits, which will be achieved by maximizing participation levels. It therefore makes sense for the aim of the plan to be to maximize participation and for the success of the plan to be measured in terms of participation levels achieved. The starting-point and subsequent progress can best be measured by some sort of community survey.

Focussing on levels of participation as measured by a community survey has the potential to involve a wide range of organizations in the implementation of the plan, since the local authority is only one provider of facilities and services. Further, it provides the local authority with criteria by which to judge its own activities and requests by other organizations for assistance: namely, to what extent will the activity contribute to increased participation?

It is not proposed to explore the methodology of a community leisure-participation survey here; such matters are dealt with in more specialized texts (e.g. Veal, 1997). Suffice it to say that, if the survey is to be the basis for assessing the overall success of the plan, it must be well designed and conducted and must involve a sufficiently large sample to enable comparisons to be made from one survey period to the next. Typically, at least 1000 interviews would be required and, especially if the sample is to be divided into zones, preferable more.

In addition to gathering information on participation, a community-wide survey can also be used to gather information on levels of use of specific facilities and services, as discussed under 'Existing facilities/services' above. Further, they can be used to gather opinions on the quality of existing facilities and services, on perceived deficiencies and requirements and on future proposals. The survey can therefore be seen as part of the consultation process, discussed below.

Social surveys can generally only be conducted among adults, typically from around 14 years old. Information on the leisure activities of children can be collected from parents or, with appropriate permissions, a special survey might be conducted via schools.

Step 3. Establish mission/goals

Mission vs. purpose vs. goals vs. objectives

Before considering this step in detail it is worth giving some attention to the question of the difference between mission, purpose, goals and objectives. The *mission* of an organization is its overall *raison d'être*, which is generally, if possible, summarized in a succinct phrase or two. In this book *purpose* will be considered as meaning the same as mission, so a statement of purpose could substitute for a mission statement. *Goals* are simply more detailed statements of the mission. *Objectives* are more specific, are generally linked to specific programmes or facilities and generally include a time dimension and quantification. Using the examples of the three types of facility used in Table 6.1 above, some illustrative mission statements, goals and objectives are set out in Table 6.4. In effect, there is a mission/goals/objectives hierarchy, as indicated in Fig. 6.4. The mission is the starting-point, the broad statement about the purpose of the organization. Goals are more detailed, involving a breaking

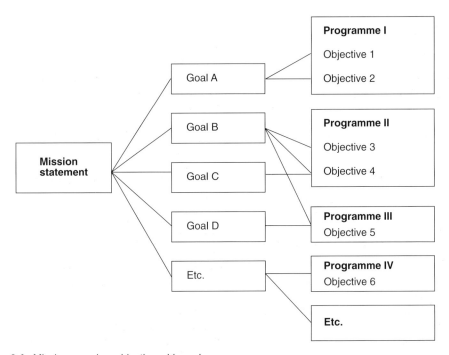

Fig. 6.4. Mission – goals – objectives: hierarchy.

Table 6.4. Mission/goals/objectives – examples.

	Leisure centre	Tourist Commission	National Park
Mission	To provide members of the local community with fulfilling recreational experiences	To maximize benefits from tourism while minimizing costs	To conserve the flora, fauna and ecological integrity of the park area while providing fulfilling recreational experiences for visitors
Goals	• To attract as wide a cross-section of the community as possible • To maximize the use of the centre • To maximize net income	• To extend the tourist season • To encourage tourists to visit areas outside the capital city • To improve the standard of service offered to tourists	• To preserve endangered species • To reduce the effects of erosion • To improve educational services for visitors
Objectives	• To double the number of elderly using the centre over the coming year • To increase utilization of the squash courts from 70% to 80% over 2 years • To reach an income of £1m by 2005	• To increase off-season tourist trips by 10% over 2 years • To increase non-metropolitan tourist trips from 20% to 30% of all tourist trips by 2005 • To increase customer-service training programmes by 50% over 2 years	• To restore species A, B, C, etc. to viability over a 5-year period • To double the programme of rehabilitation of eroded areas over the coming year • To build one new visitor interpretation centre each year over the next 3 years

down of the mission statement into components. Objectives are quite specific, and are
often quantified and linked to a time-scale;
they emerge as part of the strategic planning
process and are continually changing as priorities or circumstances change and as objectives are achieved and are replaced by
others.

Mission and goals

Drucker (1990: 3), in discussing the importance of 'getting it right', refers to the mission statements of a number of
organizations, including the Girl Scouts of
the USA: to help girls grow into proud, self-
confident, and self-respecting young
women', and a hospital emergency room: 'to
give assurance to the afflicted'. Wilkinson
and Monkhouse (1994) contrast the relatively
simple, and often inward-looking, task of
establishing a mission statement for a private
company, with the complex process involved
for public bodies, with their many stakeholders and statutory constraints.

A further feature of many public-sector
leisure agencies is their multi-purpose
nature. Over 30 years ago Hatry and Dunn
suggested the following combination of
goals and mission statement for a local-
authority recreation service.

> Recreation services should provide for all
> citizens, to the extent practicable, a variety of
> adequate, year-round leisure opportunities
> which are accessible, safe, physically attractive,
> and provide enjoyable experiences. They
> should, to the maximum extent, contribute to
> the mental and physical health of the
> community, to its economic and social well-
> being and permit outlets that will help
> decrease incidents of antisocial behaviour such
> as crime and delinquency.

> (Hatry and Dunn, 1971: 13)

In Chapter 10 the implications of such a
comprehensive statement for the on-going
management and performance monitoring of
a leisure service are explored. This formulation is an attempt to provide an all-purpose
statement to which any local authority might
subscribe. However, the discussion in the
opening chapters of this book suggests that
different people and political groups hold

different values and have differing views on
the role of the state, in relation to leisure and
tourism as much as in relation to other areas
such as education or defence. It might be
expected therefore that differing values and
philosophies would lead to differing mission
or goals statements. Table 6.5 summarizes
the main philosophical positions outlined in
Chapters 2–4 and offers suggestions as to
what effect such positions might have on the
mission/goals of a public leisure or tourism
agency.

While mission/goals statements can be
expected to reflect value positions, it is possible for statements to be devised which are so
general in nature that they are acceptable to
most shades of opinion – the differences
emerging only at later stages in the planning
process. For example, a statement to the
effect that an authority aims to enhance
health by promotion of participation in sport
might have wide acceptance, but one group
might wish to do this by making public
sports facilities freely available to all, while
another group might wish to facilitate a
private-enterprise approach. Or the authority might declare a goal to develop tourism
and only later does it emerge that one group
envisages the development of high-rise four-
star hotels, while another group envisages
chalets and backpacker hostels.

Mission/goals within the organization

The mission statement and the related statement of goals can perform a number of functions. First, they are the linchpin of the rest
of the strategic planning process – all proposals should be orientated towards the fulfilment of the mission statement and pursuit
of the goals. Secondly, if well formulated,
they can provide a common focus of attention for all members of an organization,
including elected and staff members,
whether or not they are directly engaged in
the strategic planning process, and for others
with an interest in the activities of the organization, particularly the public, as both elec-
tors and consumers of its services – the
stakeholders. Thirdly, in appropriate format,
they can also assist in establishing the corporate identity of the organization.

Table 6.5. Values/ideologies and goals.

Source/basis	Goal/objective
Leisure/travel needs and rights (Ch. 2)	
Leisure as a right	Access to facilities for chosen leisure activities for all
Leisure as a need	Ensure all needs are met
Travel as a right	Ensure freedom of travel
Holidays as a right	Ensure reasonable holiday entitlements
	Ensure access to holidays for needy
Ideological perspectives (Ch. 3)	
Conservative values	Maintenance of traditional provision and promotion of excellence
Liberal values	Minimization of state involvement
Democratic socialist values	Equality of opportunity; democratization; maximum state provision
Marxist socialist values	Facilities and opportunities that counter commercial exploitation
Feminist values	Radical: facilities and opportunities that counter patriarchy
	Reformist: access to facilities for women; child-care provision
Environmentalist values	Promotion of environmentally friendly activities; protection of the natural environment
Economic factors (Ch. 4)	
Public goods	
Externalities	
Mixed goods	Provide facilities and services that correct
Merit goods	market failures, where enhanced community
Option demand	benefit can be shown
Natural monopolies	
Infant industries	
Large projects	Public sector as entrepreneur and economic
Economic development	manager
Incidental enterprise	
Equity	Counter market inequalities and inequities through leisure provision
Tradition	Maintain existing services

In addition to complications arising from value differences among political and interest groups, most public bodies are faced with differences of outlook within the organization, both horizontally (across a range of services) and vertically (from top management via line management to the operational level). In practice the multipurpose organization is likely to have a hierarchy of mission/goals statements relating to different levels and sections of the organization. The strategic planning and management process proceeds to ask: how might this mission and these goals be best pursued? The result is a set of policies, programmes and facilities, with an organizational and management structure to go with it. Each of the sections of the organization would then be expected to subscribe to the mission of the whole organization, with its own set of contributory goals and targets. Each section will engage in its own strategic management process – considering alternative ways of achieving the broad goals that arise from the overall strategic planning process.

For example, if a local authority, as one of its goals, seeks to enhance the health of the community, as discussed above, it might decide, as a result of its planning activity, to pursue that goal by means of the provision of a public swimming-pool and the organization of an annual marathon. The pool manager is given the goal of maximizing health benefits through swimming participation, while the officer responsible for organizing the marathon is given the goal of maximizing health through marathon participation. Each of these managers now has a mini-strategic plan to prepare; each has a range of possible courses of action that might be pursued.

Diversity

Of particular note in the public sector, and in leisure in particular, is the often very diverse nature of the organizational goals involved. In the private sector the main goal is usually to make the maximum possible profit. In practice it is more complicated than that, with short-term versus long-term considerations to take into account, which leads to consideration of such issues as growth, assets, liquidity and customer loyalty, as well as profit. But all the goals and indicators of success tend to be quantitative and can be relatively easily compared between different companies (Gratton and Taylor, 1988: 150). In the public sector goals are not only diverse, but often difficult to quantify in any meaningful way – for example, goals related to excellence in the arts or to conservation of the environment or heritage. Further, goals can often be conflicting – for example, conservation versus recreational or tourism access in natural areas and some conceptions of excellence versus popularity in the arts.

Quality

Quality management is an idea imported from manufacturing, where precise quality standards for outputs are relatively easy to define and measure. In the service sector, and in the public sector in particular, definition and measurement are more of a challenge because the product – the delivery and enjoyment of the service – is:

- intangible (and so cannot be stored and tested in advance);
- heterogeneous (different customers experience the service differently and have different priorities);
- inseparable (generally delivery of the service involves interaction between supplier and customer) (Lewis and Hartley, 2001: 479).

In fact, there is considerable overlap between manufacturers and services in regard to quality management. For example, the manufacturer may subject a product to numerous tests to ensure durability, but the key test is the extent to which customers return the product and ask for their money back. Thus, customer satisfaction (or lack of satisfaction) is the key indicator in manufacturing and services. Despite the difficulties of pinning this down, the idea of quality has come to be seen as a useful focus for public services, including leisure and tourism.

Quality control is the technical, operational process of setting standards and checking whether they have been met.

Quality assurance is the process of ensuring that the system delivers the required level of quality in the first place – for example by ensuring adequate staff training or equipment maintenance. Total quality management (TQM) is a more ambitious approach designed to ensure that the whole organization, its politics and practices, are quality-orientated. An overall commitment to quality and quality improvement is likely to feature in mission and goal statements. The details of quality control and quality assurance can be seen as relating primarily to the implementation stage of planning and are discussed further in Chapter 10, while TQM is strategic in nature and is discussed further below.

TQM became fashionable as an approach to management in the 1980s and early 1990s following its apparent success in Japanese industry (Logothetis, 1992). The approach suggests that the guiding principle in any organization's planning and management should be the idea of quality. Quality is something which every person in an organization can strive to achieve in his/her own area of responsibility and it can provide common goals towards which organizations and parts of organizations can strive collectively. In the commercial sector, for example, while profit maximization may be the overall goal, few members of the organization can relate to that goal directly – they are not able to see their own particular contribution to profit. But they can see their own contribution to quality and, it is argued, if the product or service is of sufficient quality, profits will follow.

The idea readily translates to public-sector service organizations, since everyone in the organization can understand the idea of a high-quality recreational or tourism experience, although it has been suggested that leisure services present a particular challenge (Robinson, 1997). Further, the quality idea focuses attention on customer or client needs, since, ultimately, it is argued, the customer is the arbiter as far as quality is concerned. While this is broadly true for most areas of the leisure services, problems can arise in certain areas of the arts and environmental conservation, where professionals, politicians, pressure groups and the general public can differ over what is an appropriate, quality product, programme or practice. Thus, in TQM parlance, the mission/goals statement suggested by Hatry and Dunn (1971) above might be simplified into a statement of the kind:

> To provide high-quality recreation experiences for the community.

The statements about accessibility, safety and so on would then be elaborations of the basic idea of quality.

The idea of quality in management has been promulgated by the publication of British Standard 5750, and international standard ISO 9002, which provide guidelines and principles for the establishment of a quality management system within an organization (Stabler, 1996; Robinson, 1998; Lentell, 2001). The quality idea was initially welcomed as a useful tool for the leisure manager (Mills, 1992), but, in Britain, has to some extent been incorporated into the idea of best practice (Lewis and Hartley, 2001), as discussed in Chapter 10.

Visioning

Another term used in this context is *visioning*. The term is used to describe an approach in which the process of establishing a *vision* or *strategic vision* for an organization is the focus of the strategy formulation process. The idea originated in the private sector, where, in some models of management, a charismatic leader provides a vision for the organization, but, in the case of public-sector organizations, the process generally involves extensive consultation with clients and the general public. But debate, analysis and bargaining are also involved, in order to resolve differences between various stakeholder groups, the idea being to develop a shared vision. The approach is predicated on a different model of decision-making from those indicated in Chapter 5. In those models the vision is provided by the ideological/political platform of the party group that gains power, or by the aims of the members of the urban growth regime. Experience with successful visioning exercises has been recorded, such as Ritchie's (1994b) account of a Canadian city's tourism-orientated exercise and White's (2000) account of an Australian experience but, as Helling (1998) notes, such exercises can be expensive failures if they are not suitably organized.

Step 4. Consultation with stakeholders

Consultation with stakeholders – the public, clients, other organizations and members of the local authority itself – is widely seen as a vital component in the planning process. There has been a growing movement for more direct community involvement in planning and policy-making over the last 30 years. In the old model of planning, as shown in Fig. 6.5, technical inputs, such as demand or needs assessment and forecasting, held centre stage in the process; in the new model, public and stakeholder consultation and collaborative identification of issues intervene between the technical inputs and

the development of the plan or strategy. Thus planning is seen as less of a technical process and more of a collective community activity. The decision to place community consultation at the heart of the planning and policy-making process is clearly a key strategic stance.

In Chapter 7, the community-development approach to planning is put forward as a means by which public involvement and participation becomes the basis of the whole exercise. In most statutory planning activities public consultation is a legal requirement.

As with data collection, consultation can be a time-consuming process that can easily be mishandled. If not undertaken competently, far from broadening the inputs to the planning process, it can have a narrowing effect, if sectional interests are permitted to hijack the process.

As Arnstein (1969) pointed out, public participation can take many forms, from tokenism to total citizen control. The steps in Arnstein's 'ladder' of citizen participation are as follows:

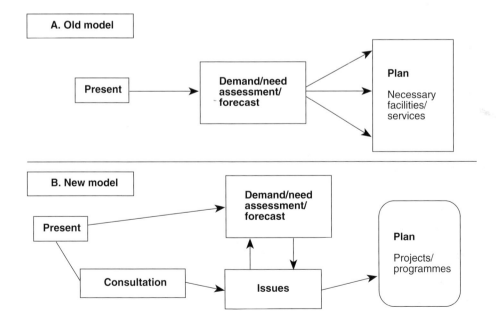

Fig. 6.5. Old and new models of planning.

1. Manipulation – a somewhat cynical use of the process by an organization.
2. Therapy – using the process to reassure the public about decisions already taken.
3. Informing – a one-way process.
4. Consultation – seeking comment on proposals already formulated.
5. Placation – a populist approach giving the public what they are thought to want, but without genuine dialogue.
6. Partnership – developing proposals together.
7. Delegated power – giving certain community groups decision-making power in specified limited areas.
8. Citizen control – full community engagement in formulation and decision-making.

In practice, most public consultation exercise involve a number of these formats, with very few venturing as far as 7 and 8.

Consultation can vary in its purpose, in the range and types of people and organizations involved, in its form and in its timing. These issues are discussed in turn below.

Purposes

Consultation may be undertaken as a means of gathering information – for example, to generate ideas, to obtain information on the issues of concern to particular groups or to obtain feedback on the feasibility of particular proposals – or it may be seen as integral to the decision-making process, involving opinions and attitudes of different groups concerning issues and proposals. Since leisure is not an issue which is thoroughly discussed on the political hustings and since it is such a wide-ranging phenomenon, involving everyone in the community, the information-gathering and decision-mak-

ing aspects of consultation are both highly relevant.

Involvement

Consultation usually involves the public at large, organizations and their representatives and the staff of the public organization doing the planning. Of particular importance in the area of leisure, which is not a statutory service in the public sector, is to produce a plan that is implemented. It is generally believed that this will only be achieved if those who are expected to be involved in implementing the plan are also involved in preparing it: many individuals and organizations must feel that they own the plan. Table 6.6 provides an indicative list of the range of individuals and organizations that might be involved in the consultation process for a leisure or tourism plan.

Form

Consultation can take a variety of forms, as listed in Table 6.7. Each of the techniques has its merits and drawbacks (Carr and Halvorsen, 2001). While involvement of the media can produce good publicity, it can result in an unrepresentative response. While a community survey ensures wide representation, it may not elicit the detailed information that can be obtained from focus groups, and so on. The Nominal Group Technique can be seen as a formalized version of the use of focus groups. Discussion groups are assembled to represent different interests in the community – for example, parents with young children, youth, the elderly, shopkeepers, hoteliers, industrialists, environmental groups – selected according to the sector being planned. Discussions are con-

Table 6.6. Individuals and organizations involved in consultation.

● Public at large	● Other departments of council
● Particular age/gender/ethnic/disability groups in the community	● Chambers of commerce
	● Owners/managers of private-sector facilities
● Current users of facilities/services	● Professional/expert groups
● Sports/arts/environmental/special interest clubs	● Neighbouring authorities
● Staff of the leisure/tourism department	● Regional/state/national governments/
● Elected members of council	agencies

Table 6.7. Public participation formats.

1. One-on-one meetings/interviews
2. Media notices
3. Competitions
4. Letters inviting comment – to residents and/or organizations
5. Public exhibitions (static or mobile) with opportunity for comment
6. Public meetings
7. Production/distribution of printed and/or video material
8. Focus groups
9. Attendance at group meetings (e.g. clubs)
10. Establishment of working parties with outside membership
11. Postal questionnaire survey of organizations
12. Community surveys
13. Nominal-group technique (NGT)

ducted with an informed leader and then the group is asked to discuss and submit their view in writing (see Ritchie, 1994b).

Timing

In Fig. 5.3 consultation is shown as 'step 4', but in fact it can take place at many stages in the whole process. If the purpose is to generate ideas, consultation might take place at the beginning of the process; if it is to obtain reactions to proposals, it would take place later in the process. If the idea of consultation is fully embraced and its political role is recognized, then it is likely to take place in various forms throughout the process.

Step 5. Develop options

At this stage the aim is to develop a range of possible programmes of action. There is no single, simple prescription for achieving this. Some will have emerged clearly from the processes already discussed. For example:

- Political statements may indicate certain programme commitments.
- Some existing policies may remain to be implemented.
- Legal issues may require a certain course of action – for example, in relation to safety.
- Facility assessment may indicate the need for renewal of certain facilities.
- User or visitor surveys may suggest some clear needs for facilities or services.
- The activities of neighbouring authorities

may suggest the need for action to remain competitive.
- Major demographic or social changes may indicate the need for additional provision.
- The consultation process will invariably produce a range of proposals.

In addition, the range of techniques outlined in Chapters 7 and 8 would be brought into play at this stage to analyse and predict demand and develop possible plans for provision.

Another approach that is often used to complement the more formal approach to data collection and analysis and which draws on the knowledge and experience of managers is a SWOT analysis, standing for strengths, weaknesses, opportunities, threats.

SWOT analysis

A SWOT analysis is usually carried out as a sort of brainstorming exercise involving senior management staff. A group of managers *brainstorms* the organization's strengths, weaknesses, opportunities and threats, based on their own knowledge of the organization and/or on information assembled as described above. Possible plans of action begin to emerge which:

- build on and reinforce strengths;
- avoid or seek to overcome weaknesses;
- seek to exploit opportunities;
- take account of or attempt to neutralize threats.

The end result of the above exercises should be a shopping list of actual and potential policies and actions, ideally related to the mission and goals of the organization. For example, if the goal is to increase attendance at the performing arts, the alternatives which might emerge could include:

- subsidizing ticket prices;
- giving people vouchers to attend the arts;
- building more performing-arts venues;
- offering larger grants to existing arts companies;
- establishing new performing-arts companies;
- launching a publicity campaign, via various media;
- providing more education programmes concerning the arts;
- developing mobile arts facilities and companies;
- offering more training for performing artists;
- offering more training for arts managers, e.g. in marketing.

In a multipurpose strategy it might be necessary to conduct a number of SWOT analyses in different sectors, involving different groups of managers and stakeholders – for example, in the arts, sport, outdoor recreation and tourism.

Some of the proposals on the shopping list will be alternative measures to achieve the same end and these must be evaluated and a choice made between them. Others may be judged to be more or less likely to be viable or to contribute to the achievement of the authority's goals. Ultimately, choices will also be necessary because of limits on human, financial and physical resources. Thus an overall evaluation of the range of options must be undertaken to arrive at the strategy. This process is addressed in step 6.

Step 6. Decide strategy

Step 6 involves evaluating and selecting from among the various options one or more projects or programmes that are to form the strategic plan. This raises some difficult issues for the public sector, especially given the diverse, sometimes conflicting and often unquantifiable nature of the goals of most public organizations, as discussed above.

The process will unfold in a variety of ways, depending on the nature of the organization, the scope and complexity of the planning task and the degree of consensus about the various options available. Given the political basis of most public sector organizations, the key decisions will often be made on the basis of political criteria, by politicians. Thus proposals that are designed to implement electoral commitments will tend to have priority. In Chapter 5 the phenomenon of urban-growth regimes was discussed, in which an informal alliance of political groups and private-sector organizations, such as developers, drives a growth agenda in a community. Also of relevance here is the area of theory known as public-choice theory, which, as mentioned in Chapter 5, suggests that political decisions are primarily driven by the self-interest and political power of various sections of the public, rather than by some overall sense of the public interest (Self, 1993). The public consultation process can be seen as linked with this idea, in that contributions invariably reflect sectional interests. The issues approach to planning, as discussed in Chapter 7, places this at the centre of the planning process.

There may, however, be a need for a formal evaluation of all or some of the options. In general the process of evaluation should seek to assess the extent to which a project or programme will contribute to the achievement of the organization's goals. Two approaches to such evaluation include: economic evaluation techniques and importance–performance analysis. Economic evaluation techniques, such as cost–benefit analysis and economic-impact analysis, are dealt with in Chapter 9, while importance–performance analysis is considered below.

Importance–performance analysis

The importance–performance technique was developed in relation to individual consumer choice (Martilla and James, 1977) but can be utilized in organizational decision-making, as indicated by Harper and Balmer

(1989) in relation to perceived benefits of public leisure services, as a form of consumer consultation (Siegenthaler, 1994) and to measure customer satisfaction (Langer, 1997: 147). It is related to the idea of conjoint analysis, as discussed by Claxton (1994). The importance–performance approach involves, in relation to the project or programme under consideration:

1. The various *performance criteria* considered to be relevant, each proposed project being given a score (say, 1–10) for its level of performance in relation to each criterion.
2. The relative *importance* of each criterion to the individual decision-maker or group of decision-makers, each criterion being given an importance score (say, 1 to 10).

The product of the two scores provides the overall preference score for the proposal. The selection of criteria and the scores given to them can arise from political philosophy, community consultation or technical analysis. Performance is likely to be more technically based and importance more subjective. Table 6.8 illustrates the method in relation to three hypothetical proposals before a local authority; on the basis of the scores in the table, project C would be favoured.

A similar decision-making approach is put forward by Shafer (1994), in which individual members of a decision-making group compare alternative projects on a pair-wise basis, assigning a score of 1 to the project considered likely to produce the greater level of benefits and 0 to the project considered likely to produce the lesser level of benefits. These scores are then summed across the group members to determine overall benefit scores. Project costs are then estimated and divided by the benefit scores to produce benefit–cost criterion values. Projects are ranked according to these values and the top set of projects whose aggregate cost falls within the overall budget is selected.

While importance–performance analysis is put forward here as a decision-making tool in relation to new projects, it can also be used at the evaluation stage, as discussed in Chapter 10.

Constraints

It will generally not be possible to implement all the projects and programmes identified as desirable, because of resource constraints. Projects and programmes have to be ranked and only the best, and those that can be financed, are implemented. Constraints may be of an organizational or economic kind. Organizational constraints refer simply to the practical problems of managing growth. Judgements have to be made about just how fast an organization can develop without losing managerial control.

In fact, financial constraints tend to be the important limiting factor. The resources available to public bodies are always limited. The limitations may be political in nature –

Table 6.8. Importance–performance decision-making – hypothetical example.

Project alternatives:
- *A*: upgrading the sea-front park and promenade
- *B*: indoor swimming-pool and leisure centre
- *C*: community centre for a range of health and community organizations

Criteria	Importance to council* (a)	Project A	Project B	Project C
		Performance score (b)†		
Benefit to residents	10	5	10	9
Benefit to tourism	6	10	5	2
Low net running costs	8	8	6	10
Political popularity	5	7	7	10
Score (sum of a × b)		209	213	232

* 1 = low importance, 10 = high importance.
† 1 = low performance, 10 = high performance.

when governments find it politically unacceptable to raise taxes. Or they may be economic – when borrowing limits are imposed as a result of macroeconomic policy. The former tends to relate to on-going running costs and the latter to capital expenditure.

The question arises as to just how a strategy should take account of economic constraints. There are two approaches. One is to outline all the community's needs/demands and the programme that would be required to meet them in the medium to long term, regardless of resource constraints, and deal with the resource questions on a shorter-term basis. Thus the plan might be costed at £50 million, but the short-term plan, over the next 2 years, say, might commit the organization to an expenditure of, perhaps, £5 million only. The second approach is to determine the resources likely, realistically, to be available over the period of plan and put forward only those projects and programmes that can be funded.

In practice, some sort of compromise between the two approaches is usually achieved. There may be little point in publishing a plan which is so ambitious that it is not treated seriously. On the other hand, a plan that contains ambit claims, and which sets out the full extent of community needs/demands, may inspire politicians and the community to find the necessary funds. Whether the ambit-claim part of the exercise is conducted publicly via a published plan, or behind closed doors, resulting in the publication of a realistic plan, varies in practice.

The strategy

The selected programmes and projects that emerge from the evaluation and decision-making process provide the basis for the strategic plan. Each programme or project will have been chosen because of its potential to achieve certain of the goals of the organization. Each programme or project will therefore have a set of goals. Specific objectives may be partially laid down in the strategic plan, but may also be worked out at the facility/programme or project level. A typical strategy document will involve:

1. Mission statement.
2. Goals statement.
3. Summary of environmental appraisal.
4. Summary of public consultation.
5. Summary of alternatives considered and evaluation process.
6. Policies/projects/programmes.
7. Goals of individual projects/programmes and objectives/targets (action plan) for the strategy period.
8. Performance measures/indicators for objectives/targets.
9. Indication of persons/departments responsible for implementation.

In some cases items 7–9 are presented in a separate document. Typically a strategy will relate to a period of a number of years, usually 3 or 5. Objectives/targets include dates for implementation; for some the time period for their achievement is the whole strategy period, for others 1 year or 2 years; in other cases the objective/target is to be achieved in specified stages throughout the strategy period.

Although most commentators on strategic management emphasize the importance of the *process* rather than end-products, the results of the process must be recorded and communicated, or 'articulated', as Mintzberg (1994: 13–14) puts it, and this is usually done in the form of a document, referred to variously as the strategic plan or the corporate plan. When the process is carried out thoroughly and realistically and with full commitment of management and other stakeholders, the resultant document can be an essential tool for management and a valuable guide for all parts of the organization and for associated organizations. However, if it is not carried out with care, the process can be seen as a waste of time and effort, producing a document that no one in the organization is committed to and which simply gathers dust on shelves.

The term document is used deliberately, since the planning process is usually focused on a document or documents. Such documents embody the results of the planning process and form the agreed basis for the implementation of the plan. It is the requirement to produce a document, usually by a specified date, that drives the process along. Later, it is the need to revise the document that provides the focus for updating the plan. Focussing on the production of a document is therefore no bad thing, as long as it is borne in mind that the document is, ultimately, a means to an end: the coordinated provision of leisure and tourism services.

The style and size of strategic planning documents have reflected the career of strategic planning over the last 30 or so years. Initial planning documents were very substantial, reflecting the attempts of organizations to be comprehensive and thorough. Thus the *Third Nationwide Outdoor Recreation Plan* produced by the American Heritage, Conservation and Recreation Service in 1979 consisted of a 91-page *Executive Report*, a 262-page *Assessment* and four substantial *Appendices*, one of which itself consisted of four reports of up to 400 pages each (Heritage, Conservation and Recreation Service, 1979). Such mammoth exercises came to be seen as too resource-consuming to produce and of doubtful value in communicating the intentions of the organization to its stakeholders. In recent years strategic planning documents have been slimmed down. In contrast, the American *National Park Strategic Plan 2001–2005* (National Park Service, 2000) is only 52 pages in length, is produced in an attractive format, including colour diagrams and photographs, and can be downloaded from the Internet. Other recent examples of national strategies include *England, the Sporting Nation: a Strategy* (Sport England, 1997), which is just 18 pages long, and in Australia, *Tourism, a Ticket to the 21st Century: National Action Plan* (Office of National Tourism, 1998), which runs to 34 pages. Thus strategic planning documents of today are designed to be attractive and accessible and to communicate to a wide audience.

Step 7. Implementation

The detail of implementation of strategic plans is the subject of management books and is not dealt with here. Clearly prepara-tion of a strategic plan is the easy part. Implementation can, however, be aided by the way in which the strategy is prepared in the first place. Among the approaches which may help are the following:

- Involvement of all sections of an organization in strategy preparation.
- Wide dissemination of the mission statement, goals and strategy outline in a readable form.
- Inclusion of features in the strategy to which all members of the organization can relate (such as the idea of quality discussed above).
- Incorporation of a reward system for achievement of targets (very difficult, but not impossible in the public sector).
- Leadership from top managers and elected leaders to ensure that the strategy is taken seriously.

Invariably the implementation of a plan is broken up into annual stages, set out in annual *action plans*. Monitoring of the achievement of these stages then overlaps with the monitoring, evaluation and feedback processes discussed below.

Steps 8/9. Monitoring, evaluation and feedback

Monitoring progress towards achievement of strategy objectives and evaluating performance generally are discussed more fully in Chapter 10. This process can be made easy or difficult depending on the design of the strategy itself. If the strategy is vague and lacks specificity, then performance will be difficult to assess.

Feedback means that, as the organization moves into the strategy period, information produced by the monitoring and evaluation process should be used to keep the organization on track. Some feedback processes are day-to-day in nature – for example, ensuring that staff are adhering to various codes of behaviour or noting income and sales figures. However, there is always the problem of day-to-day concerns blocking out consideration of the longer-term concerns of the strategy, so reporting mechanisms must be put in place at various levels to ensure that strategic matters get dealt with.

Updating of the strategy can take two forms. One approach is the annual action plan discussed above, which reports on progress in the previous year and resets the following year's targets as necessary, while the overall strategy stays in place. The alternative is to roll forward the whole strategy each year, so that there is always a 3-year or 5-year horizon. The first approach is generally favoured in the public leisure-service area, since the environment is less volatile than in some areas of the private sector.

Land-use Planning

Cullingworth and Nadin (1997: 2), in the standard UK reference for the subject, define land-use planning as: 'a process concerned with the determination of land uses, the general objectives of which are set out in legislation or in some document of legal or accepted standing'. The system has legal status, or the backing of statutes – hence it is often referred to as part of the system of *statutory planning*. Cullingworth and Nadin list over 90 Acts of Parliament relating to land-use, or environmental, planning in Britain, although the current basic system was outlined in the Town and Country Planning Act, 1968, modified by further Acts in 1990 and 1991. In federal systems, such as Australia, each state has its own planning legislation.

At the heart of the land-use planning process is the idea of *zoning* – legally designating the purpose to which land can be put. Thus land might be zoned for: residential, retail, entertainment, hotel accommodation, office, industrial, transport, education or open-space use. The zoning system also includes matters such as height restrictions and parking controls. The zoning system is set out in a published land-use plan prepared by the local authority and endorsed by a government minister. Landowners who flout the zoning regulations may be prosecuted and will be required to desist from the non-conforming use, and may even be required to demolish non-conforming buildings. The land-use plan can relate to newly developed areas or to existing areas. Thus land-use planning involves two processes: the development of an appropriate land-use plan and the subsequent implementation and enforcement of the provisions of the plan, or *development control*.

While early planning approaches were fairly simplistic in their approach to zoning, later versions have become more sophisticated. Thus the 1968 Act in Britain established the idea of *structure plans*, in which zoning was to be based on a thorough understanding of the social, economic and environmental structure of the urban or rural area under consideration. This means that, in addition to such matters as transport, housing and industry, the role of leisure and tourism in a community must be taken into account and incorporated into the structure plan. Thus the sorts of planning activity described in this and the next chapter can provide inputs into the structure-planning process.

Land-use planning is involved in a number of specialized areas, including demographic planning, transportation planning and housing. Of particular interest to the field of leisure and tourism are areas such as heritage and natural-area conservation. There is a system of protection for ancient monuments and historic buildings and precincts, even when they are in private ownership. Similarly, the designation of World Heritage Areas, National Parks and Nature Reserves – and in Australia Aboriginal Heritage Sites – have statutory protection. Also important for outdoor recreation in Britain is the network of rights of way, such as public footpaths on private land, which are often hundreds of years old.

In general the statutory land-use planning system, because of its statutory basis, remains the most powerful form of planning and one of the most effective means of securing and implementing policies. While leisure and tourism professionals are often preoccupied with management and development, it follows that they would be unwise to ignore the land-use planning process.

Further Reading

- Strategic planning/management: Wortman (1979); Wheelen and Hunger (1989); Certo and Peter (1991); Caret *et al.* (1992); Mintzberg (1994).
- Visioning: Walzer (1996); Ritchie (1994).
- Decision-making: Lindblom (1959); Ham and Hall (1984); Burton (1989); Parsons (1995).
- SWOT analysis: example in tourism: Baric *et al.* (1997).
- Public participation: Arnstein (1969), Gittins (1993); Propst *et al.* (2000); Carr and Halvorsen (2001); in tourism planning: Bramwell and Sharman (1999); Sautter and Leisen (1999).
- Importance–performance analysis: Martilla and James (1977); Claxton (1994); Siegenthaler (1994); Langer (1997).
- Quality: Logothetis (1992); Mills (1992); Robinson (1997, 1998); Lentell (2001).
- Tourism planning generally: Hill (2000).
- Land-use planning: in the UK: Cullingworth and Nadin (1997); in Australia (NSW): Department of Environment and Planning (1987).

Questions/Exercises

1. Distinguish between mission, goals and objectives in relation to one of the following: (a) a local authority park system; (b) a national sport promotion agency; (c) a regional tourism development organization.

2. Why does the definition of leisure and of tourism present difficulties with regard to the appropriate scope of a leisure/tourism plan?

3. What is the range of types of plan which public bodies might become involved with, and which have an impact of leisure and tourism?

4. Conduct a SWOT analysis of your current degree programme.

5. Set up an importance–performance decision-making process, as an individual or in a group, in relation to: (a) selecting a film to go and see (using reviews or word of mouth for performance data); or (b) buying a pair of running shoes (using collective experience and/or word-of-mouth reports for performance data).

6. Locate a local-authority, national-park agency or tourism-agency strategic plan or master-plan document in a library and assess what it has to say about public consultation in relation to the categories in Arnstein's 'ladder' of citizen participation.

7

Planning Methods

Introduction

In Chapter 6 a general approach to leisure and tourism plans and strategies was considered. In this chapter more detailed consideration is given to techniques and approaches that might be used within the planning and strategy preparation process. It might be argued that some of the more elaborate methodologies for planning for leisure and tourism are impractical because the responsible agencies – particularly local authorities – are simply not prepared to devote substantial resources to this relatively low-status activity. However, it is not necessarily the case that substantial resources are required to implement more advanced methodologies: several of the approaches suggested here make use of readily available data and can be implemented virtually on a 'back-of-an-envelope' basis. In fact, considerable resources have been devoted to planning for leisure and tourism in the past, but they have often been devoted to data collection rather than analysis: only a marginal increase in resources would have been required to make better use of the data assembled.

History

Planning for leisure in Britain can be said to have passed through three phases since the 1960s (Veal, 1993). The period 1960–1972 can be designated the *demand phase*, when planners were concerned with responding to

rapidly increasing population numbers, rising real incomes and rising car ownership. From 1973 to 1985 – the *need phase* – attention was focused less on general demand and more on the needs of particular groups in the community, such as deprived inner-city residents. From the mid-1980s to the present – *the enterprise phase* – leisure planning has reflected the dominant government view that leisure is ideally a private-sector function. Each era has spawned planning methods to meet the policy challenges presented. In fact, however, successive techniques and approaches have not necessarily replaced one another but have complemented each other. Thus a range of techniques now exist that enable the leisure planner to assess present and future demand, to focus on different groups in varying states of need, to incorporate community concerns and to consider the potential of public- and private-sector provision. This chapter draws together information on available techniques.

Planning Techniques and Approaches

A range of approaches to leisure and tourism planning are considered in turn in this chapter. In every case it is assumed that the planning activity is being undertaken for a defined geographical area – referred to here as a planning area. Typically the planning area is the defined area of a local authority. But planning is sometimes undertaken on a regional scale – for example, in relation to tourism – and in federal government systems the planning area may by a state or province. Finally, much of the discussion would be relevant to the national level of planning, although relatively few leisure activities or facilities are planned at that level.

Assuming a local-council area is the planning area, it is necessary to keep in mind the geographical considerations and flows of people indicated in Fig. 7.1. These have implications for the sources of demand for leisure and tourism in a local area. Table 7.1 indicates

that, for some leisure activities, daily commuters, day visitors and tourists must be taken into account as well as local residents.

The range of planning approaches considered below[1] is as follows: (i) standards of provision; (ii) resource-based plannings; (iii) the gross demand/market share approach; (iv) spatial approaches; (v) hierarchies of facilities; (vi) priority social-area analysis; (vii) the recreation opportunity spectrum (ROS); (viii) the matrix approach; (ix) the organic approach; (x) community development; and (xi) the issues approach.

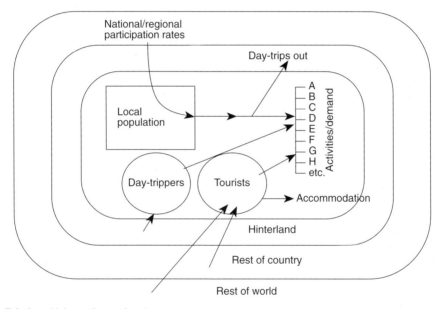

Fig. 7.1. Local leisure demand system.

Table 7.1. Spatial sources of demand.

Area/demand source*	Type of individual	Type of demand
Local area	Local residents	Leisure demand
Hinterland	Day visitors	Tourist leisure activities
	Commuters	Selected leisure activities
Rest of country	Domestic leisure tourists (ab)	a. Accommodation/transport
	Domestic business visitors (abc)	b. Tourist leisure activities
	Domestic friends and relatives (b)	c. Business/conference facilities/services
Rest of world	International tourists (ab)	a. Accommodation/transport
Short haul	International business visitors (abc)	b. Tourist leisure activities
Long haul	International friends and relatives (b)	c. Business/conference facilities/services

* See Fig. 7.1.

Standards of provision

Standards of provision generally relate to leisure planning rather than tourism planning, so most of the discussion below relates to the leisure-facility and service requirements of local communities. However, when tourists constitute a significant proportion of the users of certain types of facility, it would make sense to take their demands into account. This issue is discussed at the end of the section.

In the past, standards were probably the most commonly used method in planning for leisure. In recent years, however, other methods, such as those discussed later in this chapter, have come to the fore.

A standard in planning for leisure can be defined as a prescribed level of provision of facilities or services related to some criterion, typically the level of population.

Such standards can be developed at local level to provide guidance for the production of local plans, but a feature of leisure planning is that such standards have been developed by a number of organizations at national level. So there is a tendency for local planners to use such nationally promulgated standards rather than develop their own at local level. In a number of cases, standards developed for use in a particular locality – for example, a large city or a new town –

have been adopted by others as if they had been developed for national use: examples are the Greater London Council open-space hierarchy, discussed later in this chapter (GLC Planning Department, 1968) and, in Australia, the standards developed for the national capital, Canberra (National Capital Development Commission, 1981). Examples of nationally promulgated standards used in Britain are summarized in Table 7.2. The table includes an example of the application of the standards to a community with a population of 50,000, indicating that the application of standards is a very simple exercise.

Standards have been widely criticized in recent years and alternative approaches have been put forward to overcome their deficiencies, as outlined in the rest of this chapter. Despite this criticism, however, they have survived as one of the tools of the leisure planner, because they have a number of advantages as well as disadvantages. These are summarized in Table 7.3 and discussed in turn below.

Advantage 1. Simplicity

Standards are generally easy to understand. This can be particularly important when communicating with non-experts, such as members of the public, other professionals or politicians.

Table 7.2. Leisure facility/service provision standards.

Facility/service	Standard of provision	Body responsible	Application example: 50,000 population
1 Playing-fields	6 acres (2.4 ha) per 1000 population	NPFA	300 acres (120 ha)
2 Children's play	1½ acres (0.6 ha) per 1000 population	NPFA	25 acres (10 ha)
3 District indoor sports centres	1 per 40,000–90,000 population, plus 1 for each additional 50,000 (17 m² per 1000 population)	Sports Council	One centre
4 Local indoor sports centres	23 m² per 1000 population approx.	Sports Council	1150 m²
5 Indoor swimming-pools	5 m² per 1000 population approx.	Sports Council	250 m² (= one 25 m pool)
6 Golf-courses	One nine-hole unit per 18,000 population	Sports Council	18-hole + nine-hole
7 Libraries	1 branch library per 15,000 population. Max. distance to nearest library in urban areas: 1.6 km. Book purchases: 250 p.a. per 1000 population	DES	Three branch libraries 12,500 new books p.a.

Sources: 1. NPFA, 1971; 2. NPFA, 1971; 3. Sports Council, 1972, 1975, 1977; 4. Sports Council, 1977; 5. Sports Council, 1972, 1977, 1978; 6. Sports Council, 1972; 7. Ministry of Education, n.d.
NPFA, National Playing Fields Association; DES, Department of Education and Science.

Table 7.3. Standards: advantages and disadvantages.

Advantages	Disadvantages
1. Simplicity	1. Validity issues
2. Efficiency	2. Local conditions
3. Authority	3. Priorities
4. Measurability	4. Quality and capacity issues
5. Comparability	5. Substitutability
6. Equity	6. Spatial distribution

Advantage 2. Efficiency

Standards avoid duplication of effort. It is not necessary for every local authority to undertake detailed research to arrive at a decision on an appropriate level of provision – to reinvent the wheel. The research and consultation necessary to establish the required level, which can be costly and time-consuming, are done once only, by a central organization.

Advantage 3. Authority

In making a case to decision-makers within an organization for provision of services it can be useful to be able to refer to external, authoritative sources in support of the case. Other professionals and elected members of councils may be reassured that the expenditure of resources is justified if some external agency is, in effect, sanctioning it. This a paradox since, normally, when governments try to tell local authorities how to organize their affairs there are often complaints of threats to local democracy. And yet, in leisure provision, one of the few areas where local authorities are relatively free from government interference, they frequently look nervously over their shoulders to ensure that *they* are sanctioning their activities, by providing standards. 'They' are not necessarily the government as such, but some national or regional body whose pronouncements at least sound authoritative.

Advantage 4. Measurability

Progress towards the achievement of standards is relatively easy to assess, partly because of their simplicity, but also because of the way they are expressed, which is usually in measurable, quantitative terms. Policies based on standards can therefore be effectively monitored and progress towards their achievement can be relatively easily assessed.

Advantage 5. Comparability

Measurability makes it possible to compare levels of provision, in one area over time, between different sub-areas within a jurisdiction or between jurisdictions. This enables providing authorities or grant-giving bodies to establish where different sub-areas, jurisdictional areas or communities lie in a league table of provision. This is relevant to the Mercer/Bradshaw idea of comparative need, discussed in Chapter 2.

Advantage 6. Equity

If implemented everywhere, national standards would ensure that, regardless of where people live, they could expect to find a similar level of provision. This idea of geographical equity is related to the idea of leisure rights or rights of citizenship, as discussed in Chapter 2. Such a notion is accepted in services such as public health or education, but is an unfamiliar one in the area of leisure. It can be particularly important to national governments or agencies when making direct provision or giving grants to local providers: such national bodies would wish to appear even-handed in their treatment of different areas of the country.

Disadvantage 1. Validity issues

The ways in which standards have been derived are often open to question. It may be that those who draw them up use the best available methods and it may be that the documents setting out the standards make any limitations in the method very clear. But such qualifications are frequently ignored by users of standards. As a result, the standards are often invested with greater authority than is justified and are used with insufficient care.

Disadvantage 2. Local conditions

Documents setting out standards usually indicate that they should not be rigidly applied and particularly that local conditions are likely to vary. But rarely is any guidance given on just how standards should be varied to accommodate these local variations in conditions. Even when such advice is available it is often ignored by those applying the standards. Variations in local conditions could suggest that provision should be above or below the standard – for example, an area with a higher than average elderly population might require fewer squash courts but more golf-courses than the standards specify. But standards tend to be treated as the fixed, required level of provision in all circumstances.

Disadvantage 3. Priorities

Standards are isolated pieces of advice. In themselves they take no account of the real world, in which all desirable facilities and services cannot always be provided. Decisions on priorities have to be made within the leisure-service area and also between leisure services and other areas of public expenditure.

Disadvantage 4. Quality and capacity issues

Most standards in leisure provision fail to take account of the quality of provision and, in many cases, its capacity. Good-quality provision could, in some circumstances, compensate for a low level of provision. In addition, apparently similar facilities can vary a great deal in their capacity to accommodate leisure visits – as a result of either design or management features – for example, a well-drained or maintained sports pitch can accommodate more games than a poorly drained or maintained one.

Disadvantage 5. Substitutability

Very little is known about substitutability between leisure activities. If there are no squash courts in an area, will people play badminton? If there is no theatre, will they attend the cinema more? It is possible that concentration on a few good facilities and a limited range of activities could produce more beneficial results – however assessed – than an attempt to provide facilities across the board. For example, in an urban area where land costs are high, good indoor sports facilities may represent better value for money than a vain attempt to increase the area of open space to bring it up to standard.

Disadvantage 6. Spatial distribution

Standards usually present some gross assessment of requirements and do not of themselves provide guidance on the appropriate spatial distribution of the facilities prescribed. Spatial aspects are discussed in detail later in this chapter.

Standards – the key problem

The most serious criticism of standards lies in the first disadvantage mentioned above – that is, that their validity is sometimes questionable. This is exemplified by the most commonly used standard: the open-space standard of the National Playing Fields Association (NPFA). The standard dates from 1925, when it was observed that, for every 1000 population, 500 were below the age of 40; of these it was assumed that 150 would either not want to play sport or would be unable to because of infirmity. A further 150 would use school facilities. Thus 200 people in every 1000 would need to be catered for. Given the size of sports teams and frequency of play, it was estimated that the needs of these 200 people could be accommodated on:

> 1 senior football pitch
> 1 junior football pitch
> 1 cricket pitch
> 1 three-rink bowling-green
> 2 tennis-courts
> 1 children's playground of 0.5 acre (0.2 ha)
> 1 pavilion

The facilities would occupy 2.4 ha: hence the standard of 2.4 ha of open space per 1000 population. The standard excluded school playing-fields, military sports grounds, verges, woodlands, commons, gardens and parks, golf-courses, large areas of water and indoor facilities.

The NPFA reviewed the standard in 1971 and 1993 and concluded that the effects of rising living standards (which would have increased the standard) and changing age structure (which, because of the growth in the numbers of elderly, would have reduced the standard) cancelled each other out and left the standard at 2.4 ha (NPFA, 1971, 1993).

What then is wrong with this standard? A number of criticisms can be levelled at it, reflecting the disadvantages of standards of provision generally, as discussed above.

1. Being based on current participation rates which are themselves partly dependent upon the level of supply of facilities, the standard is somewhat tautological.
2. Age structures vary from area to area, but the standard assumes one common age structure.
3. Tastes vary from area to area: rather than playing team sports, people in one area may prefer, or have a tradition of, for example, swimming or (as in Scotland) playing golf, but neither of these activities is included in the standard.
4. Successful management and/or promotion efforts could result in participation rates well in excess of those suggested by NPFA.
5. The environment varies from area to area: where land is expensive and housing needs are pressing, as in inner-city areas, the standard of 2.4 ha may be unrealistic, and areas with access to the sea or the countryside may have fewer needs for formal provision.
6. Hard porous and artificial surfaces or floodlighting affect the capacity of sports pitches, thus reducing the overall demand for land.
7. The effect of joint provision or dual use of school facilities is not clear in the standard.
8. The standard as such gives no guidance on the spatial distribution of open space.
9. The standard implicitly assumes that all demand should be met: this rarely happens in other areas of social provision.
10. While the standard may provide a set of ultimate goals, it does not provide a plan of action in the usual conditions of limited resources.

As already indicated, the NPFA was aware of many of these problems and suggested that application of the standards should take local conditions into account. But a methodology to indicate just how local conditions should be taken into account, how local conditions should be assessed and how they would affect the application of the standard was not proposed.

The NPFA standard and similar standards promulgated in other countries, such as the USA (Buechner, 1971) and Australia (National Capital Development Commission, 1981), have a long history, and numerous studies and reports having been produced over the years to attempt to wean planners off them (e.g. Sports Council, 1968, 1993; Willis, 1968; Greater London and South East Council for Sports and Recreation, 1982; Mertes and Hall, 1996), but their longevity, despite their limitations, is evidence of the importance of the advantages of standards as discussed earlier.

Standards and tourism

Tourists are members of a community for a short time, they tend to be concentrated in certain areas and, for the most part, they do not expect to engage in the full range of community leisure activities for which standards have been produced (e.g. library use or children's play). It is generally the case that tourists make use of leisure facilities for which there are no provision standards, such as beaches, informal 'hard' open spaces (promenades, squares, streets), museums and restaurants. It is also often the case that tourists' leisure needs are met by hotel facilities, such as swimming-pools, gyms or golf-courses. Despite these complexities, it would be advisable to take account of the presence of tourists when considering the application of standards – or any planning method based on population levels.

In considering likely tourist demands for local leisure facilities, it would be advisable to draw on any research data available on tourists' use of such facilities – either from tourist surveys or from facility surveys in which tourists and locals are identified. Thus, for example, if it was found from a park user survey that 20% of users of a certain open space were tourists, a notional 20% of that open space might be considered provision for tourists and be excluded from calculations of open-space provision for the residents of the area. Alternatively it could be said that, if, for example, during the tourist season, 1000 tourists a day made use of the available open space, this would be equivalent to boosting the local population used in the standards calculation by 1000.

Moving on from the standards approach

Sufficient advantages of standards have been set out for it to be clear that, in this book, it is not being suggested that standards be abandoned entirely. The suggestions for alternative planning methods made later in this chapter are intended to offer methods by which a more local perspective can be injected into the planning process. The proposed methods go some way to overcoming some of the disadvantages of standards.

Resource-based planning

A form of planning that probably predates the use of standards is resource-based planning – the resources referred to being the natural resources of land and water (Jubenville, 1976: 141ff.).

The planning of urban areas has always had to take account of such matters as topography and watercourses. Leisure planning has sometimes suffered from this practice with, for example, open space being developed in residual flood-plains where building was not possible, rather than in areas accessible to residents. Within areas of open space reserved for recreation, planning and design have often been based on landscape aesthetics rather than recreational requirements (although, conversely, some recreation-orientated development, such as barren playing-fields, has been decidedly unaesthetic). Shipping and associated industry were naturally attracted to major waterways and, now that traditional docklands have become obsolete, there is a worldwide trend to reclaim the waterfront for recreational purposes (Craig-Smith and Fagence, 1995).

Even more so, rural planning is about the landscape. Here there have been wins and losses for leisure and tourism. While large areas of land that might have provided opportunities for leisure and tourism have been taken up by other forms of development, large areas have also been reserved for recreation and tourism in the form of protected national parks and coastline and green belts around cities. While resource issues can never be ignored, much effort in recent decades has been spent in developing planning methods that take account of human behaviour and needs – as indicated by the content of this chapter. The ideal is to find a balance between the dictates of the resource and human needs.

Resource-based planning has, however, come to the fore again with the growth of tourism. For a great deal of tourism the attraction is a static resource – either the natural or the historic built environment. A key element of planning for tourism in such situations is an appraisal of the resource. Often a resource that has been taken for granted by residents becomes a resource that can be exploited for tourism, as well as being protected from tourism. The development of guided tours, printed tour guides and information and interpretation centres demands systematically gathered information about the flora, fauna and history of an area. Such survey and research work requires specialist skills, which are beyond the scope of this book.

Gross-demand/market-share approach[2]

The *gross-demand/market-share* (GDMS) approach to planning for leisure overcomes certain of the advantages of the normal standards approach, but not all. Its advantages and disadvantages are discussed below, following a description of the general approach. Public bodies such as local authorities are often not aware of the scale of demand with which they are dealing because of absence of data. Even when data are available they are often misinterpreted – for example, a community with a population of, say, 100,000 could have a swimming-pool that attracts, per-haps, 200,000 visits a year and, because the number of visits is twice the level of the population, the impression is given that the community is being well served by the provision of the swimming-pool. But, if every member of the community visits the pool equally, this represents only two visits per person per annum – hardly a very impressive figure. In practice, most users of swimming-pools are fairly regular users, the average user visiting probably once a week. Allowing for holidays, illnesses, etc., if it is assumed that the average user visits 40 times a year, then 250,000 visits are made by only about 5000 people – that is, only 5% of the population; that is, 95% of the population are not using the pool – again a less than impressive statistic. Numbers of admissions or visits alone are therefore not an adequate measure of demand upon which to base policy: infor-mation is required on frequency of visit to establish the actual number – and propor-tion – of the community involved.

The GDMS approach involves estimating the total (gross) demand, or market, for an activity based on available national or regional participation data and considering how that demand might, or should, be met by various providers. It therefore involves three steps:

1. Estimate demand.
2. Determine facility/service requirements.
3. Decide market-share target.

In practice, steps 2 and 3 may be conducted in reverse order or simultaneously, particu-larly in the case of tourism. The three steps are discussed in turn below.

Step 1. Estimate demand

LEISURE. Leisure demand can be estimated with varying degrees of complexity or sophistication. The simple version of the GDMS approach takes a single overall level of participation for a particular activ-ity, as derived from a national or regional participation survey, and applies it to the local community. A number of such national or regional participation surveys exist which might be utilized (see Cushman *et al.*, 1996). For example, an Australian national survey indicates that the proportion of the adult population who participated in squash in Australia in 1999 was 2.0% (ABS, 2000: 17). An average com-munity with a population aged 18 and over of, say, 100,000 would therefore be expected to contain approximately 2000 squash players. The survey indicated that the average participant played once every 2 weeks, which therefore suggests a likely gross demand of 1000 players per week in the hypothetical community.

The use of national or regional survey data is deliberate. Often there are no local survey data on leisure participation avail-able, but, even if there are, national or regional data are preferable for this exercise, because the aim is to indicate *potential* demand. A local survey indicates the *current* participation level for an activity, but this is inevitably constrained by existing facilities and service availability. The use of such local survey data, when they exist, is discussed further below.

A more sophisticated version of the GDMS approach involves dividing the pop-ulation into age-groups and basing the demand estimate on age-specific participa-tion rates, as shown in Table 7.4. This exam-ple shows that the participation rate for 25–34-year-olds is double the overall aver-age, while that for people aged 45 and over is less than half the overall rate. Therefore a community with a higher-than-average pro-portion of 25–34-year-olds could be expected to have a higher overall rate of participation than the national average of 2.0% and consequently a higher-than-aver-age requirement for squash courts. Thus the hypothetical community in Table 7.4 has a demand of 1232 players a week, which is 232 more than the simple method esti-mated. In practice it should be noted that it would be necessary to add an estimate of the number of participants aged under 18; this would not be a large number in the par-ticular case of squash, but for some activi-ties, such as swimming or cinema attendance, it could be highly significant.

Table 7.4. GDMS age-specific example: squash demand by age-group.

Age-group	National data			Local data	
	A % participating p.a.*	B Frequency of participation per week*†	C No. of players per week per 100 population (A × B)	D Local community population*	E No. of players per week (C × D/100)
18–24	2.6	0.5	1.3	10,000	130
25–34	4.1	0.5	2.05	35,000	717
35–44	2.1	0.5	1.05	30,000	315
45+	0.8	0.5	0.4	25,000	100
Total	2	0.5	1.0	100,000	1232

*Hypothetical.
†No age-specific frequency data available.
Source of information: A and B: national survey; D: census.

The age structure of the population makes a difference to demand for most activities, but so do other factors, such as the occupational or socio-economic composition of the community or its level of car ownership. Any divergence from the national average in these factors is likely to change the level of demand from the average. Combining all of these factors into a single measure, using multiple regression techniques, is a theoretical possibility but not generally a very practicable one (this is discussed further in relation to forecasting, under 'Cross-sectional analysis' in Chapter 8). But a number of separate demand estimates based on these various social factors could be prepared and an average used for planning purposes. Thus, if the age structure of the population were likely to push demand above the average but the socio-economic composition seemed likely to pull it down, then it might be concluded that these factors cancelled each other out and that use of the national average participation rate would be appropriate.

Of course, the local environment and culture make a difference to leisure demand as well. For example, seaside towns are likely to have differing patterns from inner-city areas, although this may only be so for some activities. In some cases national participation data are subdivided by area type – for example, urban/rural – but this is not always the case. If these differences are thought to be so significant that the use of national data would be misleading, the GDMS method

may not be suitable, and one of the other approaches discussed later in the chapter may need to be used.

This first, demand-estimation, stage of the GDMS approach can be useful in the local planning process in its own right. It provides estimates of potential numbers of participants in various activities in a local area, which can be useful information, even for activities where the figure cannot be directly translated into facility requirements. The relative popularity of different leisure activities can be demonstrated; for example, to know that there are potentially, say, 1000 people who play squash in the community but 14,000 people who go swimming helps to put the two activities into perspective. Such figures are meaningful to the non-expert, such as the elected representative or the ratepayer. Bearing in mind that the survey referred to above relates only to people aged 18 and over, the sort of picture that might be presented for a typical community of 100,000 adult population is as set out in Table 7.5.

It is a short step from estimating current demand levels to considering future potential demand levels. This merely requires the substitution of the future population level and/or age structure in the above exercise. This is considered in more detail in Chapter 8, under 'Cross-sectional analysis'.

TOURISM. In the case of tourism, the gross demand estimate is not based on the local population, but, potentially, on the popula-

Table 7.5. Gross demand, selected physical activities, for community of 100,000 adult population.

Activity	% participating p.a.*	Estimated no. of participants
Walking	18.8	18,800
Swimming	13.9	13,900
Golf	9.6	9,600
Tennis	7.4	7,400
Fishing	5.3	5,300
Cycling	4.9	4,900
Running	4.7	4,700
Lawn bowls	2.7	2,700
Squash	2.0	2,000
Cricket	1.9	1,900
Riding	1.6	1,600

*Source: Australian data, based on ABS (2000).

tion of the rest of the world. Demand is the number of tourist trips to the area and the number of visitor bed-nights, subdivided into various market segments, for example, day-trippers, package tourists, backpackers, visiting friends and relatives (VFR) and conference-goers. For most local planning exercises, it is advisable, initially, to estimate tourist trips to the region in which the planning area is located and to use the market-share part of the process, as discussed under 'Decide supply deficit and market-share target' below, to estimate the proportion of regional visitors likely to visit the local area. This can be done at a number of levels. For example, an international city, like London, might initially obtain data on the total number of visitors to Britain or the number of visitors to major cities in Europe. An individual resort on the Spanish coast would first estimate the total number of visitors to the Spanish coast. Generally, such regional visitation statistics are available from international or national tourism bodies.

Visitors come potentially from the whole of the rest of the world, but will generally be divided into groups according to the tourist-generating region, as indicated in Table 7.1, namely: the hinterland (day visitors); the rest of the country (domestic tourists); nearby countries (international short haul); and more distant countries or regions (interna-

tional long haul), usually divided into regions, for example, Europe, North America, Japan, others. Since the key facility for tourism, as discussed below, is the availability of beds, demand needs to be expressed not just in terms of number of visitors but in terms of the number of visitor bed-nights. An example is shown in Table 7.7.

Daily commuters, as indicated in Table 7.1, can generate a demand for some leisure facilities, which similarly needs to be taken into account.

Step 2. Determine gross and net facility/service requirements

Having determined a level of demand, planning requires the translation of this into facility or service requirements. Such a method can be applied to a wide range of leisure activities where facility capacity can be measured in terms of number of users or visits. Table 7.6 lists examples of such facilities and possible measures of capacity. In the case of the squash example, the demands of 1250 squash players, each wishing to play once a week, could be accommodated in five squash courts if the courts could be used to full capacity; but, assuming that they were used at, say, 75% capacity, the requirement would be for six or seven courts.

Table 7.6. Facility capacities (see Appendix 7.1 for source).

	Visits/week
Indoor sports hall (two courts*)	1500
Community hall (one court)	450
Grass playing pitch	220
Outdoor hard court	140
Squash court	250
Weights room	330
25 m indoor pool (year-round)	3500
50 m indoor pool (year-round)	7000
25 m outdoor pool (summer)	3500
50 m outdoor pool (summer)	7000
Athletics track	500
Golf-course (18-hole)	800
Bowling-green	270
Informal park	235 per ha

*Refers to tennis or basketball court size.

In the case of services, rather than facilities, capacity is more variable. Services might include learning/training activities (e.g. learning to swim or to draw) or experiential activities (e.g. trekking or white-water rafting). Capacity is likely to be partly determined by pedagogical and safety considerations and partly by facility and equipment availability.

The key capacity measure in the case of tourism is not leisure facilities, but bed spaces. The *number of visitors* must be multiplied by the *length of stay* to arrive at a measure of *bed-nights*.

Step 3. Decide supply deficit and market-share target

If local demand (and the corresponding supply of facilities) is already higher than the national or regional figure (and it is bound to be in some areas, since the national/regional figure is an average), this can be taken to suggest that there is no need for additional provision or that alternative planning methods, as discussed later in the chapter, might be used. It would also be advisable to consider the question of future demand trends, as discussed in Chapter 8. The GDMS approach is, after all, seen as a simple, initial, broad-brush approach to planning.

The final step in the GDMS approach is to compare the gross demand and facility/service requirements with the actual situation and decide on a suitable response. The squash example provides the simplest illustration. If, as indicated above, there is a gross demand of 1000 squash players a week, which could be accommodated in five squash courts, and there are already three courts in the planning area, there is a deficit of two courts. However, it does not follow that the local council should provide the two courts: the facilities may be provided by a private or non-profit organization or by another public-sector body, such as a school with community access.

The question of who provides is a complex one, partly guided by the ideological, theoretical and political issues discussed in Chapters 2–4, and partly by the policy and strategic planning issues, discussed in Chapters 5 and 6. Thus, for some facilities, such as parks, the public sector is invariably the provider. In other cases, for example, restaurants, the private sector is invariably the provider. In other cases, including most sporting and arts facilities, there is a mixture of providers. While the local authority should, arguably, have an interest in the overall pattern of provision, as the GDMS method implies, it does not necessarily have to be the provider. This stance is common in other areas of planning – for example, local authorities are involved in planning shopping and office space, but are not the providers – but, in planning for leisure, there has been a tendency for local-council planning to be concerned only with facilities which local councils themselves provide. In the context of the contemporary mixed economy of leisure this no longer seems appropriate. While some may see this move as a diminution of councils' traditional role, it can also be seen as an expansion: councils could be seen to be engaging in planning for a much wider range of facilities than hitherto. Again, there has been a tendency to ignore such matters as the provision of pubs, restaurants, pinball parlours and cinemas, but these facilities can be seen as being as important to the quality of life of an area as many of the traditional public-sector facilities, so there is every reason why councils should be involved in their planning.

Tourism is, in fact, a classic case where local councils, or consortia of councils and businesses, have traditionally been involved in planning, but are just one of the stakeholders, and are generally not involved at all as providers in the key accommodation sector. In tourism the idea of market share is quite familiar. Local hoteliers are particularly familiar with the idea of market share. The building of new hotels is often undertaken on the basis that, provided location, pricing, design and management are all competitive, the hotel will attract a fair share of the market in proportion to its share of total capacity (Horwath and Horwath Services Pty, n.d.: 14). Thus, for example, if a local area has 5000 beds, a new hotel opening with 500 beds can expect to attract 9% of the market (500 out of 5500). An example of the application of the method for tourism is shown in Table 7.7.

Table 7.7. Gross-demand/market-share (GDMS) approach and tourism.

	Domestic visitors	International visitors	Total
Visits to the region p.a.			
Holiday tourists p.a.	350,000	200,000	550,000
Business tourists p.a.	30,000	5,000	35,000
VFR tourists p.a.	20,000	7,000	27,000
Total tourists	400,000	212,000	612,000
Average no. of nights per visit	6	4.5	5.5
Bed-nights*	2,400,000	954,000	3,354,000
Hotel beds, no.*			12,250
Average occupancy rate*			75%
Visits to planning area			
Current share %	35%	25%	31%
Current share, no.	140,000	53,000	193,000
Current share, bed-nights	840,000	239,000	1,079,000
Current hotel beds			3,800
Projected share %			35%
Projected hotel beds*			4,300
Projected bed-nights*			1,175,000

VFR, visiting friends and relatives.
*75% occupancy = 274 nights p.a.

The less formal the activity the less appropriate the gross-demand method is. Thus, while it may be interesting to have an estimate of the number of people who visit facilities such as parks or museums, it is difficult to translate that number into a specific facility requirement. For activities such as countryside recreation or major spectator attractions, such as motor racing or horse-race meetings, where the pattern of travel transcends local boundaries, the method would need to be applied at a regional rather than a local level.

Another advantage of the approach is its relative flexibility. It allows local authorities to adjust their targets according to trends. Thus, if the level of participation in squash rose, according to the General Household Survey, from 2.6% in 1987 to, say, 2.9% in 1995, then the number of squash players and the required number of squash courts could be expected to rise by some 10%. Assessments of requirements can be constantly adjusted in the light of new information.

Despite the advantages of the gross-demand approach, it is still subject to many of the limitations of the standards approach, as discussed above. In particular, the tautological element remains, in that prescribed levels of provision are based on participation rates, which are themselves partly dependent on current levels of provision. Because the gross-demand approach uses national or regional survey data, the participation rates used are not constrained by local supply conditions, but the widespread use of the method would tend towards a very uniform level of demand and provision. The lack of guidance on spatial aspects of demand is also a limitation. Other approaches discussed below attempt to overcome these limitations.

Spatial approaches

The catchment-area idea

A great deal of information has now been accumulated on the spatial aspects of leisure-facility use. The potential of this information has, however, not generally been fully exploited in the leisure planning process. The basic fact upon which spatial approaches are built is that leisure facilities have *catchment areas*: that is, there are generally identifiable areas from which most users travel to visit a facility. The size of such catchment areas varies depending on the type of facility. Thus theatres generally have larger catchment areas than swimming-pools; and, among swimming-pools, larger, newer pools generally have larger catchment areas than smaller, older pools.

Catchment areas can be an important basis for planning. Figure 7.2 illustrates the catchment-area idea, using two hypothetical facilities. The shaded areas are the areas from which the majority, say 75%, of the users of the two facilities A and B are drawn. It can therefore be seen that the facilities serve the populations living in the shaded areas but do not serve the populations living in the unshaded areas. There is a tendency for providers of leisure facilities to believe that, once they have provided a certain type of facility, their job is done – the community is served. But information of the type presented in Fig. 7.2 enables the extent to which the community is being served to be assessed.

The unshaded areas in Fig. 7.2 therefore become areas for further investigation. Provided there are people actually living in these areas, then, assuming that the policy of the authority is to make the service available to all, the findings point to the need for additional provision to serve these areas. This is couched in public-service terms, but could equally well be expressed in market terms: an organization wishing to maximize usage and income would also be well advised to investigate the market potential of the unshaded areas in Fig. 7.2.

Measuring catchment areas

It is possible to establish the catchment area of a facility by means of a user or visitor survey – interviewing users of existing facilities to discover where they have travelled from. Although a user survey is desirable, it is not always necessary, at least for initial appraisals: it is possible to infer catchment areas from user surveys carried out at similar facilities elsewhere. Thus, for instance, it has been found that about 75% of users of swimming-pools travel from within 1 mile of a pool (Veal, 1979a). Thus an approximate assessment of requirements using 1-mile-radius circles is a possibility.

In cases where membership schemes exist, membership records can be used as the basis for estimating catchment areas: this has, for example, traditionally been done in the case of libraries. The problem with membership records is that the spatial distribution of membership may not reflect the distribution of regular users – for example, people who live close to a facility may use it more frequently than people who live far away. This information would be captured in situations where records are kept of actual attendances of members, rather than simply records of membership. It should also be noted that some people actually travel to use leisure facilities from their place of work or school rather than from their home address, so the spatial distribution of home addresses may not provide an accurate picture of the catchment area.

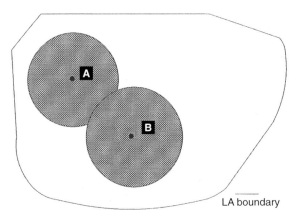

Fig. 7.2. Hypothetical facility catchment areas. LA, local authority.

Ideally the question of catchment areas is best examined in terms of *visit rates* – that is in terms of the number of visits to a facility per 1000 population per week from different zones[3]. Figures 7.3–7.5 show how such visit rates can be established in the case of three hypothetical swimming-pools in a local-authority area. The data relate to 1-mile catchment zones surrounding each pool and data are gathered as follows:

- Visits per week (Fig. 7.3): from the pools' own ticket-sales data, which gives total visits per week, and a user survey, which gives the proportion travelling from each catchment zone.
- Population (Fig. 7.4): from the population census.
- Visit rate (Fig. 7.5) = Visits per week ÷ (Population ÷ 1000).

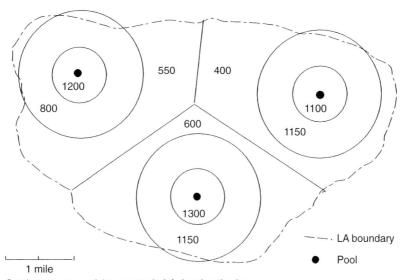

Fig. 7.3. Catchment areas: visits per week. LA, local authority.

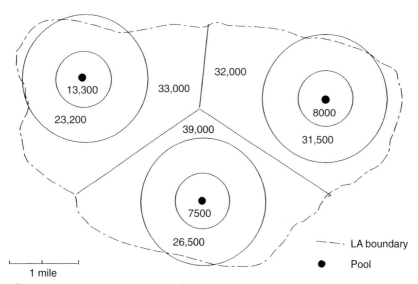

Fig. 7.4. Catchment areas: population levels. LA, local authority.

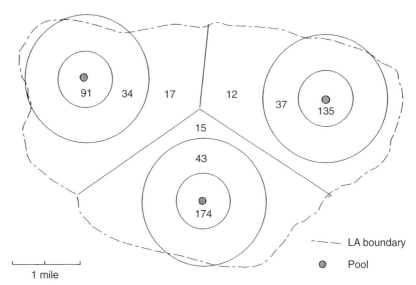

Fig. 7.5. Visit rates (visits per 1000 population per week). LA, local authority.

Thus, for example, for the inner zone of the top left-hand pool in the diagram:

Visit rate = 1200 ÷ 13,300 ÷ 1000 = 1200 ÷ 13.3 = 90 visits per 1000 population per week

Catchment areas have been discussed so far only in terms of people and population. In fact, catchment areas are likely to be different for different groups in the population. Thus car-owners are likely to be able to travel greater distances than non-car-owners and adults are likely to be able to travel greater distances than young children. Research has shown that in this respect the more deprived and less mobile groups of the community are less well served by facilities than the rest of the population – simply because they are not able to travel to facilities (Hillman and Whalley, 1977). Findings of this sort from user surveys would lead the planner to designate even larger areas as unserved.

In developing policy on this basis, it is necessary not only to identify unserved areas, but also to quantify the level of unmet demand in such areas. The swimming example is used to illustrate this approach, as shown in Fig. 7.6. Demand for a hypothetical new pool is estimated using an average of the visit rates for the three existing pools applied to the population in the area (visits per week = visit rate × population ÷ 1000). Total visits to the new pool are estimated at 2900 per week. It should be noted that the new pool also affects the catchment area and level of use of the existing facilities, but the effect is minimal because the hypothetical new facility impinges only on the fringes of the existing catchment areas, where visit rates are low.

The example in Fig. 7.6 produced a 'viable' result – that is, the estimated level of demand in the unserved areas was sufficient to justify a new facility. But what if this were not the case? It is clear that, in the example in Fig. 7.6, even with the new facility, there would remain areas which would still be poorly served, but the chances are they would not generate enough demand to justify the provision of large facilities such as a swimming-pool.

The idea of viability is a potentially contentious one. In a commercial context it is relatively unproblematic: if there are not enough customers to support a minimum-sized facility in a particular area, then such a facility will not be provided. Planners in companies such as Marks and Spencer, McDonald's Restaurants and cinema chains are fully aware of the minimum size of population necessary to support one of their facilities. In the

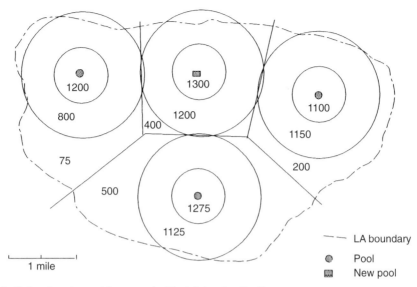

Fig. 7.6. Estimating demand for a new facility. LA, local authority.

public sector, however, things are not so simple: questions of equity have to be addressed. Thus, while the commercial organization could ignore the remaining unserved areas in the example shown in Fig. 7.6, public bodies must give them some consideration. Solutions could lie in the development of small-scale facilities, which, while they may be costly to run in relative terms (e.g. in subsidy per head), may be acceptable in absolute terms (Veal, 1979b). In addition to simply reducing the size of the facilities provided to match the scale of local demand, the form of the provision could be changed, involving, for example, dual use of education facilities, possibly at primary-school level (Murphy and Veal, 1978), the development of multipurpose facilities and the provision of mobile facilities.

Catchment areas in a rural setting

So far it has been assumed that the setting for the spatial analysis is urban, with facilities located within substantial residential areas. In rural areas the situation is different, with points of population located in small settlements within a green-fields setting. Catchment areas still apply, although rural residents generally travel further for their recreation than urban residents.

Knowledge of catchment areas of existing facilities can be just as useful in rural settings as in urban settings, but the approach to planning and provision is different, because of problems of access. In fact, the 'Hierarchies of facilities' approach discussed later in this chapter would be more appropriate than some of the methods described here. In addition, because of the rural tradition of community self-help, the 'community-development approach' discussed later would also be more appropriate.

Catchment areas and countryside recreation

In the case of countryside recreation the pattern is different again. In this case recreation sites are dotted around the countryside and the bulk of the visitors come from urban centres. If the urban centres are beyond day-trip distance, the activity becomes tourism rather than recreation. In fact, this is one of those areas where the difference between tourism and non-tourism becomes difficult to sustain. For example, a day-tripper from London to the Cotswolds would have the same recreation demands as someone from Wolverhampton, who may be staying overnight and is thus classified as a tourist.

In the case of the countryside, recreation planning must be examined at the regional rather than the local level. Catchment-area analysis, showing which parts of the country-side are utilized by residents of which urban centres, becomes vital. While the analysis could conceivably be achieved by means of a series of user surveys at recreation sites throughout the region, it is probably best done by means of a household survey throughout the region. Knowledge of spatial patterns of recreation demand can be used as the basis for planning countryside recreation provision. Population growth is not currently a common feature of British urban areas, but it is still a factor in other countries and could become so again in Britain. Catchment-area analysis makes it possible to identify those areas of the countryside that would come under increased demand pressure from population growth in particular urban areas. Use of visit rates would enable the growth to be quantified.

Modelling

The descriptions of catchment areas and resultant planning approaches have been presented here in conceptual rather than highly quantified terms. However, the quan-titative nature of the basic data lends itself to quantitative modelling – that is, using the catchment-area data to simulate the spatial process mathematically. This process, how-ever, is intimately bound up with the idea of forecasting and so is dealt with in the 'Spatial models' section of Chapter 8.

Hierarchies of facilities

The idea of hierarchies

The idea of hierarchies of facilities is a spatial one, but is sufficiently distinct to be dis-cussed separately from other spatial approaches. It is nevertheless founded on the idea that different sizes and types of facility have different catchment areas. A further principle is also invoked: that different sizes and types of facility require different num-bers of customers to be viable, as discussed above, and therefore are suited to the needs of different sizes and types of community.

The Greater London Council (GLC) parks hierarchy

Perhaps the most well-known example of the hierarchy approach is that developed for parks by the then GLC, in the late 1960s. Surveys conducted by the GLC had estab-lished that people travelled different dis-tances to visit different types of park with different functions. For example, people travelled relatively short distances to small parks to exercise the dog or to use children's play facilities, whereas they tended to travel longer distance to larger parks for family pic-nics or formal sporting activities. The GLC planners used this information to establish a parks hierarchy (see Table 7.8), which became the basis for strategic parks planning by many of the London Boroughs and by the GLC until its abolition in 1986.

Comprehensive hierarchies

Hierarchies come into their own in the com-prehensive planning of new communities – an activity that has been rare in Britain in recent years, because of the lack of growth in the population. In the 1960s and 1970s, how-ever, numerous new towns were developed, including such places as Harlow, Stevenage, Telford and Milton Keynes. It was necessary to specify the whole range of facilities required in such communities. The new towns were themselves usually developed on a hierarchical basis, with neighbourhoods at the lowest level, a cluster of neighbour-hoods forming some sort of district and finally a town or city level. Services of all kinds, including leisure, were planned within this framework, with education facili-ties often being the key organizing factor.

Three examples of such hierarchies devel-oped for different new-town situations are summarized in Table 7.9. The size and nomen-clature of the various levels of community vary, as does the range of facilities prescribed. The hierarchies nevertheless offer a compre-hensive picture of leisure provision and ways in which leisure facilities relate to other social and commercial provision and to the idea of community. While it is recognized that new-community building is no longer undertaken

Table 7.8. Greater London Council hierarchy of parks (from Greater London Council Planning Department, 1968).

Park type	Main function	Size (approx. minimum ha.)	Max. distance from place of residence (miles)	Characteristics
Metropolitan	Weekend and occasional visits by car or public transport	61	2	Either (i) areas of attractive landscape (heathland, downland, commons, woodlands, etc.), or (ii) formal parks containing both pleasant surroundings and a variety of facilities for both active and passive recreation
District	Weekend and occasional visits – mainly pedestrian	20	0.75	Open space containing both pleasant surroundings and general facilities for active recreation
Local	Short-duration pedestrian visits (including from workplaces)	2	0.25	Small spaces containing facilities for court games and children's play, and old people's sitting-out areas, all set in a pleasant landscaped environment
Small local	Shorter pedestrian visits by less mobile members of the population and workers	Under 2	Below 0.25	Small gardens, sitting-out areas, children's playgrounds

in Britain, it is perhaps surprising that, while local councils in London were prepared to take on board and utilize a parks hierarchy as a framework for planning within existing settled areas, councils have not taken up these more comprehensive hierarchical frameworks as a basis for comprehensive planning.

Priority social-area analysis

In existing developed areas, while the hierarchy idea might provide a useful framework for an overall planning strategy, a short- to medium-term strategy might well be based on social priorities: that is, it could be decided that public leisure provision should be directed towards those areas with the greatest social or recreational need. Early experiments using this approach were conducted by the GLC (Nicholls, 1975) and by the Tourism and Recreation Research Unit (TRRU) (1982) in Scotland.

The GLC study was based on a supply/need matrix. Wards across the whole GLC area were given a recreational *supply-index* score and a *need-index* score based on

the scoring systems shown in Table 7.10. They were then grouped according to their two scores, as shown in Table 7.11. The results of this analysis were then presented in map form, as shown in Fig. 7.7. The pattern shown was one of deprivation in the inner areas of London, as might be expected, but the analysis also showed a number of pockets of relative deprivation throughout the metropolitan area.

The prerequisites for such analysis are small-area census data, which are now readily available to all local authorities, and a spatially identified facilities inventory. Modern computer technology makes the latter also relatively easy to assemble. Such census–inventory analysis was pioneered in Scotland by TRRU in their study for the Lothians Regional Council. By basing their analysis on kilometre grid squares rather than wards, they were able to measure not just the number of facilities located within local areas but the distance to the nearest available facilities. The analysis was carried out for particular social groups – e.g. youth and the elderly – in relation to a range of facilities (TRRU, 1982).

Table 7.9. Hierarchies of social facilities (from Veal, 1975).

Needs of New Communities report	Telford master plan	Washington new town master plan

'Others' level
  Facilities which might be singly
  located in areas of housing:
  Church
  Public house
  Meeting rooms
  Local shops
  Children's playgrounds
	Dwelling group (100 people)
	  Immediate contact
	  Toddlers' play area
		Group (75–100 people)
		  Community open space, parking
		
		Place (1500 people)
		  Nursery school
		  Community kickabout
		  Minor walkways, vending machines
		  Telephone booths, post boxes

Local level (4000–5000 people)
  Primary school with play centre
  and pre-school playgroup
  Meeting rooms
  Maternity and child welfare clinic
  Local shops
  Children's playground
	Intermediate community unit
	  (4000 people)
	  Equipped play areas
	  Nursery schools, primary schools
	  Local shops
	  Neighbourhood police officer
	  Public house
	  Petrol filling station
		Village (4500–5000 people)
		  Youth club, village common room
		  Primary school, school playing-field
		  Organized play area and park
		  Intervillage walkway
		  Shop cluster
		  Filling station
		  Public house

Local centre
  Maternity and child welfare clinic
  School health clinic
  Library
  Primary school
  Secondary school with multiple-
  use recreation facilities
	Community unit (8000 people)
	  Middle school
	  Supervised playground
	  Small supermarket
	  Subpost office
	  Community centre
	  Miniclinic
	  Old persons' club
	  Religious facilities
		Local centre (18,000–20,000 people)
		  Working men's club
		  Youth centre, community centre
		  Secondary school
		  Indoor sports hall, playing-fields
		  Intervillage walkway
		  Local health centre, shop cluster
		  Subpost office, private offices
		  Filling station/garage/used-car sales
		  Public house

District centre (50,000 people)
  New town corporation district office
  Social services (various)
  District recreation centre, including:
    Sports hall
    Swimming-pools
    Library
    Meeting rooms
    Hall
    Catering
  Extensive shopping
  Nursery schools
  Old people's homes
	District unit (24,000–30,000 people)
	  Secondary school with adult
	    social centre
	  Senior school with adult social
	    centre
	  RC primary school
	  Adventure park
	  District shopping
	  Health centre
	  Group practice
	  Old persons' home
	  Youth club
		Town (80,000 people)
		  Entertainment centre
		  Arts centre
		  Private playing-fields
		  Main library
		  School for physically handicapped
		  RC comprehensive school
		  Indoor and outdoor sports centre
		  Riverside recreation parks
		  Town playing-fields
		  Golf-course
		  Town park–garden
		  Major health centre
		  Hospital
		  Old people's home
		  Ambulance station
		  Adult retraining centre
		  Mentally handicapped training centres
		  Town shopping centre
		  Central post office
		  Central fire station
		  Town police HQ
		  Professional services
		  Bus station
		  Hotel, motel
		  Public houses
		  County administration offices
		  Local-authority offices
		  Crown buildings
		  Magistrates' courts
		  Civil defence

City-wide/regional (750,000 people)
  City hall/local-government offices
  Main shopping centre
  Restaurants and clubs
  Theatres
  Cinemas
  Dancehalls
  Art gallery
  Museum
  Central library
  Churches
  Sports stadium
  Central clinic
  Centre for youth organization
	City (250,000 people)
	  Retailing
	  Banks
	  Government offices
	  Other offices
	  Hotels
	  Pubs, restaurants
	  Hairdressers, betting shops, cleaners, etc.
	  Filling stations and car sales
	  Cinemas
	  Halls
	  Library, art gallery, etc.
	  GPO sorting office
	  Wholesaling
	  Manufacturing	

RC, Roman Catholic; GPO, General Post Office; HQ, Headquarters.

Table 7.10. GLC recreation priority areas: scoring system (from Nicholls, 1975).

Facility	Supply index Score	Need index factor
Swimming-pool	6	% in shared dwellings
Local sports hall	5	% living at high density
Pitches	3	% with no car
Netball court	1.5	% manual workers
Bowling-green	1.5	
Tennis-court – hard	1.5	
– grass	1	

Table 7.11. Grouping of wards on supply/need indices (from Nicholls, 1975).

		Score letter for supply				
	Worst	a	b	c	d	e
Score	a	aa	ab	ac	ad	ae
letter	b	ba	bb	bc	bd	be
for	c	ca	cb	cc	cd	ce
social	d	da	db	dc	dd	de
need	e	ea	eb	ec	ed	ee

A B C D E — Best

Variations on this approach are the various geo-demographic-analysis packages, the most well-known of which in the UK is a classification of residential neighbourhoods (ACORN) (CACI Ltd, 2000). Data on the characteristics of residential areas are subjected to multivariate analysis to produce residential-area types. While these tend to reflect the housing, socio-economic and demographic data upon which they are based, it is also believed that residents of the various area types will have distinctive leisure and consumption patterns – or lifestyles.

Based on analysis of some 40 census variables, covering age structure, mobility, socio-economic factors and housing, the ACORN analysis results in some 11 area types:

- Areas of modern family housing for manual workers.
- Areas of modern family housing for white-collar workers.
- Areas of better terraces and mixed housing.
- Poor-quality older terraced neighbourhoods.
- Rural areas.
- Areas of urban local-authority housing.
- Severely deprived tenement areas and council estates.
- Low-status multioccupied and immigrant areas.
- High-status non-family areas.
- High-status suburbs.
- Resort and retirement areas.

Any ward or census-enumeration district can be classified according to one of the above types. The commercial company that produces ACORN can provide printouts and maps for any specified geographical area. Shaw (1984) demonstrated that there is a relationship between leisure participation and the ACORN type area in which people live. Commercial and public-sector organizations can therefore use ACORN to target neighbourhoods in which their priority client groups are concentrated – whether this be for the purposes of marketing or provision of services to alleviate deprivation. The potential of ACORN has been explored in a number of studies (Bickmore *et al.*, 1980; Nevill and Jenkins, 1986; Williams *et al.*, 1988; Jenkins *et al.*, 1989), but whether the

Fig. 7.7. GLC priority areas (from Nicholls, 1975).

lifestyle variable is superior to more traditional variables, such as social class or life
cycle, as a basis for market and leisure analysis, has been questioned (O'Brien and Ford,
1988; Veal, 1991a).

The recreation opportunity spectrum

An idea related to the idea of hierarchies is
the recreation opportunity spectrum (ROS) –
a framework developed in America by Clark
and Stankey (1979) for classifying open
space. The ROS classifies areas in which people might seek outdoor recreation along a
continuum from the totally undeveloped,
such as pristine wilderness ('primitive'), to
the highly developed, such as a fully serviced camping site and recreation area
('modern'). Against this are set the sorts of
activity which the management and users of
these areas might engage in to maintain the

appropriate ambience of the site and com-
patibility with visitor expectations. These
ideas are summarized in Table 7.12.

While the spectrum is designed primarily
as a management tool, it can also be used for
planning purposes in the same way as hierarchies are used – that is, to provide guidelines
for ensuring that a full range of recreational
provision is available to the user. Conflicts
arise when one group of users attempts to
use an area for a purpose that is incompatible
with the use of the space by other user
groups – for example, trail-bike riders
attempting to use an area that is being used
for picnicking. The ROS reminds the planner
and policy-maker that outdoor recreation is a
multifaceted phenomenon requiring a variety
of types of provision and management.
While it has been developed primarily in the
context of resource-based outdoor recreation,
ROS is also adaptable, in modified form, to
the urban setting (Jackson, 1986).

Table 7.12. The recreation opportunity spectrum (from Clark and Stankey, 1979; Pigram, 1983: 27).

Management/on-site activities	Spectrum of settings			
	Modern	Semi-modern	Semi-primitive	Primitive
1. Access (roads, etc.)	Easy	Moderately difficult	Difficult	Very difficult
2. Non-recreation resource uses (e.g. forestry)	Compatible on large scale	Depends on circumstances	Depends on circumstances	Not compatible
3. Management site modification	Very extensive	Moderately extensive	Minimal	None
4. Social interaction (contact with other users)	Frequent	Moderately frequent	Infrequent	None
5. Visitor impact	High	Moderate	Minimal	None
6. Regimentation (overt visitor control)	Strict	Moderate	Minimal	None

The ROS can be seen as part of the move away from a purely resource-only-based approach to natural-area planning, in which land areas are designated for conservation on the basis of their environmental qualities and are then managed to conserve those qualities. Recreational access, in such a situation, is almost an afterthought and it is simply assumed that recreation demand would align itself with the conservation principles. While the integrity of the resource must generally remain paramount, approaches such as ROS provide the planner and manager with tools to proactively consider the nature of recreation demand and how it might be met, and how the recreational experience might be optimized. Later developments, such as the 'limits of acceptable change' concept (Stankey *et al.*, 1999) and the benefits approach to leisure, as discussed in Chapter 10, take this process a stage further.

The matrix approach[4]

A goal of local councils, which is often expressed but rarely very fully addressed, is the desire to meet the requirements of all sections of the community. However, while councils may express such goals and may seek to provide a wide range of opportunities to achieve them, it is rare that any evaluation is carried out to assess the extent to which it is being achieved. In fact, in the case of public leisure policy, this is extremely difficult, because of the wide range of groups and interests that must be served.

The matrix approach to planning accepts this complexity from the beginning. It involves recognizing that it may be impossible to serve all groups equally; indeed, the policy may be to favour certain groups, but that policy should be based on information about the patterns of provision among different groups. Essentially the matrix approach is a methodology for studying the current situation with regard to leisure provision in general in any community. It is a means of examining the impact of currently available facilities and services – the interaction between facilities and people.

The matrix in question has two dimensions: the first refers to the range of groups comprising the community and the second refers to the range of facilities and services available to the community. The body of the matrix contains an analysis of the extent to which each group is served by each facility or service. Table 7.13 shows a matrix in simplified form. The development of the matrix approach can be considered under three headings: the groups, the facilities/service and the analysis.

The groups

A number of possible criteria that could be used to define groups which make up the community and which might have distinct leisure demands. Among these are the following.

- Age/life cycle.
- Gender.
- Economic status/socio-economic group.

Table 7.13. Planning matrix in simplified form.

| Facilities/ services | Groups in the community | | | | | |
	A	B	C	D	E	etc.
I	√√	•	–	√√	–	
II	√	√	–	√√	–	
III	–	√√	√	√	–	
IV	√√	√	•	√√	√√	
etc.						

√√, Very well served; √, well served; •, poorly served; –, not served at all.

- Ethnicity.
- Degree of mobility (i.e. primarily: with car/without car).
- Health/disability.
- Housing type.
- Geographical areas/neighbourhoods.
- Residents/businesses/workers.
- Visitors.

The choices of grouping for the matrix would depend on council corporate policies and priorities and on data availability. One of the requirements of a fully developed matrix system is information on the numbers of individuals in each group defined; in general this would come from the census, but in some cases data would need to be gathered from other sources – for example, health- or social-service authorities or, in the case of tourists, visitor surveys.

Facilities/services

The range of facilities and services or programmes available for leisure from the public, voluntary and private sectors is enormous. Ordering information on this range of provision therefore presents a considerable challenge. While councils have, over the years, developed inventories of their own facilities, they have been slow to consider the range of facilities and services provided by the voluntary and commercial sectors. With privatization, compulsory competitive tendering (CCT) and increasing emphasis on 'user pays', the sharp dividing line between public and private sectors has faded. In considering the requirements of the whole community therefore, councils might be expected to make greater efforts to inventory all facilities avail-

able within their communities. The idea of examining all of the leisure facilities available to a particular group is at the heart of the matrix approach, since it could be found that a group which is poorly serviced by the public sector is in fact being adequately served by the private sector.

Facilities and services might be classified on two or three levels. Level 1 would be types of provision – for example, children's play, sports facilities, arts facilities. Level 2 would further subdivide these groups, as suggested in Table 7.14, while Level 3 would involved individual, named facilities or programmes. It would be possible to carry out a matrix analysis at any one or all three of the levels.

Analysis

The cells of the matrix should indicate the extent to which a particular item of provision serves the particular social group or area. Information for this process could come from a variety of sources, including the following:

- Common sense (for example, children's play facilities should be serving children).
- Observation (for example, a particular pub is known to cater for younger people).
- Published research (for example, national or, if available, regional leisure surveys that indicate which social groups engage in particular activities or use a particular type of facility or regional tourism data indicating numbers and types of tourists visiting particular areas).
- Special research (for example, a survey of leisure centre users which indicates the socio-economic characteristics of users and where they live).

Table 7.14. Facility/service inventory for matrix analysis.

Level 1	Level 2	Level 3
Children's play	• Adventure playgrounds • Conventional playgrounds – supervised • Unsupervised playgrounds • Play centres	• Individual facilities
Youth facilities	• Youth centres • Electronic games parlours	• Individual facilities
Sports facilities/programmes	• Outdoor pitches • Outdoor courts • Bowling-greens • Indoor halls • Gyms • Squash courts • Outdoor pools • Indoor pools • Ice rinks • Spectator sport • Cycle tracks • Sports development programmes • Fun-runs/sports carnivals	• Individual facilities/ programmes
Parks/open space	• Gardens • Small parks • Major parks • Country parks • Events in parks	• Individual facilities
Social facilities	• Community centres • Day centres • Pubs • Clubs	• Named facilities
Arts/entertainment	• Theatres • Galleries • Museums • Arts centres • Cinemas • Exhibitions • Libraries • Disco/clubs • Restaurants/bars	• Individual facilities
Tourism-related	• Tourist information centres • Guided tours • Festivals/events	• Individual centres/tours/ events

An initial assessment can be made on the basis of incomplete, informal or non-local data, as indicated in the first three of these sources. In practice, a programme of surveys at individual facilities would be necessary to provide the most detailed information, or a household community survey, if conducted on a large enough scale to provide an acceptable sample of target social groups and areas, would be even more effective in providing information across the whole range of provision. Special surveys would be necessary to provide complete data on tourists and day visitors.

Using a matrix for planning

The gaps and inequities that arise from the matrix analysis can provide the basis for developing leisure policy in an area. Table 7.15 provides an example of how the results

Table 7.15. Detailed matrix analysis.

Facilities	Total visits	Age-groups					Groups (visits per week) Gender			Neighbourhoods				Tourists and day visitors
		Under 15	15–24	25–39	40–59	60+	Male	Female	W	X	Y	Z	
Swimming-pool 2	2,500	1,500	500	430	50	20	1,400	1,100	300	1,700	300	200	50
Sports centre	3,000	300	1,500	800	350	50	2,000	1,000	400	500	700	1,400	350
Tennis-courts	2,800	250	1,200	950	350	50	1,500	1,300	700	950	350	800	100
Football pitches	2,000	400	1,350	200	50	0	1,980	20	600	700	500	200	10
Library 1	5,500	800	1,250	1,000	950	1,500	2,000	3,500	3,000	1,500	750	250	150
Library 2	3,000	650	850	750	350	400	1,100	1,900	500	1,800	600	100	50
Library 3	6,000	1,100	850	1,700	1,050	1,300	2,500	3,500	500	800	3,500	1,200	250
Community centre 1	550	50	350	75	25	50	200	350	50	50	100	350	20
Community centre 2	800	50	200	250	150	150	250	550	100	200	400	100	5
Community centre 3	1,100	200	350	250	100	200	300	800	750	250	100	0	15
Parks	9,000	1,200	1,950	1,750	2,300	1,800	4,400	4,600	3,100	2,400	1,700	1,800	350
Cinema	2,200	350	1,100	400	200	150	1,200	1,000	800	500	650	250	150
Pubs	10,000	0	4,700	2,800	1,450	1,050	6,850	3,150	4,100	2,200	2,100	1,600	300
A. Total visits to facilities	52,450	9,350	16,900	11,985	7,475	6,740	28,280	24,170	17,000	14,850	12,250	8,350	2,050
B. Population '000s	100	22	15	20	23	20	48	52	30	24	25	21	4*
C. Participation ratio	525	425	1,127	599	325	337	589	464	566	619	490	397	512.00

*Total number of visitors/tourists to the area per week, '000s.

of the process might look. The data relate to a hypothetical local-authority area with a population of 100,000 and 4000 tourist visitors a week. The data on total numbers of visits to facilities per week are derived from ticket sales or counts. The distribution of these visits among the demographic groups and neighbourhoods is based on site or household-survey data.

Row A of the table shows the total number of visits made by the particular group to the range of facilities represented, from ticket sales or counts. Row B indicates the population in each group, from the census, and the number of tourists, from tourism surveys. Row C is the participation ratio relating visits to population and gives a broad indicator of the level of use of services made by each group. This hypothetical example shows that the older age-groups are the least well served of the age-groups, that females are less well served than males and that neighbourhood Z is the least well-served geographical area. It would be possible to use separate sub-ratios – for example, for sports or the arts or for local-authority services only.

In the case of leisure services for the local community, the evaluative process is completed with an assessment of the level of access apparently enjoyed by each group, in the light of the council's overall leisure policies in relation to different services and different social groups. Attention would be expected to be given to those groups with low participation ratios. In the case of tourists, equity issues are not the focus, but the extent to which leisure services are contributing to and benefiting from tourism in the area.

The organic approach

The use of the organic or incremental approach can be seen as an adjunct to the matrix approach. It would relate to a specific row of the matrix, particularly when the concern is with spatial inequalities in provision. In that sense it also relates very much to the spatial analysis discussed earlier. The organic approach is concerned with how to justify and go about planning the development of a particular type of leisure facility.

The approach is predicated on one main principle: that the case for additional provision should be based on analysis of levels and patterns of use of existing facilities. It is therefore ideally suited to areas and facility types where a facility or facilities already exist – for example, a local-authority area with two existing swimming-pools looking for a means for developing future policy for swimming-pool provision.

The process is summarized in Fig. 7.8. Various decision-making points are numbered in the diagram 1–11, while research tasks are lettered A–E. The approach consists of two decision-making processes; one related to existing facilities and the areas they serve (steps 2–7) and one related to those areas not served by existing facilities (steps 8–9). Both processes come together in the plan preparation and implementation stage (steps 10–11).

Step 1. Start: existing facilities

The basis of the method is to begin by examining existing facilities of a particular type – for example, swimming-pools or community centres. In situations where there are no existing facilities, other planning methods are more appropriate.

Step 2. Use levels of existing facilities

This seems an obvious starting-point in any planning, but seems rarely to be part of the formal planning process. If existing facilities are underused, then the case for additional provision will need to be considered very carefully. Conversely, evidence of heavily used – and even overused – facilities can provide support for further provision.

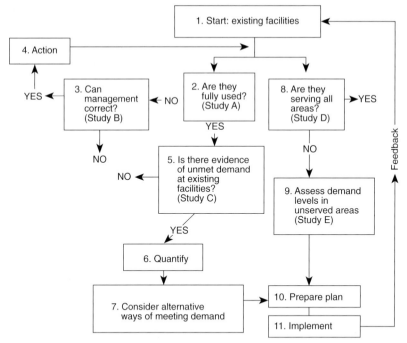

Fig. 7.8. An organic approach to planning.

Study A. Capacity and Use Levels

In order to discover whether facilities are being fully used, it is necessary to determine: (i) the capacity of the facilities and (ii) their level of use. This is more or less demanding, depending on the type of facility. Thus, for example, in the case of a theatre, capacity is related to the number of seats and use levels are measured by the number of tickets sold: assessments of level of use are therefore routine. Similarly, in the case of squash courts, the number of booking slots available and the number of those slots sold is clear. In the case of a swimming-pool, the process is a little more difficult in that the level of use is usually carefully monitored through ticket sales, but the capacity of a pool is more difficult to assess because, while safety determines the number of people who are permitted in the pool at any one time, such factors as the length of sessions and use for special events can affect overall capacity considerably. At the other extreme, in the case of parks, both usage levels and capacity present problems. In all cases overall management practices, such as opening times, affect the capacity of a facility. Table 7.6 presents the results of an exercise to estimate facility capacities in general terms, but every facility is unique, so these figures can be taken only as a guide. The basis of the capacity assessments is presented in Appendix 7.1, while Appendix 7.2 provides an overview of the measures necessary to assess usage levels.

Step 3. Management correction

If it is decided that facilities are under-used, then, before considering the planning of new facilities, the question must first be asked as to whether this situation can be corrected. As a result of study B, it may be found that remedial measures can be taken (progress to step 3) or it might be decided that nothing can be done, that the situation must be lived with (progress to step 8).

Study B. Management Study

More detailed studies of underused facilities will be required. Underuse may be due to poor management, poor design, poor maintenance or wrong decisions made in the past on scale, type and location of the facility.

Step 4. Action

This step involves implementation of the measures investigated in step 3. It would be hoped that the measures result in full use of the facilities so that, on repeating step 2, the answer is 'Yes'.

Step 5. Unmet demand

It is possible that existing facilities are overused and not adequately serving their local areas, due to changing tastes, increasing population or changing population characteristics, because the facilities provided had been inadequate from the start or because of the success of management in stimulating demand. Discovering the extent of any unmet demand would require a monitoring study (study C). If there is unmet demand, the process moves to step 6. If there is no unmet demand, the process, as far as existing facilities are concerned, comes to an end and attention turns to step 8.

Study C. Monitoring

The managers of existing facilities are in possession of useful information on latent demand in the local community, but it is not usually systematically recorded. This is information on demand that they are unable to meet, which is evidenced by requests for bookings which they are unable to meet, overuse of facilities and the results of any market research conducted within their catchment areas. A monitoring study could be instituted to ensure that, over a specified period of time, this information is recorded. Such data may then be supplemented by other survey data and gross-demand estimates of potential demand in the area. Quantifying the demand would be difficult, involving judgement about just how real the expressed demand is.

Step 6. Quantify unmet demand

As indicated under study C, quantifying unmet demand is difficult, but it must be done if provision is to be made to meet it.

Step 7. Consider alternatives

If the unmet demand is substantial, considerable additions to facilities may be contemplated on existing sites or on additional sites within the area. However, if the unmet demand is not great, it might be possible to accommodate it in existing facilities by, for example, extending opening hours, changing programmes, increasing staff or adopting off-site programmes, or by minor alterations to physical plant. The conclusions of this step are then fed into the plan preparation stage, step 10.

Step 8. Areas served and unserved

This step, and steps 9 and 10, refer to the spatial approach to planning already discussed. Facilities have catchment areas and so the corollary is that, in most cases, there are areas which are not being served by the facilities provided because they lie outside the catchment areas. It is these unserved areas that are the focus for planning in this part of the process. Of course, if study D indicates that all areas of the local authority are being served, then no further action is required in this part of the process.

Study D. Catchment-area Study

This study follows the approach suggested in the discussion of spatial approaches above. Membership records, where available, or user surveys are used to identify catchment areas of existing facilities and those unserved areas outside the catchment areas. This might be done for all potential users or for separate socio-economic groups.

Step 9. Demand assessment

In order to determine what provision should be made in the unserved areas, it is necessary to assess the level of demand for the activity/facility involved in those areas. This is done by study E.

Study E. Demand Assessment

As discussed in the spatial-analysis section of this chapter, the catchment-area studies of existing facilities provide one means of assessing likely levels of demand for facilities in currently unserved areas (see Fig. 7.1 and discussion). In addition, gross-demand methods could also be used.

Steps 10 and 11. Prepare plan and implement

The analysis contained in steps 1 to 9 and resulting from studies A to E provides data and proposals for input to a plan or strategy, which might be for leisure as a whole in the community or just for the one specific type of facility studied. Plan preparation and implementation are discussed in Chapter 6.

The community-development approach

The essence of the community-development approach to planning is public involvement and planning at the neighbourhood level. Activities such as *community development, animation* and *public participation* are all relevant to this process, but have generally been peripheral to recreation planning and management. Community development has been shaped by community workers under the auspices of education authorities in Britain, and so, except for some specific experiments, has not featured greatly in the toolkit of the leisure professional. The related idea of *animation* was developed in France and elsewhere in Europe and by the arts community in Britain and so again has not been central to the more hard-nosed management approach of the leisure professional. Public participation has been most fully developed by the planning profession, largely because of statutory requirements, but has had some impact on leisure (Limb, 1986).

There are two main elements in these processes. The first is the concern to increase the level of public involvement in decision-making, particularly at the neighbourhood level. The second is a concern with the communal and human aspects of leisure and tourism, as opposed to the facility-orientated and individual aspects. Each of these aspects is discussed in turn below.

Public involvement and consultation are discussed in the context of plan-making in Chapter 6. Direct public involvement in the planning process generally has had a chequered history since the publication of the Skeffington Report on public participation over 30 years ago (Ministry of Housing and Local Government, 1969). Public response to meetings and questionnaire surveys on broad planning policies has often been minimal. Formal public inquiries are seen as inflexible and too expensive for all but the most powerful pressure groups to become involved in. At local level, more success can be claimed: people can more readily understand and relate to problems and issues concerning their own neighbourhoods.

An early plea for more involvement of people in decision-making on leisure planning came from Gold (1973), who argued that such involvement should be routine rather than a feature of special schemes. Also in the 1970s, the *Quality of Life* experiments (DoE and DES, 1977) suggested that, if resources were allocated and decisions on how to use the resources were left to community groups, then useful and original schemes would emerge and could operate successfully, and public involvement was certainly a feature of the 'new culture of leisure provision' recommended in *Leisure Provision and People's Needs* (Dower *et al.*, 1981).

The other aspect of the community-development approach is more concerned with community organization and communal leisure than with participation in the formal planning process. A number of traditions can be identified in this area, including *community and social development, animation* and *community arts, youth work,* and *sports* and *play leadership.*

Community and social development and the *animation* and community arts movements reflect a concern with a perceived decline in community. The view is that, with people no longer living and working in the same geographical area and with increased mobility and the advent of television, there has been a decline in the more collective forms of leisure. Privatization of leisure has led to a sharp reduction in social interaction and mutual support at the neighbourhood level, leading to loneliness for some and alienation for others. Community-development workers and *animateurs* therefore attempt to reverse this collapse of community by encouraging and supporting community groups of all kinds, from tenants' associations to children's play groups, old people's bingo clubs and soccer teams. Some would see these activities as ends in themselves, while others take a more political view – that communities need to learn to act collectively in the political arena in order to improve their living conditions generally or even to bring about fundamental change in society.

The French words *animateur* and *animation* are more closely associated with arts-based community initiatives, which take the form of the community-arts movement in Britain (see Kingsbury, 1976; Simpson, 1976; Kelly, 1984) and elsewhere (Hawkins, 1993). As Baldry put it:

> Community artists are distinguishable not by the techniques they use ... but by their attitude towards the place of their activities in the life of society. Their primary concern is their impact on a community and their relationship to it: by assisting those with whom they make contact to become more aware of their situation and of their creative powers, and providing them with the facilities they need to make use of their abilities, they hope to widen and deepen the sensitivities of the community in which they work and so to enrich its existence. To a varying degree they see this as a means of change, whether psychological, social or political, within the community.
>
> (Baldry, 1976: 2.2)

Thus, up and down the country, numerous groups and individuals arose, some based on arts centres, some peripatetic, some grant-aided by the Arts Council, some by local authorities. Some worked in the area of drama, others, such as 'artists-in-residence' (Braden, 1979), with painting, sculpture or literature. Often such activity was viewed with suspicion by traditional authorities because of their perceived political motivation, sometimes their controversial activities and sometimes their ability to 'cause trouble' in the community (Kelly, 1984). Funding for such activities was substantially eroded during the 1980s and 1990s.

Mention should also be made of more established community workers: youth workers and leaders and play leaders. It is accepted that youth clubs and play centres need to be staffed with professionals with appropriate skills for working with their respective clients. Their emphasis is not so much on planning or managing facilities but more on relating to and working directly with their client groups. More recently, the *sports leader* has emerged with a combination of sports-coaching and community-development skills, whose job is to be a catalyst in engaging young people in particular, often groups of unemployed, in sport.

The community approach has also been put forward in relation to tourism, particularly in smaller communities, where the introduction of tourism may have a significant impact on lifestyles and the environment. In such circumstances, it is argued, tourism can only survive and thrive if it is developed with the community on side. An early approach to community-based tourism planning was put forward by Murphy (1985) and more recently the idea has been pursued in relation to the development of ecotourism (Wearing and McLean, 1997). Community involvement in tourism policy-making and planning is promoted for a mixture of reasons, some related to the needs of community members and some to the interests of the tourism developer or industry. Thus Van der Stoep (2000: 312–314) lists the following benefits of a community approach.

- Community buy-in and empowerment.
- Reduced potential of lawsuits being used to block projects.
- Improved chances of long-term success.

- Increasing community awareness of value of local historic, cultural and environmental attributes.
- Increased sense of community identity.
- Protection of sacred places and sensitive resources.
- Minimization of negative impacts of tourism developments.
- Enhancement of community amenities for residents.
- Opportunities for shared resources.
- Keeping profits within the community.

The Nominal-Group Technique, discussed under public consultation in Chapter 6, is a formalized approach to the involvement of certain types of interested groups in the community. While it has been particularly developed in the context of tourism, it could be used in leisure planning generally, and the Delphi technique of qualitative forecasting, as discussed in Chapter 8, can be used to involve experts in considering future scenarios for planning.

Do these various forms of community worker and community involvement have a place in planning for leisure and tourism? It might be argued that they are more part of the day-to-day management of leisure resources than the longer-term planning process. A comprehensive view of planning would, however, see a need for these skills and concerns in the planning process. In seeking to provide for leisure, it is not always possible to set out plans in the conventional sense. Neighbourhoods vary, and each may require different solutions to their problems: it may be only by having people working at the grass roots that these needs can be identified and communicated. Even when a network of facilities has been provided, there may be unmet needs: those needs may be identified, given expression or even met through a catalyst, *animateur* or leader.

The issues approach

The issues approach to planning seeks to eliminate the lengthy, expensive and sometimes wasted research and preparatory work that are necessary for many of the more traditional approaches. The origin of the approach in British leisure planning lies in the Department of the Environment (1977) circular containing guidelines for the regional councils of sport and recreation on the preparation of regional recreational strategies, which suggested that the initial report in the strategy preparation process should be an *issues report*. The issues report would contain: a brief statement of principles; a background review of the state of sport and recreation in the region; and an identification of issues and initial assessment of priorities. The final strategy was envisaged as a series of reports on each of the issues identified. This is in contrast to the rational–comprehensive approach discussed in Chapter 5 and is in effect a version of the mixed-scanning approach discussed there.

What is not clear from the various guidelines suggesting the issues approach is just how the issues are to emerge. In general it is suggested that issues will emerge from the stakeholder-consultation process, although the professionals in charge of the process usually have the responsibility for producing, from such an exercise, a list of issues that is manageable and will avoid the expensive and time-consuming research and data collection of other planning exercises.

An early example of the use of the approach in the USA illustrates how demanding the approach can be in practice. The US *Third Nationwide Outdoor Recreation Plan* (Heritage, Conservation and Recreation Service, 1979) started with a consultation process in which over 5000 organizations were approached. Some 3000 organizations and individuals responded, identifying between them over 1000 separate recreation issues. These 1000 issued were classified into 30 groups and reduced to 21 'issues of national significance', through discussion, analysis by departmental staff and consultation and meetings with interested organizations. However, the published report does not state what the original 1000 issues were, what the 30 groups were, what the 21 issues selected were or what the criteria for selecting them were. The 21 issues were submitted to the Secretary of the Interior, who selected 16 priority issues – but again how or why was not reported. The 16 issues identified were as follows:

- Appropriate roles of government and profit and non-profit organizations (3 issues).
- Federal land acquisition programme.
- Methods to protect significant open-space and recreation resources.
- Methods to protect coastal resources.
- Evaluation of National Wild and Scenic Rivers and National Trails systems (2 issues).
- Federal water programmes and recreation.
- Recreation needs of special populations.
- Contribution of recreation to physical and mental health (2 issues).
- Federal role in urban recreation.
- Federal agency research.
- Outdoor recreation and energy conservation and environmental education (2 issues).

As with mixed scanning, the danger with the issues approach is that key issues will in fact be overlooked and that issues will be identified on the basis of the lobbying skills of various interest groups or the 'flavour of the month' rather than by any objective evaluation. Against this, however, must be posed the various defects of rational–comprehensive planning, as discussed in Chapter 6.

Conclusion

This review of eleven alternative planning approaches is intended to offer the leisure planner a range of tools commensurate with the diversity of the phenomenon of leisure

and tourism and of the various organizations responsible for planning for it. Two issues should be addressed before leaving this topic: first the question of goals and objectives and secondly the question of feasibility.

Goals and objectives

In Chapter 6 it was seen that the mission and goals of an organization are the starting-point for all planning activity and that, as a result of policies, projects and programmes adopted, the strategic management process results in a set of more detailed objectives that the various parts of the organization seek to achieve. Table 7.16 summarizes the goals that are implicit or explicit in the planning techniques discussed in this chapter. These and the goals discussed in Chapter 6 are taken up again in Chapter 10 on 'Performance evaluation'.

Feasibility

The greatest difficulty in implementing any of the planning approaches discussed in this chapter is not their intrinsic complexity but the availability of resources. The question of resources for planning for leisure is a fraught one. As suggested at the beginning of the chapter, the leisure profession itself is management-orientated rather than planning-orientated: leisure professionals are action people! They have also learned, over the years, to be opportunistic – to exploit the

Table 7.16. Planning approaches related to goals/objectives.

Approaches	Goal/objective
Resource-based standards	Meet standards (various)
	Utilize natural resources
Gross demand/market share	Raise demand at least to the average
	Maximize participation
Spatial analysis	Serve all areas
Hierarchies	Ensure full range of facilities at all community levels
Priority area analysis	Meet needs of target groups in specified areas
Recreation opportunity spectrum	Provide full range of experiences
Matrix	Appropriate provision for all groups and areas
Organic	Maximize utilization of facilities
	Provide service for all areas
Community development	Meet community/group wishes
Issues approach	Meet concerns of community groups/professionals/politicians

fact that the whim of a powerful politician can achieve more in a few months than the most carefully researched plans and strategies, which may have been gathering dust on shelves for years. However, every anecdote of such whims producing positive outcomes can be matched by stories of disasters, white elephants, wasted resources and real needs neglected.

The ideal approach is surely a combination of research-based planning and opportunism – what might be called informed opportunism. This means that, when a politician has a whim, a pressure group arises or a disaster, crisis or other media event focuses the public's attention, the professionals are ready with information and ideas rather than 'off the top of the head' solutions. This may appear to be '*Yes, Minister*' style manipulation but in fact it is not. The role of the professional in the public service is to offer professional expertise in the decision-making processes. Such expertise must be based on sound information and analysis.

Summary

- A range of approaches to and methods of planning for leisure and tourism are reviewed in the chapter, including the following: the use of standards; resource-based planning; the GDMS approach; spatial approaches; hierarchies of facilities; priority social-area analysis; the ROS; the matrix approach; the organic approach; the community-development approach; and the issues approach.
- Most of the methods discussed can be seen as attempts to move away from reliance on the standards- and resource-based methods alone and to incorporate user and potential user demands and stakeholder views as much as possible. Increasingly sophisticated methods call for more extensive data collection and analysis, which have been seen as a disincentive in the past. However, increasingly sophisticated management, control and evaluation methods are leading to increasing availability of data, thus facilitating the use of some of the methods outlined here.

Further Reading

- General approaches to planning: see Further Reading list in Chapters 5 and 6 and: Hillman and Whalley (1977); Kelsey and Gray (1985); Gratton and Taylor (1988); Ravenscroft (1992); Torkildsen (1999).
- Outdoor recreation: Lieber and Fesenmaier (1983); Williams (1995); Anderson *et al.* (2000).
- Standards: Buechner (1971); NPFA (1971); Torkildsen (1999: 168); Mertes *et al.* (1996).
- Resource-based planning: Chapters 11 and 12 of Jubenville (1976).
- Recreation opportunity spectrum: Clark and Stankey (1979); Driver *et al.* (1987); as applied to tourism: Butler and Waldbrook (1991).
- Spatial methods: Coppock and Duffield (1975); Ewing (1983); Smith (1995: 111–120).

Questions and Exercises

1. Name three advantages and three disadvantages of using a standards approach in leisure planning.
2. In what areas of leisure/tourism can resource-based planning still play an important role?
3. Which drawbacks of the standards approach does the gross-demand/market-share method overcome and which does it fail to overcome?
4. Define the catchment area of a facility.
5. What is a visit rate and how can it be used in planning?
6. What is a facility hierarchy?
7. What is the essence of the recreation opportunity spectrum?
8. What is the main drawback of the matrix approach to planning?
9. What other forms of public service are related to the community-development approach to planning?
10. What are the defects of the issues approach to planning?

Notes

[1] This is an updated and evolved version of the range of planning techniques originally outlined almost 20 years ago (Veal, 1982b) and revised in the first edition of this book (Veal, 1994b: 73–108). I have taken account of the contributions of a number of writers and researchers in the field who have drawn on and contributed to the evolution of the list (e.g. Gratton and Taylor, 1985: 116–117; Williams, 1995: 66–69; Torkildsen, 1999: 168–202).
[2] In earlier discussions of this approach (Veal, 1982a; 1994b: 78–82) it was referred to as just the

gross-demand approach, on the basis that it involved estimating total, or gross, demand for an activity in the community as a basis for making provision. The changing nature of public leisure provision, in which the public sector is increasingly seen as just one among many providers of leisure facilities and services, and the more explicit treatment of tourism in this edition of the book suggested that the idea of market share should be included.

[3] It should be noted that the visit rate is not the same as the proportion of the population visiting the pool in a week, because one person may make more than one visit (see Table 8.1). So, for example, the top left-hand pool in Fig. 7.3 attracts 1200 visits from its central zone. Expressed as a percentage, this would be 9%. This implies that 9% of the population visits per week. But, if the average user makes two visits per week, the number of people visiting the pool is 600, or 4.5% of the population. The visit rate, calculated on a base of 1000, rather than 100, is deliberately used to avoid this confu-

sion. NB: in developing his own illustration of this method, Torkildsen (1999: 176) uses a percentage figure, which he calls 'per cent penetration'. I believe the visit-rate concept is a preferable measure.

[4] In the 1994 edition of the book and in the publications in which this range of planning methods was first outlined (Veal, 1982b, 1984, 1986), the term 'grid' approach was offered as an alternative term used to describe this method. In the latest edition of his standard text on *Leisure and Recreation Management*, Torkildsen (1999: 182) uses the term 'grid' to refer to a spatial method of planning based on 0.5 km grid squares. To avoid confusion for readers using both books, the term 'grid' has therefore been dropped from the presentation here. Torkildsen's 'grid' approach is in fact similar to the priority social-area analysis approach presented here. Torkildsen, in turn, refers to a version of the priority social-area analysis as a need-index approach (1999: 183).

Appendix 7.1. Estimation of Facility Capacities

The estimates in this appendix are not meant to be definitive, but indicative. They are intended to illustrate an approach. Capacities may vary from community to community, depending on local conditions, including the design of facilities and management practices.

Grass playing pitches

It is assumed that one match or practice session involves 30 participants – players, referees, coaches, reserves, etc. It is assumed that a pitch accommodates four practice sessions (typically during the week) and four matches (typically at the weekend) per week.

8 sessions × 30 participants = 240

In wintertime weekday evening practice is not possible without floodlights. However, it is assumed that such pitches are used for lunchtime practice and for schools. During daylight-saving periods, non-floodlit pitches can be fully used by non-school users. It is assumed, therefore, that, on average, the non-school use of pitches without floodlights is 200 participants per week.

Averaging the floodlit and non-floodlit pitches gives 220 users per week.

Hard courts, outdoor

Tennis

A court can be used for singles or doubles. Assuming 1-hour bookings and an equal number of singles and doubles bookings, it can be assumed that a court will accommodate three users per hour on average. In summer a court is usable for some 80 hours a week, but 100% bookings would be most unusual, because of weather factors, unpopular hours, etc. Assuming 60% usage gives a capacity of 144, say, 150, users per week. In winter a floodlit court would have a similar capacity, but a non-floodlit court would have a capacity of 100 users per week, giving an

annual average of 125. Averaging floodlit and non-floodlit courts gives about 140 users per week per court.

Netball/basketball

One match can be assumed to involve 16 participants, referees, coaches and reserves. Courts are available for the same number of hours as tennis-courts, but, because of the team nature of the sports, usage, by non-school groups is likely to be similar to that of grass pitches – that is, a certain number of evening practice sessions and weekend games. Assuming nine 2-hour sessions per week gives 144 users per week, which is similar to that for tennis.

Squash courts

Squash courts are typically available for up to 90 hours per week. It would be very rare to achieve 100% usage, but 70% usage would involve some 250 users per week.

Sports hall

A two-court hall can accommodate two tennis, basketball/netball or indoor soccer courts or eight badminton courts. It can also be used for activities such as aerobics. Assuming opening hours of 90 per week, 100% usage for badminton with half singles and half doubles would provide for 2160 players with 1-hour bookings. In fact, a hall would not be programmed entirely for badminton and would be unlikely to achieve 100% usage. Some of the time a hall would be unused; some of the time it would be used by 32 people an hour (all badminton, doubles), some of the time it might be used by 150 people an hour (aerobics), some of the time by only 20 per hour (basket/netball, 2-hour booking). Careful management and marketing, including sessions for the elderly or for mothers and babies during daytime, should be able to achieve 2000 users a week. However, this might only be achievable with school bookings. Non-school capacity could therefore be put at, say, 1500 per week.

Community halls and scout halls may be capable of accommodating some of the sporting activity indicated. Such halls are likely to be of one-court size at most. They are generally not managed for maximum opening hours, are sometimes available only to certain groups and are less flexible in use. The capacity of a two-court hall is therefore likely to be less than half of that of a one-court hall. It is therefore assumed that such halls accommodate 350 visits per week.

Weights room

The capacity of a weights/exercise room will of course depend on its size and the amount of equipment. Such a room would be open for some 90 hours per week. Supposing a typical room has a maximum capacity of ten but a typical use level of five people and 70% capacity is achieved, using 1-hour bookings gives a capacity of 330 per week.

Golf-course (18-hole)

Assuming a course is open for 7 days a week, 8 hours a day on average (up to 12 in summer, down to 6 in winter), and that one person can tee off every 4 minutes gives 120 rounds a day – say, 800 per week.

Bowling-green

Assuming three sessions a day on 6 days a week, during the season, with 15 participants in each session, gives a total of 270 visits per week.

Athletics track

Bearing in mind that we are dealing with public use only and any purpose-built track would probably be used during school time by schools, public use might be for, say, 30 hours a week (summer and winter average). Assuming 25 people using the facility for 90-minute sessions gives 500 visits per week.

Informal open space

The idea of capacity for informal open space is almost a contradiction in terms, since there is almost no limit to the amount of open space which the individual can enjoy. Nevertheless, it is possible to argue that, for certain types of open-space experience, people expect to look outside their immediate urban area – to state and national parks and the coast.

Within walking distance of their homes people might expect to be able to find areas for day-to-day walking and informal out-door games and not too far away they might expect to find district-level open space for such walking and perhaps for picnicking and public events. A reasonable approach would seem to be to take a well-used park and examine its use levels.

Appendix 7.2. Measuring Levels of Use

The aim here is not to devise total management appraisal systems, but merely to consider the question of use as against capacity.

Grass playing pitches

Where formal bookings are required, these can be used as a guide, but, if clubs are given season-long bookings for a very low fee, there may be no incentive to use the pitch fully, so sample observations of actual use levels may be advisable. In any case, a club booking is not necessarily a good guide to numbers of users. Some clubs may pack in more activity – and more users – into a booking period than others. In addition, pitches located in parks may attract informal use, which can only be ascertained by observation. Sample spot counts of use over a period of time may therefore be necessary (see Veal, 1997: Chapter 7). Measures might be as follows:

- Number of bookings as a percentage of maximum possible number of bookings.
- Absolute number of bookings (differentiates well-drained and floodlit facilities which have a higher capacity than others).
- Number of users per annum as per cent of theoretical maximum (see Appendix 7.1).
- Absolute number of users per annum.

Hard courts, outdoor

The same considerations apply as for grass pitches, although informal use may be less of an issue. While tennis-courts are used less by clubs, there is still a need for sample counts to discover the average number of players per booking.

Measures as for grass pitches.

Squash courts

Measures:

- Bookings as a per cent of slots available.
- Number of bookings per week.

Sports hall

The question arises here as to whether to use bookings or use levels or both. The variety of activities possible in a hall presents problems. It is assumed that full data are available to compile any chosen measure, but in some situations, organizational bookings may mean that management does not have a record of numbers attending; this would need to be overcome by sample counts.

Measures:

- Bookings as percentage of booking slots available.
- Absolute number of bookings per annum.
- Users per square metre of space per annum.
- Absolute number of users.
- Number of different activities catered for.

Weights room

Measures:

- Number of visits per annum per square metre.
- Number of visits per major piece of equipment.
- Absolute numbers of visits per annum.

Golf-course

Since golf-courses are such a standard facility, the number of rounds per annum is an adequate measure; 18-hole and nine-hole courses would need to be considered separately.

Bowling-green

Same considerations as for grass pitches.

Athletics track

Same considerations as for grass pitches.

Informal open space

As the discussion of capacity indicates, this is much more difficult than the more formal facilities. Assessment of use levels on the basis of counts is now a well-established technique. The problem arises in evaluating the results. When is a park underused as opposed to offering a quiet, uncrowded experience? When is a park overused and crowded as opposed to offering a lively, vibrant recreational experience for users? While quantitative information is useful, it is clear that, in this case, a great deal of qualitative judgement is needed to decide whether provision in an area is adequate or not.

8

Forecasting Leisure and Tourism Demand

Introduction

All policies and plans are concerned with the future, whether the future extends over days, months or years. Typically the policy and planning activity discussed in this book is focused on a time period of several years. When built facilities are involved, the consequences of decisions can remain with a community for decades. Many policies and plans are concerned with meeting current deficiencies and solving current problems but, even in these situations, it is necessary to include a future-orientated perspective to ensure that the proposed solutions do not have unacceptable long-term consequences. The successful leisure- and tourism-service organizations will surely be those which plan for the future rather than for the problems of the past – while of course learning from the past.

In this chapter the aim is to consider ways in which the future can be considered by policy-making and planning agencies. The techniques discussed vary considerably. They include highly technical approaches designed to produce quantified demand forecasts and less technical approaches concerned with qualitative issues and the big picture.

The discussion of strategic planning in Chapter 6 emphasizes the need for leisure and tourism organizations to be forward-looking. This need is ever more apparent as the rate of social and technological change accelerates. In recent decades leisure and tourism organizations in the public sector have reacted differently in response to such change.

Because tourism has been one of the fastest-growing industries in recent years, there has been considerable interest in tracking trends and predicting growth and fluctuations in demand. Internationally, the World Tourism Organization produces regular demand forecasts: its current predictions are for international tourist arrivals to increase from some 700 million to a billion in 2010 and 1.5 billion in 2020 (World Tourism Organization, 2001). National governments, public tourism agencies and large tourism-related private companies, such as airlines, continue to commission demand forecasts, although for many these have been thrown into disarray by the attacks on the World Trade Centre in New York in September 2001 and, in Britain, by the 2000/2001 outbreak of foot-and-mouth disease. In Australia, tourism forecasting merits its own quango, the Tourism Forecasting Council (see Tourism Forecasting Council, quarterly). Such developments have not taken place in leisure-demand forecasting.

The origins of modern leisure-demand forecasting lie in the early 1960s work of the American Outdoor Recreation Resources Review Commission (ORRRC, 1962). Data from the extensive research programme of the ORRRC were used to develop a quantitative modelling approach to recreation-demand forecasting using multiple-regression equations, which related levels of demand to demographic and socio-economic variables, such as age, income and level of education. This modelling approach was used extensively in recreation planning in the USA and to some extent in Europe. In the 1980s and 1990s, however, the approach fell out of favour with planners and policy-makers, for technical reasons (Kelly, 1980), and because of the demonstrated inaccuracy of some of the early US forecasts (Brown and Hutson, 1979). In Britain researchers produced models that were statistically quite satisfactory (e.g. Coppock and Duffield, 1975; Settle, 1977; Veal, 1987: 146–154), but their lifespan as the basis of planning and policy was, nevertheless, even more short-lived than that in the USA. It is possible that, with more research, the technical limitations of the quantitative modelling experiment might have been overcome, but public-sector policy-makers in the leisure area appeared to place much less emphasis on demand forecasting after the 1970s. This rejection of forecasting can be related to three main factors: first, a slowing of the pace of change in certain key areas, such as population levels, car ownership and incomes; secondly, suspicions about the accuracy of forecasts; and, thirdly, problems in making practical use of forecasts. In all three cases it can be argued that this response has been misguided, as is demonstrated in the discussion below.

In this chapter, firstly, we consider of all the various ways in which leisure and tourism demand might be measured and secondly, a range of social, economic and political factors that are likely to determine or affect leisure and tourism demand and which therefore need to be taken into account in any forecasting exercise are reviewed. Then various techniques used in forecasting are considered.

Forecasting What?

It is argued in Chapter 6 that planning for leisure and tourism should be based on an understanding of demand. This chapter focuses on demand – estimating its current nature and dimensions and predicting its future nature and dimensions. The term demand is used primarily in the economist's sense – that is, the amount of a service people consume or are willing to consume at a particular price. As far as leisure and tourism services are concerned, therefore, demand is equated with participation. But in participating people spend time and, often, money. In fact, there is a range of measures used in leisure-demand analysis, as set out in Table 8.1.

There has been considerable discussion in the literature over the appropriateness of participation levels as a measure of demand. Burton, for example, classifies demand into the following:

- Existing demand – currently taking place.
- Latent demand – demand frustrated by lack of facilities or services.
- Induced or generated demand – demand that only materializes when facilities are provided (e.g. the person who never considered playing squash until the leisure centre was built in his/her neighbourhood).
- Diverted demand – demand transferred from an old facility to a new one.
- Substitute demand – demand transferred from one activity to another as a result of a new facility or service becoming available (Burton, 1971: 26; Gratton and Taylor, 1985: 99–100).

It is necessary to consider these various types of unmet or contingent demand because, for most people, the range of leisure goods and services they would like to have is severely constrained by, among other things, money and access to facilities. So what people *actually* do (expressed need/demand) is not necessarily what they would really *like* to do if some of these constraints were removed. In particular, if prices for some activities were reduced, transport access were improved, or there were more capacity at peak periods, demand (participation) would probably be higher than is currently observed. So a statement such as 'the demand for cinema visits in this community is 50,000 visits a year' should really be qualified to say: 'given current prices and availability of cinemas, demand for cinema visits in this community is 50,000 visits a year'. This is true of any good or service in the

Table 8.1. Measuring leisure and tourism demand.

Leisure				Tourism*			
Measure	Definition	Relationships	Examples	Measure	Definition	Relationships	Examples
A. Participation rate	The proportion of the population of an area who engage in an activity in a given time period		6% of the adult population of area X went swimming at least once a week in 2001	Visit rate	The proportion of the population of a TGR that visits a TDR in a given time period		5% of the adult population of region Y visited region X in the year 2001
B. Participants	Number of people in an area who engage in an activity in a given time period	$A \times$ population of area X or $C \div$ mean frequency†	20,000 of the residents of area X went swimming at least once a week in 2001	Trips	a. The number of departures from a TGR to a TDR b. The total number of arrivals in a TDR in a given time period	a. $A \times$ population of region Y by frequency of visit b. Aggregate of a. across all TGRs	a. There were 100,000 tourist departures from region Y to region X in 2001 b. There were 1.2 million tourist arrivals in region X in 2001
C. Visits	The number of engagements‡ in an activity in a defined area in a given time period	$B \times$ mean frequency	There were 1.2 million visits to swimming-pools in area X (1 million by residents) in 2001	Visits	Number of visits to particular attractions or locations by tourists in a given time period	a. – b. $B(a) \times$ visits per trip	a. There were 50,000 tourist visits to theme-park X in 2001 b. Tourists from region Y made 300,000 visits in region X in 2001
D. Time	Time spent by an individual in a given area on a specific activity	$C \times$ time per visit	The average person spends 2.5 hours a day watching television	Visitor-nights	Number of visitors to a TDR multiplied by average length of stay in nights	$C \times$ length of stay (nights)	Tourists spent 3 million visitor-nights in region X in 2001
E. Expenditure	Amount of money spent per individual or by residents of a defined area on a leisure activity, activities, goods or services in a given time period	$C \times$ spending per visit	Consumer expenditure on leisure in Britain is £50 billion a year	Expenditure	Expenditure by tourists in a TDR in a given time period	$C \times$ expenditure per visit per head or $D \times$ expenditure per day per visitor	Tourists spent £50 million in region X in 2001

*In this table, the leisure measures are probably more appropriate for tourists who are day visitors.
†Frequency = number of engagements in a given time period, e.g. twice a week.
‡Engagement = one episode devoted to an activity, e.g. a visit to a facility, a game played.
TGR, tourist-generating region; TDR, tourist destination region.

economist's sense: the classic economist's demand curve shows a particular level of equilibrium consumption/demand at the point where the demand and supply curve intersect, as shown in Fig. 8.1. The demand curve extends to the right of this point, indicating that, if prices were lower, people would buy more.

In this classic economic model, latent, induced, diverted and substitute demand are not ignored – they all come into play when a shift occurs in the demand or supply curve. Thus existing demand increases if the supply curve moves downwards (there is an overall reduction in prices) or if it moves to the right (there is an increase in supply). Since a demand/supply curve for a particular leisure activity is only one of many which the consumer faces for the many products and services available (it is one element in the economist's general equilibrium system), diversion and substitution are built into the system (e.g. in the form of the economist's cross-elasticities).

As shown in using the Clawson method in Chapter 9 and in relation to various spatial planning techniques in Chapter 7, planning is very much about considering the extent to which these various forms of unmet demand might be transformed into actual demand in various supply scenarios.

Demand-change Factors

Factors likely to influence leisure and tourism demand are endless; some are easily measured and incorporated into forecasting models while others are difficult and sometimes impossible to measure. The extent to which various factors can be taken into account also varies with the geographical level at which any forecasting exercise might be undertaken. Certain trends are applicable and measurable at national level but at local level they may be inapplicable as there may simply be no locally based data. Further, at local level the considerable research resources required to fill data gaps may not be available. Even in such circumstances, however, an awareness of change factors and an informal, possibly qualitative, assessment of their likely impact can be valuable.

Eleven factors are considered below: (i) leisure and work time; (ii) demographic change; (iii) transport; (iv) income levels; (v) technological change; (vi) changing tastes and lifestyles; (vii) the activities of producers; (viii) the media; (ix) the environment; (x) changing attitudes and values; and (xi) postindustrialism, postmodernism and globalization. This is an indicative rather than an exhaustive list and a number of factors are interconnected and overlapping. They can each be discussed only briefly here, but a guide to further reading is given in each case.

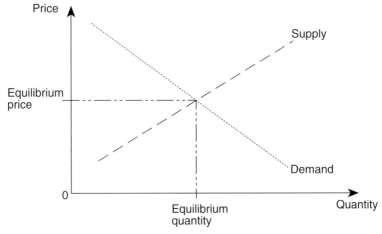

Fig. 8.1. Demand and supply.

Leisure and work time

Leisure time is often discussed as the complement of work time, so, although direct measurement of leisure time is only a recent phenomenon, it is generally accepted that leisure time has increased since the beginning of the 20th century, since annual working hours for full-time employees have fallen from over 3000 to less than 2000 (Veal, 2002), and the amount of domestic labour time needed to maintain the average home has also fallen. In the 1960s this process of work-time reduction was still in full swing in the developed economies, with the working week falling from 48 to 40 hours and holiday entitlements, at least in Europe, rising to 4 weeks a year in addition to public holidays. Thus, in a period of about 15 years, full-time working hours fell some 20%, from about 2300 a year to 1850.

In subsequent decades there was relatively little change in the work/leisure balance, indeed, in the early 1990s Juliet Schor (1991) observed that, in the USA in the 1970s and 1980s, there had been a reduction in leisure time, resulting in the emergence of the *Overworked American*. More recent research, based on direct measurement of leisure time rather than just working hours, confirms this pattern in some countries, but suggests contrary trends in others. For example, weekly leisure time in Holland was reported as falling by 4% for women and 10% for men between 1975 and 1995 (Peters, 2000: 88), but in Britain people in employment experienced an increase of 7% in leisure time between 1971 and 1996 (Martin and Mason, 1998: 143) and in Australia between 1974 and 1992 leisure time was static for men, but grew 12% for women (Bittman, 2000), although it appears to have fallen back by 5% for women by 1997 (Australian Bureau of Statistics, 1998). Thus it would seem that the amount of leisure time is changing more slowly than in the 1960s and is moving in different directions in different countries. Cross-national comparisons are, however, notoriously difficult to make and it is anticipated that moves to establish comparability through the multinational time-use study will make comparisons easier and more reliable in future (Gershuny, 2000).

From time to time there are claims that people in work are working longer hours, often unpaid, because of economic pressures. Such claims were made during the 1990s as Western economies experienced economic growth but in the context of technological and globalizing forces that threatened to take jobs off-shore to cheap-labour countries. Firms and individuals working for them felt threatened, resulting in pressure to work long hours to minimize costs and retain market share. Such terms as 'time squeeze' and 'time bind' were introduced to describe the result (Robinson, J.P., 1993; Hochschild, 1997). The extent to which this experience was felt in all parts of the economy and the extent to which it was a passing, cyclical, as opposed to long-term, phenomenon remain to be seen (Zuzanek and Veal, 1999).

Of particular importance in affecting trends in work and leisure time has been the increasing involvement of women in the paid workforce. Women in the paid workforce generally have less leisure time than men because they continue to carry the bulk of unpaid domestic work and child-care responsibilities. Thus increasing levels of female labour-force participation reduce the overall average amount of leisure time per person (Bittman and Wajcman, 1999; Gershuny, 2000) and this process is continuing.

Other changes affecting the work/leisure balance are the truncation of the working lifetime – at both ends. Increasing numbers of young people are involved in higher education in most economically developed countries, delaying entry into the workforce and the taking on of domestic responsibilities. At the other end of the working lifetime, there are increasing trends towards early retirement, again affecting the average per capita amount of available leisure time.

As unemployment grew in the Western economies during the period 1975–1995, as technology displaced labour across all sectors of developed economies, offering no alternative source of jobs, there was no shortage of commentators prepared to predict *The Collapse of Work* (Jenkins and Sherman, 1979), a *World out of Work* (Merritt, 1982), a *Jobless Future* (Aronowitz and DiFazio, 1994) or *The End of Work* (Rifkin,

1995). As unemployment fell during the late 1990s, particularly in the USA, the more cataclysmic of the predictions became rapidly outdated. But many still see an emerging crisis in work and employment in capitalist economies, due to the changing structure of the workforce brought about by technology, changing industrial management practices and the forces of globalization, as discussed below (Aronowitz *et al.*, 1998; Beck, 2000). In this scenario, there is a shift of routine manufacturing jobs to developing and newly industrialized countries and a squeeze on some of the service sectors, such as banking and the public sector generally, which have in the past absorbed substantial numbers of workers. This leaves the developed economies with the daunting task of finding sufficient high-technology, creative and service jobs in growth sectors to provide full employment. The USA and the UK appeared to have achieved this by the end of the 1990s, but whether this is sustainable and whether other developed economies will be able to emulate them remains to be seen. The future could therefore be characterized by a polarized labour force, with a favoured few working long hours in highly skilled, creative, highly paid jobs, enjoying high incomes but little leisure time, while many are unemployed or underemployed, with plenty of leisure time but low incomes and little security (what Beck, 2000, refers to as the 'Brazilianization' of the economy). This sort of polarization would clearly have implications for future patterns of leisure behaviour and for leisure markets.

Thus the phenomenon of increasing leisure time, while it may not have been transformed into *decreasing* leisure time for all, can certainly not be viewed as the certain engine of growth for leisure activity and expenditure that it was in the 1960s and 1970s.

Demographic change

In 1965 the projected population of the UK for the end of the 20th century was 77 million, an increase of 23 million, or 650,000 per year. This focused the attention of planners on the massive increase in demand for services which this additional population would generate – including housing, education and leisure services. The contraceptive pill and the increasing involvement of women in the paid workforce resulted in a marked reduction in the birth rate, such that by the mid-1980s the projected population for the year 2000 had fallen to 57 million – some 20 million less! Suddenly the urgency to predict and plan for large increases in demand was gone. In Britain and much of the Western world birth rates are now at less than replacement levels; in some countries overall population levels are falling, while in others they are maintained by the ageing of the population and immigration. Today, it is not the size of the population that is changing but its composition. The population of Britain is expected to grow from 58.2 to 61.8 million, or just 6%, between 2001 and 2021. Figure 8.2 indicates the projected dramatic changes in population age-groups, showing the effects of the movement of the baby-boomer generation (born between 1946 and the early 1960s) into the retirement phase.[1] The effects of this shift on leisure demand are explored later in the chapter.

A demographic change that has some implications for some leisure services and products is the declining size of the average household. Between 1971 and 1996 the average household size in Britain fell from 3.0 to 2.4 (National Statistics Office, 2001). This reflects the ageing of the population and women having fewer children at a later age. Thus, if the average household size were to fall to 2.0 over the next 20 years, while the population is expected to grow by 6% , the number of households would grow by more than a quarter. For those products which are sold to *households* rather than *individuals* – such as television sets, lawn-mowers and barbecues – sales would therefore grow faster than the overall population growth rate.

Income levels

It is not surprising to find that the level of income has a marked effect on patterns of leisure behaviour and consumption. Figure 8.3

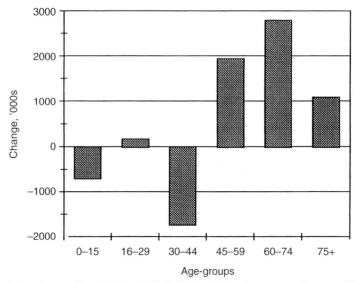

Fig. 8.2. Population change, Great Britain, 2001–2021 (based on Government Actuary, 2000: 50).

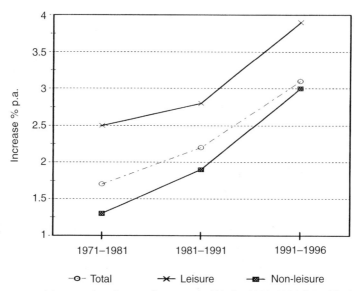

Fig. 8.3. Leisure, non-leisure and total expenditure trends, Britain, 1971–1991 (from Martin and Mason, 1998: 151).

shows how, in Britain during the period 1971–1996, the rate of growth of consumer expenditure on leisure was consistently higher than the rate of growth of total expenditure, while non-leisure expenditure grew more slowly. Thus any growth in incomes is likely to lead to more than pro-portionate growth in leisure expenditure. There is no direct relationship between increasing leisure expenditure and increasing levels of participation in leisure activities, since consumers can simply purchase better quality with higher expenditure (e.g. a larger television set), but it is likely that at least some of the increased expenditure facilitates increased participation.

Income is also important for any forecasting that seeks to take account of social inequality. For example, a recent comparison of per capita household expenditure of the top 20% and bottom 20% of households in Australia indicates that, while the top group spent 1.6 times as much as the bottom group on all household expenditure, they spent nine times as much on leisure items (Veal and Lynch, 2001: 138), suggesting that inequality is more pronounced in leisure than in other areas, but also indicating that, as incomes rise, an increasing proportion tends to be spent on leisure.

Thus any forecasting exercise over a period of time more than a year or two should take account of likely future changes in incomes and consumer spending.

Transport

Improvements in access to transport increase the range of options for leisure outside the home, resulting in increases in out-of-home leisure participation rates. This is true of access to public and private transport. In the 19th and early 20th century improvements in public transport, notably trains, resulted in a massive growth in travel for leisure. Later in the 20th century jet aircraft facilitated a similar surge in international leisure travel but the rapid spread of private car ownership transformed patterns of day-to-day leisure activity. While car ownership continues to grow, the relative rate of growth is much slower than it was in the 1950s and 1960s, as Fig. 8.4 illustrates.

Table 8.2 shows the level of car ownership in a range of countries in 1996. It indicates that the level of car ownership in the USA is one-third higher than that in Britain. Because of income and geographical factors, it seems unlikely that car ownership in Britain will ever reach the levels achieved in the USA, since public transport will probably continue to provide an acceptable service in urban areas. Despite a static population in Britain, car-ownership levels can rise as a result of second cars in multi-adult households, increases in the number of households, due to smaller household size, and more young singles and elderly people having cars, compared with previous generations. Many of these groups – particularly young singles and the elderly – are likely to use cars

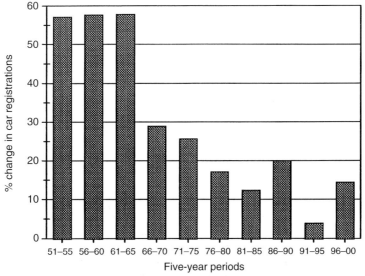

Fig. 8.4. Trends in car registrations, Great Britain, 1951–2000 (from Department of the Environment, Transport and the Regions web-site (www.detr.gov.uk) Transport Statistics Table 9.1, accessed March 2001).

Table 8.2. Car ownership, selected countries, 1996 (from Statesman's Yearbook, 2000).

	Number of cars (millions)	Cars per 1000 population
USA	138	520
Australia	8.6	480
Canada	13.6	472
Great Britain	21.2	390
Japan	48.6	390

substantially for leisure purposes, leading to increased out-of-home leisure activity. More cars mean more out-of-home leisure activity.

An increase in car ownership to, say, 450 cars per 1000 population would produce an additional 3 million cars in Britain. If each car facilitates just one recreational trip a week that would not otherwise be undertaken, the additional 3 million trips would clearly be significant for leisure facilities and services.

Technological change

Technological change is now endemic to the capitalist system, with billions of pounds being spent on research and development in industry, government and universities throughout the world. While relatively little of this research effort is explicitly aimed at leisure and tourism products, its effects do, as past experience has shown, inevitably have an impact on leisure. In the past, technology such as transistors and computers, lightweight materials, jet engines and satellites, often developed initially for military purposes, became the basis of significant leisure and tourism industries.

Many of the scientific and technological breakthroughs which will impinge on leisure and tourism in the future have already been made, but are still confined to laboratories and such television programmes as *'Beyond 2000'*. Technological forecasting is an art in itself, generally undertaken using the Delphi method, as discussed below (Halal, 2000). The art is to predict not just what items of technology will be invented or developed but which of them will successfully translate into products or services that people will want and at a price they will be prepared to pay. Thus tech-

nological forecasting is not just technological, but also social and economic. The 'top ten breakthroughs for the next decade' from the forecasts produced by the George Washington University exemplify this mix of technological and social features. The ten items, of which at least half can be seen as directly relevant to leisure, are as follows:

1. Portable information devices (the post-personal computer (PC) world).
2. Fuel-cell-powered automobiles.
3. Precision farming (computer-controlled to suit climatic conditions).
4. Mass customization (customers specifying product needs via the Internet).
5. Teleliving ('use of information devices and the Internet for shopping, working, learning, playing, healing, praying and conducting all aspects of life seamlessly').
6. Virtual assistants (customized control, filtering, managing of information flows).
7. Genetically altered organisms.
8. Computerized health care.
9. Alternate energy sources.
10. Smart, mobile robots (Halal, 2000).

We are currently living through a technological revolution, which may have considerable implications for leisure – namely the growth of new technologies based on computers, mobile telephones and broad-band broadcasting and 'narrowcasting'. In recent years, there have been press reports of some children forsaking the playground for the computer screen, with consequent implications for their physical fitness and socialization. For the majority, however, it would appear that computer games take their place alongside other attractions and may even be played at the expense of watching television. Overall, television-watching is such a pervasive leisure activity that any new activity is likely to be at the expense of television-watching. More leisure time spent in front of a computer screen rather than a television screen may represent a significant change in leisure behaviour, but not a revolutionary one. The computer may be more interactive than the television, but is likely to be more solitary, involving less social interaction. For leisure-services providers outside the home, the effect is minimal.

New products, whether technological or cultural in origin, are not adopted instantaneously by consumers: they are subject to a product life cycle. The product life cycle is a marketing term referring to the way products are taken up by innovative consumers, achieve a period of sales growth and then go into decline. Here it is used in a modified form, focusing on the proportion of households or individuals who own the product. As illustrated in Fig. 8.5, ownership of new products often develops slowly when they are untried and expensive. Often there is then a period of rapid growth, followed by a peak, or saturation level. This process takes several years. From the point of view of the producers of consumer products, reaching the peak presents a problem since sales are then primarily for replacement purposes only, and this will represent a dramatic slowdown in sales unless the product can be rejuvenated in some way. Given the pace of technological change and the efforts of designers, it would seem that persuading consumers that they should replace technologically-based goods for a newer, superior product has become routine, as any owner of a personal computer will know to his/her cost! In the 1960s this process was

sometimes referred to as built-in obsolescence – a phenomenon, particularly related to cars, where quality and surface design changes were apparently manipulated to persuade people to replace vehicles unnecessarily. While this practice is no doubt still a factor, genuine technical improvements to products over, say, a 5-year period now seems common.

From a leisure-behaviour point of view, however, the decline in product sales does not necessarily represent a decline in participation in the associated leisure activity. For example, in the case of television-set manufacture, the rapid growth phase, as sets were purchased by households for the first time, took place in the 1950s and 1960s; the product was then given a second lease of life by the introduction of colour television in the 1970s. But, once virtually all households were equipped with colour sets, sales fell because only replacement sets and the slow growth of two-set households produced sales – hence, in part, the decline of the British television-set manufacturing industry from the late 1970s. But the associated leisure activity television-watching, while it would have followed the same growth and peak, did not experience the

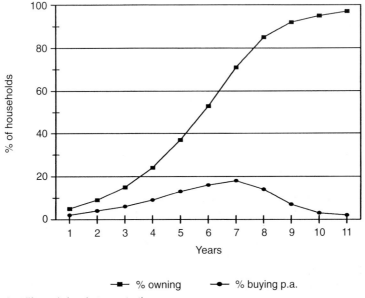

Fig. 8.5. Product life cycle/market penetration.

same subsequent decline. A similar pattern would have been seen with the subsequent introduction of video-cassette recorders – the sale of equipment goes into decline once saturation ownership is achieved, but the leisure activity and any services associated with it, such as television-show production or video hire, carry on. Indeed, the associated leisure activity and services associated with it develop a product life cycle of their own – for example, the growth of television channels and changes in viewing habits over the years.

For forecasting, therefore, the product life cycle and the associated patterns of participation are of interest. For some products the life cycle can be very short, but for others, for years after a product has been introduced and even after it has passed its very rapid growth phase, there may be significant growth still feeding through the system and consequent leisure-participation patterns to be plotted and predicted.

Over and above the purely technical questions are broader issues about whether the introduction of new technologies is demand-driven or supply-driven. As Richard Rhodes puts it: 'As methodologies, science and technology are demonstrably objective and effective; but they're unquestionably bound up with power relations as social systems' (Rhodes, 1999: 24). As discussed below, the question arises as to whether the producers determine what happens or the consumers.

The activities of producers

The activities of leisure and tourism service and product providers and the issues to which they give rise have already been discussed in relation to technological change and changing tastes, particularly in relation to the activities of the private sector. Thus the future is, to some extent, determined by the activities of producers of goods and services: how they decide to research, to invest, to produce and to market. This is true not only of the private sector but also of the public sector. For example, publicly funded campaigns, such as 'Sport for All' in Britain

(McIntosh and Charlton, 1985) and 'Life. Be in it' in Australia (Watkins, 1981), are designed to influence people's behaviour – in so far as they are successful they influence the future. In Britain in the last 30 years of the 20th century, some 2500 indoor leisure centres were built by the public sector: if they had not been built in the way that they were, from public funds, it is most unlikely that they would have been built on anything like that scale with private or voluntary resources. Therefore the millions of sporting and other leisure activities which they now accommodate each year would not have happened. The building activities of public providers determined the future.

This is not to say that providers act without constraint: campaigns and products fail. There are three groups involved in making decisions about future patterns of leisure behaviour and demand: the industry itself, the consumers and the people in between – the media, communicators, critics, culture brokers – an independent force, with an arguably significant influence in determining the 'latest thing'. Just how consumer taste arises is a matter of some sociological debate (Tomlinson, 1990; Featherstone, 1991): while some products and designs may be foisted on to a gullible public, successful products and designs are, it can be argued, those which strike a chord with the public, reflect the mood of the buying public and meet their – often psychic – needs. Complex though this scenario is, it needs to be taken into account in any forecasting exercise.

The environment

The growth of the population and its leisure needs and the growth of international tourism both pose threats to the natural environment. The drive for development and growth places increasing pressure on already degraded resources. The short-term and long-term effects of these pressures are well known and have long been debated (e.g. Ehrlich and Ehrlich, 1990). Governments have responded with a variety of policies and measures, from tree-planting to new sewerage systems to the designation of new national parks and declarations of commitment to sustainable development – that is, development which 'meets the needs of the present without compromising the ability of future generations to meet their own needs' (World Commission on Environment and Development, 1990). While this connection is obvious for noxious industries, it has been less obvious for innocent activities like leisure and tourism. But golf-courses require water, many feet compact soil in natural areas and cause runoff and erosion; hotels and resorts generate sewage and litter; and all these activities take land which may be the habitat of other creatures. The future of leisure and tourism will partly depend on society coming to terms with these impacts and finding ways of ameliorating their worst effects. The question is whether human organizations, including leisure and tourism organizations, will respond by modifying their practices to achieve sustainability, or whether some sort of crisis will develop, leading to restrictions on activities.

These questions are particularly relevant to tourism. Local leisure demand is generally increasing but, in recent years, tourism has been the major leisure growth sector, and this can be expected to continue over the coming decade. The World Tourism Organization predicted that international tourist arrivals in Europe will grow by a third, or 125 million, in the 10 years between 2000 and 2010 (World Tourism Organization, 2001). This will clearly have a significant effect on the leisure industries, since tourists eat meals in restaurants and visit parks and beaches, museums and galleries, casinos and other attractions.

This additional demand has an economic impact on the providers of leisure services in tourist areas which is generally seen as positive, but it could also make public spaces, such as urban parks and national parks, beaches, streets and shopping areas, overcrowded, particularly at peak periods. In some urban areas the effects may be insignificant or at least manageable by means of pedestrian and vehicle traffic controls – additional people can even give some urban areas an additional 'buzz' which adds to their attraction – but in some,

such as central London, tourism levels may reach saturation level, presenting challenges for city planners and managers. In many natural areas, increased visitor numbers are already presenting challenges to managers with conservation responsibilities, especially as the phenomenon of ecotourism increases in popularity.

Changing tastes and lifestyles

Tastes are the most difficult of all the factors to predict (Bikhchandani *et al.*, 1992) and few forecasting exercises attempt to do so. Some changes are long-term, while others are short-term fads. In some industries, such as fashion, regular changes in taste are institutionalized – led by the industry. Young people in particular seem to be susceptible to short-term fads or crazes – for example, for skateboards or in-line skating (Davidson, 1985) – partly because very often any activity or product would be new to them when passing through a certain age-range and there is no reason why they should adopt an established activity or product any more than a new one.

Since fads, fashions and crazes are, by definition, fickle, it is almost impossible to predict them, although they also tend to have product life cycles like consumer goods, often extending over a number of years. But longer-term change in taste patterns may be mapped, monitored and even predicted.

It might be thought that consumer taste and fashion are a private-sector concern and therefore of little interest to the public sector. However, the private and public sectors are competing for the public's time and, to some extent, their money. The public sector has a range of products which it wishes the public to consume. Admittedly, in many cases the public-sector product has its own unique image and competition with the private sector is not an issue – for example the traditional urban park. In other instances, for example, leisure services for young people – the private sector tends to set the pace and the public sector must adapt accordingly if it is to stay competitive.

Changing attitudes and values

More fundamental than changing tastes and lifestyles, although connected, is the idea of changing attitudes and values. Various commentators have argued that coping with the changing economic, technological and social environment will require significant changes in social attitudes.

In the 1920s, in a famous essay entitled 'In Praise of Idleness', the philosopher Bertrand Russell argued:

> If every man and woman worked for four hours a day at necessary work, we could all have enough ... it should be the remaining hours that would be regarded as important – hours which could be devoted to enjoyment of art or study, to affection and woodland and sunshine in green fields ... Man's true life does not consist in the business of filling his belly and clothing his body, but in art and thought and love, in the creation and contemplation of beauty and in the scientific understanding of the world.
>
> (Russell and Russell, 1923: 50)

In the 1930s, John Maynard Keynes, whose economic theories provided the basis for the post-Second World War economic growth, anticipated the effects of technology and growing productivity and wealth, suggesting that the main challenge facing future societies would not be economic survival, but what to do with the resultant increase in free time:

> If the economic problem is solved mankind will be deprived of its traditional purpose ... I think with dread of the readjustments of the habits and instincts of the ordinary man, bred into him for countless generations, which he may be asked to discard within a few decades ... there is no country and no people, I think, who can look forward to the age of leisure and abundance without dread. For we have been trained too long to strive and not to enjoy.
>
> (Keynes, 1931: 328)

The idea of the Protestant work ethic is, it has been argued, deep-seated in Western culture. The German sociologist Max Weber made the connection between Protestant teaching and the development of industrial capitalism, summarizing the Puritan, Protestant view as follows:

> Not leisure and enjoyment, but only activity serves to increase the glory of God ... Waste of time is thus the first and in principle the deadliest of sins. Loss of time through sociability, idle talk, luxury, even more sleep than is necessary for health ... is worthy of absolute moral condemnation.
>
> (Weber, 1930: 157)

The extent to which the work ethic has been internalized among the mass of the populations of Western countries is debatable, but numerous commentators are sufficiently convinced that it is to call for major attitude changes to cope with the future. In the past commentators have called for the development of alternatives to the work ethic, including a 'life ethic' (Clemitson and Rodgers, 1981: 13), a 'contribution ethic' (Clarke, 1982: 196), a 'non-work ethic' (Ritchie-Calder, 1982: 16) and a 'leisure ethic' (Argyle, 1996: 282). The call for changed values was also reflected in the manifesto of French Marxist sociologist André Gorz (1980a), who urged the working class to liberate themselves from the burden of wage labour, a call he reiterated in the 1990s (Gorz, 1999). But Marxist Ed Andrew (1981: 180) declared that: 'Any demand for a change in values, whether a return to a work ethic or an advance to a socially involved leisure ethic ... is, for the Marxist, just empty chatter.'

There is, however, little evidence of significant changes in attitudes towards work having taken place in the 20 years since these calls were made. More recently, Juliet Schor (1991: 164) proposed that Americans should break the 'insidious cycle of work-and-spend', arguing that: 'There will be more leisure only when people become convinced that they must have it.' Aronowitz *et al.* (1998) have proposed a 'Post-work Manifesto' and British forecasters Bill Martin and Sandra Mason have called for 'the emergence of new attitudes to paid work and free time', but note that this will be difficult because 'the structure of work time is something that is ingrained in daily life' (Martin and Mason, 1998: 108). While these calls attract media attention from time to time, there is little sign of them having an impact on Western politics or culture, but it is nevertheless advisable for the forecaster to keep a watching brief on this issue.

The media

The modern mass-communication media, particularly television, dominate modern leisure, but are frequently ignored in leisure forecasting – perhaps because they largely relate to home-based leisure. Cinema and radio invaded people's leisure in the 1920s and 1930s but, as with changes in leisure time and the growth of car ownership discussed above, television emerged as a major force in the 1960s and subsequently became far and away the major leisure activity of the majority of people. What changes in this phenomenon will affect leisure behaviour in future? The average individual already spends 2 or more hours a day watching television and it seems unlikely that there is scope for this to increase significantly. Increases in multiple television sets within the home, the proliferation of available channels, delivered by a variety of technologies, and the convergence of television with Internet-linked technologies are all likely to have some effect on viewing habits and will no doubt result in higher levels of expenditure on niche-market products, but, in terms of broad patterns of leisure behaviour, the effects are unlikely to be major.

Postindustrialism, postmodernism and globalization

The industrial revolution in Europe in the 18th and 19th centuries ushered in the industrial era, with its unprecedented levels of economic growth and development. From around the 1970s a number of commentators began to suggest that the economically developed part of the world was entering a *postindustrial* era, in view of the decline in the importance of manufacturing in highly developed economies and the growth in the importance of services, particularly in such areas as information technology, leisure and tourism (Bell, 1974; Jones, 1995), although some argue that the observed changes are merely a further stage in the development of the industrial era (Veal, 1987: 46–62; Kumar, 1995). Whether the economic and industrial changes that have taken place over the last 25 years, and are still taking place, represent a new type of economy or merely a new stage in the development of industrial economies, they are certainly highly significant. In particular, they are significant in moving more and more economic activity into the services sector. Typically in developed economies, less than 5% of the workforce is engaged in primary industries (agriculture, mining) and less than 20% in manufacturing, leaving over 70% in services. Within the services sector, leisure and tourism are becoming increasingly significant, as the expenditure trends discussed under 'Income levels' above indicate.

In cultural terms, the 19th century and much of the 20th century have been seen as the culmination of the modern era, characterized in particular by the increasing secularization and rationalization of the Western world and the associated ideas of continuous technical, economic and social progress. *Postmodernism* implies the end of the modernist era. The idea of a postmodern era has particular implications for the cultural world and is clearly seen in areas such as architecture and literature, where the notions of progress and a hierarchy of excellence have been challenged. Further, postmodernism suggests that cultural phenomena, such as fashion, popular music, mass-communications media, advertising and individual consumption, now determine the fundamental nature of society, rather than simply reflecting underlying economic, production-based relationships (Tomlinson, 1990; Featherstone, 1991; Docker, 1994; Rojek, 1995: 129–145).

Linked with these ideas is the concept of *globalization*, a concept discussed in Chapters 3 and 4 in relation to the role of the state. Here we consider the phenomenon as a force for change affecting the future. Anthony Giddens identifies four defining features of globalization: (i) the worldwide communications revolution; (ii) the growth of the weightless economy or the knowledge economy – financial markets being the most important, but including services such as entertainment, tourism and sport; (iii) the collapse of the Soviet Union and its Communist allies, leading to an unchallenged worldwide capitalist system; and (iv) social change – for example, the growing equality between men and women (Giddens and Hutton, 2000: 1–2). One feature of globalization that is not captured by these four dimensions is the role of the multinational firm or transnational corporation (Gratton, 1996). While many of these organizations, such as AOL-Time-Warner and News Limited, are involved with the first of Giddens's features, the communications revolution, others are involved in traditional activities like manufacturing and are centrally involved in the shift of such activities from the developed countries to the developing or newly industrialized countries. Further, many of these companies – Nike being the most notable – are part of the leisure-industry sector. A related theme is that, because of the activities and the financial muscle of such companies, as well as the activities of stock and currency markets, there is a loss of sovereignty of the nation state, an issue discussed in Chapter 4.

These developments are clearly relevant to any consideration of the future of leisure and can be related to developments in such areas as: the organization of work and leisure; developments in urban leisure and tourism, such as the growth of theme parks and leisure/retail complexes; changes in electronic home entertainment; and the growing economic and cultural significance of events such as major sporting events and film and arts festivals.

Forecasting Techniques

Most leisure-demand forecasting exercises, as reported in the literature, have been carried out at the national level (e.g. Kelly, 1987; Veal, 1991b; Martin and Mason, 1998). This is perhaps curious considering that, as far as the public sector is concerned, the major providers of leisure facilities and services are local authorities. Part of the explanation for the lack of forecasting activity at local level may be that the data requirements of leisure-demand forecasting and the perceived complexity of many of the techniques used may have suggested that forecasting at local level was not possible. However, as this chapter indicates, most techniques are usable at any level of government and, if transport and shopping demand can be forecast at local or subregional level, then so can leisure. A further reason for the lack of forecasting activity at local level would, however, appear to be related to the leisure planning and policy-making process, which, as discussed in Chapter 5, has not generally faced up to the idea of demand or participation, either in the present or in the future.

Some of the factors reviewed above remain resistant to systematic forecasting techniques, but they must be borne in mind nevertheless. There are, however, many influences on the future of leisure that can be addressed in a more or less systematic manner and the techniques available for such a task are outlined below. They fall into nine groups: (i) informed speculation; (ii) asking the public; (iii) asking the experts (the Delphi technique); (iv) scenario writing; (v) time series analysis; (vi) spatial models; (vii) cross-sectional analysis; (viii) comparative analysis; and (ix) composite methods.

Techniques are often divided into qualitative and quantitative groups, with informed speculation, the Delphi method, scenario writing and comparative analysis being seen a qualitative, asking the public and composite methods as both quantitative and qualitative and the rest quantitative. While it is true that the techniques indicated can handle qualitative data, they are also capable of including quantitative data, and many of the quantitative techniques can take account of non-quantitative data, often using dummy variables. The quantitative/qualitative divide is therefore more complex than most reviews suggest.

Each of these techniques is examined in turn below and a summary of their main features is provided at the end of the chapter in Table 8.3.

Informed speculation

We have already noted the 1920s and 1930s speculations of Bertrand Russell and John Maynard Keynes on the social implications of economic growth. Even more speculatively, some 25 years ago Isaac Asimov

(1976), the science-fiction writer, published an essay entitled 'Future Fun', in which he considered the potential of such things as space travel for leisure purposes. Many essays and concluding chapters of leisure texts consist of speculation about the how the future of leisure will or should be. For example, Roberts (1999: 222) offers the view that 'leisure during the next 20 years is most likely to be much the same as leisure in the 1980s and 1990s'. Godbey (1989, 1997) has published whole books that serve the same purpose; while being concerned with the future, they do not present forecasts as such, but a broad overview of current and future social trends and the impact they might have on leisure and leisure services. In some cases, such speculation is published in statements arising from conferences or workshops, an informal version of the Delphi technique discussed below (see Kraus, 1998: 397–399, for a synopsis of examples of these).

Such speculations are not necessarily based on any specific techniques or analysis, but represent a distillation of the thoughts and impressions of the authors. Their value therefore arises from the wisdom and experience of the writer. Often they are not intended to present forecasts or predictions as such, but to open up issues for thought and discussion. There is no specific methodology to be described for these exercises, but their value is often substantial, since they represent the product of considered thought. They are therefore an invaluable element of the leisure-forecasting literature.

Asking the public

Some leisure-participation surveys go beyond asking what people currently do in their leisure time and ask what they would like to do or are planning to do in future or would like to do in the absence of constraints. This sort of question is often designed to assess expressed needs or demands, but they can also be seen as indicators of future behaviour patterns. Responses to such questions cannot be relied on as even approximate indicators of the scale of future demand since they often reflect wishful thinking which may never be acted upon. But they can be seen as indicators of sentiment, of what people may be drawn to do in favourable conditions, of what the popular and unpopular activities currently are. For example, a survey of leisure participation in Australia found that, among men, 7% had wanted to play golf but had not done so in the survey period and a similar proportion had wanted to go fishing; for women the two activities most commonly not done were tennis (5%) and aerobics (5%) (DASETT, 1991). In every case the most common reason for not participating was lack of time. Such information provides useful market data and can in some circumstances be indicators of possible future trends in behaviour. In so far as the information is acted upon by providers, the popular activities are facilitated by the provision of venues and services, and people's aspirations become self-fulfilling prophesies.

The 'asking the people' approach is used in a systematic way in short-term economic forecasting, where regular surveys of business and consumer confidence or sentiment are undertaken and the results used as leading indicators of likely changes in business investment or consumer demand. Examples are the Michigan University Consumer Sentiment Index and the Australian Westpac Melbourne Institute Consumer Sentiment Index. Research on the track records of such indices suggests that they can predict actual business and consumer behaviour (Bram and Ludvigson, 1998).

Asking the experts – the Delphi technique

The Delphi technique exploits the fact that experts of various sorts are likely to have particular insights into future developments in their field of expertise. The term Delphi relates to the Delphic oracle of ancient Greece, a priestly entity who, in return for petitioning and often generous payment, could be persuaded to foretell people's future fortunes – often expressed in a cryptic manner.

The modern Delphi technique involves asking a panel of experts to express their views of the future and distilling this information into a forecast or forecasts. The number of experts involved could be as few as a dozen or so, or could number several hundred; they can be assembled in one place, as at a conference (e.g. Seeley *et al.*, 1980; Jones, S., 1990) or, more commonly, they can be contacted by mail. In a questionnaire, the experts are asked a series of questions, which can be in various forms, for example:

• What are the major changes you expect to see in your field of expertise over the next 5/10/20/etc. years?
• When, if ever, do you expect the following events to take place?
• What is the likelihood of each of the following events happening in the next 5/10/20/etc. years?

The first question format produces responses in the form of lists of events and the number of times they are mentioned by members of the panel. The second produces a range of dates and a mean or median date. The third produces a range of probabilities and a mean or median score.

The technique involves a number of rounds of questioning. The first question format could be used in the first round to establish a list of possible events. Alternatively, if a list of events of interest is already available, the first round would use the second or third question format. Subsequent rounds use the second or third format. In the early rounds it could be expected that a range of experts is likely to produce a wide range of differing opinions. The technique involves the collation of the responses into lists of events (format 1) and ranges and means of years (format 2) or probabilities (format 3) and feeding this information back to the panel of experts for subsequent rounds. In the subsequent rounds the panel members are asked the same questions, but they have available the collated views of their colleagues from the previous round. The panel members are then invited to revise their opinions, if they wish, in the light of this information. The process is repeated for as many rounds as necessary to produce a stable situation –

that is, where panel members are no longer changing their views. In practice the number of rounds may be limited by available time and resources and by a desire not to lose panel members through non-response. The collated views of the panel from the final round then provide the basis of the forecast.

One of the earliest uses of the technique in the leisure area was by Shafer *et al.* (1975), who asked a panel of 400 American recreation professionals and academics to indicate the most significant future events likely to take place in the area of outdoor recreation. Among those predicted were:

• By 1985: Most people work a 4-day, 32-hour week.
• By 1990: US census of population includes questions on recreation. Most homes have video-tape systems.
• By 2000: Small recreational submarines common.
           Average age of retirement 50 years.
• 2050+:   First park established on the moon.
           Average worker has 3-month annual vacation.

Clearly the experts do not always get it right! However, much of the value of the technique could be said to lie in its ability to open up debate and promote thought, rather than in the precise accuracy of its predictions.

In some cases a quasi-Delphi method is employed in forecasting, involving informal consultation with experts, but not involving the scaling of responses and rounds of consultation discussed above. An example is the World Tourism Organization Business Council (1999) international study of *Changes in Leisure Time: the Impact on Tourism*.

Scenario writing

Scenario writing is a technique that involves the devising of alternative pictures of the future as characterized by alternative values of key variables and the relationships between them.

The initial task in drawing up scenarios is to decide the key variables to be used to characterize the future. For example, a simple approach for an exercise at national level might select politics and the level of unemployment as two key variables. Alternative political scenarios for a country for the year 2010 might envisage either a right-wing conservative government or a left/centrist social democratic government. And there could be high unemployment or low unemployment. These two dimensions offer four alternative scenarios, as indicated in Fig. 8.6. Scenario A, with high unemployment and a conservative government, could be characterized by low public-sector spending and minimal unemployment benefits, whereas scenario B, with a leftist government, might be characterized by higher government spending and more generous unemployment allowances, but possibly more economic crises as government attempted to solve the unemployment problem by spending money. Scenario C would be characterized by a prosperous private-enterprise culture with low taxes and low government spending, whereas scenario D would probably involve a more substantial role for public enterprise with higher taxes and government spending.

Once the general social and economic implications of the scenarios had been worked out, any more detailed forecasting of leisure or tourism demand would now be undertaken in the context of the scenarios, so that four sets of alternative forecasts would be produced instead of one. The commissioning agency would then be aware of the range of possible demand scenarios, depending on future political and unemployment outcomes. The detailed forecasts might use any of the other techniques discussed in this chapter.

The development of scenarios need not be restricted to two variables and two dimensions. For example, a third variable could be introduced into the above scenario, such as growth in leisure time, which might be proposed as zero, moderate or substantial. The resultant 12 scenarios would then be as shown in Fig. 8.7. It would become unmanageable to produce 12 sets of forecasts, so in practice just a selection of scenarios would be chosen for more detailed study, representing the widest range of possibilities and/or those considered to be most likely. Thus, for example, in Fig. 8.7, only the scenarios in bold might be selected for detailed study.

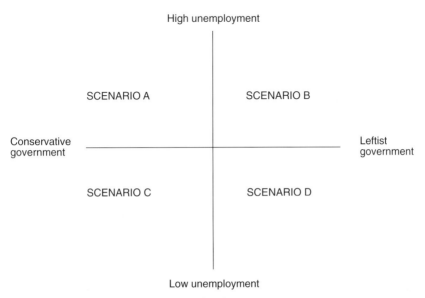

Fig. 8.6. Scenarios for the year 2010: two-dimensional.

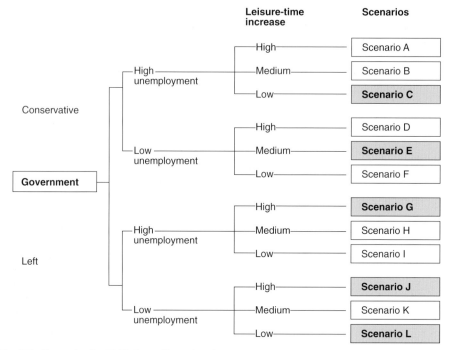

Fig. 8.7. Scenarios for 2010: three-dimensional.

In the case of inbound international tourism it would, of course, be necessary to develop either international scenarios or a series of scenarios for the markets from which tourists were generated.

An early example of the use of scenarios with leisure implications was produced by Miles *et al.* (1978) in their *World Futures* study. More recently Martin and Mason (1998: 89) have developed their forecasting work on leisure in Britain on the basis of four scenarios, based on the dimensions of economic growth (high/low) and social attitudes (conventional/ transformed). They select two scenarios for detailed work: 'conventional success', which involves continuing current trends, and 'transformed growth', which is a less materialistic and more sustainable course.

Time-series analysis

Time-series analysis is the most commonly used technique in tourism forecasting. It is a quantitative technique in which the future is predicted on the basis of past or current trends in the phenomenon being studied. A prerequisite of the technique is the availability of data extending over a substantial time period. The technique is therefore most well developed in the area of international tourism because information on tourist arrivals and departures is available extending back over many years. This cannot be said of other forms of leisure activity.

Time-series analysis has become very sophisticated, involving complex mathematical formulae and specialist computer software. The Further Reading indicates sources for such techniques, but, in the discussion below, quite simple approaches are presented to illustrate the underlying principles. The more sophisticated methods are appropriate when good data are available and the processes driving changes in demand are well understood; if these conditions are not met, then some of the simpler methods might be used to provide ballpark forecasts.

At its simplest the technique can be seen as the visual extension of a trend line, as shown in Fig. 8.8. The diagram uses data on gambling expenditure in Australia, for which there is an annual data series extending back to 1973. The lines extending from the year 2000 to 2010 are simply freehand extensions of the 1973–1999 line. The existence of two lines illustrates the limitations of the method. Projection A extends the trend of the 1990s, while projection B attempts to reflect the longer-term trend. The difference in the projected level of expenditure for the year 2010 is substantial. In fact the 1990s were an exceptional period, with casinos and gaming machines being licensed for the first time in most of the states of Australia, giving a boost to gambling that is unlikely to be repeated, so projection B is the more plausible.

A more sophisticated approach would be to fit a line mathematically, by means of regression techniques, so that a formula could be used to produce the forecast, as shown in Fig. 8.9. In this instance the regression line, shown as a dotted line in the diagram, can be represented by the equation:

$$Y = -21418.4 + 317.01X$$

where Y is the level of expenditure and X refers to the time period. Thus:

Expenditure (\$ million) = −21418.4 + 317.01 × time period.

A forecast of expenditure for the year 2010 is:

−21418.4 + 317.01X 3.15 × 2010 = \$13,451 million

In fact, visual examination of Fig. 8.9 indicates that the regression line is not a very good fit to the original data, which is a curved line. Regression techniques exist to fit a curved line, as shown in Fig. 8.10. However, although this is a better statistical fit to the data, in light of the events during the 1990s, as discussed above, it does not necessarily produce a better forecast.

Tourism and many outdoor leisure activities are often seasonal in nature, as indicated by the actual line in Fig. 8.11. The trend line is established by means of a moving average, calculated as shown in Table 8.3. The figure in columns 3 and 6 is the average of the preceding four quarterly figures and produces a trend line that can be used for forecasting purposes, as shown in Fig. 8.11. More sophisticated approaches study the pattern of seasonal variation and smooth the line by including seasonal adjustments.

In the case of tourism it has been found

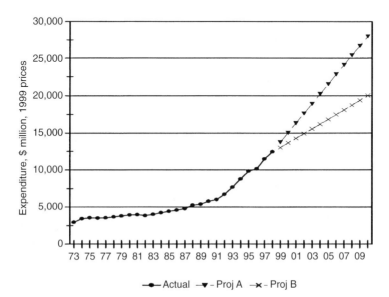

Fig. 8.8. Simple trend analysis: gambling expenditure in Australia (1973–1999 data from Tasmanian Gaming Commission, 2000).

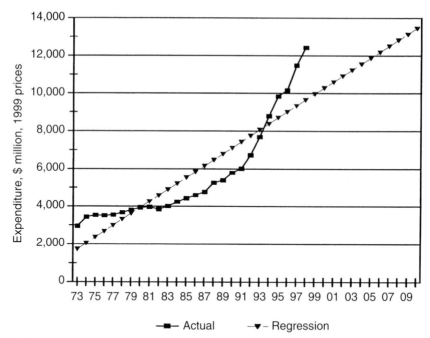

Fig. 8.9. Linear regression: gambling expenditure trends in Australia (1973–1999 data from Tasmanian Gaming Commission, 2000).

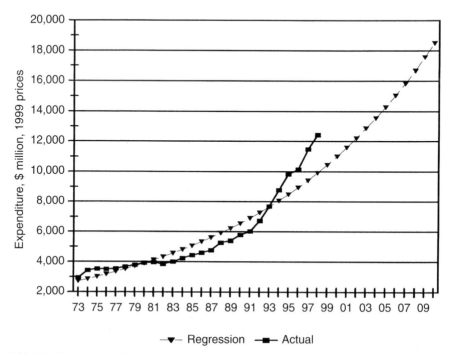

Fig. 8.10. Non-linear regression: gambling expenditure trends in Australia (1973–1999 data from Tasmanian Gaming Commission, 2000).

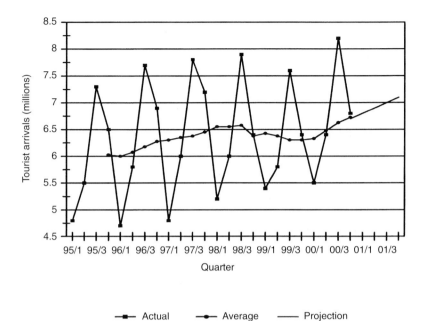

Fig. 8.11. Moving average (hypothetical data).

Table 8.3. Moving average (hypothetical data).

Year/ Quarter	Tourist arrivals (millions)	Moving average	Year/ quarter	Tourist arrivals (millions)	Moving average
1995/1	4.8		1998/1	5.2	6.6
1995/2	5.5		1998/2	6.0	6.6
1995/3	7.3		1998/3	7.9	6.6
1995/4	6.5	6.0	1998/4	6.4	6.4
1996/1	4.7	6.0	1999/1	5.4	6.4
1996/2	5.8	6.1	1999/2	5.8	6.4
1996/3	7.7	6.2	1999/3	7.6	6.3
1996/4	6.9	6.3	1999/4	6.4	6.3
1997/1	4.8	6.3	2000/1	5.5	6.3
1997/2	6.0	6.4	2000/2	6.4	6.5
1997/3	7.8	6.4	2000/3	8.2	6.6
1997/4	7.2	6.5	2000/4	6.8	6.7

that the best predictor of tourist numbers over the short term is the last available figure, so that the forecast of tourist arrivals in year X is based on an equation involving the number of arrivals in year $X - 1$. It is possible to build equations that simulate such cycles, by taking account not just of the previous year's figure, but, say, the previous 10 years' figures. Sophisticated modelling techniques, such as the autoregressive integrated moving average (ARIMA) technique, have

been developed to capture these trends, in both annual and more frequent time-series, such as quarterly and monthly arrivals, and to produce forecasts based on them. These techniques are described by Athiyaman and Robertson (1992), Witt and Witt (1992), Archer (1994), and Frechtling (1996) and computer packages are available – for example, within the Statistical Package for the Social Sciences (SPSS) – to carry them out.

An alternative time-series approach is to

explore the possibility that the past trend in demand is related to some underlying factor, such as trends in real incomes, prices or exchange rates. Such a model is referred to as *structural*, because it reflects an understanding of the underlying structure of relationships between the phenomenon and causal factors. For example, the hypothetical data in Fig. 8.12 show a demand trend following the trend in real incomes, but lagged by a couple of years. An equation could be developed with income as the independent variable and leisure or tourism demand as the dependent variable, and forecasts of demand based on forecasts of real income. The technique therefore requires access to time-series data and forecasts for the independent variable. In fact, such a structural model need not be restricted to a single independent variable. Crouch and Shaw (1991), for example, review a wide range of international tourism forecasting studies, involving as many as 25 different structural variables.

Spatial models

The idea of spatial models of leisure demand is explored as a planning technique in Chapter 7 and in the Clawson technique of cost–benefit analysis outlined in Chapter 9. These techniques rely on the observed fact that, where specific facilities or attractions are involved, patterns of leisure or tourism demand are influenced by the locations of those facilities or attractions. These patterns are not random but are often sufficiently systematic to provide the basis for prediction. It has been observed in a wide range of facilities and attractions that the further people live from the facility or attraction, the less likely they are to visit it. Visitation falls off with increased distance, either because of the additional cost and effort in travelling or because of leisure-time availability compared with the time needed to undertake the visit and associated travel.

In Fig. 8.13, the location of a hypothetical leisure or tourism facility is indicated by the letter X; the rings might be at kilometre inter-

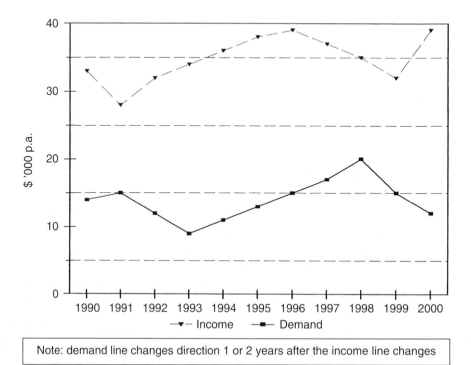

Note: demand line changes direction 1 or 2 years after the income line changes

Fig. 8.12. Structural trend line (lagged).

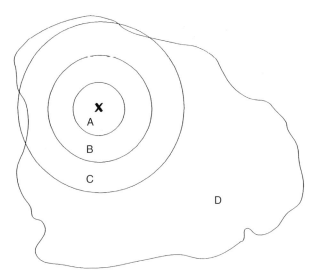

Fig. 8.13. Hypothetical facility/attraction catchment area.

vals in the case of an urban leisure facility, at perhaps 10 km intervals for a countryside recreation facility and at 100 or more kilometres in the case of a tourist attraction such as a ski resort. Area A is likely to have the highest level of visits as a proportion of the population, followed by areas B and C, and then D. For some types of facility this phenomenon is not marked, or the effect is only apparent over quite substantial distances – for example, live theatre, where people generally expect to have to travel long distances. In other cases, such as swimming-pools or libraries, the effect can be quite marked, over comparatively short distances.

These patterns are relevant to forecasting because the *future* patterns of demand will be affected by:

- changes in the population distribution within the catchment area;
- changes in transport infrastructure (for example, new roads that make travel to the site cheaper and/or faster);
- provision of additional facilities in the study area.

The process of quantifying the potential demand under different scenarios is a special case of a transportation modelling exercise and is examined in Chapter 7 in relation to spatial planning methods. The Clawson

method, as outlined in Chapter 9, is a method for relating such distance-related patterns of demand to economic factors, namely the cost of travelling to the site. The Clawson method is used primarily for cost–benefit analysis, but can also be used for predicting the impact of new facilities or transport infrastructure or the effect of price rises.

Recent published examples of the use of spatial methods are rare, although they are often used in feasibility studies for new facilities. Early pioneering examples of the approach include Coppock and Duffield (1975) in relation to countryside recreation in Scotland and Milstein and Reid (1966) in relation to outdoor recreation in the USA.

Cross-sectional analysis

The cross-sectional technique is based on analysis of the variation in leisure participation within – or across – the community and is used particularly when time-series data are not available. Cross-sectional analysis can be based on a single survey. Participation in most leisure activities is known to vary according to certain factors, such as age, occupation, level of education and income. As the structure of the population changes with regard to these underlying factors or variables (for example, the ageing of the population or increasing levels of education and professionalization), so, it might be expected, will leisure participation. The method therefore relies on forecasts of the underlying variables being available from other sources. Such sources include government agencies, which produce, for example, demographic forecasts and short-term economic forecasts, academic and independent research organizations and, possibly, Delphi and scenario-drawing exercises.

Two approaches can be used in cross-sectional analysis: (i) the cohort method; and (ii) regression-based techniques. These are discussed in turn below.

Cohort method

The cohort method can best be demonstrated by an example, as shown in Table 8.4. The table gives data from a hypothetical community, in which surveys show activity X is participated in primarily by young people (column A). Applying the survey participation rates to current age cohorts of the population (column B) gives an estimate of the current total numbers of participants in the community by age-group (column C). Applying the same participation rates to a population forecast, in this case for the year 2011 (column D), gives an estimate of future participation numbers (column E). It can be seen in this example that, because there is

expected to be a fall in population numbers in the young, active age-groups and an increase in the older, less active age-groups, an overall fall in numbers of participants in activity X is predicted, even though there is a slight increase in the total population. If the activity had been one with high participation among older age-groups, the analysis would, of course, have shown an increase in number of participants. Thus the predicted participation level depends on the cross-sectional pattern of participation and the predicted pattern of cross-sectional change in the underlying variable, in this case age.

One weakness of the approach is that the basic cohort-specific participation rates (column A) are not assumed to change. But this is not in fact intrinsic to the method. If different participation rates can be established using other methodologies – for example, time-series analysis – then such rates could be used for the prediction.

Additional underlying, or predictor, variables could be used – for example, occupation or incomes. However, predictions of such variables are less readily available than for age, particularly for local communities. The technique could be used in combination with the scenario method, where hypothetical projections of the underlying variables could be used. For example, the impact of alternative income-growth and distribution scenarios on participation could be explored.

Table 8.4. Cohort method – prediction for activity X, hypothetical community.

| | | Current year | | | Prediction: Year 2011 | | |
| | Participation in activity X: % per week | Population | | Estimated no. of participants per week | Population | | Predicted no. of participants per week |
Age-group	A Survey*	B Census	%	C (A × B)/100	D Planning dept.	%	E (A × D)/100
14–19	14.9	15,600	19.5	2,324	12,000	14.9	1,788
20–24	11.5	15,200	19.0	1,748	12,100	15.0	1,391
25–29	7.4	11,360	14.2	841	10,000	12.4	740
30–39	5.2	16,880	21.1	878	17,100	21.2	889
40–49	4.8	7,200	9.0	346	10,300	12.8	494
50–59	3.5	6,160	7.7	216	9,200	11.4	322
60+	2.5	7,600	9.5	190	9,800	12.2	245
Total	8.2	80,000	100.0	6,543	80,500	100.00	5879

*Can be a local survey or regional/national data as discussed in 'gross demand' method in Chapter 7.

Ideally, more than one underlying variable should be examined. For example, it might be predicted that, not only will there be more older people in a community, but they will be relatively better off financially, because of improved superannuation provisions. Age–income cohorts would therefore reflect these changes. While current participation rates for such cohorts may be readily obtained from surveys, forecasts would be difficult to obtain, although, as discussed above, hypothetical predictions could be utilized for scenario purposes.

The cohort method is not as useful for tourism-demand forecasting because the community for which the calculations have to be done is the tourist origin community, rather than the host community. However, the method may be appropriate for some exercises in domestic tourism forecasting or, in international tourism, when the market is concentrated in a small number of origin communities.

(ii) Regression-based techniques

Regression-based techniques can cope more readily with a number of underlying variables because the activity forecasts are based on predictions of mean values rather the size of cohorts. The technique involves two steps. In the first, a regression equation is estab-

lished using the available cross-sectional data, in which the dependent variable is a measure of leisure or tourism demand and the independent variable or variables are the factors determining or influencing demand, such as age or income. In the second step, the equation, together with forecasts of the independent variable obtained from elsewhere, are used to provide a forecast of demand. The regression technique is usually applied to individuals but can also be applied to cohorts, the latter being, in effect, a combination of two approaches.

REGRESSION METHOD USING COHORTS. *Step 1.* Table 8.5 presents data on sport participation in Great Britain for age cohorts. Figure 8.14 is a graphical presentation of the actual data and the regression line. In this case, the regression equation is non-linear, involving using the logarithm of the dependent sport-participation variable (Y). The calculations were undertaken using a spreadsheet computer program. The equation is:

Log $Y = 1.93 - 0.012\,X$ or:
log of % participation $= 1.98 - 0.012 \times$ age

Step 2. Using the average age of the population in this equation produces an estimate of the average participation rate; inserting the predicted average age of the population for

Table 8.5. Sport participation by age, Great Britain, 1996 (based on data from Government Actuary, 2000; Gratton, 2000).

	Actual			Regression equation estimates	
Age-group	Midpoint of age range (X)	% participating in last year	Log of % participating (Y)	Log of % participating	% participating
16–19	17.5	53	1.7243	1.7103	51.3
20–24	22.5	44	1.6435	1.6482	44.5
25–29	27.5	35	1.5441	1.5862	38.6
30–34	32.5	34	1.5315	1.5241	33.4
35–39	37.5	30	1.4771	1.4621	29
40–44	42.5	25	1.3979	1.4	25.1
45–49	47.5	21	1.3222	1.338	21.8
50–54	52.5	20	1.301	1.2759	18.9
55–59	57.2	18	1.2553	1.2176	16.5
60–64	62.5	14	1.1461	1.1518	14.2
65+	72.5	10	1	1.0277	10.7

Equation: $Y = 1.98 - 0.012X$ ($R^2 = 0.988$).

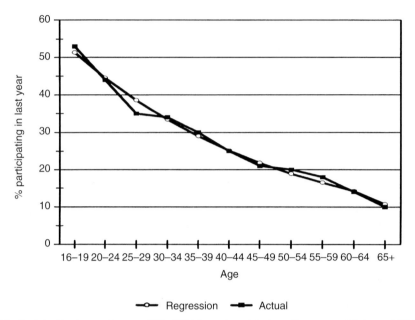

Fig. 8.14. Participation in sport by age, UK, 1996 (based on data from Government Actuary, 2000; Gratton, 2000).

some time point in the future produces a forecast of the average participation rate at that time. Based on Government Actuary (2000) data, the current average age of the British population is approximately 38.5 years and is expected to rise to 41.5 years in 2021. The equation therefore gives the following estimates:

Current:
Log of % participation = 1.98 – 0.012 × 38.5 = 1.518 (antilog = 33.0)
Therefore estimated % participation = 33.0% = 19.2 million participants

Year 2021:
Log of % participation = 1.98 – 0.012 × 41.5 = 1.482 (antilog = 30.3)
Therefore estimated % participation = 30.3% = 18.7 million participants

The participation rate and the number of participants would be expected to fall because of the ageing of the population. The number of participants does not fall as much as the decline in the participation rate might imply because it is partially offset by a predicted population increase of 3.6 million in

Great Britain in the period. Examples of the use of this method using Australian data can be found in Veal (1994a) and Veal and Lynch (2001: 418).

Using a single independent or predictor variable, the regression is not very different from the simple cohort method, except that the regression line smooths the relationship between the participation variable and the predictor variable – a phenomenon that may or may not be beneficial, in that the kinks in the actual data line may represent real fluctuations rather than aberrations in the data.

The regression method comes into its own, however, when dealing with two or more predictor variables. For example, suppose it were decided that income, as well as age, should be introduced into the analysis and that five income groups should be used. If there were seven age-groups, this would then produce 35 income/age cohorts. Producing current participation data for these cohorts from surveys would not be difficult, but, as discussed above, finding available forecasts of the future numbers in each of the 35 cohorts to use in the forecasting step could be difficult or impossible. Additional variables would multiply the difficulties. With regression, it is only necessary to have available forecasts of overall average age and overall average income to produce the demand forecast.

REGRESSION METHODS USING INDIVIDUALS. One disadvantage of the cohort method is that the very act of classifying people into cohorts and characterizing them by the cohort average may introduce distortions. With regression, it is possible to perform the regression analysis using survey data from individuals. The participation variable for each individual can be:

- a yes–no variable, with the individual scoring one if he or she has participated in the activity and zero if not;
- the frequency of participation in a given time period, with zero for those who have not participated at all;
- the level of expenditure on the activity – often used in the case of tourism.

The variable in the regression analysis is then the individual's own level of participation and characteristics (for example, age), rather than the mean of the cohort. The analysis presents particular statistical problems in the case of measuring demand for or participation in individual leisure activities, since most are very much minority activities, so most respondents in a survey are non-participants and score zero. This problem may be overcome in the case of grouped activities, such as the sport example above. The technicalities are beyond the scope of this text, but are discussed elsewhere, for example, by Ewing (1983). Tourism presents fewer problems, because going on holiday is not a minority activity, and often the measure used is not a yes/no variable on whether or not a person has been on holiday, but the amount of money he/she has spent.

Bowker *et al.* (1999), in using regression techniques to forecast outdoor recreation and tourism activities in America, used four independent variables, namely: age; income; race (whether a person was white or non-white); and gender (whether a person was male or female). A simple equation involving these variables would be of the following form:

$$\text{Participation} = a + b\text{AGE} + c\text{INCOME} + d\text{RACE} + e\text{GENDER}$$

where a, b … e are determined by the regression analysis. Race and gender are dummy variables, which can have values in the regression analysis such as white = 0 and non-white = 1, and male = 0 and female = 1. In the forecasting stage (step 2) it is necessary to have available predicted percentages of white/non-white population and of males/females, in addition to predicted changes in the average age and average income of the population.

Table 8.6 presents some of the forecasts resulting from the study. It is not possible to illustrate this graphically because it would require a four-dimensional illustration! The USA, like all economically developed countries, is expected to experience an ageing population, with the average age increasing by 5% by 2010 and by 12% by 2050. Thus, it is notable that, while the volume of trips in most of the more physically demanding activities is predicted to increase at or below the population growth rate of 44% by 2050, less physically demanding activities, such as sightseeing and visiting historic places, are expected to have a much higher level of growth. Cycling is an exception, which may reflect the product life-cycle syndrome, discussed above, or may reflect a growing interest in cycling among older age-groups.

Such multivariate analysis begins to resemble the methods used in economic or econometric forecasting, which is based on an individual or household *consumption function*. The consumption function is an equation that relates purchasing patterns to income and other characteristics of the household or individual. The advantage of this econometric approach is that it has been developed to consider the whole of the individual or household budget and is not confined to single products or activities. Such consumption-function equations may be developed in isolation, or they may be associated with equations related to other parts of the economy, such as government expen-

Table 8.6. Forecasts of outdoor recreation participation, USA (extract from Bowker *et al.*, 1999).

	1995	2010	2050	% change 1995–2050
Independent (predictor) variables used in forecasting – indices				
Age	1	1.056	1.126	12.6
Income	1	1.209	1.888	88.8
Per cent white	1	0.970	0.900	−10.0
Per cent male	1	1.002	1.006	0.6
Selected recreation activities – millions of trips				
Cross-country skiing	33.5	35.2	48.2	44
Canoeing	49.3	52.7	63.6	29
Visiting a beach/waterside	1667.1	1833.8	2367.3	42
Backpacking	79.2	81.6	103.0	30
Cycling	1386.8	1719.6	2995.5	116
Sightseeing	1209.5	1451.4	2394.8	98
Visiting historic places (days)	482.4	607.8	1042.0	116
US population (index)	1	1.126	1.439	43.9

diture, private investment and imports and exports, which constitute a model of the whole economy. Such models are developed by national treasuries and by economic consultants and academic economists. While some are based on equations, as discussed here, others use the input-output modelling technique, which is discussed briefly in the context of economic impact in Chapter 9.

The econometric approach is well suited to tourism forecasting, but some leisure activities are not well reflected in terms of expenditure. The potential exists, however, to apply the econometric approach, with its multiple expenditure choices and financial-budget constraints, to choices in allocation of time, with time-budget constraints. The technicalities of the econometric approach are beyond the scope of this text, but reference material is indicated in the Further Reading.

Comparative method

Dumazedier (1982: 187–205) argued that a given society might consider alternative futures for itself by examining the experiences of more economically advanced societies. In particular, societies approaching the postindustrial phase of development could examine the impact of postindustrialism and ways of coping with it, as experienced by the most economically and technologically advanced countries, particularly the USA. Such an approach to considering the future has certain similarities to scenario writing, with the scenarios being provided by the experiences of existing countries rather than having to be devised hypothetically. The approach was not developed in detail by Dumazedier, and such factors as cultural and climatic conditions would seem to raise considerable problems in its application, but the approach is used informally by forecasters and may offer potential for developing countries wishing to consider alternative models of development.

Dumazedier proposed the comparative method in an international context, but it has been applied most successfully intranationally, in the USA, by John Naisbitt, the author of *Megatrends* (1982; Naisbitt and Aburdene, 1990). Naisbitt's technique involves the examination of social trends in different parts of the USA, via content analysis of local media. Certain states are identified as bell-wether states that set the pace for social change, which other states then follow. While Naisbitt's megatrends for the 1980s virtually ignored leisure, his 1990s version included renaissance in the arts as one of ten megatrends, prompting the following assertion.

> In the final years before the millennium there will be a fundamental and revolutionary shift in leisure time and spending priorities. During the 1990s the arts will gradually replace sport as society's primary leisure activity.
>
> (Naisbitt and Aburdene, 1990: 53)

The basis of the claim that sport is currently society's primary leisure activity is not clear, but, with the passing of the millennium, it would seem safe to say that this particular prediction has not been realized, at least not yet.

Composite approaches

Many leisure forecasters tend, in practice, to utilize a combination of techniques, rather than relying on any one. One method can be used to complement or to overcome the weaknesses of another. Thus the mechanical nature of some of the more quantitative techniques can be modified by results of Delphi exercises, and the broad-brush results of national forecasts can be combined with spatial analysis for application at local level. Martin and Mason (1998) use a combination of time-series, cross-sectional and scenario-writing techniques in their forecasting of UK leisure patterns. Kelly's (1987) study of recreation trends in the USA utilized cross-sectional cohort methods, time-series analysis and consideration of trends in lifestyles and leisure styles and this was repeated in a more recent study (Kelly and Warnick, 1999). In a study of Australian leisure futures, a basic cohort-based cross-sectional analysis was complemented by consideration of such factors as product life cycles and the effects of changing household composition (Veal, 1991b).

Summary

- Forecasting of leisure and tourism demand is seen as one of the key inputs to the planning process. Such forecasting has its origins in the early development of leisure and tourism research in the 1960s. While interest in tourism-demand

forecasts has been consistent, static populations and levelling off of some demand factors have resulted in fluctuating levels of interest in leisure forecasts in recent years.

- Demand for leisure and tourism can be measured in a number of ways, including participation rates, trip volume and expenditure.

- Changes in demand for leisure and tourism are affected by many factors, all of which are not equally susceptible to prediction. Among the change factors that are reviewed in this chapter are: leisure and work time; demographic change; income levels; transport; technological change; the activities of producers; the environment; tastes and life styles; attitudes and values; the media; and postindustrialism, postmodernism and globalization.

- A range of forecasting techniques are reviewed in the chapter, namely: informed speculation; asking the public; asking the experts – the Delphi technique; scenario writing; time-series analysis; spatial models; cross-sectional analysis; comparative analysis; and composite methods. In tourism forecasting, the time-series method has been most common, because of the ready availability of time-series data. In leisure forecasting, cross-sectional methods have been the most common but are now being replaced by composite methods, which draw on a number of techniques and data sources.

Further reading

- Leisure-demand forecasting techniques: Gratton and Taylor (1985: 99–114); Field and MacGregor (1987); Veal (1987); Burton (1989); Zalatan (1994).
- Leisure futures and trends: Godbey (1997); Martin and Mason (1998); Kelly and Warnick (1999); Chapter 18 of Veal and Lynch (2001).
- Tourism forecasting techniques: Witt and Witt (1992); Var and Lee (1993); Archer (1994); Lundberg *et al.* (1995: 149–165); Smith (1995: 116ff.); Frechtling (1996).

- Technological forecasting: Halal (2000); PricewaterhouseCoopers (2001).
- Forecasting methods generally: Makridakis *et al.* (1998).
- Informed speculation: Burton (1970); Asimov (1976); Jennings (1979); Pigram (1983); Jackson and Burton (1989); Kelly and Godbey (1992: 479–512).
- Asking the people: Coppock and Duffield (1975: 84).
- Asking the experts – Delphi: Chai (1977); Linstone (1978); Moeller and Shafer (1983, 1994); Ng *et al.* (1983); Kaynak and Macaulay (1984); Green, H. *et al.* (1990); Jones, S. (1990).
- Time-series analysis: Hill (1978); Stynes (1983); Athiyaman and Robertson (1992).
- Scenarios: Miles *et al.* (1978); Henry (1988); Martin and Mason (1998).
- Spatial techniques: Coppock and Duffield (1975); Ewing (1983); Smith (1995: 131–142).
- Cross-sectional technique: Young and Willmott (1973); Coppock and Duffield (1975); Veal (1980).
- Econometric methods: Ewing (1983); Adams (1986).
- Comparative method: Dumazedier (1982); Naisbitt (1982).
- Composite techniques: Kelly (1987); Veal (1991b); Martin and Mason (1998); Kelly and Warnick (1999).

Questions/Exercises

1. Of the various demand-change factors discussed, which are most likely to affect, over the next 10 years: (a) domestic tourism demand in a coastal resort; (b) international tourism demand in a large capital city; (c) demand for youth sport facilities; (d) demand for the performing arts; (e) demand for countryside recreation close to a large city?

2. What is the difference between time-series and cross-sectional forecasting methods?

3. What are the respective advantages and disadvantages of quantitative and qualitative forecasting methods?

4. Using library or Internet sources, locate a time-series leisure- or tourism-demand data set in an area of interest and produce a simple trend forecast.

5. Conduct a Delphi exercise on a topic of your choice among the class members with whom you are studying.

6. Replicate the exercise in Table 8.3 for a local area, region or country for which population forecasts are available.

Note

[1] The trends for other Western countries are similar. For example, a similar diagram for Australia can be found in Veal and Lynch (2001: 387).

9

Economic Evaluation Techniques

Introduction

In this chapter two forms of economic evaluation are considered: cost–benefit analysis and economic-impact analysis. *Cost–benefit analysis* seeks to replicate for public-sector investment projects or services the sort of financial evaluation that is usually undertaken in the private sector. But, in addition to the financial outlays and incomes that are taken into account by a private-sector enterprise evaluating an investment, the public enterprise must consider the many additional, non-market, costs and benefits of the sort discussed in Chapter 4. *Economic-impact analysis* relates particularly to the economic management/development criterion for government activity (see Chapter 4); governments at all levels feel justified in becoming involved in various projects if they will create jobs and incomes – economic-impact analysis seeks to quantify the impact of a project on the local community, in terms of jobs and incomes.

While they are concerned with the public sector, both techniques assume the acceptability of the basic capitalist market framework for analysis – that is, that the state exists alongside the market and the market process is considered to be a broadly acceptable way of ordering economic affairs and wages and prices are determined in the market sector and are considered to be useful measures of economic costs and values. For those who believe that the market system is fundamentally flawed or, for instance, that the distribution of incomes in society is fundamentally

unjust, the techniques are largely irrelevant. However, for those who believe that the market system is flawed but capable of being reformed, the techniques can be useful tools, because they use market-based thinking and analysis to justify non-market, government activity, and so can be used to achieve shifts in resources away from the market in favour of the public sector – a move that most reformists would see as beneficial.

Both techniques can be used to evaluate projects in advance, as part of a feasibility study designed to consider whether a project should go ahead, or they can be used when a project is up and running, or has been completed, to examine whether it has fulfilled its promised potential and/or to provide guidance when considering decisions on similar projects in future.

It should be noted that, whereas economic analysis is very often scorned or viewed suspiciously by enthusiasts for such areas as the arts, heritage, the environment or sport, because they feel that their area of interest is threatened by it, it is usually the case that analyses are carried out by economists who are also enthusiasts for the particular area. Economists who specialize in studies of the arts, sport or the environment are often personally committed to the field. And, more often than not, the analysis demonstrates that the benefits or impacts from the leisure phenomenon being studied are currently being grossly undervalued by the decision-makers. It is rare for a cost–benefit or economic-impact study of a public leisure project to find that a project is poor value for the community. Economic analyses have invariably been supportive of public enterprise rather than a threat to it.

It cannot be stressed too much that the techniques described here are inputs to decision-making processes rather than complete decision-making procedures in their own right. Apart from the innate limitations of the procedures, as outlined in the discussions below, it should be borne in mind that any public-sector leisure or tourism project exists in the context of other calls on public-sector resources, including such areas as health, education, roads and defence. While some economic decision-making procedures enable a degree of comparison to be made between projects in different sectors, in the end decisions will be influenced by political and moral values, with economic factors playing, possibly, only a minor role.

Cost–Benefit Analysis

Introduction

Cost–benefit analysis is a technique designed to estimate and compare all the costs and all the benefits of a project in money terms. This sounds straightforward enough, but is far from it. While actual financial outlays and incomes can generally be estimated fairly readily, in the case of public-sector projects other factors need to be taken into consideration. For example, in many cases the users of a public service pay nothing to use the service – for example, a park, beach or library – so how is the value of such usage – the benefits – to be quantified? Conversely, a project may have negative impacts – such as noise from a city Grand Prix race or loss of an informal play space to development – how are such negative impacts – costs – to be quantified?

Cost–benefit analysis has had a chequered career in leisure research. In the early days of leisure research, it was a key feature of the quantification and modelling school of research, exemplified by the work of Clawson and Knetsch (1962) and Lieber and Fesenmaier (1983) in the USA and Coppock and Duffield (1975) in the UK. Subsequently, in the late 1970s and early 1980s, it fell out of

favour, along with quantification generally. But in recent years there has been increasing interest in the technique, as economic policy based on liberal principles has sought to cut back the size of the public sector and it has become necessary to account for public investment in economic terms. Thus cost–benefit analysis has been used to evaluate, for example, sporting and cultural events and environmental and heritage projects. However, there are also objections to the use of cost–benefit analysis.

There are those who object to the use of economic criteria in certain areas, on the grounds that the value of certain things is beyond measure, intangible or priceless. In fact the public does put a value on priceless things when, for example, money is raised by public appeal to buy a major painting for the public collection, to prevent it being sold overseas. Occasionally the required amount of money is not raised for such purchases, implying that the price asked for the 'priceless' painting is too high and that there is a limit to the price people are prepared to pay for such an item. At a more mundane level, when local councils decide on the specific level of grant to give to the local repertory theatre or on the budget for the municipal museum, they are indicating some sort of monetary valuation of those services to the community. Private individuals also make decisions on what to spend on intangible things, such as the enjoyment of a Beethoven symphony, when they decide whether or not to pay the required price for a recording or to attend a concert.

It could be argued that in such circumstances the community or the individual is not placing a value on the intangible item but simply indicating what they can afford. The argument then becomes semantic: the economist's definition of value is what someone, or some organization, will pay for something. This is somewhat different from, for example, the value an individual might place on a personal relationship or the value of a human life. These two senses of value are, however, not entirely distinct. For example, massive savings of lives could be made if all country roads were lit, but the cost would be huge. No community is prepared to spend such sums, indicating a sort of limit to the value of (saving) human life. The amount the community, or individual, is willing or able to pay is therefore what is meant when the term value is used in the discussions below (see Peterson and Loomis, 2000, for an extended discussion of the concept of value).

Cost–benefit analyses can be used in three different situations:

1. Study of a single proposed project.
2. Comparison between alternative proposed projects.
3. Study of an existing project or projects.

Situations 1 and 2 would be used as an aid to decision-making on whether to embark on a project. Situation 3 is part of the process of evaluating ongoing projects. There is a great deal of literature giving examples of applications of cost–benefit analysis to leisure and tourism, especially to outdoor recreation/tourism (see Further Reading). However, the technique has generally been used to evaluate projects when they are up and running, rather than being used as a tool for investment decision-making. One of the areas where the technique is, however, actively used in this way is in transport, particularly road building. New roads produce savings in terms of travel-time savings and reductions in accidents (whose costs can be measured). These savings can be compared with the costs of construction and maintenance and various road proposals can then be ranked in order of the levels of the net benefits they are expected to produce. Many highway authorities in the Western world adopt this approach, but there is no comparable use of the technique in the leisure area. While cost–benefit analysis is sometimes used for investment appraisal where leisure is an adjunct to an economic product, such as in the recreational use of reservoirs or forests, generally the examples of its use in leisure and tourism are *post hoc*.

Measurables and unmeasurables

Defenders of cost–benefit analysis accept that there are limitations to the technique, pointing out that in practice there are often costs and benefits which, for various reasons, cannot be measured. The technique seeks to put money values on those things which *can* be valued economically, so that decision-making of a more qualitative kind can concentrate on those elements which *cannot* be valued in money terms. The process can thus be an aid to clarifying decision-making procedures by distinguishing between those aspects of a project which can be quantified and valued in money terms and those which cannot.

Four types of cost and benefit are therefore involved in any project. As shown in Table 9.1, they are:

A. Costs which can be measured.
B. Costs which cannot be measured.
C. Benefits which can be measured.
D. Benefits which cannot be measured.

Cost–benefit analysis involves identifying and listing all the above costs and benefits, but it concentrates on *quantifying* the measurable aspects, A and C, only. Whether or not C exceeds A, the decision–makers must still decide whether C + D is greater than A + B, and that will still involve an element of qualitative judgement. However, if there are no unmeasurable costs of type B and the measurable benefits (C) can be shown to be greater than the measurable costs (A), then the project has been shown to be viable without having to consider the unmeasurable benefits (D).

The cost–benefit approach

Since cost–benefit analysis seeks to replicate private-sector investment-appraisal methods for the public sector, we should briefly consider these methods. In the private sector the main criterion generally used to determine whether an operation or project is viable – that is, profitable – is whether it can generate sufficient income to pay its costs and provide

Table 9.1. Measurable/non-measurable costs and benefits.

	Costs	Benefits
Measurable	A	C
Non-measurable	B	D

an acceptable return on the capital employed. In the planning phase the income and expenditure streams must be estimated and, if the projected figures do not add up, then the project will not be proceeded with – the facility or service will not be provided. If the figures do add up and the project is proceeded with, the projected figures may or may not turn out to be correct. If they are wrong in an unfavourable way (costs higher than expected or income lower than expected, or both), then, sooner or later, the facility or service will be closed or will be sold at a loss to another owner, who may be able to run it at a profit because of reduced capital costs.[1] The investment market in the private sector is competitive, so that entrepreneurs only put their money into projects they think will produce profits that are expected to be at least equal to the going rate of return on capital invested. The precise level of this rate of return will vary, depending on the degree of risk associated with the project, and must be higher than the rate of interest investors would obtain by placing their money in very low-risk investments – for example, depositing their money in a bank. The combination of perceived risk and expected level of return must be acceptable to the investment market. Generally leisure and tourism projects are seen as high-risk areas (compared with, say, retailing or food manufacture), so the rate of return demanded is comparatively high.

In the public sector, different criteria apply – generally facilities or services make a loss financially. With few exceptions, there is generally a subsidy to the users of the service. This makes sense in terms of the various non-market social benefits that public services are believed to provide, as discussed in Chapter 4. If a public service can be run profitably, and still achieve the objectives of the public agency concerned, then it might be expected that a private-sector operator could and would run it. There are very few truly financially profitable public-sector operations that cover all their operating costs and provide a return on realistically valued capital resources. The question then arises as to how to decide which proposed projects in the public sector are worthwhile. How can alternative projects be compared and the best

selected? How can we ensure that the money spent in one area of public expenditure – say, roads – is as effective in producing benefits as money spent in another sector, such as parks? If fewer benefits are being obtained per pound or dollar spent in one area than in another, then, as in the market situation, it would seem sensible to transfer resources until some sort of balance is achieved. Indeed, it should also be possible to demonstrate that money spent in the public sector is producing benefits at least as great as would be obtained from returning the subsidy moneys to taxpayers' pockets and allowing them to spend the money themselves in the market-place.

In the private sector a firm assesses a project's viability in terms of:

Expenditure vs. Income

In the public sector, the corresponding terms are:

Costs vs. Benefits

In the private sector *income* must exceed *expenditure* by the required amount for the project to be viable; in the public sector *benefits* must exceed *costs* by the required amount. The two systems are compared for a hypothetical £10 million project[2] in Table 9.2. In the public-sector project, the capital is assumed to be entirely borrowed money, so there are interest and repayment charges (capital charges). In the private-sector case it is assumed that half the capital is provided by a bank loan and half by the risk-taking investors.[3]

In the private-sector case the investor would assess the anticipated 20% return in the light of the level of risk involved and decide whether to invest. In the public-sector case, the income is less, resulting in a cash deficit of £3 million. For the project to go ahead, the net social benefits (social benefits minus social costs) must be deemed to be at least worth this amount. The task of cost–benefit analysis is to identify and quantify these social benefits and to assess whether they are worth the £3 million each year. Quantification involves expressing them in the same terms as the tangible costs and benefits – namely, in money terms. This

Table 9.2. Private-sector vs. public-sector project evaluation.

Private sector	£'000	Public sector	£'000
a. Capital cost (investor: £5m, bank loan: £5m)	10,000	a. Capital cost	10,000
Annual expenditure		Annual costs	
b. Bank interest (10% on bank loan)	500	b. Capital charges (10%)	1,000
c. Running costs	3,500	c. Running costs	3,500
d. Total expenditure (b + c)	4,000	d. Total costs (b + c)	4,500
Annual income		Annual income	
e. Sales	5,000	e. Fees and charges	1,500
Annual profit		Annual deficit/subsidy	
f. Profits (e − d)	1,000	f. Net cost/loss (e − d)	−3,000
g. % Return on investors' capital (100 × f/5000)	20%	g. Net social benefits	?

process is described in the next four sections, which deal with: identifying and measuring costs; identifying and measuring benefits in general; measuring private benefits; comparing the costs and benefits.

Identifying and measuring costs

The question of identifying and measuring costs would seem to be straightforward, and, indeed, it is more straightforward than measuring benefits. In fact, many studies in the literature involve only benefit measurement because the measurement of costs is seen as unproblematic or because, when comparative studies are being conducted, the costs of two or more projects may be similar and the study is then concerned only with identifying which project produces the most benefits. Costs can be of four types; (i) capital costs; (ii) running costs; (iii) externalities; and (iv) opportunity costs. These are discussed in turn below. Although, as mentioned above, the analysis can be undertaken to evaluate a project when it is up and running, the discussion is couched in terms appropriate for assessing a proposed new project.

Capital costs

Capital costs are those costs which are necessary for purchase, construction and equipping a project and generally getting it started – in other words, the investment. These costs can be measured in two ways: as a lump sum or as an annual cost. The lump sum is easy enough to understand: if a project costs £1 million to start up, then that is its capital cost. But if, to set up the project, £1 million is borrowed at an interest rate of 10% per annum, the annual cost will be £100,000 in interest payments. Since it will also be necessary to pay back the £1 million over, say, 20 years – a mortgage – then the annual costs will be somewhat more than £100,000 a year. In conducting the cost–benefit analysis, it is this total annual capital charge which is generally used.

The capital charge may be partially offset by the increasing value of the asset, but more commonly an asset falls in value over time and therefore an annual depreciation charge must be included. Until recently this was ignored in public-sector accounting, but it is now commonly included.

Running costs

Running costs are a relatively simple concept. The costs of staffing, materials, heating, lighting, transport and so on are easily envisaged and often quite easy to estimate.

Externalities as costs

While there is much theory on negative externalities – costs borne by a third party not directly involved in the project, as discussed in Chapter 4 – there are few empirical data. This is largely because most public projects are aimed primarily at producing benefits, and so externalities of a negative type are generally seen as insignificant or ignored. A study of the Adelaide Grand Prix is a rare example of research on such negative externalities as traffic congestion (Dunstan, 1986), noise and property damage (McKay, 1986a) and accident costs (Fischer *et al.*, 1986), as shown in Box 9.1. Three specific examples of negative externalities are discussed in turn below; they are: traffic congestion, noise and accidents.

Traffic congestion is an inevitable consequence of some leisure phenomena, such as special events or tourism. A new project can increase traffic congestion in its vicinity. This imposes costs on local residents, who now take longer to get from A to B. Surveys can be conducted to establish just how many

vehicles are involved and the time delays suffered. A hypothetical example is shown in Table 9.3, showing how time lost and extra vehicle fuel costs might be valued. In addition to time loss, congestion causes vehicles to use more fuel; however, if each vehicle used, say, an extra 50 pence worth of fuel per trip because of the delays, this would amount to only £500,000 – a smaller sum than the time costs.

Noise is another negative externality that may be caused by leisure facilities and events. One way of valuing the cost of noise to the sufferers is to estimate the cost of soundproofing their homes. This is done, for instance, in cost–benefit studies of airports, in relation to houses under the flight path. It may be only a partial solution, how-

---

Box 9.1. Adelaide Grand Prix Study (from Burns *et al.*, 1986).

A study of the 1985 Formula One Grand Prix held in Adelaide, South Australia (SA). The project included studies of tourism, the transport sector, the accommodation sector, the restaurant industry, residents' reactions, road accidents, the promotion of entrepreneurship and exports in SA and public-sector finance. Some of the key findings are summarized below.

Benefits:	Tangible benefits: visitor expenditure (including multiplier effects)	$9.9m
	Tangible benefits: event costs funded from outside SA (including multiplier effects):	$13.7–14.9m
	Social benefit: psychic income (general excitement, etc.)	$28m
	Total benefits	$51.6m–52.8m
Costs:	Tangible costs: event and capital costs funded from SA sources	$6.6m–$7.5m
	Social costs: traffic congestion	$6.2m
	Social costs: property damage	$0.03m
	Social costs: accidents	$3.2m–5.8m
	Total costs	$16.0m–$19.5m
Benefit : cost ratio		2.7–3.2

Psychic benefits – method
(a) % of population who experienced extra travel costs	20%
(b) Total extra travel costs	$6.2m
(c) % of group (a) who were still in favour of the Grand Prix being held	90%
(d) Total extra travel costs of group (c) (90% of $6.2 million)	$5.6m
(e) Psychic value of Grand Prix to group (c), at least	$5.6m
(f) Psychic value of Grand Prix for whole population ((e) $\times$ 5)	$28m

For group (c) the enjoyment of the Grand Prix must at least have compensated for the extra travel costs. So this was seen as a minimum measure of the psychic benefit for that group. It was argued that the 80% of the population who did not experience extra travel costs would have enjoyed a similar level of psychic benefit. The study concludes that, since one fifth of the population had benefits of $5.6 million then, extrapolating to the total population ... total benefits are at least $28 million (p. 26).

Table 9.3. Estimating costs of traffic congestion.

a. No. of vehicles experiencing delays (data from a survey)	1,000,000
b. Average increase in journey time (data from a survey)	0.25 hours
c. Aggregate delay time (a × b)	250,000 hours
d. Value of time per hour (average wage-rate)*	£8.00
e. Value of time lost (c × d)	£2,000,000
f. Average fuel costs per vehicle per hour (from motoring organization)	£2.00
g. Aggregate fuel costs of congestion (c × f)	£500,000
h. Total costs of congestion (e + g)	£2,500,000

*If, as is likely, some of the travel time is lost by people not working in paid jobs, the valuation of their time is more complex, and this is discussed in more detail below under benefits.

ever, in that people are still inconvenienced in the use of their gardens and in not being able to leave their windows open. In this instance some estimate of the compensation for loss of amenity might be assessed, of the sort that might be awarded by a court. One way in which the monetary value of the cost of noise pollution might be assessed is by examining property prices. The difference between the price or rent of identical houses under and not under a flight path indicates the value that house buyers or renters place on peace and quiet. Note that, in this case, the cost is a one-off cost imposed on the owner at the time the airport is built. When the house is sold, the new owners are already compensated for the noise by the fact that they have bought a cheaper house. Interview surveys of affected people may also be used to assess the extent of noise inconvenience.

Accidents may increase as a result of increased traffic generated by major events and tourism. As with the congestion example above, some assessment must initially be made of the amount of additional traffic likely to be generated and the corresponding likely numbers and types of accident. Such assessments can be made by reference to similar events in the same community or elsewhere, and in discussion with local transport authorities. An estimated cost per accident is then multiplied by the anticipated number of accidents to establish the accident costs of the event.

How is the cost of an accident assessed? Although, in one sense, a money cost cannot be put on death and injury caused to humans by accidents, people nevertheless do frequently associate such phenomena with money. The courts, for instance, award financial damages for everything from death to minor injury. There is a 'going rate' in insurance cases for such things as loss of limbs, macabre though it may seem. Two inputs are made into assessment of these costs: medical costs and loss of income/output by the victim. Distress to victims and families is more difficult to assess in money terms, although, again, compensation ordered by the courts can give some guide. Since cost–benefit studies are routinely carried out for road projects and savings from accidents is one of the major benefits from new or improved roads, transport authorities are able to provide up-to-date valuations of accident costs.

Opportunity costs

The *opportunity cost* of something is measured by the value of that something in its best possible alternative use. It is a measure of benefits foregone and underlies the concept of cost throughout economic theory. It is important in cost–benefit analysis and perhaps particularly so in leisure and tourism. The idea is best explained by an example.

Large city-centre parks are dedicated to recreational use, but the opportunity cost of the decision to dedicate that land to recreation can be measured by considering the value of the land in its next-best alternative use. For example, the land occupied by Central Park in New York or Hyde Park in London would be worth billions of pounds if sold on the open market for development. The community is foregoing that income as the cost of providing the open space. Thus, if the going rate of interest is 10% per annum, then a park which could, in theory, be sold for £100 million is costing £10 million a year in income foregone – £10 million is its annual *opportunity* cost.

The opportunity cost of resources, especially land, arises frequently in the case of leisure/tourism because such phenomena as urban parks, national parks, coastline and prestige city sites tend to feature prominently. Since these resources have often been in the public domain from time immemorial and have generally not recently involved any cash outlay, they are popularly considered to be costless. But the economist would argue that it is wrong to consider them so. Even when it would be impossible to sell the land – for example, because of legal constraints – the decision to impose such constraints was made by the society and has a cost.

Even where cash costs have been incurred – for instance, in recently acquired land – there may be a temptation to ignore such sunk costs if they were met from reserves or grants. Again the economist would say this is erroneous. If opportunity cost is ignored, then projects that have real capital costs rather than opportunity costs are disadvantaged.

Identifying and measuring benefits in general

Social or non-market costs and benefits generally correspond to the examples of market failure discussed in Chapter 4. The first five forms of market failure identified were: public goods; externalities; mixed goods/services; merit goods; and option demand. Each of these implies some sort of benefit (or cost) accruing to the community at large or to particular third-party groups in the community, with externalities being capable of also imposing costs on third parties, as indicated above.

Among the other arguments for government involvement in leisure and tourism discussed in Chapter 4 were: infant industries; size of project; natural monopolies; economic management/development; incidental enterprise; tradition. If a project is justified on these grounds, then economic-impact rather than cost–benefit analysis would be the appropriate technique for evaluation, as discussed in the second half of the chapter. The tradition argument for government involvement is not easily susceptible to economic analysis unless the sense of tradition is itself seen as a public good. The remaining argument discussed in Chapter 4 was equity. Equity issues are not intrinsic to cost–benefit analysis, since, in mainstream economic analysis of market, no distinction is generally made between groups of consumers, it being assumed that the question of equitable income distribution has been dealt with through taxation and welfare policies. However, distributional effects of projects can be taken into account in the process of undertaking a cost–benefit study – that is, it is possible to indicate which groups will reap the benefits of a project and which groups will bear the costs. These factors can then be taken into account by decision-makers.

The benefits arising from the various forms of market failure, as discussed in Chapter 4, are discussed in turn below.

Public goods

The classic type of public provision is the public good – which is non-rival and non-excludable. Examples include fireworks displays, public broadcasting, preservation of the landscape and provision of marine navigational assistance, such as marker buoys. The fireworks display is the easiest of these to examine. Suppose it costs £100,000 to mount a fireworks display: how do we know this is worth it to the community? The benefits are enjoyed by the people who watch the display. If the display is in a public area, such as the Thames Embankment, then these people are unable to actually pay for the experience, but they are obtaining a benefit. How do we find out what the value of this benefit is to them and therefore whether the total value of the benefits enjoyed is greater than the £100,000 spent? A common approach to measuring such benefits is the *willingness-to-pay* or *contingency* method. A social survey could be mounted, after the event, which would ask people whether they had seen it and how much they would have been prepared to pay if asked. If it is found that, say, 200,000 people had seen the event and would, on average, have been prepared to pay £1 each, then the valuation of the users, at £200,000, is greater than the £100,000 cost, so the display is justified. If the exercise were being done before the event, people could be asked whether they *intended* to watch and, if so, what they would, in theory, be prepared to pay.

There are problems with this approach because, if people thought they might actually be charged for the display, they might be tempted, in their response to the survey, to deliberately underestimate the amount they would be prepared to pay, so that any charge actually imposed would be small. In the case of a purely public event, like a fireworks display, where imposing a charge would be almost impossible, this tendency can be expected to be small. On the other hand, if respondents to the survey thought that there was no prospect of being charged and the question was entirely hypothetical, they might exaggerate the amount they would be willing to pay in order to ensure that the event continued in future. It is possible that these two tendencies cancel each other out to some extent in willingness-to-pay surveys, thus giving, on average, a true figure. But there is some doubt about the validity of the technique generally, given its hypothetical nature.

A similar approach can be used to place a value on the public-good dimension of maintenance of heritage, where vicarious enjoyment, psychic benefit or national pride is involved. The general public could be asked what they would be prepared to pay per annum, for example, to preserve the Lake District, the Parthenon or the Pyramids.

An alternative valuation method is to base the valuation on the amounts people pay for similar events or services which are charged for. This would not be suitable for the psychic-income example, but it might be possible for the fireworks-display example.

The *Adelaide Grand Prix* study (Burns *et al.*, 1986) came up with an ingenious inferential method of measuring the psychic income

which the residents of Adelaide gained from having the Formula One Grand Prix in their city, as shown in Fig. 9.1 above.

Where the public good involves direct enjoyment by users and the users have to travel to a specific site or area, as in the case of a public event or visiting a park, it is possible to assess valuations on the basis of travel patterns and costs. This methodology is discussed below under 'Measuring private benefits'.

Externalities as benefits

Externalities are one of the most important types of benefit associated with public leisure facilities; they are similar to public goods, except that the beneficiaries are identifiable third parties, rather than the public at large.

The existence of a public leisure facility can often give rise to increased trade for neighbouring businesses – for example, nearby pubs and restaurants benefiting from the presence of a theatre; the value of this externality would be reflected in property values or rents or in the turnover of these businesses. The expenditure, the increased business and the increased property values or rents are all indicators of the same thing; so in a cost–benefit study care must be taken to count this phenomenon only once.

A further factor to be considered in relation to this type of externality is whether it represents a real net benefit of the project or whether it results from a transfer of activity from elsewhere. For example, if the increased business of restaurants and pubs is counterbalanced by a decrease in the business of restaurants and pubs elsewhere in the city, then there is no net benefit. On the other hand, if the concentration of facilities causes an overall increase in pub and restaurant spending or attracts more visitors from outside the city, then there can be said to be a net increase in economic activity and therefore a net benefit to the city community.

A large public organization can provide externality benefits to smaller organizations in an industry. For example, a large public cultural organization, such as a national theatre or opera or broadcasting organization, will often provide training and professional experience for workers in the industry and will underpin a technical-support industry that others can make use of. While the training costs of such organizations can be estimated, the value of the other externalities which they produce can be difficult to estimate.

Mixed goods/services

In nearly all cases of public leisure provision, there are private consumer benefits involved in a project as well as public benefits. Very often that private benefit is not reflected in the price paid by the consumer of the service – as it would be in the private sector – because the price has been reduced, sometimes to zero, in order to achieve other social objectives. Reducing the price of something means that more people are able or willing to buy more of it. In addition to the wider social benefits (e.g. public-good aspects enjoyed by non-users, externalities, merit-good or economic aspects), the users are obtaining an individual benefit, which should also be taken into account. Examples are outlined in Table 9.4. In these instances, the public and the private benefits must be measured for the purposes of the cost–benefit analysis. The public or social benefits are all examples of public goods, externalities, merit goods, etc., which are discussed under appropriate headings. The measurement of private benefits is a major issue that is discussed later in the chapter.

Merit goods

Merit-good arguments (see p. 60) would appear to be unquantifiable. It is not the general public or the leisure-facility user who makes such judgements but professional groups, pressure groups or politicians. However, in a democratic society, it might be expected that such decisions would be approved of by a majority of the general public. The value of the merit-good dimension of a service might therefore be assessed in a similar manner to public goods, primarily by means of the willingness-to-pay or contingency method.

Option demand

Option demand or existence value – where people are willing to see government expenditure on something to ensure its availability for possible future use – can be evaluated by surveys using the willingness-to-pay or contingency method.

Comparing costs and benefits

The results of a cost–benefit analysis exercise must be drawn together in a summary table, as shown in the hypothetical example in Table 9.5. This extends the public-sector example given in Table 9.2: both the costs and the benefits increase as a result of the cost–benefit analysis, but the result is a surplus of £750,000 a year rather than the former £3 million

Table 9.4. Benefits from mixed goods/services.

Examples	Public-good and other social benefits	Private user benefits
Performing arts	Cultural spin-off Tourist attraction	Enjoyment of performance
Urban parks	Amenity for local properties and passers-by Pollution dispersal	Enjoyment of the park
National parks	Merit good, option demand, vicarious enjoyment, amenity for properties and passers-by	Enjoyment of the park
Sports facilities	Health effects, enjoyment of sporting success	Enjoyment of participation Health benefit
Youth facilities	Reduction of antisocial behaviour	Enjoyment of facilities
Facilities for elderly	Physical- and mental-health effects	Enjoyment of facilities Health benefit

Table 9.5. Summary cost–benefit analysis (annual flows).

	Cash assessment* £'000 p.a.	Cost–benefit analysis £'000 p.a.
Costs		
Capital charges	1000	1000
Opportunity costs	–	300
Running costs	3500	3500
Externalities	–	450
Total costs	4500	5250
Benefits		
Private/user benefits paid for in fees and charges	1500	1500
Private/user benefits not paid for (consumer surplus, etc.)	–	1000
Non-user benefits (e.g. public good, option demand, externalities)	–	2500
Total benefits	1500	5000
Surplus/deficit	−3000	+750

*As in Table 9.2.

deficit. Of course, the cash situation remains the same, but the analysis shows that the cash deficit is exceeded by the net social benefits.

In Table 9.5, the data are presented in terms of annual amounts. This is suitable for a project where the annual costs and benefits are relatively constant, but this is not often the case. Very often, costs are high early on and benefits are initially low, but increase over time. Rather than a single annual cost and annual benefit figure, therefore, it is necessary to examine the flow of annual costs and benefits over the life of the project – that is, over a reasonable time period, by which time major

replacement or rebuilding might be expected.

The simple solution to this would be to add the flows for, say, 20 years and compare the two totals. However, two projects could have the same aggregates arising from very different sequences of costs and benefits. For example, in Table 9.6 and Fig. 9.1, it can be seen that, although both have the same aggregate net benefits, project A has more net benefits early on in its life, but project B net benefits are not produced until later. Project A would therefore be preferred because, generally, other things being equal, people would prefer to obtain benefits earlier rather than later. This is

Table 9.6. Two projects compared over 10 years.

	Project A			Project B		
Year	Costs (£m)	Benefits (£m)	Net benefits (£m)	Costs (£m)	Benefits (£m)	Net benefits (£m)
1	10	9	−1	11	8	−3
2	8	9	+1	10	8	−2
3	7	10	+3	9	7	−2
4	7	10	+3	9	8	−1
5	6	11	+5	9	9	0
6	8	12	+4	8	12	+3
7	9	11	+2	7	12	+6
8	10	10	0	7	14	+7
9	9	9	0	7	13	+6
10	8	9	+1	8	12	+4
Total	82	100	+18	85	103	+18

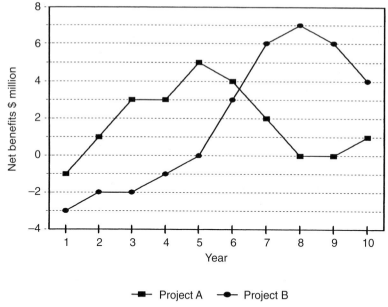

Fig. 9.1. Two projects – net benefits over 10 years.

reflected in the realities of interest payments that must be paid on borrowed money. Project A is in the black from year 2, when the £1 million first-year deficit has been paid off. But project B is in the red until year 7, when the net benefits cancel out the accumulated deficits. This sort of consideration is applied by accountants to projects in the private sector. Even though, in a public-sector cost–benefit analysis, all the costs and benefits may not represent cash, but a combination of estimated cash and social costs and benefits, economists argue that they should be treated in the same way when evaluating projects.

Accountants overcome the problem of uneven flows of income and expenditure (costs and benefits) over the life of the project, by use of a *discount rate*, which can be seen as the other side of the coin to interest rates. If the current rate of interest is 10%, then £100 invested for a year will be worth £110 in a year's time. Looked at another way, £110 in a year's time is worth £100 at present. The flow of net benefits can be discounted to the present to give the *net present value* (NPV) of the project. At an interest rate of 10%, the NPV of project A is £11.3 million, whereas the NPV of project B is £7.6 million.

Measuring private benefits – travel-cost and other methods

In private-sector leisure facilities and in a few public-sector facilities, the market price for the service is charged to the user and, in economic terms, this is seen as an indicator of the minimum value of the benefits enjoyed by the user. For example, if 100,000 people a year pay £5 each to visit a leisure facility, then they can be said to be placing a collective value of at least £500,000 on the experience. In the case of public leisure facilities that are mixed goods and in some cases of public goods, the price of entry is either zero or subsidized, in recognition of the public good, externality or other dimension, so the price paid for entry is not a reflection of the value the user attaches to the experience. How are the user benefits to be measured in such cases? The willingness-to-pay approach, and its limitations, have been considered in the discussion of public goods above. Two alternatives discussed here are the *travel-cost* or *Clawson method* and the idea of *switching values*.

The travel-cost or Clawson method

The travel-cost, revealed-preference or Clawson method of valuing individual recreation benefits is based on measurement of the *consumer surplus*. The economic concept of consumer surplus requires explanation. It arises in any market situation and is based on the proposition that, when a price is set by the provider of a service, the same price is paid by all but some would be willing to pay more than the set price if they had to. This can be explained using the familiar economic demand curve, as shown in Table 9.7 and Fig. 9.2.

Suppose, in this example, the actual price charged is £5. Sales are then 280. There are 220 potential customers, who would have been prepared to pay only between £2 and £4.99 and so do not buy. The 280 customers who actually buy are all charged £5, but:

- 30 of them would have been prepared to pay at least £15 but less that £17;
- 70 would have been prepared to pay at least £10 but less than £15;
- 100 would have been prepared to pay at least £7 but less than £10;
- 80 would have been prepared to pay at least £5 but less than £7.

All the customers except those who were prepared to pay just £5 are getting a bonus – they are getting the item for less than they would have been prepared to pay for it: they enjoy a *consumer surplus*. They can be divided into four groups as above:

Group A (*n* = 30) prepared to pay between £15 and £16.99 – say, £16 on average

Group B (*n* = 70) prepared to pay between £10 and £14.99 – say, £12.50 on average

Group C (*n* = 100) prepared to pay between £7 and £9.99 – say, £8.50 on average

Group D (*n* = 80) prepared to pay between £5 and £6.99 – say, £6.00 on average.

The total consumer surplus enjoyed by the 280 customers can therefore be estimated as in Table 9.8. The £1285 total of the consumer surplus is a measure of the benefit which the buyers are getting over and above what they paid. It can be represented diagrammatically as the shaded area in Fig. 9.3. The consumer

Table 9.7. Price vs. sales (hypothetical data).

Price	Sales
£2	500
£5	280
£7	200
£10	100
£15	30
£17	0

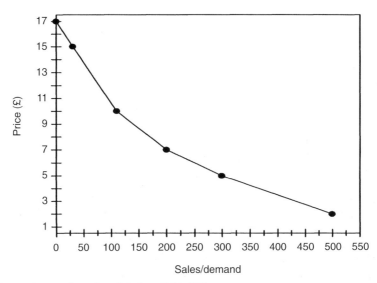

Fig. 9.2. Demand curve (based on data from Table 9.7).

Table 9.8. Estimate of consumer surplus.

Group	Number of customers a (*n*)	Price actually paid b (£)	Price range would have paid c (£)	Average price would have paid d (£)	Difference (d − b) e (£)	Consumer surplus (a × e) (£)
A	30	5	15.00–16.99	16.00	11.00	330
B	70	5	10.00–14.99	12.50	7.50	525
C	100	5	7.00–9.99	8.50	3.50	350
D	80	5	5.00–6.99	6.00	1.00	80
Totals	280			−	−	1285

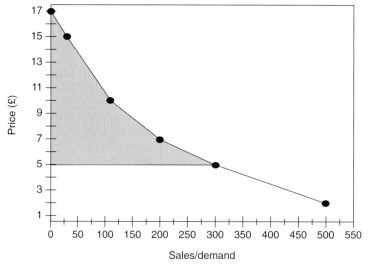

Fig. 9.3. Consumer surplus.

surplus is seen as a useful measure of the benefit users obtain from a leisure service. If, as is the case with many public facilities, the price charged were reduced to zero, it would still be possible to estimate the consumer surplus because it is based on what various groups of users would be prepared to pay. The question is, how can the latter list of prices and quantities – the demand curve – be established in practice?

Two methods are used by economists to find out what people might be prepared to pay to use a leisure facility. The first is to ask them – the willingness-to-pay or contingency method, as already discussed. This has limitations, as outlined above. An alternative method, which overcomes some of the limi-

tations of the willingness-to-pay approach but has drawbacks of its own, is the travel-cost, Clawson or revealed-preference method, devised in the 1960s by American researchers Clawson and Knetsch (1962). This procedure was developed particularly in the context of outdoor leisure/tourism trips and is based on the idea of deriving a demand curve – and hence the consumer surplus – from a study of the costs that users of a leisure/tourism site incur in travelling to the site.

Suppose that the travel catchment area of a site can be divided into four zones A, B, C and D, as shown in Fig. 9.4. For each zone there are different travel costs to the site. A user survey could establish how many people

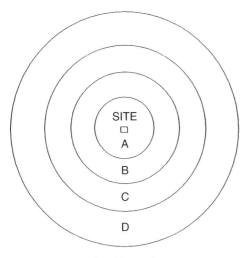

Fig. 9.4. Leisure site with travel zones.

travelled from each zone and the population census could be used to find out the resident population of each zone, to produce data of the sort given in Table 9.9. It can be seen that the visit rate – the level of visits per 1000 population – falls as the travel costs increase, as shown in Fig. 9.5. It is assumed that entry to the site at present is free. How do we use this information to estimate the level of use for different price levels – that is, determine a demand curve?

The process proposed by the Clawson method is set out in Table 9.10. It uses the information on how people react to changes in travel costs to infer how they would react to changes in entry charges. The effects of a range of hypothetical entry charges are explored.

Table 9.9. Hypothetical leisure/tourism site.

		Zone				
	Source of information	A	B	C	D	Total
a. Travel costs per head	Survey	£5	£10	£15	£20	
b. Total no. of visits to site p.a.	Survey/counts	40,000	60,000	25,000	0	125,000
c. Zone population, '000	Census	20	40	50	60	170,000
d. Visit rate (visits per 1000 population per annum)	Calculated (b/c)	2000	1500	500	0	

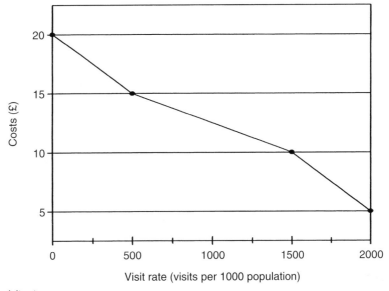

Fig. 9.5. Costs vs. visit rates.

Table 9.10. Travel-cost analysis.

	Source of Information	Zone A	Zone B	Zone C	Total visits
a. Population '000s	Census	20	40	50	
Entry charge nil – actual situation, as in Table 9.9					
b. Total cost	Survey	£5	£10	£15	
c. Total visits	Survey/counts	40,000	60,000	25,000	125,000
d. Visits per 1000 population	c/a	2000	1500	500	
Hypothetical entry charge £5					
e. Total cost	b + 5	£10	£15	£20	
f. Visits per 1000 population	d	1500	500	0	
g. Estimated no. of visits	f × a	30,000	20,000	0	50,000
Hypothetical entry charge £10					
h. Total cost	b + 10	£15	£20	£25	
i. Visits per 1000 population	d	500	0	0	
j. Estimated no. of visits	i × a	10,000	0	0	10,000
Hypothetical entry charge £15					
k. Total cost	b + 15	£20	£25	£30	
l. Visits per 1000 population	d	0	0	0	
m. Estimated no. of visits	l × a	0	0	0	0

For example, if an entry fee of £5 were to be introduced, people living in zone A would be faced with total costs of £10 (£5 travel and £5 entry). This is the same as the travel costs for zone B. If people react to entry charges as they do to travel costs – that is, if Fig. 9.5 could be said to relate to aggregate travel and entry costs, rather than just travel costs – then it might be expected that the *visit rate* for zone A would fall to 1500 per 1000 – the level that zone B residents produced when faced with total costs of £10.

Similarly, with an entry charge of £5, zone B costs would rise to £15 and the visit rate would fall to 500 (the visit rate which zone C originally had). Zone C costs would rise to £20 and their visit rate to zero, since zone D had zero visits when faced with costs of £20. A similar analysis could be done for a £10 and £15 entry fee, as shown in Table 9.10 (zone D is omitted because it generates no trips).

The resultant price/visits schedule is as shown in Table 9.11, from which a demand curve could be drawn. The consumer surplus can then be calculated as follows:

- 10,000 prepared to pay £10–14.99 (£12.50 average): consumer surplus = £125,000.

- 40,000 prepared to pay £5–9.99 (£7.50 average): consumer surplus = £300,000.
- 75,000 prepared to pay 0–£4.99 (£2.50 average): consumer surplus = £187,500.
- Total consumer surplus = £612,500.

This means that the 125,000 visitors to the site are obtaining £612,500 of benefits, even though they are not paying for them. Such a sum could be entered on the benefit side of a cost–benefit analysis.

The travel-cost/Clawson method is not without its critics, since it makes a key, challengeable, assumption that people would react to entry charges as they react to travel costs. Nevertheless, it is one of the few alternatives to the willingness-to-pay method.

Switching values

The switching-values approach avoids the problem of direct measurement of user benefits. Rather than measuring benefits it suggests to decision-makers the minimum value of the benefits if a project is to be approved. This is illustrated by the example in Table 9.12. In this case the net annual costs of the project are £800,000 and the number of visits is 400,000, so that each visit costs £2 in sub-

Table 9.11. Price/visit (demand) schedule (from Table 9.10).

Entry price	Visits (demand)
0	125,000
£5	50,000
£10	10,000
£15	0

Table 9.12. Switching values (hypothetical).

Annual costs of project	£3,000,000
Annual income of project	£2,200,000
Net annual costs	£800,000
Number of visits per annum	400,000
Cost per visit – switching value	£2

sidy. The decision-makers (e.g. councillors) make the decision as to whether visits are worth that level of subsidy (Manidis, 1994). The subsidy per visit, or switching value, is the focus of attention; decision-makers could, for instance, say that a subsidy of £1 only is acceptable – the project officers would then need to see if a viable plan could be devised at such a level of subsidy – if not, the project would be abandoned.

The value of time

A type of benefit that arises in mixed-goods situations is the saving of *leisure time*. This arises particularly when recreation or tourist traffic is a significant factor in new road schemes. It can also be incorporated into the travel-costs element of the Clawson method – that is, total travel costs can incorporate time costs as well as such things as fuel and vehicle wear and tear.

In cost–benefit studies of road developments the value of time savings by travellers is usually the major benefit arising. Thus, for example, if a proposed road scheme saves 15 minutes of travel time for 2 million motorists a year (i.e. 500,000 hours) and if time is worth £10 an hour, the saving would be £5 million a year.

Leisure enters into the road cost–benefit analysis, since a proportion of the motorists using the road will be at leisure or on holiday – is their time worth anything?

For someone involved in paid work – truck drivers or couriers, for example – their time (and time savings) can be valued at the wage rate. This, incidentally, means that the value of time savings of highly paid workers is higher than that of lower-paid workers; so road schemes which save more time of the former will produce more savings and more economic benefits. It can be argued that leisure time should be valued at the wage rate because, at the margin, workers can be said to value their leisure time at the wage rate. If they valued it less, they should, in theory, work longer hours; if they valued it more, it would make sense for them to work shorter hours. But this sort of analysis suggests that it should be the overtime rate rather than the normal hourly pay rate that should be used. Or it could be pointed out that the existence of collective bargaining and fixed working hours means that the individual has little choice about working hours, so this is not a useful basis for valuation.

There are, however, instances where individuals can be seen to pay to save their own leisure time. In such situations people appear to put a value on their leisure time for themselves. Examples where this can be observed are in the choice of travel mode – people fly rather than drive to a holiday destination to save time, but they pay more to do so, thus putting a value on the time saved. People also pay tolls on motorways and bridges rather than taking the slow road or the long way round. Studies have been conducted in such situations and have usually come up with leisure-time valuations somewhat less than the wage rate – usually between half and two-thirds of the wage rate, in fact.

This raises an important equity issue. Wealthy people are able to place a higher monetary value on their leisure time than poor people. The leisure-time savings of a road scheme that affects residents of a wealthy area would therefore be valued more highly than the leisure-time savings from a road scheme serving residents of a poor area; so the former scheme would be favoured. But it is generally accepted that this would not be equitable, so all leisure-time savings are valued by road planners at an average rate.

Conclusion

Overall, cost–benefit analysis is a rigorous methodology that is consistent with liberal market thinking but is also clearly focused on establishing a legitimate role for the public sector. The rigour of the method is also, however, a limitation, because thorough applications of the method quickly generate economic jargon and substantial data-collection costs. This is perhaps why less rigorous, more limited and less expensive techniques tend to find favour with leisure managers – for example, techniques that concentrate on customer satisfaction or that concentrate on benefits only. Examples of these are discussed in Chapter 10.

Economic-impact Analysis

Introduction

While cost–benefit analysis is concerned with the overall viability of an investment project, economic-impact analysis is more limited in scope, being concerned mainly with the extent to which the project generates jobs and incomes in an area, and not with other benefits or with detailed examination of costs. Thus giving everybody £100 cash from council coffers to spend as they please is unlikely to be seen as a wise use of funds in cost–benefit terms but would have a measurable economic impact.

In terms of the economic arguments for state involvement in leisure, as discussed in Chapter 4, economic-impact analysis is linked to the economic-development argument; government activity is justified in terms of its impact on jobs and incomes, in contrast to cost–benefit analysis, which is related to the market-failure arguments, such as public goods and externalities.

If government activity is to be justified in terms of economic development, then the main criterion for decision-making should be to obtain the maximum impact in terms of increased incomes and employment per pound or dollar of government expenditure. Economic-impact studies are therefore designed to produce statements of the form:

'The outlay of X pounds of government money on this project will produce Y pounds of increased income and/or Z new jobs.'

Economic-impact studies may be undertaken:

- before initiating a project, as an aid to decision-making;
- after completion of the project, as a form of evaluation;
- after one event (e.g. a festival) in order to persuade government to continue to support future events;
- in relation to whole sectors of industry – e.g. sport or the arts.

Studies may be undertaken by government for its own needs, or by an interest group or organization (including a quango, such as the Arts Council) to persuade government and/or the community of the worth of a project or sector. The form of economic-impact study that examines the economic impact of a whole sector, such as the arts or sport, on the economy might be better termed economic-significance studies and these are discussed separately below.

Often an economic-impact study is concerned primarily with a private-sector development – for example, studies of tourism development in a host community or of a privately run sporting event – but the motivation for doing the study is invariably related to government and its role. The private sector does not generally undertake economic-impact studies for its own use. Economic-impact studies are undertaken to persuade government, from an economic-management point of view, to support a project. Often an event cannot run profitably and requires a subsidy from government – the subsidy is justified by demonstrating the amount of additional income the event generates for the host community. For example, a report on the *Adelaide Grand Prix* study (as described in Box 9.1), states that the Grand Prix 'regularly makes a financial operating loss of from £1 million to £2.6 million, but generates over £20 million in extra income in South Australia' (Burgan and Mules, 1992: 708).

The outline of economic-impact studies below considers, first, the principles and practice of identifying and quantifying the expenditure associated with the project whose impact is being assessed; secondly the phenomenon of the multiplier is considered; and, finally, studies of the economic significance of the leisure and tourism sectors are examined.

Counting the cost

The initial stage in economic-impact analysis is to specify the area to which the analysis is to relate and to identify and quantify the expenditure items that are to be counted.

The definition of the study area is of key importance for the analyses. The net economic impact of a project is affected by the flows of money it generates into and out of the study area. Thus, if the study area is small, such as a local-government area, the impact of a project is diminished by the considerable sums of money generated by the project which will inevitably flow outside the area to non-local firms, organizations and individuals. The larger the area the less chance there is of these leakages occurring, since a project will be able to source its supplies and labour needs from within the area. The extent to which an area can do this and therefore retain the maximum proportion of the income generated depends not only on its size but also on its overall economic structure. Thus an area with a furniture-manufacturing industry or high-tech design capabilities would not need to import these goods and services and so would retain the benefit from expenditure on such items.

The smaller the study area the greater the proportion of money generated by a project that leaks. For example, if the study area is a single city, the leakages are likely to be substantial; if it is a region the leaks will be less because more supplies will be sourced from within the region. If the study area is a whole country, the leakages include only imports and overseas holiday expenditure. The level of leaks is also affected by the diversity of the economy. For example, an area with very little manufacturing will, in effect, import most of its material supplies. At national level, small countries are likely to need to import more supplies than large countries.

As with a cost–benefit analysis, some of the data requirements for the analysis arise directly from the project under study: its construction and running costs. In the case of economic-impact analysis, however, we are not generally concerned with opportunity costs or non-financial aspects, such as public-good or externality effects, which form part of a cost–benefit analysis.

Data must be gathered to track the expenditure arising from a project, so it is necessary to know something about the structure of the local economy, particularly how the recipients of money from a project (firms and other organizations and private individuals) spend their incomes – for example, how much private individuals save, spend on food, housing and so on, and how much firms spend on wages, materials and rent. In the study area, surveys of organizations and private individuals may be conducted to discover this, or use can be made of existing data – for example, national surveys of consumer and industry expenditure patterns. In small study areas the vital information on how much expenditure is allocated locally can generally only be gathered by survey. In the case of firms, they might be divided into different sectors, such as construction, services, retailing, and so on, which have different expenditure patterns.

The multiplier

The multiplier idea applies to any form of expenditure, but is usually applied to expenditures that represent net increases in demand for goods and services within an economy. Thus it is usually applied to any increase in expenditure from outside the area of study – for example, export income, visitor expenditure, investment by firms from outside the area or expenditure by a higher tier of government. However, it can also be applied to new investment expenditure by local firms or increased expenditure by the local tier of government, as long as it is not funded by increased taxation, since the latter would cancel out the project expenditure. This sort of analysis would apply in the case of tourism, since tourism brings expenditure into an area from outside. Non-tourism examples do, however, exist. For example, day visitors from outside the study area have the same effect as tourists; this applies to coastal and rural areas that attract day visitors from urban settlements, and also to urban centres that attract visitors from suburban and rural hinterlands for cultural, sporting and entertainment purposes. Investment by private firms or governments in leisure projects, such as sports or entertainment facilities, also have multiplier effects.

The multiplier idea is that the initial expenditure of a sum of money is just the start of a process, not the end. For example, an investor who spends £1 million on building a leisure complex, spends that money on wages of construction workers and suppliers of building materials and equipment. The construction workers spend their money on food, transport, housing, and so on, and the suppliers of building materials and equipment spend the money they receive on wages for their workers, further supplies, and so on. And so the process continues, with more and more rounds of expenditure spreading throughout the economy, so that the effect is potentially much greater than the original £1 million.

So does the original £1 million multiply endlessly, to produce an infinite multiplier? The answer is no – because of the phenomenon of leakages. The firms and workers who receive payments in the various rounds do not spend all the money they receive in the local area – much of it leaks out. Some is spent directly outside the study area – for example, by construction firms, equipment suppliers and retailers buying in supplies from outside the area and workers and their families going on holiday or buying on the Internet. Some of the money is not spent at all, but is deducted as income tax or sales tax or is retained as savings. So, on each round of expenditure, the amount of money circulating within the local economy is reduced.

The aim of multiplier analysis is to quantify these effects so that the overall net impact of project expenditure can be quantified. There are basically two ways in which this is done in economic-impact studies. One

is by special surveys and the other is by means of an economic technique known as input–output analysis. We consider the use of special surveys first.

To simplify the explanation we shall assume that surveys have established that the various firms in the area are fairly similar in their patterns of local and non-local expenditure. Suppose the survey reveals that firms, on average, spend 25% of their income with other local firms, 40% on wages for employees and payments of profits to local residents and 35% outside the study area, in terms of imported supplies and taxes. And suppose that a resident survey establishes that the average resident spends 50% of his/her income locally and 50% goes in non-local expenditure, taxes or savings. We are now in a position to trace what happens to project expenditure, and this is shown in Fig. 9.6. The analysis is done in relation to a typical £1000 of expenditure – for a project costing, say, £500,000 the figures would need to be multiplied by 500. These calculations can be relatively easily done by computer using a spreadsheet (see Appendix 9.1).

After 15 rounds the sums involved become very small, so this analysis has been terminated at that stage. It shows that, as a result of the initial £1000 expenditure:

- Local businesses experience an increase in turnover of £1817.63, including the initial £1000.
- Private individuals – wage-earners and business shareholders – experience an income increase of £726.90.

The business turnover figure calculated in this way should be treated with some caution. It does not, in the economist's terms, represent value added – there is a certain amount of double counting in the figure. For example, if a leisure-centre café buys pre-cooked meals from a catering company, which has in turn bought supplies from a retailer in the area, who in turn bought them from a wholesaler in the area, the value of the original supplies is counted three times (including the final sale to the customer); only the mark-up at each sale constitutes value added. The totals in Fig. 9.7 nevertheless mean that an investment project of, say,

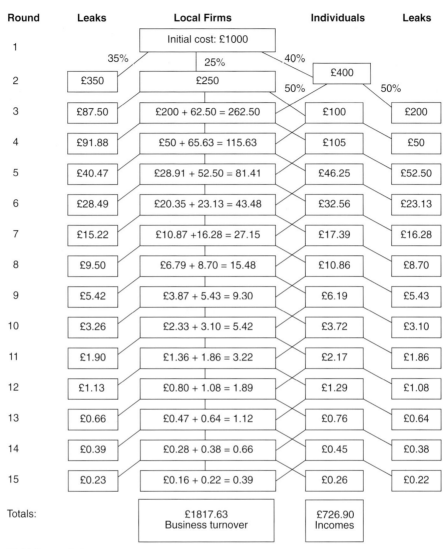

Round	Leaks		Local Firms		Individuals	Leaks
1			Initial cost: £1000			
		35%	25%	40%		
2	£350		£250		£400	
				50%		50%
3	£87.50		£200 + 62.50 = 262.50		£100	£200
4	£91.88		£50 + 65.63 = 115.63		£105	£50
5	£40.47		£28.91 + 52.50 = 81.41		£46.25	£52.50
6	£28.49		£20.35 + 23.13 = 43.48		£32.56	£23.13
7	£15.22		£10.87 +16.28 = 27.15		£17.39	£16.28
8	£9.50		£6.79 + 8.70 = 15.48		£10.86	£8.70
9	£5.42		£3.87 + 5.43 = 9.30		£6.19	£5.43
10	£3.26		£2.33 + 3.10 = 5.42		£3.72	£3.10
11	£1.90		£1.36 + 1.86 = 3.22		£2.17	£1.86
12	£1.13		£0.80 + 1.08 = 1.89		£1.29	£1.08
13	£0.66		£0.47 + 0.64 = 1.12		£0.76	£0.64
14	£0.39		£0.28 + 0.38 = 0.66		£0.45	£0.38
15	£0.23		£0.16 + 0.22 = 0.39		£0.26	£0.22
Totals:			£1817.63 Business turnover		£726.90 Incomes	

Fig. 9.6. Multiplier analysis.

£1 million, would generate an estimated £1,817,630 of business turnover in the area and £726,900 of personal incomes.

Multipliers are ratios relating the initial rounds of expenditure to aggregate effects. There are various multipliers that can be calculated. The business-turnover multiplier relates the total business turnover to the overall business turnover; the more important income multiplier relates the initial income figure in round 2 to the overall income effect.

Business turnover multiplier: 1817.64 ÷ 1000 = 1.82

Income multiplier: 726.90 ÷ 400 = 1.82

This income multiplier is known in the tourism literature as the *orthodox income multiplier*. An alternative, *unorthodox* income multiplier relates the increase in income to the initial, round 1, expenditure:

Unorthodox income multiplier: 726.90 ÷ 1000 = 0.73

The multiplier can be used to calculate the effect of projects of various size. Thus the impact of a £15 million project would be:

Business turnover impact: £15,000,000 × 1.82 = £27,300,000
Income impact: £15,000,000 × 0.73 = £10,950,000

The calculations illustrated in Fig. 9.7 can be repeated with varying levels of leakage to show the effects of an economy with low leakage as opposed to one with high leakages, as shown in Table 9.13.

Often the interest in the economic impact of a project is in its job-generating effect. The income effect can be translated into a measure of the employment effect by use of an average wage or income rate. Thus, in the example given above, where a £15 million project produced a total increase in local incomes of £10,950,000, if the average income is £10,000 per annum, the number of full-time equivalent jobs created is:

10,950,000 ÷ 10,000 = 1095 full-time equivalent jobs

The use of the term *full-time equivalent jobs* reflects the fact that such estimates rarely translate directly into *full-time* jobs. For some businesses the effect of the project will be very small and will not justify employing additional staff; it might result in increased overtime for existing staff or, if there is spare capacity, an increase in profits for the owners of the firm. Often the additional employment will be in the form of short-term or part-time jobs. The estimate of the employment effect is therefore very approximate.

An alternative method of calculating multipliers, especially for large projects, is via an economic technique known as input–output analysis. This is a form of economic modelling that seeks to emulate the interrelationships among the various sectors of the economy. This procedure is quite technical and is beyond the scope of this book, but a discussion of the use of input–output analysis in tourism can be found in Fletcher (1989) and further examples are given in the Further Reading section.

Economic-significance studies

In times when economic rationalism is guiding overall policy for many governments, representatives of certain industry sectors feel compelled to justify their existence in economic terms. This is especially true of areas of leisure that have, in the past, been viewed primarily as a cost to the community, as a consumption item – as non-essential or have simply not been recognized as a significant industry sector. To some extent all service industries in modern developed countries suffer from this problem of perception. Despite the fact that services constitute as much as three-quarters of a modern economy, including a significant proportion of international trade, the perception seems to persist in the community that the real business of the economy lies in such activities as agriculture, mining and manufacturing. Service industries suffer from an image problem. Organizations representing sport and the arts have therefore seen it as neces-

Table 9.13. High-leakage and low-leakage multipliers.

		Proportion of expenditure	
	Expenditure item	High-leakage situation	Low-leakage situation
Firms	Wages, etc.	0.3	0.4
	Local suppliers	0.2	0.4
	Leakage	0.5	0.2
Private individuals	Local firms	0.4	0.7
	Leakage	0.6	0.3
Business turnover multiplier		1.5	3.1
Income multiplier		0.4	1.2

sary to draw the attention of government and the rest of the community to the dimensions of these areas as industries.

Such studies involve collation of statistics on turnover of relevant sectors of the economy and of relevant departments of government and categories of consumer expenditure. This often entails considerable effort since official statistics do not always identify leisure expenditure as such. For example, a considerable proportion of transport and clothing expenditure is for leisure purposes.

Examples of such studies include the study of *The Economic Impact and Importance of Sport in the UK*, commissioned by the Sports Council from the Henley Centre for Forecasting (1986). This established that sport accounted for £5.6 billion of value added in the UK economy in 1985 and supported 376,000 jobs. A study of the economics of the arts in the UK conducted by the Policy Studies Institute found that consumer expenditure in the sector was over £5 billion and some 5000 supported (largely non-profit and public-sector) organizations employed over half a million people, with a combined turnover of £2.2 billion, of which £1.7 billion came from various forms of public support (Casey *et al.*, 1996). Similar studies have been conducted by the government in Australia (DASETT, 1988a, b).

Figure 9.7 shows the findings of a study conducted in the state of Michigan in the USA in relation to the arts (Touche Ross, 1985). The aim was to show the relationship between the government inputs into the arts, in the form of grants and tax concessions on gifts, and the size of the industry as a whole. As the diagram shows, in 1983, $55 million of gifts and grants went to arts organizations, which earned additional income, mainly from the box office, of $78 million and spent a total of $130 million in the local economy, mainly in the form of wages to artists. A multiplier effect of 1.5 transforms this into a total economic impact of $195 million. The aim of the exercise was to demonstrate to government that the $55 million of grants and gifts underpinned an industry with a much larger economic significance. It should not of course be assumed that withdrawal of the $55 million would result in a total loss of $195 million to the Michigan economy, since some of the $55 million might be spent elsewhere and have similar effects, and the money earned at the box office would probably also be mostly still spent in the local economy. The purpose of such an exercise should therefore be to demonstrate that activities such as the arts do play, like other forms of economic activity, an economic role in society, as well as a cultural one.

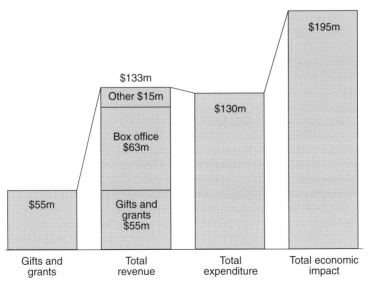

Fig. 9.7. Arts industry in Michigan (from Touche Ross, 1985).

Summary

- This chapter reviews two economic evaluation methods: cost–benefit analysis and economic-impact analysis. Both can be seen as aids to decision-making at the planning stage or part of the evaluation of projects when up and running or completed.
- Cost–benefit analysis seeks to measure all the costs and benefits associated with a project, whether or not they fall directly on the promoters of the project or its users. In that sense the method tries to capture some of the public-good dimensions and externalities associated with public projects, as discussed in Chapter 4. It is noted that some costs and benefits may not be measurable and convertible into monetary quantities, and these are identified in any cost–benefit study.
- Among the approaches explored in measuring benefits are the willingness-to-pay or contingency method and the travel-cost or Clawson method.
- Economic-impact studies are not concerned with the costs of a project but only with its effects in terms of income and jobs in an area. The approach can therefore also be used to assess the importance to an economy of an industry sector, such as the arts, tourism or sport.
- Of particular interest in economic-impact studies is the idea of the multiplier, which is explored in the chapter.

Further Reading

- Economics of sport and leisure/recreation: Cooke (1994); Gratton and Taylor (2000).
- Economics of leisure and tourism: Tribe (1995).
- Willingness to pay: Peterson *et al.* (1988); Garrod *et al.* (1993).
- Cost–benefit analysis and tourism: Smith (1995: 284–295).
- Travel–cost/Clawson method: Clawson and Knetsch (1962); Garrod *et al.* (1993).
- Input–output analysis: a simple exposition in relation to sport: Hefner (1990); a technical presentation in relation to tourism: Fletcher (1989); in relation to tourism and including a discussion of tourism satellite accounts: Smith (2000); in relation to a theme park: Sasaki *et al.* (1997).
- Tourism impacts: Mathieson and Wall (1982); Faulkner (1994); Frechtling (1994a, b); Erkkila (2000).
- The arts: Baumol and Bowen (1976); Throsby and O'Shea (1980).
- Parks and gardens: Garrod *et al.* (1993).
- Sport: in Europe: Jones, H. (1990); in UK: Henley Centre for Forecasting (1986); in Australia: DASETT (1988a, b).
- Sporting events: Burgan and Mules (1992); Gratton *et al.* (2000); KPMG Peat Marwick (1993).
- Sport stadia and teams: Noll and Zimbalist (1997).
- Outdoor recreation: including a discussion of the concept of value: Peterson and Loomis (2000).

Questions and Exercises

1. What is the difference between cost–benefit analysis and economic-impact analysis?
2. How does cost–benefit analysis deal with costs and benefits that cannot be measured?
3. What are the equivalent terms to *cost* and *benefit* used in the private sector?
4. Name three types of cost that might be included in a cost–benefit study.
5. What is the basic measure of benefit which the travel-cost or Clawson method seeks to measure?
6. What is another term for the contingency method and what are its drawbacks as a way of measuring benefits?
7. Provide a brief description of the way the multiplier works.
8. What is leakage in multiplier analysis?
9. List the costs and benefits that might arise in a local community from: (a) building a sport and leisure centre; (b) building a museum; or (c) holding an arts festival.

Notes

[1] The on-selling of loss-making projects is quite common and can ensure the survival of a project. For example, a project that cost £100 million to set up may have to generate about £12 million a year (12%) to service the capital – that is, to pay interest to banks and/or dividends to shareholders. This is in addition to covering running costs. If the project is unprofitable, the owner might sell it for, say, £50 million, taking a £50 million loss. The new owner now only has to generate £6 million a year (12% of £50 million) to service the capital. In such circumstances the project may be profitable.

[2] In a number of cases in this chapter the generic term *project* is used. In each case the reader may find it useful to imagine a specific type of project with which she or he is familiar, for example, a museum, a swimming-pool, a park, a resort or a hotel.

[3] In this example the private-sector operation involves the investors' own capital of £5 million and £5 million borrowed from the bank; the inter-est on the borrowed money is fixed at 10% and is therefore a running cost. The profit is therefore seen as a return on the money put up by the investors. The public sector may also involve money that is not borrowed (e.g. a grant from a higher level of government, or cash from reserves), but the simpler option is shown for illustrative purposes.

Appendix 9.1. Multiplier Analysis Spreadsheet

	A	B	C	D	E	F	G
1	Proportions:	Firms:	to leaks:	0.35	Individuals:	to leaks:	0.5
2			to firms:	0.25		to firms:	0.5
3			to individuals:	0.4			
4							
5	Round	Leaks	Firms	Individuals	Leaks		
6	1		1000.00				
7	2	350.00	250.00	400.00			
8	3	87.50	262.50	100.00	200.00		
9	4	91.88	115.63	105.00	50.00		
10	5	40.47	81.41	46.25	52.50		
11	6	28.49	43.48	32.56	23.13		
12	7	15.22	27.15	17.39	16.28		
13	8	9.50	15.48	10.86	8.70		
14	9	5.42	9.30	6.19	5.43		
15	10	3.26	5.42	3.72	3.10		
16	11	1.90	3.22	2.17	1.86		
17	12	1.13	1.89	1.29	1.08		
18	13	0.66	1.12	0.76	0.64		
19	14	0.39	0.66	0.45	0.38		
20	15	0.23	0.39	0.26	0.22		
21			1817.63	726.90			

Formulae:
Cell B7: +$D$1*C6 (copy to cells B8 to B20)
Cell C7: +$D$2*C6 + $G$2*D6 (copy to cells C8 to C20)
Cell D7: +$D$3*C6 (copy to cells D8 to D20)
Cell E8: +0$G$1*D7 (copy to cells E8 to E20)
Cell C21: @SUM(C6..C20)
Cell D21: @SUM(D6..D20)
Proportions in D1–D3 and G1–G2 can be changed, but each should add to 1.0.
A copy of this spreadsheet is available on the web-site for the book – see Preface.

10

Performance Evaluation

Introduction

The logic of formal models of the planning/management process is that outcomes of programmes or projects should be *evaluated*: that is, they should be examined to assess the extent to which they are achieving what they were intended to achieve (effectiveness) and whether they are doing so at an acceptable cost (efficiency). Evaluation is seen as an important part of the cycle of decision-making, as illustrated in Fig. 5.3 (p. 82). In the rational–comprehensive model, and its derivatives, decisions on future policies and project initiatives are made to a large extent on the basis of experience of current and past policies and their outcomes; evaluation feeds into subsequent rounds of decision-making.

In this chapter, the aim is to explore the evaluation stage of the policy and planning process. As Fig. 5.3 indicates, evaluation is concerned with the implementation of a plan, policy, project or programme and therefore engages with its on-going management. The *management* of a project involves a range of processes and skills not covered in this book, including human-resource management, promotion and sales and financial management. The outcomes of a project that are to be evaluated clearly depend intimately on the effectiveness of these management processes. In this chapter, while performance indicators that bear directly on these management processes are considered, the management processes themselves are not considered; other texts, such as Torkildsen (1999), deal with these aspects.

The rest of the chapter is divided into four sections. First, there is broad-ranging discussion of the context of evaluation. Secondly, the steps in a typical evaluation process are outlined. This is followed by an outline of some examples of evaluation systems, including the best-value process currently in operation in Britain, the benefits approach to leisure (BAL) developed in North America, customer-service approaches and importance–performance analysis. This is followed by examples of applications of evaluation systems in community recreation, arts, cultural venues and events, sports facilities and tourism. Finally, there is a discussion of the overall relationship between corporate goals and the evaluation process.

Evaluation in Context

One key method of evaluation is economic evaluation, and two economics-based techniques are examined in Chapter 9, namely cost–benefit and economic-impact analysis. As indicated in Chapter 9, these techniques can be used to evaluate projects before they happen, when they might be viewed as part of the planning process, or they can be used to evaluate projects after they have been implemented or partially implemented, when they become part of the evaluation process. However, in most areas of public policy these techniques tend to be used for major, high-cost, high-profile projects and tend to be treated as research or special-inquiry techniques rather than routine tools of management. For day-to-day or year-to-year decision-making, public organizations tend to use less formalized and less expensive techniques.

Most observers would agree that, in the Western world, there will continue to be pressure on public-sector organizations to evaluate their activities in a formal manner, and leisure- and tourism-service organizations will not be exempt from this trend. Pressures to do this will come from outside leisure- and tourism-service organizations – mainly from elected governments, which provide the money – and also from inside these organizations, as staff with professional management skills, who are familiar with the processes involved and see them as a legitimate part of professional management, gain ascendancy.

It might be thought that privatization and competitive tendering have simplified the evaluation process by reducing it to primarily financial considerations. But this is not the case; while financial dimensions are invariably part of the evaluation process, inevitably other quantitative and qualitative considerations also come into play.

- If the management of a service is contracted out to a commercial operator, then the public body doing the contracting out must decide just what terms to include in the management contract and still has the responsibility to decide, on behalf of taxpayers and ratepayers, whether or not the resultant service is effective as well as being worth the management fee.
- Even where a contracted-out service is apparently financially self-sufficient, it is rarely the case that capital or opportunity costs are covered; thus the authority still has to decide whether the nature and quality of the service provided are worth the allocation of land and buildings.
- In the case of tourism-development policies, while the ultimate objectives of public policy are generally financial/commercial, the results are widely dispersed among tourism and other businesses and impacts are experienced more widely in the community, so evaluation of outcomes generally involves a wide range of measures.

- The decision to leave all or the bulk of leisure and tourism provision to the private sector is itself a policy decision, the outcomes of which should, logically, be monitored and evaluated; and, if a local council is concerned about the quality of life of the community as a whole,[1] then such monitoring and evaluating could be quite complex.
- The same argument can be applied in the case of a single-sector agency, such as an arts, sport or tourism commission – if the agency has responsibilities in relation to the sector as a whole – for example, boosting participation – then it will need to monitor and evaluate beyond its own immediate programmes.

In fact, as pointed out in Chapter 6, competitive tendering has, if anything, focused attention on the need for public agencies to clarify objectives and, consequently, on the need for evaluation. In Britain, this focus has been reinforced by the *best-value* system, which has succeeded *compulsory competitive tendering* (CCT).

The results of evaluation can take a variety of forms; they may be:

1. A routinized element in the organization's management information system, with the performance of particular programmes or departments being evaluated on a regular and frequent basis, perhaps weekly or monthly. This is comparable to the regular financial reports managers receive on profit centres in private-sector organizations.
2. Ad hoc, one-off exercises – policy or programme reviews – in the form of reports commissioned by senior management or external authorities, as required.
3. Designed primarily to appear in the annual report which most public organizations are required to produce. Whereas in the past such annual reports were primarily window-dressing (and many still are), they are increasingly structured around or contain evaluative information, linked to strategic corporate plans.
4. Reports that form part of the organization's corporate planning cycle, following the conventional management/planning

model, involving the setting of objectives and evaluation of outcomes on an annual basis and/or over a set planning-cycle period – for example, 3 years.

Evaluation can be seen as either *internal* or *comparative*. *Internal evaluation* is designed to assess the performance of a programme or project in its own terms – it is a self-contained exercise. For example, if a programme is established to spend £5 million to increase the numbers of a certain category of visitor to a site by 25% in a given time period, the programme can be evaluated in those terms – that is, whether it has stayed within budget and has resulted in the specified increase in visitors in the time period specified. Internal evaluation has the advantage that the criteria for success are decided by the organization or section of the organization which is responsible for the programme and which should therefore be most familiar with it. This feature, however, can also be seen as a disadvantage because it can be abused by those individuals or organizations who choose unambitious targets or criteria, so that, in effect, they cannot fail. This is overcome to some extent by comparative evaluation.

Comparative evaluation is more difficult to implement because it involves deciding how one programme is performing compared with another. This is manageable when dealing with similar types of programme/facility with similar objectives – for example, comparing the performance of two or more outdoor swimming-pools. This idea is sometimes referred to as *benchmarking*, a process by which external benchmark performance measures are established for certain types of management unit. In the commercial sector a range of largely financial measures are used, such as the rate of return on capital and share price/earnings ratio. Internally, non-financial measures are also used, for example, because of waterfront labour disputes over recent years, one of the most well-known benchmarks in industry is the number of shipping containers which a port can load or unload from a ship in an hour.

In the public sector some of these measures can be used as part of the evaluation process, but, because many of the objectives tend to be non-financial, other measures must be developed. A public example of this is the information published about universities, which includes such things as student/staff ratios, the proportion of staff with PhDs, the proportion of graduates who gain employment and the evaluation of teaching quality by students (Ashenden and Milligan, annual). Of course, differences between leisure facilities – for example, in their age, building quality and design, transport access or the nature of the catchment population – may produce differences that make comparisons of performance difficult, if not impossible.

At a higher level, government may seek to evaluate across different sectors; for example, they may wish to decide whether a museums service is performing as well as a national parks service, or how arts programmes compare with health programmes in terms of value for money. It is at these levels that the pressure to use economics-based methods comes to the fore, since such methods reduce all factors involved to the common denominator of money, based on consumer preference and costs. However, the loss of detail and of qualitative differences between the measures of performance or outcomes used often causes such an approach to be resisted.

Two similar-sounding terms are used continually in evaluation and the difference between them should be clearly understood; they are: *effectiveness* and *efficiency*. Effectiveness is the extent to which a project has achieved what it was intended to achieve. Efficiency is the cost per unit of output. It is here where evaluation often becomes particularly threatening to the public service, because, even if measures of effectiveness can be agreed on and a programme or project is evaluated as being very successful in terms of its effectiveness, it can still be seen as inefficient.

The public-sector professional is often motivated by professional values concerned with quality of output and standards appropriate to the culture of the service involved; so talk of efficiency, particularly when it is associated with cost-cutting, can be seen as a threat to all that – indeed, as a threat to the very substance of the professional's judgement. In contrast, in the commercial sector, where making a profit is the main aim, cost-cutting is more likely to be seen in a positive light, especially if things are arranged so that the person or department achieving the savings is seen to get the credit for doing so. However, this does not preclude problems in the private sector where certain groups in an organization may be less profit-orientated and more quality-orientated than others – for example, the design, engineering or research sections of a manufacturing company or the creative workers in the broadcasting or entertainment sector.

Despite fears and misgivings, the pressure is on to measure efficiency as well as effectiveness. This requires public organizations to measure outputs as well as inputs. In Fig. 10.1, as output (effectiveness) increases, an organization would expect to move along a line such as A – that is, costs would rise proportionately. This, however, means that efficiency – costs per unit of output – remains constant. Increasing efficiency involves moving on to a lower line, such as B. While the proponents of corporate management and evaluation would claim to be attempting to move organizations on to a more efficient line, such as B, others would claim that often the effect of reducing costs per unit of output is simply cost-cutting, which can only be achieved by moving the organization back down along line A – thus reducing costs, but also reducing output and therefore effectiveness.

Steps in the Evaluation Process

In essence the evaluation process involves, for every policy, facility, service, programme or subprogramme, 12 steps, as listed in Table 10.1. Ideally, steps 1 and 2 will already have been established as part of the policy-making and planning process. But this is not always the case. When particular programmes, projects or facilities are being evaluated, it may be that the corporate, strategic planning process has provided only some very broad terms of reference or none at all, and a *post hoc* formal rationalization of the project must be devised.

The heart of the process is the specification of *performance indicators* (PIs), generally quantified measures of effectiveness or efficiency of the outcomes of a project that will indicate the extent to which objectives are being met. PIs are common in the private sector, in the form of the basic measures,

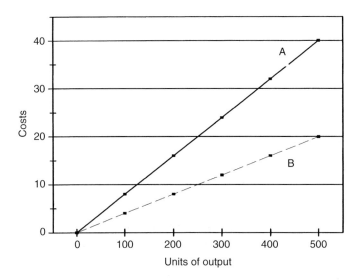

Fig. 10.1. Effectiveness vs. efficiency.

Table 10.1. Steps in the evaluation process.

1. Identify goals
2. Specify objectives
3. Devise measures of effectiveness – performance indicators (PIs)
4. Devise measures of efficiency – PIs
5. Specify data collection methods
6. Collect baseline PI data
7. Set targets
8. Collect PI data collection at specified times (e.g. weekly, quarterly, annually)
9. Identify and obtain external benchmark data
10. Compare baseline values of PIs with current values, targets and external benchmark data
11. Deliver verdict
12. Consider implications

such as profit rate, sales growth and price/earnings ratios. Gratton and Taylor (1988: 150, 152) list a number of ratios commonly used in the private sector generally and Huan and O'Leary (1999) review a wide range of indices used in the tourism industry to monitor performance in individual firms and whole industry sectors. In the public sector the use of PIs is at an earlier stage of development and, because of the diverse nature of public-sector goals, the process of developing PIs is more complex than in the private sector, where financial ratios predominate.

In some cases the specification of a PI follows simply and logically from a stated goal and objective. In other cases, the process will be more complex. Some hypothetical examples are given in Table 10.2, ranging from a simple case of visitor-number targets to a more complex issue to do with awareness. In the practical management situation, the important phenomenon is the target set for the particular year, week or month, which might be used by management to galvanize the staff.

It should be noted that this discussion does not include consideration of just what managers might do to achieve the targets set. While some targets might be achieved at no financial cost – just by working more smartly – others might involve measures that cost money. In such circumstances, efficiency PIs, might come into play – for example, a PI could be the cost per additional visitor, compared with overall costs per visit.

The examples concentrate on internal evaluation. External evaluation requires, as indicated in step 9 in Table 10.1, comparable data from comparable facilities or services, or benchmarking. This might be partially achieved internally by some organizations – for example, an authority with three swimming-pools could compare their performances. But obtaining data from outside the organization requires cooperation among organizations or some sort of central agency or broker to collate appropriate data (Ogden and Wilson, 2001). Such activity is in its infancy in the leisure and tourism field, but the applications in the next section include examples of this in practice.

Approaches

In this section various examples of performance evaluation are considered, including overall systems of evaluation – best value, the BAL and customer service. In the subsequent section, applications in various sectors are considered.

Best value

As mentioned above, the best-value performance management framework was introduced by the British Labour government in the late 1990s to replace CCT in local-authority services. The political dimensions of this transition are discussed in Chapter 4; here we are concerned, more pragmatically, with

Table 10.2. Objectives – PIs – targets – examples.

	Visitor numbers example	Market segments example	Community awareness example
1. Goal	Maximize visitor numbers	Increase user diversity	Increase community awareness of facility
2. Objective	Increase visitor numbers by 10% next year	Increase use by: a. Elderly by 20% b. Tourists by 50%	Increase recognition factor by 25%
3. Effectiveness PIs	No. of visitors	a. No. of elderly users b. No. of tourist users	Awareness indicated by (a) survey and (b) telephone/email enquiries
4. Efficiency PIs	Cost per visitor	Cost per visitor	Cost per enquiry
5. Data collection method	Ticket sales	User survey + ticket sales	a. Community survey b. Keep record of telephone/e-mail enquiries
6. Baseline PI value – this year	Visits: 200,000	a. No. of elderly: 4000 b. No. of tourists: 2000	a. Current awareness score from last year's community survey: 40% b. No. of telephone/e-mail enquiries received: 10,000
7. Targets – next year	Visits: 220,000	a. No. of elderly: 4800 b. No. of tourists: 3000	a. Awareness score: 50% b. Enquiries: 12,500

the operational aspects of best value as they apply to leisure and tourism.

The framework sets out a process of rational management of policies and programmes, including the monitoring and evaluating of outcomes. While it provides a framework for operational management, the initial target-setting stages of the process and subsequent evaluation of outcomes mean that it can be seen as an integral part of the policy process.

The principles of best value were set out in a 1999 White Paper, *Modern Local Government: In Touch with the People* (Department of the Environment, Transport and the Regions, 1999a) and involved the following:

- Setting clear objectives.
- Having targets for continuous improvement.
- Input from users.
- Independent inspection and audit.
- Comparison with the best in the public and private sectors.
- Addressing cross-cutting issues – i.e. those which cut across departmental boundaries.
- Sharing performance data with other agencies.
- Monitoring and evaluation of performance.
- Use of PIs.

The principles are encapsulated in the four Cs:

- Challenge – being able to justify the provision of services on the basis of changing needs.
- Consult – involvement of the community in decision-making.
- Compare – comparison of performance with other agencies, and aiming to reach the standards of the top 25%.
- Compete – while CCT is abolished, the services provided must still be competitive, with access for private operators.

Local councils are required to prepare annual *best-value performance plans* and to review their performance annually, a process that is monitored by the Audit Commission. A number of local authorities were selected to conduct a pilot programme in 1999–2000, a process that was judged a success (Lewis and Hartley, 2001) and on the basis of which all authorities were brought into the scheme.

The Department of Environment, Transport and Regions and the Audit Commission specify PIs that must be collected each year by every best-value authority (including all local authorities and national park boards) and which are published on the Audit Commission's web-site (www.audit-commission.org.uk) as part of a benchmarking exercise. The Audit Commission also deploys a team of inspectors to evaluate and report on each authority's overall best-value performance.

Table 10.3 lists the PIs specified for use in 2000–2001 for a range of local-authority leisure services. Because of the requirement that the data be available from all councils, the range of PIs involved is quite limited and also appears somewhat *ad hoc*. It is notable that many of the PIs relate only to counts of the number of facilities provided and a number make use of existing standards or accreditation from outside bodies. Of the 19 PIs, only two require survey data (2b and 3b) and three are efficiency measures (3a, 4b and 6f). The expenditure per head item (2a) is difficult to interpret, since a high level of expenditure could indicate a high level of service or a low level of efficiency.

The benefits approach to leisure

The Benefits Approach to Leisure (BAL) management, formerly referred to as benefits-based management (BBM), was developed in the USA by Driver and his associates to provide a framework for the management particularly of natural recreation areas, such as national parks and forests (Driver and Bruns, 1999). The method was developed in order to move natural-area recreation managers away from resource-only, activity-based and experience-based planning and management (Anderson *et al.*, 2000). In a resource-only approach, environmental concerns predominate and the needs of recreation are considered only as an afterthought,

Table 10.3. Best-value culture and related services performance indicators 2000/2001 (from Department of the Environment, Transport and the Regions, 1999a).

1. Planning	a. *Does the local authority have a local cultural strategy? Yes/No
2. Cultural and recreational facilities and activities – general	a. *Spend per head of population on cultural and recreational facilities and activities b. *% of residents, by targeted group, satisfied with the l.a.'s cultural and recreational activities
3. Libraries	a. *Cost per visit to public libraries b. *% of library users who found the book(s) they wanted and/or the information they needed and were satisfied with the outcome c. *Number of physical visits to libraries per head of population d. Number of books and other items issued per head of population
4. Swimming-pools/sports centres	a. Number of swims and other visits per 1000 population b. Net cost per swim/visit
5. Playgrounds	a. Number of playgrounds and play areas per 1000 children under 12. b. % conforming to national standards for local unequipped play areas c. % conforming to national standards for local equipped play areas d. % conforming to national standards for larger, neighbourhood equipped play areas.
6. Museums/galleries	a. *Number of pupils visiting museums and galleries in organized school groups b. Number of museums operated or supported by the authority c. Number registered under the Museum and Galleries Commission registration scheme d. Number of visits to museums per 1000 population (including web-site, etc.) e. Number of visits in person per 1000 population f. Net cost per visit/usage

* Starred items are *essential* best-value PIs specified by the government; the rest are Audit Commission PIs, which may be used in the best-value process.
l.a., Local authority.

as discussed in Chapter 7. *Activity-based* planning and management simply bring facilities for activities (e.g. camp-sites, car parks) into the picture without any direct consideration of recreation demands. *Experience-based* approaches are concerned with recreationists' satisfaction and demands, but do not consider wider social dimensions, beyond the immediate experience or beyond the individual recreationist.

The BAL approach seeks to remedy this by considering all benefits arising from recreational activity. In that sense it is similar to the discussion of benefits in Chapter 3, but without the theoretical economic trappings. Thus Driver and Bruns (1999: 352–353) list no fewer than 105 types of benefit that have been identified by research as arising from leisure participation. A summary of these is provided in Table 10.4. Each benefit is potentially capable of being evaluated by means of one or more performance indicators, although some – for example, community spirit or self-confidence – would present a challenge to the researcher, particularly in attributing any change in the indicator to participation in a leisure activity. In practice, in any one situation, all the benefits listed would not be relevant; planners or managers would be expected to target particular benefits in light of the strategic policies of the agency, the nature of the facilities or natural resources involved and the nature of the actual and targeted users.

Driver and Bruns's outline of the BAL approach clearly indicates that, in order to be implemented, a full-scale objectives–performance–evaluation system must be established:

Table 10.4. Benefits of leisure – summary of Table 21.1 of Driver and Bruns, 1999.

I. Personal benefits	A. Psychological
	1. Better mental health and health maintenance (5 items listed – e.g. holistic sense of wellness; catharsis)
	2. Personal development and growth (24 items listed – e.g. self-confidence; leadership; problem solving)
	3. Personal appreciation and satisfaction (14 items listed – e.g. self-actualization; exhilaration; challenge; nature appreciation)
	B. Psychophysiological (18 items listed – e.g. cardiovascular benefits; reduced/prevented hypertension; increased life expectancy)
II. Social and cultural benefits	25 items listed – e.g. community satisfaction; pride in community; reduced social alienation; ethnic identity; prevention of problems of at-risk youth
III. Economic benefits	8 items listed – e.g. reduced health costs; less work absenteeism; local and regional economic development
IV. Environmental benefits	11 items listed – e.g. maintenance of physical facilities; environmental ethic; ecosystem sustainability

Plan implementation requires the collaborative development of outcomes-directed management objectives, prescriptions, and guidelines and standards that will be supported at the policy level and implemented on the ground using the concept of total quality management. Managerial objectives define and target the type of benefit opportunities that will be provided at designated places and times, both on and off-site. Management prescriptions define managerial actions that will be taken to assure the delivery of the targeted benefit opportunities. The guidelines and standards are used during monitoring as objective measures of the degree to which the types, quantity, and quality of targeted benefit opportunities are actually being delivered.

(Driver and Bruns, 1999: 362).

The terms 'guidelines and standards' used by Driver and Bruns are equivalent to performance indicators. While published papers on BAL mention the possibility of negative effects of leisure participation – which could include matters such as noise, pollution or injuries – the cost/efficiency aspect of services does not appear to be fully addressed; it therefore remains valuable but incomplete as an evaluation system.

Customer service

Customer-service models derive from market research. The most well-known approach to customer-service monitoring is the SERVQUAL system developed by Parasuraman and his colleagues (Parasuraman *et al.*, 1988), the main focus of which is to assess service quality by comparing customers' *expectations* of service quality with the level of service quality actually received. Service quality is broken down into components, and scores on these components can be seen as PIs. Scores are obtained from customers via a standardized survey instrument including Likert-style rating scales. Being limited to customer satisfaction, SERVQUAL is not a complete evaluation system, since customer satisfaction is generally a necessary, but not sufficient, criterion upon which to base an evaluation. For example, a facility could enjoy very high customer-satisfaction ratings because it is providing a costly and unsustainable level of staffing or is admitting only a narrow range of customer types.

Parasuraman *et al.* have provided a standardized survey instrument to administer to customers, with service components covering: reliability, empathy, responsiveness, assurance and tangibles. Christine Williams (1998a, b) used the instrument in surveys at a range of leisure facilities in the UK – an art gallery, museum, amusement park, leisure centre, golf-course and theatre – and concluded that a specialist instrument adapted to the leisure-service environment would be desirable.

One such instrument has been developed by Gary Crilley and Gary Howat and associates at the Centre for Environmental and Recreation Management (CERM), at the University of South Australia, and has been tested in a range of Australian and UK leisure centres (Howat *et al.*, 1996). The list of customer service quality attributes, which constitute PIs, is given in Table 10.5. The CERM team is also developing efficiency measures to widen the scope of the system in the CERM system.

A number of leisure centres collect data on a regular basis using this system and submit it to CERM for analysis. CERM is then able to provide centres with average data from a number of comparable centres for comparison, or benchmarking, purposes. Thus, with the inclusion of efficiency and other measures, this system offers the prospect of a complete performance-evaluation system for sport and leisure centres.

Importance–performance analysis

Importance–performance analysis was discussed in Chapter 6 in relation to decision-making about possible projects, but it is probably true to say that it is more often used as an evaluation technique, when a project or programme is up and running, or completed. The SERVQUAL approach discussed above uses a form of this general approach, in that it normally involves gathering ratings of customer expectations and satisfactions – the scores are gathered in relation to the customer's prior expectations from each dimension of the service and the actual experience or level of satisfaction with the service received. The results of the two assessments are listed, side by side, and the differences noted. Large negative differences on particular components are deemed to be contributors to overall customer dissatisfaction and are a trigger for management or marketing action.

Expectations and satisfaction may not, however, be the best guide to the source of customer satisfaction/dissatisfaction because some components may be more important than others. Scoring poorly on some components may be more significant than on others; conversely, making great efforts to increase customer satisfaction on unimportant components may be a waste of resources. Further, low expectations may be coloured by previous experience of the service, possibly leading to continued management complacency. In some versions, therefore (e.g. Langer, 1997), *importance* is used rather than *expectations*.

This leads to a useful visual tool for assessment, in that the component scores on

Table 10.5. CERM customer-service quality attributes (from Howat *et al.*, 1996).

1. Parking – parking area safe, secure
2. Cleanliness – facilities clean, well maintained
3. Information – up-to-date information available on activities, events, etc.
4. Punctuality – programmes start and finish on time
5. Choice – offer a broad range of activities
6. Organization – centre well-organized and run
7. Comfort – centre physically comfortable and pleasant
8. Value for money – programmes/facilities provide value for money
9. Quality equipment – equipment of high quality and well maintained
10. Food and drink – a good canteen or kiosk
11. Child-minding – adequate child-minding service
12. Staff responsiveness – staff friendly and responsive
13. Staff presentation – staff presentable and easily identified
14. Staff knowledge – staff experienced and knowledgeable
15. Officials – umpires, judges, etc. qualified, experienced and consistent

the two scales – importance and satisfaction/performance – can be plotted on a graph, as shown in Fig. 10.2. In this case average scores (each on a 1–5 scale) have been plotted for 12 components (A–L) from a survey of a group of users of a service. The graph can be interpreted as follows.

- For components in the top half of the graph (L, B, D, A, H, J) performance is high, so the outcomes are making a positive contribution to user satisfaction. But, in the case of component L, the importance is low, so, if this is a costly or difficult component of the service to provide, efforts may be being wasted.
- For items in the bottom half of the graph (C, E, F, G, K, I) performance is low, so having a negative effect on user satisfaction. But items C and E in the bottom left-hand corner of the graph are not important to the users, so are not of high priority. The components for priority attention are K and I, which are important to the users.

Examples of this type of presentation can be found in Langer (1997: 147) in relation to users of a travel company and Hudson and Shephard (1998) in relation to a ski resort.

This particular example of the application of the importance–performance method deals only with customer or user evaluation. A similar approach could be adopted with PIs provided they could be placed on a common scale. Thus, as with the example in Chapter 6, the importance scores for a range of PIs could be based on assessments made by decision-makers, such as board or council committee members, or some wider group. The performance scores (PIs) might all be expressed in terms of percentage of target achieved or, if benchmarking with other agencies is involved, being in, say, the first, second, third or fourth quartiles of scores – as in the Sport England example below.

The advantage of the importance–performance method is that, rather than merely judging a service as successful or unsuccessful, it provides guidance on priorities for improving the service.

Applications in Leisure and Tourism

In this section applications of evaluation systems in various sectors of leisure and tourism are considered, in community recreation, the arts, cultural venues and events, sports facilities and tourism.

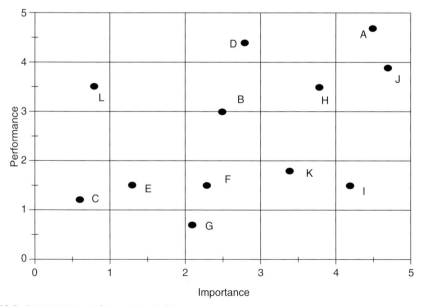

Fig. 10.2. Importance–performance graphic.

Community recreation

Hatry and Dunn (1971) give an example of how such qualitative assessments might be incorporated and how the evaluation process can be related to objectives. Their suggested objectives for a public recreation service are set out in the statement quoted in Chapter 6. Implicit in the statement are a number of criteria for effectiveness, each of which can be assessed by means of measures, which in turn can be derived from a number of data sources, as shown in Table 10.6. Some of these items of data could be collected routinely (for example, the number of attendances at swimming-pools, which can be obtained from ticket sales) but others would require special data-collection exercises (for example, attendances at parks, which require special counts) and some would require quite detailed research (for example, citizen or user attitudes, which must be based on surveys).

Arts, cultural venues and events

There has been growing interest in performance appraisal in the area of the arts for some years. More than in most sectors, however, this field presents difficulties in handling the question of quality versus popularity, since the general public may have different tastes from those of the arts *aficionados*, as discussed in Chapter 11 (Cohen and Pate, 2000). This is illustrated in an episode in Australia in 1989/90, when, following a national review of museums, the federal Department of Finance produced a report, entitled *What Price Heritage?* (Department of Finance, 1989), which proposed PIs for museums, relying largely on cost per visit and cost per square metre. This provoked considerable criticism from the museums sector and arts industry in general, including, unusually, a critical response from the federal Department of the Arts, entitled: *What Value Heritage?* (DASETT, 1990), and a specially convened conference (Skates, 1990). Little has been heard about PIs for Australian museums since then.

As indicated above (Table 10.3), in England and Wales PIs for some arts facilities, notably libraries and museums, are included in the current best-value framework. During the era of CCT in the UK, the Audit Commission produced a study of *Local Authorities, Entertainment and the Arts* (Audit Commission, 1991), which set out a wider range of possible PIs, as summarized in Table 10.7. The summary list is compiled from three different tables in the report and so consists of a mixture of objectives, policies and targets. There is just one attempt here to tackle the artistic-quality issue, in the inclusion of newspaper reviews of productions as one of the PIs.

Sports facilities

As part of the best-value process, Sport England commissioned the Leisure Industries Research Centre (LIRC) of the University of Sheffield to devise a set of PIs for sports halls and swimming-pools and to survey 155 such facilities to gather data for benchmarking purposes. The list of PIs developed is reproduced in Table 10.8. It includes six 'key indicators', which are considered essential, and 29 other indicators.

The benchmarking part of the study illustrates the principle that, to be valid, comparisons of performance should compare, as far as possible, like with like. The study therefore grouped facilities in three different ways, referred to as 'families'. Three family types were identified, based on facility type, location and size; details are given in Table 10.9, together with the number of facilities in each category included in the study. The best-value framework relates performance to the top quarter of facilities in a category – the 75% benchmark – and to the bottom quarter – the 25% benchmark. Table 10.10 shows the results for the first PI, 'access for youth'. The PI is a ratio, so that a figure of 1.0 indicates that the use of the facility by 11–19-year-olds is in line with the proportion of 11–19-year-olds in the catchment population. A PI of less than 1.0 indicates that the group is underserved and over 1.0 indicates that it is overserved. The PI calls for careful interpretation in this particular instance, since a high figure could indicate that other groups in the community are being neglected.

Table 10.6. Community-recreation performance criteria and measures (related to Hatry and Dunn, 1971, see p. 103).

Criteria	Measures	Data sources
A. Adequacy	A1. Attendances	A1. Ticket sales or counts
	A2. Participants/non-participants	A2. A1. + user surveys (frequency of visit) + population census (non-users)
	A3. Persons living within x min or y km of facilities	A3. Maps and population census
	A4. User/resident perceptions	A4. User/resident surveys
B. Enjoyableness	B1. Attendances	B1. As A1
	B2. Participants/non-participants	B2. As A2
C. Accessibility	C1. Persons living within x min/y miles of facilities	C1. As A3
D. (Un)crowdedness	D1. Crowdedness indices	D1. Combination of D2–D5
	D2. Waiting times	D2. Management study
	D3. Numbers turned away	D3. Management study/records
	D4. Capacity utilization	D4. Management study
	D5. User perceptions	D5. User survey
E. Variety	E1. Number of different activities catered for	E1. Inventory
F. Safety	F1. Accidents	F1. Management records
G. Physical attractiveness	G1. Index of attractiveness	G1. Special study + user/resident survey
H. Crime reduction	H1. Crime rates in community	H1. Police records
I. Health enhancement	J1. Illness in community	J1. Local health records or special study
J. Economic well-being	K1. Business income, jobs, property affected	K1. Cost–benefit study (see Chapter 9)

Table 10.7. Performance indicators for arts, cultural venues and events (adapted from Audit Commission, 1991: 30, 34, 37).

Area	Objective/function	Performance indicators	Data source*
Entertainment and the arts	Foster artistic excellence	No. of performers supported	Own records
		No. of engagements/recording contracts by supported performers	Survey of supported performers
		Newspaper reviews of performances	Clippings service
		No. of groups applying for grant aid	Own records
		No. of groups receiving grant aid	Own records
	Improve quality of life	Use made by local population of supported facilities	Community or user surveys + census
		No. of performances by type (e.g. cultural, popular) in supported facilities	Facility records
		Use made of supported facilities by people from different groups	Community or user surveys + census
	Promote equity of access	Breakdown of audiences by social background	User surveys
	Foster a sense of community	% of residents aware of the supported facilities	Community survey
		No. of hires of supported facilities by local groups	Booking system
	Conservation of cultural buildings	† Trading profit/loss on promotions	Own financial records
		† Cost of building maintenance	Own financial records
	Increase participation in the arts by supporting local groups	No. of groups supported	Own records
		No. of groups using council facilities	Booking system
Venues and events	Council's own programme	Number of events (performances/hirings)	Own records
		Number of different productions/presentations	Own records
		Mix of events (number and percentage of different types)	Own records
	Pricing	Admission prices charged	Own records
		Average ticket price	Own records
		Discounts offered to target groups	Own records
		Take-up by target groups	Box-office records or user survey
	Attendance	Total number of attendances	Box-office records
		Frequency of attendance by people from different segments of the population	User surveys
		% of seats sold	Box-office records
	Financial	Average ticket yield	Box-office records
		† Subsidy per attendance	Box-office + financial records
		† Subsidy per paid attendance	Box-office + financial records

		Targets[‡]	
Multipurpose Venues	Performances	Minimum number of evening performances a year	Own records
		Minimum number of different performances a year	Own records
		Minimum number of times any one production is to be performed	Own records
	Financial arrangements with performers, managers, etc.	Minimum and maximum share of hire, box-office, etc. income	Own records
		Minimum hire fee	Own records
	Programme	Maximum/minimum no. of events of different types – e.g. rock, orchestral concerts, TV comics, etc.	Own records
	Pricing	Maximum prices to charge	Own records
		Policy on discounts for target or disadvantaged groups (e.g. retired, students)	Own records
	Audience	Proportions of audience to come from particular sectors of society (e.g. young people, ethnic minorities)	User surveys
	Attendance	Minimum percentage of seats to be sold	Box-office
	Subsidy	[†] Maximum average subsidy per seat sold	Box-office + financial records

* Not in the original.
† Efficiency indicators; the rest are effectiveness indicators.
‡ This list is a mixture of targets, performance indicators and policies.

Table 10.8. Best-value performance indicators and benchmarks for sports halls and swimming-pools (adapted from Sport England, 2000: 18–24).

Groups	Policy	Performance indicator	Data source
Access (effectiveness)	* Access for youth	% of visits by 11–19-year-olds ÷ % of cp aged 11–19 years	US + Census
	* Access for disadvantaged groups	% of visits by SEG DE ÷ % of cp in SEG DE	US + Census
	* Access for ethnic minorities	% of visits by black, Asian and other (minority) ethnic groups ÷ % black, Asian and other (minority) ethnic groups in cp	US + Census
	Access for adults	% of visits by 20–59-year-olds ÷ % of cp aged 20–59 years	US + Census
	Access for older people	% of visits by 60+-year-olds ÷ % of cp aged 60+ years	US + Census
	First visits	% of visits that are first visits	US
	Use of discount card	% of visits using discount card	US and/or TS
	Use of discount card by disadvantaged groups	% of visits using discount card for 'disadvantaged'	US and/or TS
	Use by females	% of visits female	US
	Use by disabled people < 60 years	% of visits disabled people aged < 60 years	US
	Use by disabled people 60+ years	% of visits disabled people aged 60+ years	US
	Use by unemployed	% of visits unemployed	US
Financial (efficiency)	*Cost recovery	Annual income as % of annual operating costs	Acc
	*Subsidy per visit	(Annual operating costs − annual income) ÷ no. of visits p.a.	Acc, TS
	Subsidy per square metre	(Annual operating costs − annual income) ÷ area of facility	Acc, Area
	Subsidy per opening hour	(Annual operating costs − annual income) ÷ no. of hours open p.a.	Acc, PR
	Subsidy per catchment resident	(Annual operating costs − annual income) ÷ cp	Acc, Census
	Operating cost per visit	Annual operating costs ÷ no. of visits p.a.	Acc, TS
	Operating cost per sq. metre	Annual operating costs ÷ area of facility	Acc, Area
	Operating cost per opening hour	Annual operating costs ÷ no. of hours open p.a.	Acc, PR
	Maintenance/repair costs per sq. metre	Annual maintenance/repair costs ÷ area of facility	Acc, Area
	Energy costs per sq. metre	Annual energy costs ÷ area of facility	Acc, Area
	Income per visit	Annual income ÷ no. of visits p.a.	Acc, TS
	Income per sq. metre	Annual income ÷ area of facility	Acc, Area
	Income per opening hour	Annual income ÷ no. of hours open p.a.	Acc, PR
	Direct income per visit	Annual user fees ÷ no. of visits p.a.	Acc, TS
	Secondary income per visit	Annual subsidies, grants, etc. ÷ no. of visits p.a.	Acc, TS

Utilization	* Visit level	Annual visits ÷ area of facility	TS, Area
(effectiveness	Visits per opening hour	Annual visits ÷ no. of hours open p.a.	TS, PR
and efficiency)	% casual visits	No. of casual visits as % of total visits p.a. (casual + organized)	TS
	% unused programme time	% of programmed time not used	PR
	% unused usable programme time	% of programmed time available for use but unused	PR
	No. of people visiting halls as % of cp	Weekly no. of people visiting halls as % of cp	TS, Census
	No. of people visiting pools as % of cp	Weekly no. of people visiting pools as % of cp	TS, Census
	No. of users who visit other facilities as % of cp	Weekly no. of users who visit other facilities as % of cp	US, Census

* Key indicators – the rest are other indicators.

cp, Catchment population – data obtained from census – see Chapter 7 for discussion of catchment area; US, user survey; TS, ticket sales (usually a computerized system capable of capturing data on bookings and numbers and types of ticket sold/used – but NB must be programmed to calculate no. of users for team etc. game bookings); Acc, accounts; Area, area of facility in sq. metres; PR, programme/booking system; SEG, socio-economic group; DE, semi-skilled and unskilled occupations; p.a., per annum.

Table 10.9. Sport England – sports facility 'families' (from Sport England, 2000: 7–8).

	No. of facilities included in the study
*Family type 1: type of facility**	
● Dry with outdoor facilities	29
● Dry without outdoor facilities	20
● Mixed with outdoor facilities	28
● Mixed without outdoor facilities	31
● Wet	47
Family type 2: type of location	
● Less than 15% of the catchment population in social groups DE	32
● 15–19.9% of the catchment population in social groups DE	4
● 20% and over of the catchment population in social groups DE	59
Family type 3: size of facility	
● Small – less than 1500 square metres	24
● Medium – 1500–2999 square metres	33
● Large – 3000 square metres and over	33
Total number of facilities included in the study	155

* Dry = no swimming-pool; Mixed and Wet = includes swimming-pool.
DE, semi-skilled and unskilled occupations.

Table 10.10. Sport England benchmarks for youth-access PIs (from Sport England, 2000: 7–8).

	% of visits by 11–19-year-olds ÷ % of catchment population 11–19-year-olds		
	25% benchmark	50% benchmark	75% benchmark
*Family type 1: type of facility**			
● Dry with outdoor	0.9	1.4	1.7
● Dry without outdoor	1.0	1.7	2.0
● Mixed with outdoor	0.9	1.4	1.8
● Mixed without outdoor	0.8	1.3	1.6
● Wet	0.9	1.2	1.6
Family type 2: % of DE in catchment			
● Less than 15%	0.9	1.2	1.7
● 15–19.9%	0.9	1.2	1.7
● 20% and over	1.0	1.5	1.8
Family type 3: size of facility			
● Small	0.8	1.5	1.8
● Medium	0.9	1.3	1.6
● Large	0.7	1.2	1.6
All facilities	0.9	1.3	1.8

* Dry = no swimming-pool; Mixed and Wet = includes swimming-pool.
DE, semi-skilled and unskilled occupations.

Similar tables are produced for all 35 PIs, providing local authorities with benchmarks against which they can measure the performance of their own facilities. This therefore stands as the most fully developed leisure-services benchmarking system publicly available. The LIRC provides a benchmarking service to subscribing authorities similar to that provided by CERM mentioned above. The Sport England/LIRC system is seen as a supplement to the statutory government/ Audit Commission system and can be used by authorities in preparing their best-value plans and reviews.

Tourism

Langer (1997) presents a SERVQUAL approach to measure customer satisfaction in a travel company. While a travel company is not generally a public-sector organization, the principles could well apply, at least in part, to some public transport operations and public agencies operating local guided tours and reservations systems. A list of 16 quality dimensions is used by Langer, as summarized in Table 10.11, with customer ratings being gathered by survey, using a

scale of 1–5. The global customer-satisfaction score is a summary or average of the 16 individual scores, and it is this overall score that would probably be used in an overall performance evaluation for the service.

Tourism New South Wales (NSW) is a state government agency with responsibility for promotion of tourism in Sydney and the rest of NSW, Australia. Its 1998 *Masterplan* included the ten 'Indicators of success' shown in Table 10.12. Because Tourism NSW is a development and promotion organization, the success of its actions must be inferred from the success of the tourism industry as a whole; the indicators therefore rely extensively on surveys of visitors, host communities and the tourism industry.

Goals and Performance Indices

In the course of this book a wide variety of goals and objectives for leisure facilities have been alluded to. Some arise from political philosophies and some are implicit in the planning and evaluation techniques discussed. Figure 10.13 summarises these various goals and objectives and relates them to appropriate measures of effectiveness. This

Table 10.11. Travel-company service-quality dimensions (from Langer, 1997: 141).

1. Helpfulness in case of special requests
2. Travel motivation through travel consultants
3. Courteous, friendly travel-consultant behaviour
4. Consultation quality (professional, competent)
5. Appearance of employees
6. Price–performance ratio of agency
7. On-schedule holiday-booking processing
8. Helpfulness in case of short-term enquiries
9. Friendly response to telephone enquiries
10. Location of travel agency
11. Extensive variety of travel brochures
12. Clear office arrangement of travel agency
13. Extent of supplementary travel services
14. Understandable tour confirmations and documents
15. Fairness in event of complaints
16. Clear, understandable holiday travel prices
17. Global customer satisfaction (average of above)

Table 10.12. Indicators of success – Tourism New South Wales Masterplan (adapted from Tourism New South Wales, 1998: 18–19).

Outcome	Indicators of success	Data source
1. Consistent industry profitability that delivers increased local investment and employment	• Consistent profitability • Changes in the level of investment • Accommodation houses average/median occupancy rates	• Industry performance data as analysed by Tourism NSW • Tourism NSW Tourism Accommodation Development Register • ABS quarterly occupation surveys
2. Tourism products and a marketing system that attract high-yield markets	• Increase in average daily visitor expenditure (net of accommodation and air fares) • Increase in proportion of visitors identified as 'special interest' • Diversity of product in inventory and/or tourism database	• Visitor surveys • Visitor surveys • Tourism NSW register
3. Effective management of mass tourism from existing and emerging markets	• Increased repeat visitation from identified markets	• Visitor surveys
4. Sydney as a cultural capital and one of the world's leading convention cities	• Increase in NSW market share of international and interstate visitor-nights in Sydney over the period of the plan • Measured increase in convention delegates and convention spending in Sydney • Progressive increase in number of conventions and average size of major conventions (above 2000 delegates) won by Sydney	• BTR survey data • Sydney Visitors and Convention Bureau + visitor surveys • Sydney Visitors and Convention Bureau
5. The environment protected and appreciated by the tourism industry	• Industry operators adopt resource/energy/waste management and/or minimization practices • Financial contribution by tourism industry to environment protection/enhancement	• Attitude survey of industry operators and other relevant groups
6. New South Wales strongly branded as the complete holiday experience	• Increased visitor participation in cultural activities and nature-tourism activities in NSW • Increased availability of international and interstate entertainment and cultural-tour packages • Increased availability of nature-tourism packages	• Visitor surveys • Industry/product surveys • Industry/product surveys
7. Wider dispersion of tourism benefits through key tourist areas	• Proportion of international visitor-nights in NSW spent outside Sydney increases to 25% by 2010 • Measured increase in level of tourist spending in major tourism nodes as identified in the plan	• BTR survey data

8. Improved standards of service to ensure high levels of visitor satisfaction	• Continuing improvement in the level of visitor satisfaction with holiday experiences in NSW	• Quantitative visitor-satisfaction surveys
	• Measured participation by industry staff on customer-service programmes such as AussieHost	• Tourism NSW data
9. Improved efficiency in government spending for tourism	• In any government measure of State economic performance, return on government investment in tourism-related areas continues to improve (e.g. increased levels of employment and tourism expenditure)	• NSW Treasury data
	• Yield to the state, based on measures of state economic performance	
10. A tourism industry highly valued by the community and government	• Community recognition of the importance of tourism expenditure to the local economy	• Community survey
	• Measured changes in attitudes towards tourism by key stakeholders at local-government and key state-agency level	• Industry/local-government survey
	• Tourism is contributing to environmental sustainability	• Visitor survey and community surveys

ABS, Australian Bureau of Statistics; BTR, Bureau of Tourism Research.

Table 10.13. Goals and measures of effectiveness and efficiency.

Goal	Measures of effectiveness/efficiency	Data sources								
		Community survey	User/ visitor surveys	Ticket sales	User counts	Inventory	Service costs	Own records	Census	Special study
Access to facilities for chosen leisure activities for all	*Effectiveness*									
	Proportion of population participating	●								
	Proportion of population within reach of facilities	●				●			●	
	Proportion of population satisfied with service		●							
	Efficiency									
	Net cost per visit/participant			●	●		●			
Provision for need for all	*Effectiveness*									
	Extent to which needs (e.g. see social priority analysis[a]) are met (e.g. see matrix method)	●	●							
	Efficiency									
	Net cost per visit/participant						●			
Maintain existing provision	*Effectiveness*									
	Qualitative measures					●				
	Efficiency									
	–									
Promote excellence	*Effectiveness*									
	Excellence: medals, awards, records, etc.									●
	Efficiency									
	Costs per medal, etc.						●			
Minimize state role	*Effectiveness*									
	Short-term: extent of privatization	●								
	Long-term: quantity and quality of service						●	●		
	Efficiency									
	Public/private service costs						●	●		
Extend state role	*Effectiveness*									
	Growth of facilities/staff/user numbers					●		●		
	Efficiency									
	Costs per visit/participant				●		●			

Objective	Measure	Indicator					
Promote equality of opportunity	*Effectiveness*	Proportion of different social groups participating (e.g. see grid)	•	•			
	Efficiency	Costs per visit by target group	•	•			•
Promote democratization	*Effectiveness*	Representation on governing bodies					•
	Efficiency	–					
Provide facilities and opportunities that counter commercial exploitation	*Effectiveness*	Qualitative measures					•
	Efficiency	–					
Provide facilities/programmes that counter patriarchy	*Effectiveness*	Qualitative indicators of change	•	•			•
	Efficiency	–					
Promote access to facilities for women	*Effectiveness*	Number of facilities/programmes	•	•	•		
		Female participation levels	•	•	•		
	Efficiency	Cost per visit/female participant	•	•	•		
Child-care provision	*Effectiveness*	Number of child-care places and utilization	•	•	•		
	Efficiency	Cost per child place/visit	•	•	•		
Promote environmentally friendly activities	*Effectiveness*	Environmental audit of programmes					•
	Efficiency	Cost per user compared with others					•

continued

Table 10.13. *continued*

Goal	Measures of effectiveness/efficiency	Community survey	User/visitor surveys	Ticket sales	User counts	Inventory	Service costs	Own records	Census	Special study
Protect the natural environment	*Effectiveness*									
	Area protected					●				
	Qualitative review									●
	Efficiency									
	–									
Provide services that provide public-good, externality, mixed-good, merit-good and option-demand benefits	*Effectiveness*									
	Willingness-to-pay surveys	●	●							●
	Measure health, etc. benefits	●	●						●	●
	Clawson method		●							●
	Efficiency									
	Costs per visit/rate of return			●	●		●			●
Promote economic activity through leisure	*Effectiveness*									
	Profit	●								
	Economic impact – jobs, incomes							●		●
	Efficiency									
	Cost per job created						●			●
Promote equity	*Effectiveness*									
	Visits by deprived groups	●	●						●	●
	Efficiency									
	Costs per visit	●	●					●		●
Meet standards (various)	*Effectiveness*									
	Facility inventory					●				
	Efficiency									
	–									
Raise demand at least to the national/ regional average	*Effectiveness*									
	Participation levels	●							●	
	Efficiency									
	Costs per visit/participant						●			

There are 11 columns in this dot matrix. I'll label them 1–11 from left to right.

Objective	Type	Measure	1	2	3	4	5	6	7	8	9	10	11
Serve all areas	*Effectiveness*	Catchment areas, access and usage in different areas	•	•									
	Efficiency	Costs per visit in different areas	•	•						•			
Ensure full range of facilities	*Effectiveness*	Facility inventory for each level of community						•					
	Efficiency	–											
Meet needs of target groups in specified areas	*Effectiveness*	Access and facilities in target areas	•	•									
	Efficiency	Costs per visit/target participant	•	•						•			•
Provide full range of experiences	*Effectiveness*	Inventory of facility/resource types						•		•			
		Consumer reaction	•	•									
	Efficiency	Cost per visit/experience type	•	•	•	•		•	•				
Appropriate provision for all groups	*Effectiveness*	Participation levels by all groups	•	•						•			
	Efficiency	Costs per visit/target participant	•	•	•	•			•				
Serve all areas	*Effectiveness*	Facility catchment areas		•									
	Efficiency	Costs per visit/different areas				•	•		•				
Maximize utilization of facilities	*Effectiveness*	Facility utilization				•	•	•				•	•
	Efficiency	Costs per unit of capacity											•
Meet community wishes	*Effectiveness*	Community satisfaction	•										•
	Efficiency	–											

[a] See Chapter 7.

appears to be a very daunting list, but many, such as the political values, are alternatives, and others, such as economic development or the encouragement of infant industries, only apply in special circumstances.

Table 10.13 points to a need for substantial data collection on a regular basis. Some of this data collection relates to the environmental appraisal, as summarized in Table 6.2 (p. 97). But the performance-appraisal process suggests that, rather than being one-off exercises for the purpose of establishing the plan or strategy, data-collection systems need to be routinized and surveys repeated on a regular basis if policies are to be fully evaluated. Reliable *management information systems* need to be established, comprising: routine ticket-sale data (and user counts when this is not available); disaggregated financial data; booking records; regular user surveys; community surveys; and local census analysis. In practice, however, the cost of collecting some of the data specified may be considered excessive and may be ignored or undertaken only rarely – this applies particularly to those items requiring research. Public-sector agencies tend to see evaluative and market research as major, exceptional, undertakings, whereas many private-sector organizations see continuous user and market research (for example, annual market surveys) as a routine activity. Public-sector bodies will increasingly need to view such matters in a similar light if they are to justify their roles and respond to the demands increasingly being placed upon them.

Performance evaluation in the public sector of leisure and tourism is still in its infancy. This is due partly to the history of public services and partly to the complexity of the policies and services involved. In the private sector, the goal generally is to maximize profits, the PI – the rate of profit – is easily measured and there is a consensus among accountants, and even a legal specification, as to how it should be measured. The indicator provides a direct measure of the achievement of the goal. In the public sector, goals are often more complex, concerned with issues such as community well-being or the quality of life. PIs in such situations are just that – indicators. Often a number of indicators are required to give even an approximation of movement towards goal achievement. In the BAL system discussed above, the idea of first-stage and second-stage benefits is put forward (Driver and Bruns, 1999: 356–357): thus, for example, numbers of participants might be an indicator of first-stage benefits, but the enhanced health and improved quality of life of those participants can be seen as second-stage – and ultimate – benefits. In practice most public agencies are a long way from assessing performance and outcomes with this degree of sophistication, but the skills and infrastructure are being developed to make it possible in future.

Summary

- This chapter addresses steps 9 and 10 in the rational–comprehensive model presented in Chapter 5 (Fig. 5.3).
- The steps involved in performance evaluation are outlined and in particular it is emphasized that performance evaluation must be linked to goals and objectives.
- At the heart of modern performance evaluation is the performance indicator, PI – generally a quantified measure of a specific aspect of performance.
- In the case of internal evaluation, PIs are measured against baseline and target values; in the case of comparative evaluation, PIs are benchmarked against the same PIs from a number of similar facilities or programmes.
- The chapter reviews a number of frameworks that have emerged in recent years to systematize evaluation, including the British best value framework and the North American BAL system, and considers applications of these and other evaluation exercises.
- A major implication of performance evaluation is that its implementation requires a reliable information system comprising: routine ticket-sale data (and user counts when they are not available); disaggregated financial data; booking records; regular user surveys; community surveys; and local census analysis.

Further Reading

- Programme evaluation in general: Quade (1989); Shadish *et al.* (1991); Rossman (1999); Chapter 19 of Rossman and Schlatter (2000).
- Leisure-programme evaluation: Hatry and Dunn (1971); Theobald (1979); Bovaird (1992); Guide 13 of Torkildsen (1993); Henderson and Bialeschki (1995); Robinson (1997).
- Best value: Audit Commission, and Department of the Environment, Transport and Regions publications; Lewis and Hartley (2001); Ogden and Wilson (2001).
- Best value and sport: Sport England (1999, 2000).
- SERVQUAL: Howat *et al.* (1996); Langer (1997); Williams (1998a, b).
- Tourism: Chapter 6 of Hall and Jenkins (1995); Langer (1997).
- The arts: Cohen and Pate (2000); Department of Finance (1989); DASETT (1990); Skates (1990); Jackson (1991).
- Importance–performance analysis: see Chapter 6 Further Reading, and: Guadagnolo (1985); Hollenhorst *et al.* (1992); Langer (1997: 147); Hudson and Shephard (1998); Rossman and Schlatter (2000: 390–394).

Questions/Exercises

1. What is the difference between efficiency and effectiveness?

2. What is a performance indicator and what role does it play in the evaluation process?

3. What is the difference between internal and comparative evaluation? What is another term for comparative evaluation?

4. Outline the limitations of the British best-value framework.

5. What are the main features of the benefits approach to leisure and how does it differ from the best-value framework?

6. Select a recent annual report of a leisure or tourism agency and assess its approach to performance evaluation.

7. Discuss the problems of assessing quality in leisure-service performance evaluation.

8. For tourism agencies the outcomes of policies and programmes are often widely dispersed in the industry, making evaluation difficult. Give examples of this problem and discuss ways of addressing it in the evaluation process.

9. Select a leisure or tourism facility, service or programme known to you and either obtain a copy of its goals/objectives or devise a suitable list of goals/objectives yourself. Now suggest a list of performance indicators based on these goals/objectives, indicating the data source for each PI.

10. Devise a list of five service performance indicators for a university/college course. Either as an individual or a group, grade your current course on the five indicators, in terms of importance and performance, and plot the results on a graph. What would be the priority areas for attention by the course providers on the basis of this assessment?

Note

[1] In England and Wales the Local Government Act 2000 requires local authorities to 'promote the social, economic and environmental well-being of their area, and … work with partners to prepare a community strategy'.

11

Policy and Planning for Particular Sectors and Groups

Introduction

In most of the book the common elements among the various sectors of leisure and tourism have been stressed. In this chapter the diversity of leisure and tourism and the implications of that diversity for policy and planning are examined. While leisure and tourism have been considered in general terms, so have people. The differing needs and demands of various social groups within the community are therefore also considered here. The examination is necessarily brief, so more specialized and detailed sources are listed in the Further Reading section to provide pointers to further study.

Leisure and Tourism Sectors

This part of the chapter is divided into five sections dealing with: (i) sport and physical recreation; (ii) the arts and entertainment; (iii) outdoor recreation in natural areas; (iv) urban outdoor recreation; and (v) tourism. The discussion of each sector is under four headings: the scope of the sector; the rationale and goals of policy within the sector; institutional factors; and planning. The rationale for public involvement in the sector and the consequent goals and planning activities that are generally pursued relate directly to many of the issues addressed earlier in the book.

Sport and physical recreation

Scope

Sport can be defined as competitive or challenging physical, playful activity that takes a variety of forms, ranging from informal individual, family or community-based activity to highly competitive and commercialized phenomena of worldwide significance. Physical recreation encompasses those activities which are physical in nature and leisure-orientated, but not necessarily competitive or organized, typical examples being walking, non-competitive cycling and some forms of water-based recreation.

Public-policy rationale and goals

In general, public policy in sport has two goals:

1. Mass participation – to maximize participation in sport and physical recreation among the general population (sport for all).
2. Élite success – to promote maximum high-level achievement in competitive sport, both locally and internationally.

These goals are believed to be justified because of:

- the health benefits that mass participation can bring;
- the fostering of the community cohesiveness and pride that can come from sporting success;

- economic factors, such as the attraction of industry or tourists to a community or the economic benefits expected from the hosting of major events, such as the Olympic or Commonwealth Games.

Those involved in sport and physical recreation tend to enjoy them for their own sake and may be somewhat bemused at others' need to justify public support in instrumental terms. As a result, much political support for sport can be said to arise as a result of the self-interested lobbying activity of sporting organizations and their supporters – the public-choice model discussed in Chapter 5 – rather than from some appraisal of the benefit of sport to the wider community.

The two goals of sports policy – high-level performance and sport for all – are to some extent complementary and to some extent in competition, if not in contradiction. One view is that sport thrives on a sort of pyramid or 'trickle-down' model, as shown in Fig. 11.1. A strong, broad, mass-participation base should, it is argued, provide the breeding-ground for talent to produce the élite athletes for national and international competition. Conversely, a successful élite and a strong local and national competitive structure should provide inspiration and a suitable environment to encourage grass-roots participation.

An alternative view is that the trickle-down effect simply does not work: that the dynamics of mass participation are governed by local culture and infrastructure and other lifestyle trends, rather than by any inspira-tion coming from the élite (Roche, 1993). It can be argued that, for many sporting activities, the relationship between the mass, grass-roots level is not pyramid-shaped at all, but more as portrayed in Fig. 11.2, with what might be called 'selective élitism' beginning quite low in the system.

A third view is that, even if the trickle-down effect does work in theory, it is frustrated in practice because government resources inevitably flow to the élite level at the expense of the less glamorous mass-participation level, as a result of the lobbying activity of sporting organizations and the profile that association with élite sport can give politicians. Often, however, this conclusion is based on analysis of national and federal government expenditure patterns, ignoring expenditure on the grass roots by local government (e.g. McKay, 1986b).

Institutional factors

While the pyramid scenario may indeed work or may be a goal to aim at, the planning and management of organizational structures to achieve it can be complex. Each level involves public, private and commercial organizations, with different sets of goals and different modes of operation. Those professional and voluntary managers and policy-makers involved in opposite ends of the pyramid may not subscribe to, or even understand, the pyramid philosophy: they have their own, differing perspectives. Indeed, someone involved in élite sports

Fig. 11.1. Sports participation pyramid.

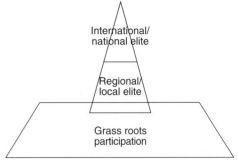

Fig. 11.2. Sport and selective élitism.

competition may have a low opinion of recreational sport and resent the public resources devoted to it, while someone involved in community recreation may be philosophically antagonistic towards the very concept of élitism and resent the public resources being devoted to the support of élite sport.

At the community level in the pyramid, the distinction between sport, physical recreation and social recreation becomes blurred: the manager of a community sport and leisure centre may feel that it is just as useful, or even more useful, to provide opportunities to enable elderly people to get out of the house for a game of bingo at the leisure centre or to encourage teenagers to engage in exercise through attendance at a discothèque, as it is to provide for formal sports activities. On the other hand, management's desire to reach as wide a cross-section of the community as possible and to maximize attendances at leisure facilities may, in the view of some, lead to superficial dabbling in a wide range of sporting activities and neglect of facilities, resources and organizational structures for those who wish to progress or improve and take sport seriously.

At the élite level questions can arise over just how far individuals should push themselves or be pushed to excel and win for the benefit of national pride, if this is at the expense of long-term physical and mental health. The concept of élitism raises issues concerning the relationship between public policy, amateurism, professionalism and commercialism. While public resources are provided to support the development of athletes in the context of an amateur ethos, increasing commercialization and professionalization of sport often result, ultimately, in great personal financial rewards for some, raising questions of 'who pays?' or 'who should pay?'

In sport, professionalism usually implies financial self-sufficiency – that is, those sectors where the athletes are professional do not generally look to the public sector for subsidy; they derive their income from spectators, television fees and sponsorship. In traditional sports different relationships have grown up between the publicly funded amateur sector of the sport and the commercially funded, professional sector, although the relationship has not always been amicable, as witness the relationship between Rugby League (professional) and Rugby Union (amateur). Different sports have had different relationships with the public sector, for a mix of historical, cultural and technical reasons. In the case of boxing, for example, the modest facilities required for training have enabled the sport, even at amateur level, to be fairly self-sufficient. Tennis has relied on private clubs, sometimes helped by public funds and sometimes using public facilities. In the case of golf, amateurs pay their way and often use the same facilities as the professionals, while publicly provided facilities also tend to be financially self-sufficient. In the case of soccer, the amateur game is extensively supported through subsidized access to publicly provided playing pitches.

Planning

As Chapter 6 indicates, planning for sport facilities for the community on the basis of standards of provision for playing-fields is a long-established tradition. From its establishment in the early 1970s, the British Sports Council was instrumental in widening the scope of public planning to include such facilities as indoor sports and leisure centres and swimming-pools and dual-use of education facilities, utilizing relatively sophisticated planning techniques and the development of interlinked national, regional and local planning strategies for the provision of facilities (Sports Council, 1972, 1975, 1978, 1982, 1988, 1991a,b, 1993).

Planning for the promotion of mass participation by means other than the provision of facilities is a less certain process. Direct promotion through publicity campaigns has been difficult to evaluate, as have educational programmes (Watkins, 1981; McIntosh and Charlton, 1985).

Planning for the top part of the pyramid is complicated by the involvement of numerous national and international governing bodies of sport, commercial promoters, professional players' organizations, media interests and, in the pubic sector, a range of quangos, often with ministers looking closely over their shoulders, despite the supposed existence of the arm's-length principle. The core of planning at this level is the formal strategic plan of the governing body; such a plan is a necessity if the aspirations of the sport are to be supported by public funds (Elvin, 1990: 73).

Because of the institutional structure and the devolved management structure of modern built sport and recreation facilities, this sector has been at the forefront of the recent developments in management and provision, such as compulsory competitive tendering (CCT) and best value.

The arts

Scope

The arts cover a wide spectrum of human activity, including the performing arts (drama, music, opera and dance), painting and sculpture, craft activities, literature, poetry, architecture and design, film, television and radio. The arts industries cover the various activities and institutions that facilitate or conserve these activities and their outputs, including theatres, galleries, museums, heritage conservation, libraries and the various public and private bodies that provide financial support for the sector.

Rationale and goals

Public subsidy of the arts has traditionally been justified on the grounds of the wider cultural benefits they bring to the community (Baumol and Bowen, 1976). Other arguments relate to their growing importance in the economy (Wall, 1983; Casey *et al.*, 1996); and, especially in relation to galleries, museums and libraries, their educational value (Baumol and Bowen, 1976).

The arts have certain similarities to sport and certain stark differences. The similarity lies in the duality of objectives: excellence versus mass involvement. The differences lie in the structure of the industry and its relationship with the public.

Unlike sport, where the publicly subsidized sector and the commercial sector are both considered, unequivocally, to be sport, in the arts those elements of the industry that are financially self-sufficient, such as commercial film and theatre, recorded music and commercial television and publishing, tend to be classified as *entertainment* or *popular culture* rather than part of the arts. Thus it would seem that, to exaggerate just a little, only if an activity does not make money is it classified as art.

A further contrast between sport and the arts is that, whereas in sport public resources are largely devoted to enabling direct participation in sport by members of the public and professionals are largely financially self-supporting, in the case of the arts, public resources are required to support professionals, with the public role being largely that of audience only. The area of the arts that corresponds to grass-roots sports participation is amateur theatre or amateur music, and, whereas the amateur is a celebrated phenomenon in sport, in the arts such activity is generally looked down upon or largely ignored. Active participation in the arts is left to voluntary effort (for example, amateur music and drama), to the public or commercial education sector (for example, adult education classes in painting or pottery or commercial dance studios), or to self-help (for example, amateur rock and jazz bands). When the arts community itself ventures into the area of participation – in the form of community arts – it is often controversial (Kelly, 1984; Hawkins, 1993).

There is a further difference between sport and the arts which is notable because it leads to a particular difficulty in arts policy and management that does not arise in sports policy and management. This is that, in the arts, the concept of excellence is often disputed, whereas it is not in sport. There is generally no dispute about who is the number-one ranking tennis player or what team won the World Cup. In particular, there is a consensus among athletes, sports administrators and the general public about what excellence is – even if there is lively debate from time to time as to which team or player is currently demonstrating such qualities. This is not the case in the arts: what artists or administrators think of as excellence is often at variance with the tastes of the general public. While there are, of course, exceptions, in general the public will flock to performances of the familiar and the unchallenging, but will stay away in droves from productions that are new or difficult. Hence arts managers are continually being faced with the task of balancing artistic challenge and integrity with the commercial realities of getting 'bums on seats'. All this, of course, makes application of traditional, rationalist, decision-making and performance evaluation difficult.

Libraries are often neglected in discussion of the arts, and yet they are the most pervasive and significant of the publicly funded arts/cultural services. Of course, libraries have an educational and information-providing role, which may well be the primary basis of their political support, but most of their use is for leisure purposes (Taylor and Johnson, 1973). While it is, no doubt, their educational and information roles that provide much of the basis for their continued political support as free public services, the leisure function of libraries offers an interesting case-study of public provision. Lending libraries are obviously socially desirable and make efficient use of resources, since several hundred people can read one library book compared with only a few in the case of private ownership. But why should the borrower not pay? Private lending libraries existed into the 1950s, where people paid a small sum to borrow books, in the same way that people currently hire videos. But they were eventually undermined by the arrival of the cheap paperback. The free public lending library has the advantage of making a wider range of titles available to the reader (not all books are available in cheap paperback editions) and makes books available to those for whom even paperback prices would be a deterrent. As a leisure service, therefore, the public lending library is both efficient and equitable. Against this must be balanced the financial interests of publishers and authors, who would no doubt prefer people to buy books rather than borrow them for free from libraries. But this has been

addressed to a certain extent by the Public Lending Right Act, 1979, which requires public libraries to pay into a central fund that compensates authors and publishers for library use of their work.

Similar arguments apply to art galleries and museums: an infinite number of people may enjoy works of art and heritage items in galleries, compared with just a few if they were privately owned. To this extent galleries and museums meet the non-rival, although not strictly the non-excludable, criterion for public goods, as discussed in Chapter 4. In addition, the natural-monopoly criterion applies in relation to single works of art or collections of national or even world cultural importance. In the case of galleries and museums, however, the mixed-good concept has prevailed in some countries in recent years and there has been a trend towards charging an entrance fee – albeit one that only partially covers costs. As with libraries, however, it is likely that the broader cultural-heritage and educational role of galleries and museums is the basis of their political support, rather than their purely leisure functions. Increasingly, such institutions are also being seen as worthy of support because of their role as part of the infrastructure of tourism and potential for urban economic regeneration (Voase, 1997).

Broadcasting is a quintessential public good even if provided entirely for leisure purposes and even if commercially supported through advertising. It is likely, however, that public broadcasting bodies, such as the BBC in Britain and the ABC in Australia, generally receive their political support not because of their leisure role but because of their educational, information and national cultural-identity role.

Institutional factors

Because of the high cost of supporting professional performers in a subsidized environment, the central preoccupation of much of the arts management community would appear to be funding. While a large proportion of funding in the performing arts is generated from the box office and other entrepreneurial activities, the balance is sought in the form of grants from local, state or central government. It is the latter which attracts the most debate and controversy.

Clearly, if governments were to provide more money for the arts, then directors, writers and performers would have more freedom to pursue their artistic aims and would be less constrained by the discipline of the box office. The controllers of the public purse-strings, however, might well look askance at such a proposition: surely less dependence on the box office could mean fewer people attending performances – surely that would not be achieving the public objective of bringing the arts to the people! Of course, the arts organizations could be saying: if we had more money we could mount more lavish productions, provide more variety and put on more performances in more locations – this would bring the arts to more people. In so far as the public funding bodies are suspicious of the earlier argument but are sympathetic to the latter, they have an interest in knowing just how any additional funding will be used. It is not uncommon, therefore, for governments to offer additional funds that are earmarked for specific activities, such as regional touring.

In the case of other art forms, notably galleries and museums, the preoccupation with funding is equally prevalent. While blockbuster, money-making exhibitions and entrance fees are becoming more common, galleries and museums are usually even more dependent on public subsidy than are the performing arts. This has traditionally been justified on the educational grounds discussed above. The demand for additional funding is nevertheless endemic. Museum and gallery trustees and managements always need money for acquisitions, for expansion to exhibit the artefacts they have stored away or for staff to pursue research and conservation activities.

Planning

With the exception of libraries, planning for the arts can best be described as an *ad hoc* process. Since the *Housing of the Arts* reports of the 1960s (Arts Council of Great Britain, 1959, 1961), there has been no apparent national strategic planning in Britain comparable to the then Sports Council's detailed plans for the provision of sport facilities. At local level, again with the possible exception of libraries, planning for the arts would appear to be more a matter of municipal pride rather than assessment of community need. The principle seems to be that any urban authority of any size feels that it should have a civic theatre, a museum and, possibly, an arts centre – indeed, the philosophy might well have been summed up by the title of one of the early, and few, books on arts centres, which was: *Arts Centres: Every Town Should Have One* (Lane, 1978).

Before its abolition by the Thatcher government in 1980, the Greater London Council pioneered attempts at developing a strategic approach to local cultural planning. In subsequent years, a number of researchers kept alive the idea that *cultural industries* might be taken seriously as a key feature of urban life and an important economic sector and that local strategies might be produced to address the development of such an industry and to secure community benefits from it (e.g. Garnham, 1987; Bianchini *et al.*, 1991; Landry and Bianchini, 1995; Zukin, 1995). In the new political environment in Britain, the establishment of a Department for Culture, Media and Sport has brought responsibility for the arts and sport into one government department, which has resulted, in turn, in nationally promulgated guidelines for the production of local *cultural strategies* (Department for Culture, Media and Sport, 1999). This recognizes that local authorities have responsibilities across the whole range of leisure and tourism, including outdoor recreation, sport, tourism, heritage and the arts.

It is notable that, during the brief period at the end of the 1980s and in the early 1990s, the Australian federal government included a similarly broad department, with the unwieldy title of the Department of the Arts, Sport, the Environment, Tourism and Territories (DASETT). A forward-looking national cultural-policy document emerged, dealing with the arts (Commonwealth of Australia, 1994), but the various junior portfolios within the ministry remained separate, as they do at state level, and no local planning guidance emerged. In Britain, however, it is possible that, with central government support, more planning for the arts, alongside planning for other aspects of culture, will be seen in local government in future.

Outdoor recreation – natural areas

Scope

Outdoor recreation in natural areas takes place in national parks and country parks, in forests, on the coast and on footpaths and, through the phenomenon of driving for pleasure, throughout the countryside. The visiting of heritage and other attractions in the rural environment is also included.

Rationale and goals

As with sport and the arts, public policy with regard to outdoor recreation in the natural environment – in national parks and country parks and on the coast – is faced with two potentially conflicting goals: conservation and recreational access. Conservation of flora, fauna, landscape, ecosystems and heritage seems a clear enough mandate, until it is realized that, in the case of Britain, hardly any area of the country has been untouched by human activity over the centuries. Before human beings made their mark, the whole of Britain was covered in forest, but now even the national parks are grazed by sheep! Even in supposedly pristine environments, such as the Australian bush, the landscape we see today results from thousands of years of management by human beings through hunting and gathering activity and the use of fire (Flannery, 1994). So what is natural and to be conserved? In some areas, phenomena such as abandoned mines, which would, in modern times, be seen as a desecration of the natural landscape, have now become a part of the cultural heritage.

But the real problems arise when considering recreational access. For virtually any ecosystem, human activity – certainly on any scale – poses a threat. Walking tracks, car parks, toilet blocks and camp-sites usurp space that might have been used by flora and fauna, and their use inevitably disturbs flora and fauna: ultimately conservation implies the exclusion of the species *Homo sapiens* in its modern form.

And yet national-parks authorities are required by law to facilitate recreational access as well as conserving the environment; and facilitating such access is a necessary part of their continued community and political support. But, as a result of the dual goals, the sort of overt promotional and marketing activity we see in the sports and arts sectors is not part of the countryside recreation scene. In natural areas a balance has to be struck between recreational access and conservation.

Institutional factors

A unique feature of countryside recreation – particularly in Britain – is that much of it takes place on private property, with the public role being to ensure and to manage rights of access. This is true of large parts of Britain's national parks, of footpaths and of coastal access (although actual beaches are in the public domain). While initial campaigns for public access were organized by voluntary effort (Glyptis, 1991: 28), today the public's interest in recreational access to the countryside is represented by elected councils and quangos (such as national parks agencies and the Countryside Commission), although non-profit-sector organizations, such as the National Trust, remain important.

Providing for countryside recreation faces the further special problem that, typically, the population being planned for is not the resident rural population, but the nearby – and distant – urban population. Consequently rural residents are seen to be providing for the recreational needs of urban residents. Of course, this might be seen as a balance to the cultural and other services provided by urban areas for rural residents, but things are rarely seen in such a light, especially given that the rural population is generally smaller in numbers and less wealthy than the urban population. This demographic and financial imbalance is, of course, an argument for national and regional government providing financial support for local rural councils and for national park organizations, and this is generally what happens in practice. In some federal systems the problem is partly solved by state governments having responsibilities for natural areas.

Planning

One way in which policy-makers seek to balance the demands of conservation and recreational demand is by designation and zoning processes. Thus, at one end of the spectrum, nature reserves and, in some countries, wilderness areas are established, from which humans are virtually excluded. Within national parks, efforts are made to concentrate high-volume visitation in limited areas, where services can be provided and the impact on the natural environment can be contained. At the other extreme, in the UK country parks are created that are primarily devoted to recreation and can sometimes be indistinguishable from larger urban parks. The recreation opportunity spectrum idea, as outlined in Chapter 7, is one way in which this spectrum approach is formalized.

The fact that the clients for countryside recreation are urban residents, as discussed above, is a key feature of planning for countryside recreation. This means that, ideally, planning should be undertaken on a regional rather than a local basis. Thus, for example, planning for outdoor recreation in the various counties in the south-east of England is dominated by demands of the population of London; any one individual county cannot be expected to encompass this process in its entirety – researching and planning for the phenomenon must be a cooperative, regional, process. A similar situation exists along the south-east coast of Australia, dominated by the major cities of Melbourne, Sydney and Brisbane. However, in the UK, the need for this sort of approach to planning has become less urgent as static or declining populations and economic recession have slowed the rate of growth of recreation demand and, in some cases, put it into reverse (Rodgers, 1993). Planning for outdoor recreation, in a no-growth situation, can become more resource-based and less concerned with demand pressures.

Urban outdoor recreation

Scope

Urban outdoor recreation takes place primarily in parks, playing-fields, playgrounds and squares and plazas. The provision of open space in urban areas constitutes the largest single public leisure service sector, in terms of expenditure, the value of land allocation and staff, and is the longest established. Parks include formal and informal landscaped areas for walking and relaxation and specific-purpose facilities designed for more physically active recreation, including boating facilities, playgrounds, hard sports areas, such as tennis-courts, and grass playing pitches. And they may contain catering facilities and performance spaces. Parks accommodate events, such as music performances, sports matches, demonstrations and rallies and peripatetic phenomena, such as funfairs and circuses. Other forms of urban public open space should not be ignored, including public squares and plazas, harbour and riverside areas, seaside promenades, market-places and village greens and, indeed, streets, especially where they have been pedestrianized.

Rationale and goals

This sector does not face the conflicting goals of recreational access versus conservation to anything like the extent that they are faced by its countryside counterpart. Urban parks can, however, extend to the urban fringe, where environmentally sensitive areas can be involved, and, even within urban areas, parks may encompass areas that are valued for their nature-conservation value rather than their direct recreational value. In addition, parks can include natural or built items of heritage value, such as mature trees, or monuments and buildings, the conservation of which may conflict with some recreational objectives. In general, however, parks have been planned, designed and developed specifically for recreational purposes.

Nevertheless, there is an excellence factor in park management that parallels that in sport or the arts, namely horticultural and landscape values. The horticulturalist or landscape planner has a set of professional values that may or may not be compatible with the needs and demands of the recreational user of an area of open space. In general, the horticulturalist or landscaper wants to do things with plants or with the aesthetics of the landscape. This is not necessarily in conflict with recreational needs – for example, elaborate floral displays are generally popular with the public, although expensive to maintain.

Parks for informal recreation offer the same sorts of community benefits as natural areas, in the form of opportunities to relax, commune with nature and take mild exercise. Generally the aim of the providers of such facilities is to provide opportunity rather than to actively promote or maximize participation. In so far as parks contain sports facilities, the goals should, logically, be similar to those discussed under sport and physical recreation, and areas developed in relation to cultural and entertainment, such as the recent growth of harbourside developments, have a promotional ethos similar to commercial enterprises – the more the merrier – and therefore a more proactive approach to promotion of participation is appropriate. There should therefore be a difference between the resource-based focus of green, open-space recreation-area management and the people-based promotional orientation of sports and entertainment-related facilities

Institutional factors

Generally urban open space is in the ownership and control of local government. In large urban centres, however, other agencies may be involved, such as the Royal Parks in London, run by the Department of the Environment. In some federal systems the state government tends to have responsibility for national parks and some major urban parks. Often in local government, parks are administered separately from other leisure services, so the resource-based, facility-maintenance approach has tended to be predominant.

Planning

As indicated in Chapter 7, planning for open space in urban areas on the basis of standards is a long-established practice, and many of the alternative methods discussed also have their basis in open-space planning. In Britain the opportunity to develop new parks, even in areas with very low levels of provision, is very limited. In fact it is in the areas of greatest relative deprivation, in the centres of large cities, that the opportunities are most rare, because of the price of land. Planning of these areas today is therefore much closer to management – the task is to determine how to make the best use of the facilities available. Optimizing use can involve management practices (for example, increasing staff patrols in areas where usage is limited because of safety fears) or development work (e.g. improving drainage of pitches or providing artificial surfaces). However, in growing cities, such as those in Australia and in developing countries, the challenge of providing suitable open space for a growing population is significant.

Tourism

Scope

Tourism is defined differently by different writers and agencies. Definitions of a tourist generally involve an overnight stay away from home in a place other than the person's normal place of residence. Some definitions distinguish between those who travel for leisure purposes and those who travel for non-leisure purposes, such as business, and yet the business traveller's requirements overlap considerably with those of the leisure traveller. Similarly, day-trippers to holiday areas are not normally included in the strict definition of tourist, but many of their requirements and activities are similar to those of the staying tourist in all respects except the requirement for accommodation. While the high-profile sector of tourism is international travel, in most developed countries domestic tourism – people taking holidays in their own country – is larger in both the number of trips and financial turnover.

Tourism is often viewed and analysed in terms of the industry rather than the tourist. The tourism industry is fragmented, not only in terms of the dominance of small businesses (such as hotels and camping-sites, restaurants and gift shops), but also in terms of the variety of subsectors involved, including travel agents, transport, the accommodation sector, cafés and restaurants and natural environment and built attractions. As with leisure generally, many sectors of the so-called tourism industry are only partly in the tourism industry – for example, transport, catering and many of the attractions (when they are used by locals as well as visitors).

Tourism is increasingly being seen as consisting of mass tourism and a series of specialist tourism markets – although in practice one tourist might be involved in a number of markets in any one trip. Among the specialist areas are: ecotourism or nature-based tourism; cultural tourism; the meetings, incentives, conventions and events (MICE) sector; urban tourism; wine tourism; the backpacker market; sports tourism; and the short-breaks market. Each of these areas is developing its own body of research and expertise.

Rationale and goals

Public policy and planning for tourism have in common with countryside recreation planning the characteristic that they are not focused on the needs and demands of local residents. Thus, even though the public agency responsible for policy and planning is democratically elected or answerable to a democratically elected body, policy and planning are not directed at meeting the holiday-making needs and demands of the electorate; rather, they are generally aimed at maximizing the benefits local residents might obtain from other people's holiday-making and minimizing the negative effects the tourists might generate. The benefits are seen almost exclusively as economic – the generation of jobs and incomes – and the negative effects are almost exclusively seen as environmental.

Paralleling the ambivalence of the dual goals of countryside recreation, tourism policy is generally juggling with two contradictory goals: the maximization of tourist numbers and their expenditure in a destination and the minimization of their environmental impact on the destination. The maximization part of the equation is much stronger. The conflict between the two goals is often resolved – or permitted to remain unresolved – by separating them institutionally, as discussed below.

A key feature of tourism policy is the way public bodies intervene in what is essentially a private-sector industry. Public bodies generally undertake a marketing and promotional role on behalf of the industry. Public money is spent generating customers for private industry with a view to reaping social benefits in the form of increased jobs and incomes (and tax income). Often the main resource around which tourism develops is publicly owned and managed – for example, lakes, mountains and beaches or museums, galleries and historic buildings. Why does this sort of intervention happen in tourism and not in other industries, such as car-manufacturing? Two factors would seem to explain it: one is the fragmentary nature of the industry, as discussed above, and other is the fact that the markets which must be addressed are, by definition, not local. Thus marketing and promotion costs are high and, although they can be justified and effective for the industry as a whole, they are too costly for many of the individual commercial organizations involved. So government bodies step in as the promotional arm of the industry, claiming to represent the economic interests of the host community.

A form of state involvement in tourism that is not given a great deal of prominence in tourism policy or the literature is the idea of *social tourism* (Finch, 1975), a process by which deprived groups in the community are helped to go on holiday, usually via some form of subsidy, but also by direct provision. The idea is particularly appropriate for carers – generally family members who take care of people with severe disability or chronic illness. Provision of relief for such individuals, in the form of a holiday, is a humanitarian gesture, but can also be very cost-effective for the state, the provision of periodic relief helping the carer to continue in that role, rather than the burden of care falling on the state.

Institutional factors

The contradiction between the maximization of tourist numbers and minimization of environmental impacts is often avoided as a result of the fact that the responsibility for tourism development and promotion is in the hands of the private sector and regional and national public marketing bodies such as tourism commissions and associations, while the responsibility for local environmental planning, protection and conservation lies with local planning authorities. Thus the option of reducing or stabilizing tourist numbers is not really available to the environmental planners – all they can do is seek to influence where developers and tourists are allowed to go and what they are allowed to do where.

Planning

Planning for tourism is, like planning for countryside recreation, characterized by the fact that demand comes from outside the area. Planning activity is influenced by the institutional factors discussed above. Unlike many other fields of leisure planning, demand forecasting has played a significant role in tourism planning, but mainly at the national level. National tourism commissions and ministries produce tourism-demand forecasts and targets, as discussed in Chapter 8. On the basis of such forecasts and targets, attention is then given to the question of future accommodation and airport capacity, but little attention is given to the capacity of the leisure environments and attractions that tourists come to see. That this is a problem is to some extent recognized in attempts by national and regional tourist bodies to spread the tourist load, both spatially and temporally – that is, it is recognized that certain places (e.g. London) become overcrowded at certain times of the year. At the regional and local level, the tourism-planning task is to cope with a level of demand that is seen as more or less an externally given. As tourism is a relative newcomer to the local planning scene, its integration into local planning is less fully developed than are other sectors (Dredge and Moore, 1992; Long, 1994).

The concept that has caught the imagination of tourism researchers, policy-makers and planners in recent years is *sustainability*. The output of literature concerned with sustainability and tourism in the last decade has been extraordinary. As indicated in Chapter 3, the concept arose from the environmental movement; thus the tourism industry and its academic community can be said to have effected a clever move in adopting the concept as their own, since tourism development in natural areas has traditionally been seen as one of the *bêtes noires* of environmental conservationists. The term has been cemented into place in tourism planning by the suggestion that sustainability not only refers to environmental sustainability, but also to economic and social sustainability, in the sense of acceptability to the host community. In urban areas the natural environment is replaced by the built heritage as the focus of sustainability concerns (Fyall and Garrod, 1998). Thus the potential 'wolf' of tourism development is packaged within 'sheep's clothing' of sustainable development strategies and made to appear less threatening. Meanwhile, as the plan unfolds in practice, as in any industry, the developers and operators of tourism facilities – and the often associated urban-growth regimes, as discussed in Chapter 5 – follow their natural bent, which is to maximize profits, and there is little evidence to suggest that members of the community do not also wish to maximize their incomes from tourism. Thus the environmentally sustainable development, with the best possible credentials, can lead to unintended creeping urbanisation in rural areas (Craik, 1987) or marketing and development that is culturally inappropriate or contested (Hale, 2001).

Groups

In this section seven social groups with particular leisure or tourism needs are considered. Every individual is unique and so could be said to have unique leisure and tourism requirements. In family settings and some organizational settings this uniqueness can be catered for, but human beings are also social animals with interests, demands and needs in common. Common experiences can be as important as individual experiences – people want to belong and to share. Classifying people into groups and considering their common characteristics and needs is not therefore to deny their individuality; in fact, it has been the failure of providers to consider the common needs of some groups that has, in the past, denied members of such groups their individuality. As a result of campaigns, regulations, research and the spread of ideas such as market segmentation and niche marketing, some of these problems are now beginning to be overcome.

Four perspectives can be considered in examining social groups and their needs and demands: (i) a welfare perspective; (ii) a human- and citizens'-rights perspective; (iii) a market perspective; and (iv) a diversity and inclusion perspective.

The *welfare perspective* dominated thinking about certain groups, such as people with disabilities and the elderly, in the past, but is rapidly being replaced by the other three perspectives. The idea that various individuals should be viewed as relatively passive recipients of assistance from the rest of the community is being replaced by more active, subject-centred, perspectives.

The *rights perspective* reflects the discussion of human rights and citizens' rights in Chapter 2. This is based on the premise that all individuals have the same rights of access to services and participation in the social, political and economic life of the community. Following the various international declarations referred to in Chapter 2, many of such rights are enshrined in national constitutions and legislation. Thus equal opportunity and antidiscrimination legislation designed to protect the rights of various minority or traditionally disadvantaged groups is now common. This in turn means that individuals or organizations that infringe the legislation can be sued or prosecuted. Such changes have, however, often only been brought about by a considerable amount of campaigning by members of the groups concerned and their supporters. Often the campaign continues after legislation and regulations are in place, to ensure compliance through such measures as publicity and bringing test cases to court.

The *market perspective* draws attention to the power of particular groups as consumers in the market-place, suggesting that it is in the commercial interest of manufacturers, retailers and service providers to consider the needs of such market segments. While this has traditionally been part of commercial thinking in relation to the youth market or women as consumers, more recently the tourism market has come to realize the value of the retired market, the gay and lesbian 'pink pound' or dollar has been recognized, and others, such as minority ethnic groups and people with disabilities, have begun to quantify their market power.

Diversity and inclusion are concepts more commonly used in the public sector (Dattilo and Williams, 1999; Patterson and Taylor, 2001). Rather than thinking of society as a mainstream mass and various additional special groups with special needs, it is suggested that society as a whole be considered to consist of a host of groups with a variety of common and special needs – there is no mainstream, but rather a kaleidoscope of diversity. This reflects social change brought about by immigration, changed family and household structures and globalization, and reflects thinking in the commercial sector, which increasingly sees the market in terms of a wide range of overlapping lifestyle groups.

In this section the following groups are discussed in turn: (i) women; (ii) ethnic groups; (iii) people with disabilities; (iv) children; (v) youth; and (vi) the elderly.

Women

Women comprise more than half the population, but early leisure and tourism research, policy and planning often gave the impression that women were at best a minority and at worst non-existent. In Chapter 3 the way women's leisure and tourism needs are viewed from feminist perspectives was considered. Here we consider the question: how should policy and planning for leisure and tourism in contemporary society seek to reflect the particular needs of women? Such an approach is avowedly reformist in feminist terms since, in a society of full equality between men and women there would be few particularly women's needs – all would be human needs. Thus, if child-care were shared equally, child-care facilities would be demanded by parents rather than mothers. If male violence were to be eliminated, then travel after dark for leisure or any other purpose would not be a problem experienced by women or men. If all sports were open to both sexes – for mixed or single-sex competition – then particular provision for women's sports would not be necessary: access would be available to all. But society is not equal, so measures must be taken to redress the imbalances that exist and to put in place transitional arrangements, few of which would be necessary in a fully equal society.

The main problem area in leisure policy and planning for women would appear to be the area of sport. This is reflected in the substantial literature on women and sport; even in general discussions of leisure, sport is often the form of leisure used as an example to demonstrate existing inequalities. Women's comparatively low level of participation and the reasons for it are discussed in terms of cultural expectations and constraints (e.g. Scraton, 1993), male organizational power (McKay, 1998), media sports coverage (e.g. Brown, 1993) and lack of facilities (Mowbray, 1992, 1993) and are recognized in specific targets in policy documents, such as the current Sport England (1997) strategic plan.

Participation statistics suggest that in most other areas women's participation levels are greater than or equal to those of men. It is rarely suggested that the arts or entertainment sectors discriminate against women audiences or that libraries, parks or countryside recreation facilities do not cater to the needs of women.

While women participate in tourism to the same extent as men, there is concern that women are not free to travel alone or unaccompanied by men, partly because of safety concerns. Research on the gendered nature of tourism has begun to address this issue (Kinnaird and Hall, 1994; Swain, 1995; Pritchard, 2001).

Increased access and provision for women's leisure has implications for men. Some of the difficulties women face in gaining access to resources is explained by the fact that resources – for example, land – are limited, and men's sporting organizations may be required to give up some of the facilities which they have hitherto enjoyed exclusively by default. In theory, to meet equal demand for women, provision of facilities and services in some areas would need to be almost doubled – and men would have to share the cost through taxation and/or other revenue-raising methods, in the same way that women have shared the burden of funding men's public leisure provision to date. In fact, a more equal society could lead to qualitative changes in men's leisure, especially in the area of sport, and such ideas are already being addressed in literature on the topic of masculinity (e.g. Miller, 1990; Lynch, 1993; Webb, 1998).

Gender awareness has also led to the development of research on the leisure and tourism experiences and provision for gay men and lesbians (e.g. Markwell, 1998a; Pritchard *et al.*, 2000).

Ethnic groups

Ethnic groups are groups of people with a common culture – so everyone belongs to an ethnic group, whether it be a majority or minority in a particular society. While ethnicity is often associated with race, this need not be the case, as the experience of Northern Ireland illustrates. In general, minority ethnic and racial groups are at a disadvantage, in leisure and tourism as in other spheres of life. The challenge in contemporary societies is to achieve racial and ethnic equality and to gain the positive cultural benefits that ethnic diversity can offer. As discussed above and in Chapter 2, policies for equity and inclusion can also be seen in terms of the rights of citizenship. Leisure-service providers are at the forefront of these processes and, indeed, face the dilemmas these objectives can bring. For example, is it wise to encourage ethnically based sports teams to bring different groups together in friendly competition, or will the rivalry actually damage community relations? Will ethnically based cultural festivals result in the sharing of cultural experiences or greater separation between groups?

In Britain, most ethnic-minority groups have their origins in immigration from various parts of the British Commonwealth/ Empire. Often immigrants were recruited by British employers specifically as cheap labour in periods of labour shortage. Whole groups of migrants therefore suffered from low incomes and, as a result of this and racial discrimination, also suffered from poor housing and a cycle of deprivation. Policy for ethnic-minority groups, including leisure policy, has tended to be orientated towards alleviating or compensating for general social deprivation. Such policies need to be handled sensitively, whether aimed specifically at ethnic-minority groups or deprived groups in general, since, while public leisure services may be provided with the aim of achieving equity, as discussed in Chapter 4, such provision can be viewed as a cynical exercise in placation if other services and opportunities, such as housing, health and education, not to mention jobs, are not being attended to at the same time.

Another dimension of policy related to ethnic groups relates not to deprivation but to differences in social customs and values. In particular, as discussed by Green, E. *et al.* (1990: 70–81), women and girls from Moslem or conservative Christian communities are restricted in terms of permitted public recreation behaviour. Such restrictions have slowly been recognized by public leisure providers and catered for by special programmes.

People with disabilities

Disabilities come in a variety of forms and degrees of severity and affect a substantial proportion of the population. Included are mental illness and physical disability, suffered from birth or as a result of illness or accident, and including deafness, dumbness, blindness, disabilities related to the nervous and the muscular–skeletal systems, and chronic conditions, such as diabetes and asthma. Such a wide range of conditions calls for a correspondingly wide range of policy responses. Since a number of disabilities arise with ageing, there is considerable overlap between people with disabilities and the elderly population.

When the majority of people with severe disabilities lived in institutions, the question of access to leisure provision was seen as largely an institutional issue. Over the last 20 years a process of deinstitutionalization has been taking place in the belief that people with disabilities can live more dignified lives in the community. Leisure services have a clear role to play in such a process, since leisure activities can be not only be therapeutic for the individual, but also a direct means of integration with the wider community.

Provision of leisure and tourism services for people with disabilities was traditionally viewed in welfare terms, but is increasingly being seen in terms of rights, market power and inclusive diversity, as discussed above. Attitudes towards people with disabilities and the policies and practices of public- and private-sector agencies in regard to people with disabilities as clients, customers or users have often been shaped by a medical perspective that serves to marginalize and exclude people with disabilities from mainstream society. In the days of institutionalization, the result was that people with disabilities were largely out of sight and out of mind. Within this perspective, people with disabilities are seen as difficult and requiring special facilities and arrangements, which cause trouble and expense for the provider. This has resulted in buildings, transport facilities and infrastructure and many services being designed in ways that deter or prevent people with various disabilities from using them.

While modifications can be expensive once buildings and facilities have been constructed, suitable designs adopted from the very beginning can be relatively cheap or even costless – for example, the width of doorways, design of kerbless showers in hotel rooms, elimination of steps, positioning of light switches and the size of lettering in print and on computer screens. Following legislation to uphold the rights of people with disabilities – such as the UK Disability Discrimination Act, 1995 – building guidelines and regulations for access have been promulgated in many countries, but are not always willingly or fully observed.

Tourism opportunities for people with disabilities have attracted research and policy attention in recent years (Murray and Sproats, 1990; Darcy, 1998; Burnett and Bender Baker, 2001). This research has focused particularly on the market perspective, drawing attention to the actual and potential size of the market and, in particular, to the fact that people with disabilities are generally accompanied by family and friends, so accommodation and hospitality facilities and attractions that cannot accommodate people with disabilities also lose the custom of their companions.

Children

While the origins of public leisure services can be traced to the early development of play facilities for young people (Kraus, 1998: 197–198) and children constitute a significant proportion, if not the majority, of the customers of some public leisure facilities, children's leisure needs have been relatively neglected in discussion of leisure policy. Part of the reason for this is the difficulty of conducting research with children: for practical or ethical reasons it is difficult to administer questionnaires to young children, so that leisure-participation surveys and facility-user surveys omit children who are younger than about 12 years and often older. Research therefore tends to be conducted by means of observation and is left to child psychologists who have an interest in children as individuals, but not necessarily as a social category.

As regards provision of leisure facilities and services for children, there is a tendency to think only in terms of (outdoor) playgrounds, as the playground standards mentioned in Chapter 7 indicate, ignoring the fact that children are the major customers of such facilities as swimming-pools, commercial computer games, skateboards and so on. There is an assumption that the leisure needs of children are attended to by schools and

parents and that therefore relatively little attention is required from public bodies, which carefully consider the needs and demands of all other market segments. In addition to consideration of formal provision, for young children the home and neighbourhood is their informal leisure/play environment, but often children's needs are given little consideration in the design of such environments (Young, 1980).

There are signs of an emerging wider agenda for research on children's leisure and tourism. For example, the research of Malkin *et al.* (2000) reflects increasing concerns about child abuse and safety-consciousness. Turley (2001) has recently presented research on children and zoos and Cullingford (1995) on children and holidays. Of particular concern in recent years has been the fear, partly realized, that children's fitness and health will be negatively affected by the sedentary lifestyle brought about by the growth of video-based games and the Internet (Friedman, 2000).

Youth

Much of the political sentiment behind the support for public leisure services would appear to be based on the belief that approved leisure provision should be available for young people. Indeed, the very origins of modern public leisure services are often traced to the 19th century provision of mechanics institutes (Cunningham, 1980). One belief is that provision of suitable leisure facilities for young people will prevent juvenile crime. The 1975 White Paper on *Sport and Recreation* stated: 'By reducing boredom and urban frustration, participation in active recreation contributes to the reduction of hooliganism and delinquency among young people' (Department of the Environment, 1975: 3).

At around the same time, a national organization hosted a conference entitled *Off the Streets: Leisure Amenities and the Prevention of Crime* (NACRO, 1975), which reflected the possibility of a link between crime prevention and leisure provision. In fact, there has never been any systematic research to test this proposition empirically.

A curiosity in Britain is that the main public leisure service directed explicitly at young people, the *youth service*, is in fact not seen as part of leisure services at all, but as an arm of the education service: it is therefore imbued with the education ethos. Thus the training of youth leaders is closer to that of social workers and teachers than to that of leisure managers.

Youth and their leisure and subcultures have been the subject of considerable research over recent decades (e.g. Rapoport and Rapoport, 1975; Brake, 1980; Roberts, 1983; Miles, 2000). As with research on any social group in a changing society, this work can become dated as the economic and social environment of young people changes. In the 1960s and 1970s young people were affluent. In the 1980s they bore the brunt of unemployment, so that most young people in their late teens were either in the education/training system or unemployed: so relatively few were employed and affluent. And yet new research focusing on lifestyle suggests that a creative and vibrant youth culture can exist without the underpinning of affluence (McRobbie, 1994; Miles, 2000), although there continues to be debate as to the influence of social class in determining lifestyles (Hendry *et al.*, 1993; Roberts and Parsell, 1994). There is therefore a need for continual updating of research on youth and the policies that flow from it.

For many public leisure services young people are simply one of a number of user groups or market segments. Designing programmes to meet the needs and demands of young people is therefore a challenge for the management of existing facilities. Multiple use is not always ideal, of course. Facilities designed and managed exclusively or mainly for young people – for example, ice-skating rinks – have a very different atmosphere from those where other user groups must also be catered for. The commercial sector is generally highly successful at providing facilities that tap straight into youth culture and its styles (Smith, 1975).

The leisure facility traditionally provided by the public sector exclusively for youth has been the youth club. In fact, the status of the British youth club as a leisure facility has been in question, since, as discussed above, the youth service has traditionally been an arm of the education service rather than the leisure service. The youth club, while using leisure as a medium, has therefore had other objectives, such as education or welfare work for at-risk youth, which may explain why its relative popularity has declined in favour of general community leisure facilities and commercial outlets.

The elderly

The ageing of Western societies is a phenomenon with which most are now familiar (see Chapter 8). Much research has been done over the last two decades to remedy the neglect of the particular leisure needs and demands of older age-groups. As with research on youth, there is a tendency for such research to become outdated in the light of changing social conditions. The elderly as a category are becoming younger, fitter and more affluent. They are becoming younger because of a tendency for earlier retirement, and often the definition of the elderly includes the retired. They are becoming physically fitter as a result of improvements in diet and advances in medicine and also, possibly, because of a different outlook, which encourages older people to be more active and to be more conscious of preventive lifestyle factors. They are becoming more wealthy because of inheritance (particularly related to increasing levels of home ownership) and superannuation. While a significant proportion of the elderly still suffer from financial and health/mobility problems, an increasing proportion suffer from none of these things: they present themselves to leisure providers as a market segment like any other.

It might be said that, if the elderly are just another market segment, then the market can meet all their leisure needs, but this would be an inappropriate conclusion. Younger age-groups also constitute market segments but, while commercial provision plays its part for all age-groups, the state still has a role to play. As argued in the early parts of this book, equity, deprivation and need are only part of the argument for state provision – net community benefits can also arise even if services are provided for relatively affluent people. And in some cases – for example, the provision of parks or swimming-pools – the state has a virtual monopoly of supply, so, being in that situation, it has an obligation to provide for all, regardless of socio-economic situation, even if the service involves a significant element of 'user pays'.

The net benefits to the community from providing leisure opportunities for the elderly are likely to be even greater than in providing for younger age-groups. For both the young elderly and old elderly, the mental and physical benefits to the individual and to the wider community of staying active are obvious. The challenge is therefore very much one for management and it is one that has been widely taken up. Often the facilities are available: the task is to provide programmes at the right time, in the right place and at the right price to attract this market segment. Fortunately many of the elderly demand and can use services at times when facilities are relatively underused, such as during the weekday daytime.

Similarly, retired people are able to go on holiday during off-peak periods, making them an attractive market segment for the tourism industry. While international tourism companies specializing in the elderly are a relatively new phenomenon, the public sector and traditional domestic-tourism operators have been aware of the market for many years. Many English coastal towns have become retirement resorts (Karn, 1977), resulting in the provision of infrastructure and services that can be attractive to older holiday-makers.

The *continuity theory* suggests that the proportion of the elderly who take up new activities upon retirement is relatively low (Atchley, 1989). The implications of this are either that people must be attracted to the particular activity before retirement or that new ways of marketing the idea of experimentation to retired people must be found. Thus the challenge of leisure for the elderly may begin with the establishment of a leisure-orientated lifestyle earlier in life (Carpenter, 1997).

Finally

Each of the leisure sectors and social groups discussed in this last chapter merits a book in its own right. Each could be examined in terms of the philosophical, ideological, economic, planning and demand issues raised in the bulk of the book. While public policies are developed for leisure and tourism or for the community, in practice they relate to specific types of activity for specific groups of people. The challenge for the policy-maker and planner is to enhance the quality of life of real people by seeking to understand their leisure and tourism needs and demands in the context of an understanding of the economic, political and social processes that control the distribution of community resources.

Summary

- This chapter is concerned with leisure and tourism sectors and with social groups. It includes brief discussions of five sectors: (i) sport and physical recreation; (ii) the arts and entertainment; (iii) outdoor recreation in natural areas; (iv) urban outdoor recreation; and (v) tourism; and six social groups: (i) women; (ii) ethnic groups; (iii) people with disabilities; (iv) children; (v) youth; and (vi) the elderly.
- The sectors are discussed in terms of: the scope of the sector; the rationale and goals of policy within the sector; institutional factors; and planning.
- Four perspectives for viewing the needs and demands of different social groups are discussed: (i) a welfare perspective; (ii) a human- and citizens'-rights perspective; (iii) a market perspective; and (iv) a diversity and inclusion perspective.

Further Reading

- Sport and physical recreation: Department of the Environment (1975, 1991); Hillman and Whalley (1977); Gratton and Taylor (1985, 1991, 2000); McIntosh and Charlton (1985); Kamphorst and Roberts (1989); Roberts and Brodie (1992); Houlihan (1997); and various publications from the Sports Council and Sport England.

- The arts: Baumol and Bowen (1966, 1976); Baldry (1976); Draper (1977); Lane (1978); Braden (1979); Kelly (1984); Hantrais and Kamphorst (1987); Waters (1989); Hawkins (1993); Schouten (1998); Evans (1999); Stevenson (2000).
- Outdoor recreation in natural areas: Coppock and Duffield (1975); Patmore (1983); Pigram (1983); Glyptis (1991, 1993); Groome (1993); Pigram and Jenkins (1998); Cordell (1999); Gartner and Lime (2000).
- Urban outdoor recreation: Lever (1973); Jackson (1986); Welch (1991); Ravenscroft (1992).
- Tourism: Mathieson and Wall (1982); Smith (1995); Bull (1991); Dredge and Moore (1992); Johnson and Thomas (1992); Hall and Jenkins (1995); Leslie and Hughes (1997); Faulkner *et al.* (2000).
- Social tourism: Finch (1975).
- Ecotourism: Wearing and McLean (1997); Wearing and Neil (1999).
- Groups with special needs: Thompson (1999); Allison and Schneider (2000); Patterson and Taylor (2001).
- Women: Deem (1986a, b); Wimbush and Talbot (1988); Henderson *et al.* (1989); Green, E. *et al.* (1990); Wearing (1990, 1998); Scraton (1993, 1999); Yule (1997a, b); Henderson (2000); and tourism: Kinnaird and Hall (1994); Swain (1995).
- Gay and lesbian leisure: Markwell (1998a, b); Clift and Forrest (1999); Pritchard *et al.* (2000); Chapter 3 of Patterson and Taylor (2001).
- Ethnic groups: Khan (1976); Kew (1979); Pryce (1979); Green, E. *et al.* (1990: 70–81); Kraus (1994); Lashley and Hylton (1997); Hibbins (1998); Long (2000); Ravenscroft and Markwell (2000); Chapter 10 of Patterson and Taylor (2001).
- People with disabilities: Stein and Sessoms (1977); Austin (1987); Kennedy *et al.* (1991); Levitt (1991); Aitchison (2000); French and Hainsworth (2001); Chapters 6–8 of Patterson and Taylor (2001); and tourism: Murray and Sproats (1990); Darcy (1998).

- Children: Ellis (1973); Barnett (1991); Malkin *et al.* (2000).
- Youth: Brake (1980); Roberts (1983, 1997); Hendry *et al.* (1993); McRobbie (1994); Roberts and Parsell (1994); Miles (2000).
- The elderly: Rapoport and Rapoport (1975); Atchley (1989); Green, E. *et al.* (1990: 82–84); Collins *et al.* (1993); Wearing (1995); Chapter 8 of Patterson and Taylor (2001).

Questions/Exercises

1. How do the rationales for government involvement in the arts and sport differ?

2. A number of the sectors of leisure and tourism have two or more key goals that are potentially contradictory: identify these goals and why they are potentially contradictory in relation to: sport, the arts, natural-area recreation and tourism.

3. How does planning for urban leisure differ from planning for leisure in the countryside or natural areas?

4. In what ways can the idea of sustainable tourism development be considered a contradiction in terms?

5. The traditional, mainstream pattern of provision of leisure facilities has tended to exclude or marginalize members of a number of the social groups discussed in this chapter. Select two groups and contrast the ways in which this tendency operates.

6. Discuss any two of the groups discussed in this chapter and consider their likely particular needs or demands as a tourism market segment.

7. Many public agencies produce sector-specific or group-specific plans and strategies – for example, strategies for sport or the arts or policies for ethnic diversity or for leisure provision for youth. Identify two different strategy documents from public or academic library sources and contrast the approaches used for policy-making and planning.

Bibliography

ABS – see Australian Bureau of Statistics

Adams, F.G. (1986) Forecasting – the econometric approach. In: Adams, F.G. (ed.) *The Business Forecasting Revolution: Nation–Industry–Firm*. Oxford University Press, New York, pp. 74–105.

Aitchison, C. (2000) Young disabled people, leisure and everyday life: reviewing conventional definitions for leisure studies. *Annals of Leisure Research* 3(i), 1–21.

Allen, J. (1992) Post-industrialism and post-Fordism. In: Hall, S., Held, D. and McGrew, T. (eds) *Modernity and its Futures*. Polity Press, Cambridge, pp. 169–220.

Allison, M.T. and Schneider, I.E. (eds) (2000) *Diversity and the Recreation Professions: Organizational Perspectives*. Venture, State College, Pennsylvania.

Alt, J. (1979) Beyond class: the decline of industrial labor and leisure. *Telos* 12, 55–80.

Anderson, D.H., Nickerson, R., Stein, T.V. and Lee, M.E. (2000) Planning to provide community and visitor benefits from public lands. In: Gartner, W.C. and Lime, D.W. (eds) *Trends in Outdoor Recreation, Leisure and Tourism*. Oxford University Press, Oxford, pp. 197–211.

Andrew, E. (1981) *Closing the Iron Cage: the Scientific Management of Work and Leisure*. Black Rose Books, Montreal.

Archer, B. (1994) Demand forecasting and estimation. In: Ritchie, J.R.B. and Goeldner, C.R. (eds) *Travel, Tourism and Hospitality*. John Wiley & Sons, New York, 105–114.

Argyle, M. (1996) *The Social Psychology of Leisure*. Penguin, London.

Arnstein, S. (1969) A ladder of citizen participation. *Journal of the American Institute of Planning* July, 216–224.

Aronowitz, S., Esposito, D., DiFazio, W. and Yard, M. (1998) The post-work manifesto. In: Aronowitz, S. and Cutler, J. (eds) *Post-Work*. Routledge, New York, pp. 31–80.

Aronowitz, S. and DiFazio, W. (1994) *The Jobless Future*. University of Minnesota Press, Minneapolis.

Arts Council of Great Britain (1959) *Housing the Arts in Great Britain: Part I: London, Scotland, Wales*. ACGB, London.

Arts Council of Great Britain (1961) *Housing the Arts in Great Britain: Part II: The Needs of the English Provinces*. ACGB, London.

Ashenden, D. and Milligan, S. (annual) *The Good Universities Guide*. Ashenden Milligan, Subiaco, Western Australia.

Asimov, I. (1976) Future fun. In: *Today and Tomorrow and …* Scientific Book Club, London, pp. 199–209.

Atchley, R. (1989) A continuity theory of normal ageing. *The Gerontologist* 29(1), 183–190.

Athiyaman, A. and Robertson, R.W. (1992) Time series forecasting techniques: short-term planning in tourism. *International Journal of Contemporary Hospitality Management* 4(1), 8–11.

Audit Commission (1989) *Sport for Whom? Clarifying the Local Authority Role in Sport and Recreation*. HMSO, London.

Audit Commission (1991) *Local Authorities, Entertainment and the Arts*. Audit Commission, London.

Austin, D.R. (1987) Recreation and persons with physical disabilities: a literature synthesis. *Therapeutic Recreation Journal* 17(1), 38–43.

256

Australian Bureau of Statistics (1998) *How Australians Use their Time, 1997*. ABS, Canberra.

Australian Bureau of Statistics (2000) *Participation in Sport and Physical Activities*. ABS, Canberra.

Bacon, W. (1989) The development of the leisure profession in the United Kingdom: a comparative analysis of development and change. *Society and Leisure* 12(1), 233–246.

Bailey, P. (1979) *Leisure and Class in Victorian England*. Routledge & Kegan Paul, London.

Baldry, H.C. (1976) Community arts. In: Haworth, J.T. and Veal, A.J. (eds) *Leisure and the Community*. Conference Papers, Leisure Studies Association, London, pp. 2.1–2.6.

Banks, R. (1985) *New Jobs from Pleasure: a Strategy for Creating New Jobs in the Tourist Industry*. Conservative Party, London.

Baric, A., Stevenson, Y. and van der Veen, L. (1997) Community involvement in tourism development for the Southern Highlands. In: Hall, C.M., Jenkins, J.M. and Kearsley, G. (eds) *Tourism Planning and Policy in Australia and New Zealand: Cases, Issues and Practice*. Irwin, Sydney, pp. 154–167.

Barnet, R. and Cavanagh, J. (1996) Homogenization of global culture. In: Mander and Goldsmith, (eds) *The Case Against the Global Economy and for a Turn Toward the Local*, pp. 71–77.

Barnett, L.A. (1991) Developmental benefits of play for children. In: Driver, B.L., Brown, P.J. and Peterson, G.L. (eds) *Benefits of Leisure*. Venture, State College, Pennsylvania, pp. 215–248.

Bauman, Z. (1998) *Globalization: the Human Consequences*. Polity Press, Cambridge.

Baumol, W.J. and Bowen, W.G. (1966) *Performing Arts – the Economic Dilemma*. MIT Press, Cambridge, Massachusetts.

Baumol, W.J. and Bowen, W.G. (1976) Arguments for public support of the performing arts. In: Blaug, M. (ed.) *The Economics of the Arts*. Martin Robertson, London, pp. 42–57.

Beck, U. (2000) *The Brave New World of Work*. Polity, Cambridge.

Bell, D. (1974) *The Coming of the Post-Industrial Society*. Heinemann, London.

Bennett, T. (1989) Museums and the public good: economic rationalism and cultural policy. *Culture and Policy* 1(1), 37–51.

Bennington, J. and White, J. (eds) (1988) *The Future of Leisure Services*. Longman, Harlow, UK.

Bianchini, F., Fisher, M., Montgomery, J. and Worpole, K. (1991) *City Centres, City Cultures*. Centre for Local Economic Strategies, Manchester.

Bickmore D., Shaw, M.G. and Tulloch, T. (1980) Lifestyles on maps. *Geographical Magazine* 52(11), 763–769.

Bikhchandani, S., Hirshleifer, D. and Welch, I. (1992) A theory of fads, fashion, custom and cultural change as informational cascades. *Journal of Political Economy* 100(4), 992–1026.

Bittman, M. and Wajcman, J. (1999) *The Rush Hour: the Quality of Leisure Time and Gender Equity*. SPRC Discussion Paper 97, Social Policy Research Centre, University of New South Wales, Sydney.

Bittman, M. (2000) The land of the lost weekend? Trends in free time among working age Australians, 1974–1992. *Loisir et Société* 21(2), 353–378.

Bovaird, T. (1992) Evaluation, performance measurement and achievement of objectives in the public sector. In: Sugden, J. and Knox, C. (eds) *Leisure in the 1990s: Rolling Back the Welfare State*. Conference Papers, Leisure Studies Association, Eastbourne, UK, pp. 145–166.

Bowker, J.M., English, D.B.K. and Cordell, H.K. (1999) Projections of outdoor recreation participation to 2050. In: Cordell, H. (ed.) *Outdoor Recreation in American Life: a National Assessment of Demand and Supply Trends*. Sagamore Publishing, Champaign, Illinois, pp. 323–350.

Braden, S. (1979) *Artists and People*. Routledge, London.

Bradshaw, J. (1972) The concept of social need. *New Society* 496 (30 March), 640–643.

Brake, M. (1980) *The Sociology of Youth Culture and Youth Sub-cultures*. Routledge, London.

Bram, J. and Ludvigson, S. (1998) Does consumer confidence forecast household expenditure? A sentiment index horse race. *Economic Policy Review* 4(2), 59–78.

Bramham, P. and Henry, I. (1985) Political ideology and leisure policy in the United Kingdom. *Leisure Studies* 4(1), 1–20.

Bramham, P., Henry, I., Mommaas, H. and Van Der Poel, H. (eds) (1993) *Leisure Policies in Europe*. CAB International, Wallingford, UK.

Bramwell, B. and Sharman, A. (1999) Collaboration in local tourism policymaking. *Annals of Tourism Research* 26(2), 392–415.

Brown, J. (1985) *Towards the Development of a Commonwealth Policy on recreation*. AGPS, Canberra.

Brown, P. (1993) Women, the media and equity in sport. In: Veal, A.J., Jonson, P. and Cushman, G. (eds) *Leisure and Tourism: Social and Environmental Change, World Leisure and Recreation*

Association 1991 Congress Proceedings. Centre for leisure and Tourism Studies, University of Technology, Sydney, pp. 160–163.

Brown, T.L. and Hutson, D.L. (1979) Evaluation of the ORRRC projections. In: Heritage, Conservation and Recreation Service *Third Nationwide Recreation Plan: Appendix 2, Survey Technical Report 4*. US Government Printing Office, Washington, DC, pp. 259–276.

Brownlie, I. (ed.) (1992) *Basic Documents on Human Rights*. Clarendon Press, Oxford.

Buechner, R.D. (1971) *National Park Recreation and Open Space Standards*. National Recreation and Park Association, Washington, DC.

Bull, A. (1991) *The Economics of Travel and Tourism*. Pitman, Melbourne.

Burbank, M.J., Heying, C.H. and Adranovich, G. (2000) Antigrowth politics or piecemeal resistance? Citizen opposition to Olympic-related economic growth. *Urban Affairs Quarterly* 35(3), 334–357.

Burgan, B. and Mules, T. (1992) Economic impacts of sporting events. *Annals of Tourism Research* 19(3), 700–710.

Burnett, J.J. and Bender Baker, H. (2001) Assessing the travel-related behaviors of the mobility-disabled consumer. *Journal of Travel Research* 40(3), 4–11.

Burns, J.P.A., Hatch, J.H. and Mules, T.J. (eds) (1986) *The Adelaide Grand Prix – the Impact of a Special Event*. Centre for South Australian Economics Studies, Adelaide.

Burton, T.L. (1970) The shape of things to come. In: Burton, T.L. (ed.) *Recreation Research and Planning*. Allen & Unwin, London, pp. 242–268.

Burton, T.L. (1971) *Experiments in Recreation Research*. Allen & Unwin, London.

Burton, T.L. (1989) Leisure forecasting, policymaking, and planning. In: Jackson, and Burton (1983).

Burton, T.L. and Glover, T.D. (1999) Back to the future: leisure services and the reemergence of the enabling authority of the state. In: Jackson, E.L. and Burton, T.L. (eds) *Leisure Studies: Prospects for the 21st Century*. Venture, State College, Pennsylvania, pp. 371–384.

Butler, R.W. and Waldbrook, L.A. (1991) A new planning tool: the Tourism Opportunity Spectrum. *Journal of Tourism Studies* 2(1), 2–14.

Cabinet Office (2001) *Service First: the New Charter Programme*, Cabinet Office, London, at: www.cabinet-office.gov.uk/service/index.list.htm (accessed January 2001).

CACI Ltd (2001) *PeopleUK: User Guide*, available at: www.caci.co.uk/index.html (accessed May 2001).

Caldwell, G. (1985) Poker machine playing in NSW and ACT clubs. In: Caldwell, G., Haig, B., Dickerson, M. and Sylvan, L. (eds) *Gambling in Australia*. Croom Helm, Sydney, pp. 261–268.

Caret, N., Klein, R. and Day, P. (1992) *How Organizations Measure Success: the Use of Performance Indicators in Government*. Routledge, London.

Carpenter, G. (1997) A longitudinal investigation of mid-life men who hold leisure in higher regard than work. *Society and Leisure* 20(1), 189–211.

Carr, D.S. and Halvorsen, K. (2001) An evaluation of three democratic, community-based approaches to citizen participation: surveys, conversations with community groups, and community dinners. *Society and Natural Resources* 14(1), 107–126.

Casey, B., Dunlop, R. and Selwood, S. (1996) *Culture as Commodity? The Economics of the Arts and Built Heritage in the UK*. Policy Studies Institute, London.

Cassidy, J. (1997) Why Karl Marx was right. *Weekend Australian* 20 December, 21, 24 (reprinted from *The New Yorker*).

Castells, M. (1977) *The Urban Question*. Edward Arnold, London.

Centre for Leisure and Tourism Studies (1993) *The Nation-wide Impact of CCT in Leisure Services*. University of North London, London.

Certo, S.C. and Peter, J.P. (1991) *Strategic Management: Concepts and Applications*. McGraw-Hill, New York.

Chai, D.A. (1977) Future of leisure: a Delphi application. *Research Quarterly* 48(3), 518–524.

Chairmen's Policy Group (1982) *Leisure Policy for the Future*. Sports Council, London.

Chappelle, D.E. (1973) The 'need' for outdoor recreation: an economic conundrum. *Journal of Leisure Research* 5(4), 47–53.

Clark, R. and Stankey, G. (1979) *The Recreation Opportunity Spectrum: a Framework for Planning, Management and Research*. General Technical Report PNW-98, US Department of Agriculture Forest Service, Seattle, Washington.

Clark, T.N. (2000) Old and new paradigms for urban research: globalization and the Fiscal Austerity and Urban Innovation Project. *Urban Affairs Review* 36(1), 3–45.

Clarke, A. (1995) Farewell to welfare? The changing rationales for leisure and tourism policies in Europe. In: Leslie, D. (ed.) *Tourism and Leisure – Perspectives on Provision.* LSA Publication No. 52, Leisure Studies Association, Eastbourne, UK, pp. 211–222.

Clarke, J. and Critcher, C. (1985) *The Devil Makes Work: Leisure in Capitalist Britain.* Macmillan, London.

Clarke, R. (1982) *Work in Crisis.* St Andrews Press, Edinburgh.

Clawson, M. and Knetsch, J.L. (1962) *Economics of Outdoor Recreation.* Johns Hopkins Press, Baltimore, Maryland.

Claxton, J.D. (1994) Conjoint analysis in travel research: a manager's guide. In: Ritchie, J.R.B. and Goeldner, C.R. (eds) *Travel, Tourism and Hospitality Research.* John Wiley & Sons, New York, pp. 513–522.

Clemitson, I. and Rodgers, G. (1981) *A Life to Live.* Junction Books, London.

Clift, S. and Forrest, S. (1999) Gay men and tourism: destinations and holiday motivation. *Tourism Management* 20(3), 615–625.

Coalter, F. (with Long, J. and Duffield, B.) (1988) *Recreational Welfare.* Avebury/Gower, Aldershot.

Coalter, F. (1990) Analysing leisure policy. In: Henry, I.P. (ed.) *Management and Planning in the Leisure Industries.* Macmillan, Basingstoke, UK, pp. 149–178.

Coalter, F. (1995) Compulsory competitive tendering for sport and leisure management: a lost opportunity? *Leisure Studies* 1(1), 3–15.

Coalter, F. (1998) Leisure studies, leisure policy and social citizenship: the failure of welfare or the limits of welfare? *Leisure Studies* 17(1), 21–36.

Coalter, F. (2000) Public and commercial leisure provision: active citizens and passive consumers? *Leisure Studies* 19(3), 163–182.

Cohen, C. and Pate, M. (2000) Making a meal of arts evaluation: can social audit offer a more balanced approach? *Managing Leisure* 5(3), 103–120.

Collins, M. (ed.) (1996) *Leisure in Industrial and Post-Industrial Societies.* Leisure Studies Association, Eastbourne, UK.

Collins, M.F. (1997) Does a new philosophy change the structures? Compulsory competitive tendering and local government leisure services in midland England. *Managing Leisure* 2(4), 204–216.

Collins, M.F. and Cooper, I.S. (eds) (1998) *Leisure Management: Issues and Applications.* CAB International, Wallingford, UK.

Collins, S.M., Wacker, R.R. and Blanding, C. (1993) *Leisure, Recreation and Aging: a Selected, Annotated Bibliography.* National Recreation and Park Association, Ashburn, Virginia.

Commonwealth of Australia (1994) *Creative Nation.* Department of Communications and the Arts, Canberra.

Cooke, A. (1994) *The Economics of Leisure and Sport.* Routledge, London.

Cooper, W.E. (1999) Some philosophical aspects of leisure theory. In: Jackson, E.L. and Burton, T.L. (eds) *Leisure Studies: Prospects for the 21st Century.* Venture, State College, Pennsylvania, pp. 3–15.

Coppock, J.T. and Duffield, B.S. (1975) *Recreation in the Countryside: a Spatial Analysis.* Macmillan, London.

Cordell, H. (ed.) (1999) *Outdoor Recreation in American Life: a National Assessment of Demand and Supply Trends.* Sagamore Publishing, Champaign, Illinois.

Council of Europe (1978) *Sport for All Charter.* Council of Europe, Strasburg.

Cox, E. (1995) *A Truly Civil Society: the 1995 Boyer Lectures.* ABC Books, Sydney.

Craig-Smith, S.J. and Fagence, M. (eds) (1995) *Recreation and Tourism as a Catalyst for Urban Waterfront Redevelopment: a International Survey.* Praeger, Westport, Connecticut.

Craik, J. (1987) From cows to croissants: creating communities around leisure and pleasure. *Social Alternatives* 6(3), 21–27.

Craik, J., Davis, G. and Sunderland, N. (2000) Cultural policy and national identity. In: Davis, G. and Keating, M. (eds) (2000) *The Future of Governance: Policy Choices.* Allen and Unwin, Sydney, pp. 177–202.

Cranston, M. (1973) *What are Human Rights?* The Bodley Head, London.

Crompton, J. (2000) Repositioning leisure services. *Managing Leisure* 5(2), 65–76.

Cross, G. (1990) *A Social History of Leisure Since 1600.* Venture, State College, Pennsylvania.

Crouch, G.I. and Shaw, R.N. (1991) *International Tourism Demand: a Meta-Analytical Integration of Research Findings.* Management Paper No. 36, Monash University Graduate School of Management, Clayton, Victoria.

Cullingford, C. (1995) Children's attitudes to holidays overseas. *Tourism Management* 16(2), 121–127.

Cullingworth, J.B. and Nadin, V. (1997) *Town and Country Planning in the UK*, 12th edn. Routledge, London.

Cunningham, H. (1980) *Leisure in the Industrial Revolution*. Croom Helm, London.

Cushman, G. and Hamilton-Smith, E. (1980) Equity issues in urban recreation services. In: Mercer, D. and Hamilton-Smith, E. (eds) *Recreation Planning and Social Change in Urban Australia*. Sorrett, Malvern, Victoria, pp. 167–179.

Cushman, G., Veal, A.J., and Zuzanek, J. (eds) (1996) *World Leisure Participation: Free Time in the Global Village*. CAB International, Wallingford, UK.

Darcy, S. (1998) *Anxiety to Access: Tourism Patterns and Experiences of New South Wales People with a Physical Disability*. Tourism New South Wales, Sydney.

Dare, B., Welton, G. and Coe, W. (1987) *Concepts of Leisure in Western Thought*. Kendall Hunt, Dubuque, Iowa.

DASETT – Department of the Arts, Sport, the Environment, Tourism and Territories (1988a) *The Economic Impact of Sport and Recreation – Household Expenditure*. Technical Paper No. 1, AGPS, Canberra.

DASETT – Department of the Arts, Sport, the Environment, Tourism and Territories (1988b) *The Economic Impact of Sport and Recreation – Regular Physical Activity*. Technical Paper No. 2, AGPS, Canberra.

DASETT – Department of the Arts, Sport, the Environment, Tourism and Territories (1990) *What Value Heritage? Issues for Discussion*. AGPS, Canberra.

DASETT – Department of the Arts, Sport, the Environment, Tourism and Territories (1991) *Recreation Participation Survey, February 1991*. DASETT, Canberra.

Dattilo, J. and Williams, R. (1999) Inclusion and leisure service delivery. In: Jackson, E.L. and Burton, T.L. (eds) *Understanding Leisure and Recreation – Mapping the Past, Charting the Future*. Venture, State College, Pennsylvania, pp. 451–463.

Davidson, J.A. (1985) Sport and modern technology: the rise of skateboarding, 1963–1978. *Journal of Popular Culture* 18(4), 145–157.

Davis, G. and Keating, M. (eds) (2000) *The Future of Governance: Policy Choices*. Allen & Unwin, Sydney.

Deem, R. (1986a) *All Work and No Play? The Sociology of Women's Leisure*. Open University Press, Milton Keynes.

Deem, R. (1986b) The politics of women's leisure. In: Coalter, F. (ed.) *The Politics of Leisure*. Conference Papers No. 24, Leisure Studies Association, London, pp. 68–81.

Department for Culture, Media and Sport (1999) *Local Cultural Strategies: Draft Guidance for Local Authorities in England*. DCMS, London (downloadable from: www.culture.gov.uk).

Department of Environment and Planning (1987) *The NSW Environmental Planning and Assessment Act 1979: a Guide for Local Government*. Department of Environment and Planning, Sydney.

Department of Finance (1989) *What Price Heritage? The Museums Review and the Measurement of Museum Performance*. Department of Finance, Canberra.

Department of Industry and Science (1999) *End Goal 2006: Moving the Sport and Recreation Industry to a Higher Growth Path – Discussion Paper*. Sport and Tourism Division, Department of Industry, Science and Resources, Canberra.

Department of the Arts, Sport, the Environment, Tourism and Territories – see DASETT.

Department of the Environment (1975) *Sport and Recreation*. Cmnd 6200, HMSO, London.

Department of the Environment (1977) *Guidelines for Regional Recreational Strategies*. Circular 73/77, HMSO, London.

Department of the Environment (1991) *Sport and Recreation, Planning Policy Guidance Note 17*. HMSO, London.

Department of the Environment and Department of Education and Science (1977) *Leisure and the Quality of Life: A Report on Four Local Experiments*, 2 vols. HMSO, London.

Department of the Environment, Transport and the Regions (1999a) *Modern Local Government: In Touch with the People*. Cmd 4014, Stationery Office, London (via: www.local-regions.detr.gov.uk/bestvalue/bvindex.htm, accessed January 2002).

Department of the Environment, Transport and the Regions (1999b) *Best Value and Audit Commission Performance Indicators for 2000/2001*. DETR, London (via: www.audit-commis-sion.gov.uk, accessed January 2002).

DES – see Department of Education and Science.

Dexter Lord, G. and Lord, B. (eds) (1999) *The Manual of Museum Planning*, 2nd edn. Stationery Office, London.

Docker, J. (1994), *Postmodernism and Popular Culture*. Cambridge University Press, Melbourne.

DoE – see Department of the Environment.

Doern, G.B. (1993) The UK Citizen's Charter: origins and implementation in three agencies. *Policy and Politics* 21(1), 17–29.

Dombrink, J. (1996) Gambling and the legalisation of vice: social movements, public health and public policy in the United States. In: McMillen, J. (ed.) *Gambling Cultures: Studies in History and Interpretation*. Routledge, London, pp. 43–64.

Donnelly, J. (1989) *Universal Human Rights in Theory and Practice*. Cornell University Press, Ithaca, New York.

Dow, G. (1993) What do we know about social democracy? *Economic and Industrial Democracy* 14(1), 11–48.

Dower, M., Rapoport, R., Strelitz, Z. and Kew, S. (1981) *Leisure Provision and People's Needs*. HMSO, London.

Doyal, L. and Gough, I. (1991) *A Theory of Human Needs*. Macmillan, London.

Doyle, T. (2000) *Green Politics: the Environment Movement in Australia*. UNSW Press, Sydney.

Draper, L. (ed.) (1977) *The Visitor and the Museum*. American Association of Museums, Seattle, Washington.

Dredge, D. and Moore, S. (1992) A methodology for the integration of tourism planning in town planning. *Journal of Tourism Studies* 3(1), 8–21.

Driver, B.L. and Bruns, D.H. (1999) Concepts and uses of the benefits approach to leisure. In: Jackson, E.L. and Burton, T.L. (eds) *Leisure Studies: Prospects for the 21st Century*. Venture, State College, Pennsylvania, pp. 349–369.

Driver, B.L., Brown, P.J., Stankey, G. and Gregoire, T. (1987) The ROS planning system: evaluation, basic concepts, and research needed. *Leisure Sciences* 9(2), 201–212.

Driver, B.L., Brown, P.J. and Peterson, G.L. (eds) (1991) *Benefits of Leisure*. Venture, State College, Pennsylvania.

Drucker, P. (1999) *Managing the Non-Profit Organization*. Butterworth-Heineman, Oxford.

Dumazedier, J. (1982) *The Sociology of Leisure*. Elsevier, The Hague.

Dunleavy, P. (1980) *Urban Political Analysis: the Politics of Collective Consumption*. Macmillan, London.

Dunstan, G. (1986) Living with the Grand Prix: good or bad? In: Burns, J.P.A., Hatch, J.H. and Mules, T.J. (eds) *The Adelaide Grand Prix – the Impact of a Special Event*. Centre for South Australian Economics Studies, Adelaide, pp. 105–123.

Dye, T.R. (1978) *Understanding Public Policy*. Prentice-Hall, Englewood Cliffs, New Jersey.

Edgell, D.L. (1990) *International Tourism Policy*. Van Nostrand Reinhold, New York.

Ehrlich, P. and Ehrlich, A. (1990) *The Population Explosion*. Hutchinson, London.

Ellis, M.J. (1973) *Why People Play*. Prentice-Hall, Englewood Cliffs, New Jersey.

Elvin, I.T. (1990) *Sport and Physical Recreation*. Longman, Harlow.

Erkkila, D.L. (2000) Trends in tourism economic impact estimation methods. In: Gartner, W.C. and Lime, D.W. (eds) *Trends in Outdoor Recreation, Leisure and Tourism*. CAB International, Wallingford, UK, pp. 235–244.

Etzioni, A. (1967) Mixed scanning: a 'third' approach to decision-making. *Public Administration Review* 46(1), 385–392.

Evans, G. (1995) The National Lottery: planning for leisure or pay up and play the game? *Leisure Studies* 14(4), 225–244.

Evans, G. (1999) The economics of the national performing arts – exploiting consumer surplus and willingness-to-pay: a case of cultural policy failure? *Leisure Studies* 18(2), 97–118.

Ewing, G.O. (1983) Forecasting recreation trip distribution behaviour. In: Lieber, S.R. and Fesenmaier, D.R. (eds) *Recreation Planning and Management*. E. & F.N. Spon, London, pp. 120–140.

Fain, G.S. (ed.) (1991) *Leisure and Ethics*. American Alliance for Health, Physical Education, Recreation and Dance, Reston, Virginia.

Faulkner, B. (1994) *Evaluating the Tourism Impacts of Hallmark Events*. Occasional Paper 16, Bureau of Tourism Research, Canberra.

Faulkner, B., Moscardo, G. and Laws, E. (eds) (2000) *Tourism in the 21st Century: Lessons from Experience*. Continuum, London.

Featherstone, M. (1990) Global culture: an introduction. *Theory, Culture and Society* 7(3), 1–14.

Featherstone, M. (1991) *Consumer Culture and Postmodernism.* Sage, London.

Field, B.G. and MacGregor, B.D. (1987) Recreation. In: *Forecasting Techniques for Urban and Regional Planning.* Hutchinson, London, pp. 159–231.

Filipcova, B. (ed.) (1972) Special issue on socialist life style. *Society and Leisure* 3.

Finch, S. (1975) Holidays: the social need. In: Haworth, J.T. and Veal, A.J. (eds) *Leisure and the Community.* Papers from a Leisure Studies Association Conference, University of Birmingham, pp. 6.1–6.8.

Fischer, A., Hatch, J. and Paix, B. (1986) Road accidents and the Grand Prix. In: Burns, J.P.A., Hatch, J.H. and Mules, T.J. (eds) *The Adelaide Grand Prix – the Impact of a Special Event.* Centre for South Australian Economics Studies, Adelaide, pp. 151–168.

Fitzgerald, R. (1977) Abraham Maslow's hierarchy of needs – an exposition and evaluation. In: Fitzgerald, R. (ed.) *Human Needs and Politics.* Pergamon, Sydney, pp. 36–51.

Flannery, T. (1994) *The Future Eaters: an Ecological History of the Australasian Lands and People.* Reed Books, Kew, Victoria.

Fletcher, J.E. (1989) Input–output analysis and tourism impact studies. *Annals of Tourism Research* 16(2), 514–529.

Frechtling, D.C. (1994a) Assessing the impacts of travel and tourism – measuring economic benefits. In: Ritchie, J.R.B. and Goeldner, C.R. (eds) *Travel, Tourism, and Hospitality Research,* 2nd edn. John Wiley & Sons, New York, pp. 367–392.

Frechtling, D.C. (1994b) Assessing the impacts of travel and tourism – measuring economic costs. In: Ritchie and Goeldner, 1994, pp. 393–402.

Frechtling, D.C. (1996) *Practical Tourism Forecasting.* Butterworth-Heinemann, Oxford.

French, D. and Hainsworth, J. (2001) 'There aren't any buses and the swimming-pool is always cold': obstacles and opportunities in the provision of sport for disabled people. *Managing Leisure* 6(1), 35–49.

Friedman, M. and Friedman, R. (1979) The role of government. In: *Free to Choose.* Penguin, Harmondsworth, UK, pp. 47–58.

Friedman, S.J. (2000) *Children of the World Wide Web: Tool or Trap?* University Press of America, Lanham, Maryland.

Fyall, A. and Garrod, B. (1998) Heritage tourism: at what price? *Managing Leisure* 3(4), 213–228.

Galbraith, J.K. (1973) *Economics and the Public Purpose.* Penguin, Harmondsworth, UK.

Garnham, N. (1987) Concepts of culture: public policy and the cultural industries. *Cultural Studies* 1(1), 24–37.

Garrod, G., Pickering, A. and Willis, K. (1993) The economic value of botanic gardens: a recreational perspective. *Geoform* 24(2), 215–224.

Gartner, W.C. and Lime, D.W. (eds) (2000) *Trends in Outdoor Recreation, Leisure and Tourism.* CAB International, Wallingford, UK.

Gershuny, J. (2000) *Changing Times: Work and Leisure in Postindustrial Society.* Oxford University Press, Oxford.

Giddens, A. (1998) *The Third Way: the Renewal of Social Democracy.* Polity Press, Cambridge.

Giddens, A. (2000) *The Third Way and its Critics.* Polity Press, Cambridge.

Giddens, A. and Hutton, W. (2000) Anthony Giddens and Will Hutton in conversation. In: Hutton, W. and Giddens, A. (eds) *On the Edge: Living with Global Capitalism.* Jonathan Cape, London, pp. 1–51.

Gittins, J. (1993) Community involvement in environment and recreation. In: Glyptis, S. (ed.) *Leisure and the Environment.* Belhaven, London, pp. 183–194.

GLC – see Greater London Council.

Glyptis, S. (1989) *Leisure and Unemployment.* Open University Press, Milton Keynes.

Glyptis, S. (1991) *Countryside Recreation.* Longman, Harlow, UK.

Glyptis, S. (ed.) (1993) *Leisure and the Environment.* Belhaven, London.

Godbey, G. (1989) *The Future of Leisure Services: Thriving on Change.* Venture, State College, Pennsylvania.

Godbey, G. (1997) *Leisure and Leisure Services in the 21st Century.* Venture, State College, Pennsylvania.

Gold, S.M. (1973) *Urban Recreation Planning.* Lea and Febiger, Philadelphia.

Gorz, A. (1980a) *Farewell to the Working Class.* Pluto, London.

Gorz, A. (1980b) *Ecology as Politics*. South End Press, Boston.

Gorz, A. (1999) *Reclaiming Work: Beyond the Wage-based Society*. Polity Press, Cambridge.

Government Actuary (2000) *National Population Projections 1998–based*. National Statistics Series PP2 No. 22, Stationery Office, London.

Gratton, C. (1996) Transnational corporations and the leisure industry. In: Collins, M. (ed.) *Leisure in Industrial and Post-Industrial Societies*. Leisure Studies Association, Eastbourne, UK, pp. 145–170.

Gratton, C. (2000) *COMPASS 1999: a Project Seeking the Co-ordinated Monitoring of Participation in Sports in Europe*. Draft report, Sheffield, Hallam University, Sheffield.

Gratton, C. and Taylor, P. (1985) *Sport and Recreation: an Economic Analysis*. E. & F.N. Spon, London.

Gratton, C. and Taylor, P. (1988) *Economics of Leisure Service Management*. Longman, Harlow, UK.

Gratton, C. and Taylor, P. (1991) *Government and the Economics of Sport*. Longman, Harlow, UK.

Gratton, C. and Taylor, P. (2000) *Economics of Sport and Recreation*. E. & F.N. Spon, London.

Gratton, C., Dobson, N. and Shibli, S. (2000) The economic importance of major sport events: a case-study of six events. *Managing Leisure* 5(1), 17–28.

Gray, H.P. (1982) The contributions of economics to tourism. *Annals of Tourism Research* 9(1), 105–125.

Greater London and South East Council of Sport and Recreation (1982) *Prospect for the Eighties: Regional Recreation Strategy*. GLSECSR, London.

Greater London Council Planning Department (1968) *Surveys of the Use of Open Space*, Vol. 1. GLC, London.

Green, E., Hebron, S. and Woodward, D. (1990) *Women's Leisure, What Leisure?* Macmillan, Basingstoke, UK.

Green, H., Hunter, C. and Moore, B. (1990) Application of the Delphi technique in tourism. *Annals of Tourism Research* 17(2), 270–279.

Greenwood, J. (1992) Producer interest groups in tourism policy: case studies from Britain and the European Community. *American Behavioral Scientist* 36(2), 236–256.

Groome, D. (1993) *Planning and Rural Recreation in Britain*. Avebury, Aldershot, UK.

Guadagnolo, F. (1985) The importance–performance analysis: an evaluation and marketing tool. *Journal of Park and Recreation Administration* 3(2), 13–22.

Halal, W.E. (2000) The top 10 emerging technologies. *The Futurist* 34(4), 1–10.

Hale, A. (2001) Representing the Cornish: contesting heritage interpretation in Cornwall. *Tourist Studies* 1(2), 185–196.

Hall, C.M. (1992) *Hallmark Tourist Events*. Belhaven, London.

Hall, C.M. (2000) *Tourism Planning: Policies, Processes and Relationships*. Prentice Hall, Harlow, UK.

Hall, C.M. and Jenkins, J.M. (1995) *Tourism and Public Policy*. Routledge, London.

Hall, P. (1980) *Great Planning Disasters*. Weidenfeld & Nicholson, London.

Ham, C. and Hill, M. (1984) *The Policy Process in the Modern Capitalist State*. Wheatsheaf, Brighton.

Hamilton-Smith, E. and Robertson, R.W. (1977) Recreation and government in Australia. In: Mercer, D. (ed.) *Leisure and Recreation in Australia*. Sorrett, Malvern, Victoria, pp. 75–189.

Hantrais, L. and Kamphorst, T.J. (eds) (1987) *Trends in the Arts: a Multinational Perspective*. Giordano Bruno Amersfoort, Voorthuizen, the Netherlands.

Haralambos, M., Van Krieken, R., Smith, S. and Holborn, M. (1996) *Sociology: Themes and Perspectives*. Longman, Melbourne.

Harding, A. (1994) Urban regimes and growth machines: toward a cross-national research agenda. *Urban Affairs Quarterly* 29(3), 356–382.

Harper, J.A. and Balmer, K.R. (1989) The perceived benefits of public leisure services: an exploratory investigation. *Society and Leisure* 12(1), 171–188.

Harrington, M. (1974) Leisure as the means of production. In: Kolakowski, L. and Hampshire, S. (eds) *The Socialist Idea: a Reappraisal*. Weidenfeld & Nicholson, London, pp. 153–163.

Harrison, B. (1967) Religion and recreation in nineteenth century England. *Past and Present* 38(1), 98–120.

Harvey, D. (2000) *Spaces of Hope*. Edinburgh University Press, Edinburgh.

Hatry, H.P. and Dunn, D.R. (1971) *Measuring the Effectiveness of Local Government Services: Recreation*. The Urban Institute, Washington, DC.

Hawkins, G. (1993) *From Nimbin to Mardi Gras: Constructing Community Arts*. Allen & Unwin, Sydney.

Haworth, J.T. and Veal, A.J. (eds) (1976) *Leisure and the Community.* Conference Papers, Leisure Studies Association, London.

Hefner, F.L. (1990) Using economic models to measure the impact of sports on local economies. *Journal of Sport and Social Issues* 14(1), 1–13.

Held, D. and McGrew, A. (2000) *The Global Transformations Reader,* Polity Press/Blackwell, Cambridge.

Heller, A. (1976) *The Theory of Need in Marx.* Allison & Busby, London.

Helling, A. (1998) Collaborative visioning: proceed with caution! Results from evaluating Atlanta's Vision 2020 project. *Journal of the American Planning Association* 63(3), 335–349.

Henderson, K.A. (2000) Gender inclusion as a recreation trend. In: Gartner, W.C. and Lime, D.W. (eds) *Trends in Outdoor Recreation, Leisure and Tourism.* CAB International, Wallingford, UK, pp. 17–28.

Henderson, K.M. and Bialeschki, D. (1995) *Evaluating Leisure Services: Making Enlightened Decisions.* Venture, State College, Pennsylvania.

Henderson, K.M., Bialeschki, D., Shaw, S.M. and Freysinger, V.J. (1989) *A Time of One's Own: a Feminist Perspective on Women's Leisure.* Venture, State College, Pennsylvania.

Hendon, W.S., Shanahan, J.L. and MacDonald, A.J. (eds) (1980) *Economic Policy for the Arts.* Abt Books, Cambridge, Massachusetts.

Hendry, L.B., Shucksmith, J., Love, J.G. and Glendinning, A. (1993) *Young People's Leisure and Lifestyles.* Routledge, London.

Henley Centre for Forecasting (1986) *The Economic Impact and Importance of Sport in the UK.* Study 30, Sports Council, London.

Henry, I. (1984a) The politics of the New Right: consequences for leisure policy and management. *Leisure Management* 4(9), 10–11.

Henry, I. (1984b) Conservatism, socialism and leisure services. *Leisure Management* 4(11), 10–12.

Henry, I. (1985) Leisure management and the social democratic tradition. *Leisure Management* 5(2), 14–15.

Henry, I. (1988) Alternative futures for the public leisure service. In: Bennington, J. and White, J. (eds) *The Future of Leisure Services.* Longman, Harlow, UK, pp. 207–244.

Henry, I.P. (ed.) (1990) *Management and Planning in the Leisure Industries.* Macmillan, Basingstoke, UK.

Henry, I.P. (1993) *The Politics of Leisure Policy.* Macmillan, Basingstoke, UK.

Henry, I. (1999) Globalization and the governance of leisure: the role of the nation-state, the European Union and the city in leisure policy in Britain. *Society and Leisure* 22(2), 355–380.

Henry, I. (2001) *The Politics of Leisure Policy,* 2nd edn. Pelgrave, Basingstoke, UK.

Henry, I. and Paramio Salcines, J.L. (1998) Sport, culture and urban regimes: the case of Bilbao. In: Collins, M.F. and Cooper, I.S. (eds) *Leisure Management: Issues and Applications.* CAB International, Wallingford, UK, pp. 97–112.

Henry, I. and Spink, J. (1990) Planning for leisure: the commercial and public sectors. In: Henry, I.P. (ed.) *Management and Planning in the Leisure Industries.* Macmillan, Basingstoke, UK, pp. 33–69.

Heritage, Conservation and Recreation Service (1979) *The Third Nationwide Outdoor Recreation Plan: Executive Report.* US Government Printing Office, Washington, DC.

Heritage, Conservation and Recreation Service (1979) *The Third Nationwide Outdoor Recreation Plan, Executive Report, Assessment and 4 Appendices.* United States Department of the Interior, US Government Printing Office, Washington, DC.

Hertz, N. (2001) *The Silent Takeover: Global Capitalism and the Death of Democracy.* William Heinemann, London.

Hibbins, R. (1998) Leisure and ethnic diversity in Australia. In: Rowe, D. and Lawrence, G. (eds) *Tourism, Leisure, Sport: Critical Perspectives.* Hodder Education, Rydalmere, New South Wales, pp. 100–111.

Hill, K.Q. (1978) Trend extrapolation. In: Fowles, J. (ed.) *Handbook of Futures Research.* Greenwood Press, Westport, Connecticut, pp. 249–272.

Hillman, M. and Whalley, A. (1977) *Fair Play for All.* PEP (now Centre for Policy Studies), London.

Hindess, B. (1993) Citizenship in the modern West. In: Turner, B.S. (ed.) *Citizenship and Social Theory.* Sage, London, pp. 19–35.

Hirsch, F. (1977) *Social Limits to Growth.* Routledge & Kegan Paul, London.

Hochschild, A.R. (1997) *The Time Bind: When Work Becomes Home and Home Becomes Work.* Metropolitan Books, New York.

Hodge, G.A. (2000) *Privatization: an International Review of Performance.* Westview, Boulder, Colorado.

Hollenhorst, S., Olson, D. and Forney, R. (1992) The use of importance–performance analysis to evaluate state park cabins. *Journal of Parks and Recreation Administration* 10(1), 1–11.

Horna, J. (1994) *The Study of Leisure: an Introduction.* Oxford University Press, Toronto.

Horne, D. (1986) *The Public Culture: the Triumph of Industrialism.* Pluto Press, London.

Horwath and Horwath Services Pty. (n.d.) *A Guide to the Hotel Development Process.* Horwath and Horwath Pty., Sydney.

Houlihan, B. (1997) *Sport Policy and Politics: a Comparative Analysis.* Routledge, London.

Houlihan, B. (2001) Citizenship, civil society and the sport and recreation professions. *Managing Leisure* 6(1), 1–14.

House of Representatives Standing Committee on Expenditure (1986) *Patronage, Power and the Muse: Inquiry into Commonwealth Assistance to the Arts.* AGPS, Canberra.

Howat, G., Crilley, G., Absher, J. and Milne, I. (1996) Measuring customer service quality in sports and leisure centres. *Managing Leisure* 1(2), 77–90.

Huan, T.C. and O'Leary, J.T. (1999) *Measuring Tourism Performance.* Sagamore, Champaign, Illinois.

Hudson, S. and Shephard, G.W.H. (1998) Measuring service quality at tourist destinations: an application of importance–performance analysis to an Alpine ski resort. *Journal of Travel and Tourism Marketing* 7(3), 61–77.

Hughes, H.I. (1984) Government support for tourism in the UK: a different perspective. *Tourism Management* 5(1), 13–19.

Hutton, W. and Giddens, A. (eds) (2000) *On the Edge: Living with Global Capitalism.* Jonathan Cape, London.

Illich, I., Zola, I.K., McKnight, J., Caplan, C. and Shaiken, H. (1977) *Disabling Professions.* Marion Boyars, London.

International Olympic Committee (1995) *The Olympic Charter.* IOC, Lausanne.

Iso-Ahola, S. (1980) *The Social Psychology of Leisure and Recreation.* W.C. Brown, Dubuque, Iowa.

Iso-Ahola, S. (1989) Motivation for leisure. In: Jackson, E.L. and Burton, T.L. (eds) *Understanding Leisure and Recreation – Mapping the Past, Charting the Future.* Venture, State College, Pennsylvania, pp. 247–280.

Jackson, E.L. and Burton, T.L. (eds) (1989) *Understanding Leisure and Recreation – Mapping the Past, Charting the Future.* Venture, State College, Pennsylvania.

Jackson, E.L. and Burton, T.L. (eds) (1999) *Leisure Studies: Prospects for the Twenty-First Century.* Venture, State College, Pennsylvania.

Jackson, P. (1986) Adapting the ROS technique to the urban setting. *Australian Parks and Recreation* 22(3), 26–28.

Jackson, P.M. (1991) Performance indicators: promises and pitfalls. In: Pearce, 1991, pp. 41–64.

Jansen-Verbeke, M. (1985) Inner city leisure resources. *Leisure Studies* 4(2), 141–158.

Jarvie, G. and Maguire, J. (1994) *Sport and Leisure in Social Thought.* Routledge, London.

Jeffries, D. (2001) *Governments and Tourism.* Butterworth-Heinemann, Oxford.

Jenkins, C. and Sherman, B. (1979) *The Collapse of Work.* Eyre Methuen, London.

Jenkins, C., Nevill, A.M. and Williams, E.A. (1989) Making waves: the structure of the catchment area of a leisure pool. In: Botterill, D. (ed.) *Leisure Participation and Experience: Models and Case Studies.* Conference Papers 37, Leisure Studies Association, Eastbourne, UK, pp. 137–168.

Jenkins, H. (1979) *The Culture Gap: an Experience of Government and the Arts.* Marion Boyars, London.

Jennings, L. (1979) Future fun: tomorrow's sports and games. *The Futurist* 13(6), 417–431.

Johnson, P. and Thomas, B. (eds) (1992) *Perspectives on Tourism Policy.* Mansell, London.

Jones, H. (1990) The economic impact and importance of sport: a Council of Europe co-ordinated study. *Sport Science Review* 13(1), 26–31.

Jones, S. (1990) The Australian tourism outlook forum Delphi. In: Horwath and Horwath Services (eds) *Australian Tourism Outlook Forum: Contributed Papers, Sydney, June 1990.* Bureau of Tourism Research, Canberra, pp. 51–55.

Jones, B. (1995) *Sleepers Wake! Technology and the Future of Work*, 2nd edn. Oxford University Press, Melbourne.

Jubenville, A. (1976) *Outdoor Recreation Planning.* W.B. Saunders, Philadelphia.

Kamenka, E. and Tay, A.E. (eds) (1978) *Human Rights.* Edward Arnold, Port Melbourne, Victoria.

Kamphorst, T.J. and Roberts, K. (eds) (1989) *Trends in Sports: a Multinational Perspective.* Giordano Bruno Culemborg, Voorthuizen, the Netherlands.

Karn, V. (1977) *Retiring to the Seaside.* Routledge & Kegan Paul, London.

Kaynak, E. and Macaulay, J.A. (1984) The Delphi technique in the measurement of tourism market potential. *Tourism Management* 4(1), 87–101.

Keller, P.F. (2000) Globalization and tourism. In: Gartner, W.C. and Lime, D.W. (eds) *Trends in Outdoor Recreation, Leisure and Tourism.* CAB International, Wallingford, UK, pp. 287–298.

Kelly, J. (1987) *Recreation Trends: Toward the Year 2000.* Management Learning Laboratories, Champaign, Illinois.

Kelly, J. and Warnick, R.B. (1999) *Recreation Trends and Markets: the 21st Century.* Sagamore, Champaign, Illinois.

Kelly, O. (1984) *Community, Art and the State: Storming the Citadels.* Comedia, London.

Kelly, J.R. (1989) Leisure and quality: beyond the quantitative barrier in research. In: Goodale, T.L. and Witt, P.A. (eds) *Recreation and Leisure: Issues in an Era of Change.* Venture, State College, Pennsylvania, pp. 300–314.

Kelly, J.R. and Godbey, G. (1992) *The Sociology of Leisure.* Venture, State College, Pennsylvania.

Kelsey, C. and Gray, H. (1985) *Master Plan Process for Parks.* American Alliance for Health, Physical Education, Recreation and Dance, Alexandria, Virginia.

Kennedy, D.W., Smith, R.W. and Austin, D.R. (1991) *Special Recreation: Opportunities for Persons with Disabilities.* W.C. Brown, Dubuque, Iowa.

Kenway, J. (1992) Feminist theories of the state: to be or not to be? In: Mueltzfeldt, M. (ed.) *Society, State and Politics.* Pluto, Leichhardt, New South Wales, pp. 108–142.

Kew, S. (1979) *Ethnic Groups and Leisure.* Sports Council/SSRC, London.

Keynes, J.M. (1931) Economic possibilities for our grand-children. In: *The Collected Writings of John Maynard Keynes*, Vol. 9, *Essays in Persuasion* (1972 edn). Macmillan, London, pp. 321–332.

Khan, N. (1976) *The Arts Britain Ignores: the Arts of Ethnic Minorities.* Arts Council of Great Britain, London.

Kidd, B. and Donnelly, P. (2000) Human rights and sports. *International Review for the Sociology of Sport* 35(2), 131–148.

Kingsbury, A. (1976) Animation. In: Haworth, J.T. and Veal, A.J. (eds) *Leisure and the Community.* Conference Papers, Leisure Studies Association, London, pp. 12.1–12.5.

Kinnaird, V. and Hall, D. (1994) *Tourism: a Gender Analysis.* John Wiley & Sons, Chichester, UK.

Klein, N. (1999) *No Logo: Taking Aim at the Brand Bullies.* Picador, New York.

Korten, D.C. (1996) The mythic victory of market capitalism. In: Mander, J. and Goldsmith, E. (eds) (1996) *The Case Against the Global Economy and for a Turn Toward the Local.* Sierra Club, San Francisco, California, pp. 183–191.

KPMG Peat Marwick (1993) *Sydney Olympic 2000: Economic Impact Study*, 2 vols. Report to Sydney Olympics 2000 Bid Ltd, Sydney.

Kraus, R. (1994) *Leisure in a Changing America: Multicultural Perspectives.* Macmillan, New York.

Kraus, R. (1998) *Recreation and Leisure in Modern Society*, 5th edn. Jones and Bartlett, Sudbury, Massachusetts.

Krippendorf, J. (1987) *The Holiday Makers: Understanding the Impact of Leisure and Travel.* Heinemann, London.

Kumar, K. (1995) *From Post-Industrial to Post-Modern Society: New Theories of the Contemporary World.* Blackwell, Oxford.

Lafargue, P. (1958) The right to be lazy. In: Larrabee, E. and Meyersohn, R. (eds) *Mass Leisure.* Free Press, Glencoe, Illinois, pp. 105–117 (paper originally published 1848).

Landry, C. and Bianchini, F. (1995) *The Creative City.* Demos/Comedia, London.

Lane, J. (1978) *Arts Centres: Every Town Should Have One.* Paul Elek, London.

Langer, M. (1997) *Service Quality in Tourism: Measurement Methods and Empirical Analysis.* Peter Lang, Frankfurt-am-Main.

Langhorne, R. (2001) *The Coming of Globalization: its Evolution and Contemporary Consequences.* Palgrave, Basingstoke, UK.

Lashley, H. and Hylton, K. (eds) (1997) Special issue – a black perspective. *Leisure Studies* 16(4).

Latham, M. (1998) Economic policy and the third way. *Australian Economic Review* 31(4), 384–398.

Leach, R. (1993) *Political Ideologies*, 2nd edn. Macmillan, Melbourne.

Lenskyj, H. (1991) A new ball game? Historical and contemporary models of women's sport in Canada. *World Leisure and Recreation* 33(3), 15–18.

Lentell, B. (1996) Putting clothes on the invisible man: the Audit Commission, the Citizen's Charter and local authority leisure services. In: Collins, M. (ed.) *Leisure in Industrial and Post-industrial Societies*. Publication No. 49, Leisure Studies Association, Eastbourne, UK, pp. 269–286.

Lentell, B. (2001) Customers' views of the results of managing quality through ISO 9002 and Investors in People in leisure services. *Managing Leisure* 6(1), 15–34.

Leslie, D. and Hughes, G. (1997) Agenda 21, local authorities and tourism in the UK. *Managing Leisure* 2(3), 143–154.

Lever, W.F. (1973) Recreational space in cities – standards of provision. *Journal of the Royal Town Planning Institute* March, 138–140.

Levitt, L. (1991) Recreation for the mentally ill. In: Driver, B.L., Brown, P.J. and Peterson, G.L. (eds) *Benefits of Leisure*. Venture, State College, Pennsylvania, pp. 161–178.

Lewis, M. and Hartley, J. (2001) Evolving forms of quality management in local government: lessons from the Best Value pilot programme. *Policy and Politics* 29(4), 477–496.

Lieber, S.R. and Fesenmaier, D.R. (eds) (1983) *Recreation Planning and Management*. E. & F.N. Spon, London.

Limb, M. (1986) Community involvement in leisure provision – private enterprise or public interest? In: Coalter, F. (ed.) *The Politics of Leisure*. Conference Papers Series No. 24, Leisure Studies Association, London, pp. 90–110.

Lindblom, C.E. (1959) The science of 'muddling through'. *Public Administration Review* 19(2), 79–88.

Linstone, H.A. (1978) The Delphi technique. In: Fowles, J. (ed.) *Handbook of Futures Research*. Greenwood Press, Westport, Connecticut, pp. 273–300.

Logothetis, N. (1992) *Managing for Total Quality: From Demming to Taguchi and SPC*. Prentice Hall, New York.

London M., Crandall, R. and Fitzgibbons, D. (1977) The psychological structure of leisure: activities, needs, people. *Journal of Leisure Research* 9(4), 252–263.

Long, J. (1994) Local authority tourism strategies – a British appraisal. *Journal of Tourism Studies* 5(2), 17–23.

Long, J. (2000) No racism here? A preliminary examination of sporting innocence. *Managing Leisure* 5(3), 121–134.

Lundberg, D.E., Krishnamoorthy, M. and Stevenga, M.H. (1995) *Tourism Economics*. John Wiley & Sons, New York.

Lynch, R. (1993) The cultural repositioning of rugby league football and its men. *ANZALS Leisure Research Series* 1, 105–119.

Lynn, J. and Jay, A. (eds) (1988) *The Complete Yes Minister: the Diaries of a Cabinet Minister*. BBC Books, London.

Lynn, J. and Jay, A. (eds) (1989) *The Complete Yes Prime Minister: the Diaries of the Right Hon. James Hacker*. BBC Books, London.

Ma, J. (2001) From Shanghai to Davos. *Asian Wall Street Journal* 20 February, 6.

MacFarlane, L.J. (1985) *The Theory and Practice of Human Rights*. Maurice Temple Smith, London.

McIntosh, P. and Charlton, V. (1985) *The Impact of Sport for All Policy 1966–1984*. Study 26, Sports Council, London.

McKay, J.M. (1986a) Some social impacts of the Grand Prix on residents closest to the circuit – noise and property damage. In: Burns, J.P.A., Hatch, J.H. and Mules, T.J. (eds) *The Adelaide Grand Prix – the Impact of a Special Event*. Centre for South Australian Economics Studies, Adelaide, pp. 124–150.

McKay, J. (1986b) Hegemony, the state and Australian sport. In: Lawrence, G. and Rowe, D. (eds) *Power Play*. Hale and Iremonger, Sydney, pp. 115–135.

McKay, J. (1991) *No Pain, No Gain? Sport and Australian Culture*. Prentice Hall, Sydney.

McKay, J. (1998) Gender and organizational power in Australian sport. In: Rowe, D. and Lawrence, G. (eds) *Tourism, Leisure, Sport: Critical Perspectives*. Hodder Education, Rydalmere, New South Wales, pp. 180–193.

McRobbie, A. (1994) Shut up and dance: youth culture and changing modes of femininity. In: McRobbie, A. (ed.) *Postmodernism and Popular Culture*. Routledge, London, pp. 155–176.

Maguire, J.A. (1999) *Global Sport: Identities, Societies, Civilizations*. Polity Press, Cambridge

Makridakis, S., Wheelwright, S.C. and Hyndman, R.J. (1998) *Forecasting Methods and Applications*, 3rd edn. John Wiley & Sons, New York.

Malkin, K., Johnston, L. and Brackenridge, C. (2000) A critical evaluation of training needs for child protection in UK sport. *Managing Leisure* 5(3), 151–160.

Mander, J. and Goldsmith, E. (eds) (1996) *The Case Against the Global Economy and for a Turn Toward the Local*. Sierra Club, San Francisco, California.

Manidis, P. (1994) Cost–benefit analysis in parks. In: Royal Australian Institute of Parks and Recreation Seminar Proceedings, *Who Pays – Open Space and Recreational Facilities*. RAIPR, Canberra, pp. 45–53.

Manidis Roberts (1992) *Outdoor Recreation and Open space: Planning Guidelines for Local Government*. Department of Planning, Sydney.

Marcuse, H. (1964) *One Dimensional Man*. Routledge & Kegan Paul, London.

Markwell, K. (1998a) Playing queer: leisure in the lives of gay men. In: Rowe, D. and Lawrence, G. (eds) *Tourism, Leisure, Sport: Critical Perspectives*. Hodder Education, Rydalmere, New South Wales, pp. 112–123.

Markwell, K. (1998b) Space and place in gay men's leisure. *Annals of Leisure Research* 1, 19–36.

Marshall, T.H. (1994) Citizenship and social class. In: Turner, B. and Hamilton, P. (eds) *Citizenship: Critical Concepts*. London, Routledge, Vol. II, pp. 5–44.

Martilla, J.A. and James, J.C. (1977) Importance–performance analysis. *Journal of Marketing* 41(1), 77–79.

Martin, W.H. and Mason, S. (1998) *Transforming the Future: Rethinking Free Time and Work*. Leisure Consultants, Sudbury, UK.

Maslow, A. (1954) *Motivation and Personality* (2nd edn, 1970). Harper & Row, New York.

Mathieson, A. and Wall, G. (1982) *Tourism: Economic, Physical and Social Impacts*. Longman, London.

Mercer, D. (1975) The concept of recreational need. *Journal of Leisure Research* 5(1), 37–50.

Merritt, G. (1982) *World out of Work*. William Collins, London.

Mertes, J.D. and Hall, J.R. (1996) *Park, Recreation, Open Space and Greenway Guidelines*. National Recreation and Park Association, Ashburn,Virginia.

Miles, I., Cole, S. and Gershuny, J. (1978) Images of the future. In: Freeman, C. and Jahoda, M. (eds) *World Futures: the Great Debate*. Martin Robertson, London, pp. 279–342.

Miles, S. (2000) *Youth Lifestyles in a Changing World*. Open University Press, Buckingham, UK.

Miller, T. (1990) Sport, media and masculinity. In: Rowe, D. and Lawrence, G. (eds) *Sport and Leisure: Trends in Australian Popular Culture*. Harcourt, Brace Jovanovich, Sydney, pp. 74–95.

Miller, T., Lawrence, G., McKay, J. and Rowe, D. (2001) *Globalization and Sport: Playing the World*. Sage, London.

Mills, P. (1992) BS5750 – a leisure perspective. In: Mills, P. (ed.) *Quality in the Leisure Industry*. Longman, Harlow, pp. 16–34.

Milstein, D.N. and Reid, L.M. (1966) *Michigan Outdoor Recreation Demand Study*, Vol. 1, *Methods and Models*. Michigan Departments of Conservation and Commerce, Lansing, Michigan.

Ministry of Education (n.d.) *Standards of Public Library Service*. HMSO, London.

Ministry of Housing and Local Government (1969) *People and Planning* (the Skeffington Report). HMSO, London.

Moeller, G.H. and Shafer, E.L. (1983) The use and abuse of Delphi forecasting. In: Lieber, S.R. and Fesenmaier, D.R. (eds) *Recreation Planning and Management*. E. & F.N. Spon, London, pp. 96–104.

Moeller, G.H. and Shafer, E.L. (1994) The Delphi technique: a tool for long-range travel and tourism planning. In: Ritchie, J.R.B. and Goeldner, C.R. (eds) (1994) *Travel, Tourism, and Hospitality Research*, 2nd edn. John Wiley & Sons, New York, pp. 473–480.

Mooney, C.Z. (1999) The politics of morality policy: symposium editor's introduction. *Policy Studies Journal* 27(4), 657–680.

Mowbray, M. (1992) Local government recreation planning and equity. *Urban Policy and Research* 10(2), 17–23.

Mowbray, M. (1993) Sporting opportunity: equity in urban infrastructure and planning. *ANZALS Leisure Research Series* 1, 120–141.

Murphy, B. and Veal, A.J. (1978) *Community Use of Community Schools at the Primary Level*. Research Working Paper 5, Sports Council, London.

Murphy, P.E. (1985) *Tourism: a Community Approach*. Methuen, New York.

Murray, M. and Sproats, J. (1990) The disabled traveller. *Journal of Tourism Studies* 1(1), 3–8.

Musgrave, R.A. and Musgrave, P.B. (1980) The theory of social goods. In: *Public Finance in Theory and Practice.* McGraw-Hill, New York, pp. 54–95.

NACRO – see National Association for the Care and Resettlement of Offenders.

Naisbitt, J. (1982) *Megatrends: Ten New Directions Transforming our Lives.* Warner Books, New York.

Naisbitt, J. and Aburdene, P. (1990) *Megatrends 2000.* Pan Books, London.

National Association for the Care and Resettlement of Offenders (1975) *Off the Streets: Leisure Amenities and the Prevention of Crime.* NACRO, London.

National Capital Development Commission (1981) *Urban Open Space Guidelines.* Technical Paper 21, NCDC, Canberra.

National Park Service (2000) American *National Park Strategic Plan 2001–2005.* National Park Service/ US Department of the Interior, Washington, DC (available at: www.nps.gov/planning/index.htm – accessed April 2001).

National Playing Fields Association (1971) *Outdoor Play Space Requirements.* NPFA, London.

National Playing Fields Association (1993) *The National Playing Fields Association Six Acre Standard.* NPFA, London.

Nevill, A.M. and Jenkins, C. (1986) Social area influences on sports centre use, an investigation of the ACORN method of social area classification. In: Mangan, J.A. and Small, R.B. (eds) *Sports, Culture, Society, Proceedings of the VIII Commonwealth and International Conference on Sport, Physical Education, Dance, Recreation and Health.* E. & F.N. Spon, London.

Ng, D., Brown, B. and Knott, W. (1983) Qualified leisure services manpower requirements: a future perspective. *Recreation Research Review* 10(1), 13–19.

Nicholls, M. (1975) *Recreationally Disadvantaged Areas in Greater London. Report of an Analysis of Provision for Sports and Active Recreation.* RM 467, Policy Studies Unit, Greater London Council, London.

Nichols, G. (1996) The impact of compulsory competitive tendering on planning in leisure departments. *Managing Leisure* 1(2), 105–114.

Nichols, G. and Taylor, P. (1995) The impact on local authority leisure of CCT, financial cuts and changing attitudes. *Local Government Studies* 21(4), 607–622.

Noll, R.G. and Zimbalist, A. (eds) (1997) *Sports, Jobs and Taxes: The Economic Impact of Sports Teams and Stadiums.* Brookings Institution Press, Washington, DC.

NPFA – see National Playing Fields Association.

O'Brien, S. and Ford, R. (1988) Can we at last say goodbye to social class? An examination of the usefulness and stability of some alternative methods of measurement. *Journal of the Market Research Society* 30(3), 289–332.

Office of National Tourism (1998) *Tourism, a Ticket to the 21st Century: National Action Plan.* Department of Industry, Science and Tourism, Canberra.

Ogden, S.M. and Wilson, P. (2001) Beyond data benchmarking: the challenge of managing a benchmarking network in the UK public leisure sector. *Managing Leisure* 6(2), 95–108.

Ott, A.F. and Hartley, K. (1991) *Privatization and Economic Efficiency.* Edward Elgar, Cheltenham, UK.

Paddick, R.J. (1982) The concept of need in planning for recreation. In: Howell, M.L. and Brehaut, J.R. (eds) *Proceedings of the VII Commonwealth and International Conference on Sport, Physical Education, Recreation and Dance: 4 (Recreation).* University of Queensland, Brisbane, pp. 39–47.

Papadakis, E. (1993) *Politics and the Environment.* Longman Cheshire, Melbourne.

Parasuraman, A., Zeithaml, V.A. and Berry, L.L. (1988) SERVQUAL: a multiple-item scale for measuring consumer perceptions of service quality. *Journal of Retailing* 64(1), 12–37.

Parsons, W. (1995) *Public Policy.* Edward Elgar, Cheltenham, UK.

Patmore, A. (1983) *Recreation and Resources.* Basil Blackwell, Oxford.

Patterson, I. and Taylor, T. (eds) (2001) *Celebrating Inclusion and Diversity in Leisure.* HM Publishing, Melbourne.

Pearce, S. (ed.) (1991) *Museum Economics and the Community.* Athlone Press, London.

Perez de Cuellar, J. (1987) Statement. *World Leisure and Recreation* 29 (1), 3.

Peters, P. (2000) *The Vulnerable Hours of Leisure: New Patterns of Work and Free Time in the Netherlands, 1975–95.* Thela Thesis, Amsterdam.

Peterson, G.L. and Loomis, J.B. (2000) Trends in leisure value and valuation. In: Gartner, W.C. and Lime, D.W. (eds) *Trends in Outdoor Recreation, Leisure and Tourism.* CAB International, Wallingford, UK, pp. 215–224.

Peterson, G.L., Driver, B.L. and Gregory, R. (eds) (1988) *Amenity Resource Valuation: Integrating Economics with Other Disciplines*. Venture, State College, Pennsylvania.

Pieper, J. (1965) *Leisure: the Basis of Culture*. Faber, London.

Pigram, J. (1983) *Outdoor Recreation and Resource Management*. Croom Helm, London.

Pimlott, J.A.R. (1976) *The Englishman's Holiday: a Social History*. Harvester Press. Hassocks, Sussex, UK.

Porritt, J. (1984) *Seeing Green: the Politics of Ecology Explained*. Basil Blackwell, Oxford.

Premier's Department, Treasury and Public Works Department (1992) *Total Asset Management Manual: Capital Works Investment*. New South Wales Government, Sydney.

PricewaterhouseCoopers (2001) *Technology Forecasts 2001–2003*, at pricewaterhouse coopers.com (accessed May 2001).

Prime Minister (1991) *The Citizen's Charter: Raising the Standard*. Cmd 1599, HMSO, London.

Pritchard, A. (2001) Tourism and representations: a scale for measuring gendered portrayals. *Leisure Studies* 20(2), 79–94.

Pritchard, A., Morgan, N.J., Sedgley, D., Khan, E. and Jenkins, A. (2000) Sexuality and holiday choices: conversations with gay and lesbian tourists. *Leisure Studies* 19(2), 267–282.

Propst, D.B., Wellman, J.D., Campa, H. and McDonough, M.H. (2000) Citizen participation trends and their educational implications for natural resource professionals. In: Gartner, W.C. and Lime, D.W. (eds) *Trends in Outdoor Recreation, Leisure and Tourism*. CAB International, Wallingford, UK, pp. 383–392.

Pryce, K. (1979) *Endless Pressure: a Study of West Indian Life-Styles in Bristol*. Penguin, Harmondsworth, UK.

Quade, E.S. (1989) *Analysis for Public Decisions,* 3rd edn. North-Holland, New York.

Rapoport, R. and Rapoport, R.N. (1975) *Leisure and the Family Life Cycle*. Routledge, London.

Ravenscroft, N. (1992) *Recreation Planning and Development*. Macmillan, Basingstoke, UK.

Ravenscroft, N. (1993) Public leisure provision and the good citizen. *Leisure Studies* 12(1), 33–34.

Ravenscroft, N. (1996) Leisure, consumerism and active citizenship in the UK. *Managing Leisure* 1(3), 163–174.

Ravenscroft, N. (1998) The changing regulation of public leisure provision. *Leisure Studies* 17(2), 138–154.

Ravenscroft, N. and Markwell, S. (2000) Ethnicity and the integration of young people through urban park and recreation provision. *Managing Leisure* 5(3), 135–150.

Rhodes, R. (ed.) (1999) *Visions of Technology: a Century of Debate about Machines, Systems and the Human World*. Simon and Schuster, New York.

Richter, L.K. (1989) *The Politics of Tourism in Asia*. University of Hawaii Press, Honolulu.

Rifkin, J. (1995) *The End of Work*. Jeremy P. Tarcher/Putman, New York.

Ritchie, J.R.B. (1994a) Crafting a destination vision. In: Ritchie, J.R.B. and Goeldner, C.R. (eds) *Travel, Tourism, and Hospitality Research*, 2nd edn. John Wiley & Sons, New York, pp. 29–38.

Ritchie, J.R.B. (1994b) The nominal group technique – applications in tourism research. In: Ritchie, J.R.B. and Goeldner, C.R. (eds) *Travel, Tourism, and Hospitality Research*, 2nd edn. John Wiley & Sons, New York, pp. 493–502.

Ritchie, J.R.B. and Goeldner, C.R. (eds) (1994) *Travel, Tourism, and Hospitality Research*, 2nd edn. John Wiley & Sons, New York.

Ritchie-Calder, Lord (1982) Education for the post-industrial society. In: Costello, N. and Richardson, M. (eds) *Continuing Education for the Post-Industrial Society*. Open University Press, Milton Keynes, pp. 11–22.

Roberts, K. (1978) *Contemporary Society and the Growth of Leisure*. Longman, London.

Roberts, K. (1983) *Youth and Leisure*. Allen & Unwin, London.

Roberts, K. (1997) Same activities, different meanings: British youth cultures in the 1990s. *Leisure Studies* 16(1), 1–16.

Roberts, K. (1999) *Leisure in Contemporary Society*. CAB International, Wallingford, UK.

Roberts, K. and Brodie, D.A. (1992) *Inner-City Sport: Who Plays, and What are the Benefits?* Giordano Bruno Culemborg, Voorthuizen, the Netherlands.

Roberts, K. and Parsell, G. (1994) Youth cultures in Britain: the middle-class take-over. *Leisure Studies* 13(1), 33–48.

Robinson, J.P. (1993) The time squeeze. *American Demographics* 12(1), 12–13.

Robinson, L. (1997) Barriers to total quality management in public leisure services. *Managing Leisure* 2(1), 17–28.

Robinson, L. (1998) Quality management in public leisure services. In: Collins, M.F. and Cooper, I.S. (eds) *Leisure Management: Issues and Applications*. CAB International, Wallingford, UK, pp. 211–224.

Robinson, N.A. (ed.) (1993) *Agenda 21: Earth's Action Plan, Annotated*. Oceana Publications, New York.

Roche, M. (1992) *Rethinking Citizenship: Welfare, Ideology and Change in Modern Society*. Polity Press, Cambridge.

Roche, M. (1993) Sport and community: rhetoric and reality in the development of British sport policy. In: Binfield, J.C. and Stevenson, J. (eds) *Sport, Culture and Politics*. Sheffield Academic Press, Sheffield, pp. 72–112.

Roche, M. (2000) *Mega-events and Modernity: Olympics and Expos in the Growth of Global Culture*. Routledge, London.

Rodgers, H.B. (1993) Estimating local leisure demand in the context of a regional planning strategy. In: Glyptis, S. (ed.) *Leisure and the Environment*. Bellhaven Press, London, pp. 116–130.

Rojek, C. (1995) *Decentring Leisure: Rethinking Leisure Theory*. Sage, London.

Rossman, J.R. (1999) Assessing the leisure service delivery system. In: McLean, D.D., Bannon, J.J. and Gray, H.R. (eds) *Leisure Resources: its Comprehensive Planning*. Sagamore, Champaign, Illinois, pp. 211–250.

Rossman, J.R. and Schlatter, B.E. (2000) *Recreation Programming: Designing Leisure Experiences*, 3rd edn. Sagamore, Champaign, Illinois.

Rowe, D. and Lawrence, G. (eds) (1998) *Tourism, Leisure, Sport: Critical Perspectives*. Hodder Education, Rydalmere, New South Wales.

Rugman, A. (2000) *The End of Globalization*, Random House, London.

Russell, B. and Russell, D. (1923) *In Praise of Idleness and Other Essays*. Allen & Unwin, London.

Ryan, C. (1995) *Researching Tourist Satisfaction: Issues, Concepts, Problems*. Routledge, London.

Sasaki, K., Harad, M. and Morino, S. (1997) Economic impacts of theme-park development by input–output analysis: a process toward local industrialization of leisure services. *Managing Leisure* 2(1), 29–38.

Sassen, S. (1998) *Globalization and its Discontents*. New Press, New York.

Saunders, P. (1993) Citizenship in a liberal society. In: Turner, B.S. (ed.) *Citizenship and Social Theory*. Sage, London, pp. 57–90.

Sautter, E.T. and Leisen, B. (1999) Managing stakeholders: a tourism planning model. *Annals of Tourism Research* 26(2), 312–328.

Schor, J.B. (1991) *The Overworked American: the Unexpected Decline of Leisure*. Basic Books, New York.

Schouten, F. (1998) Access to museums as leisure providers: still a long way to go. In: Collins, M.F. and Cooper, I.S. (eds) *Leisure Management: Issues and Applications*. CAB International, Wallingford, UK, pp. 65–70.

Scraton, S. (1993) Boys muscle in where angels fear to tread – girls' sub-cultures and physical activities. In: Horne, J., Jary, D. and Tomlinson, A. (eds) *Sport, Leisure and Social Relations*. Sociological Review, Keele, UK, pp. 160–186.

Scraton, S. (ed.) (1999) Special issue: the Big Ghetto: Gender, Sexuality and Leisure – 1998 LSA International Conference. *Leisure Studies* 18(3).

Sears, D.W. (1975) The recreation voucher system: a proposal. *Journal of Leisure Research* 7(2), pp. 141–145.

Seely, R.L., Iglarsh, H.J. and Edgell, D.J. (1980) Utilizing the Delphi technique at international conferences: a method for forecasting international tourism conditions. *Journal of Travel Research* 18(1), 30–34.

Self, P. (1993) *Government by the Market? The Politics of Public Choice*. Macmillan, Basingstoke, UK.

Settle, J.G. (1977) *Leisure in the North West, a Tool for Forecasting*. Study No. 11, Sports Council, London.

Shadish, W., Cook, T.D. and Leviton, L.C. (1991) *Foundations of Program Evaluation: Theories of Practice*. Sage, Newbury Park, California.

Shafer, E.L. (1994) A decision design for tourism CEOs. In: Ritchie, J.R.B. and Goeldner, C.R. (eds) *Travel, Tourism, and Hospitality Research*, 2nd edn. John Wiley & Sons, New York, pp. 23–25.

Shafer, E.L., Moeller, G.H. and Russell, E.G. (1975) Future leisure environments. *Ekistics* 40(236), 68–72.

Shaw, M. (1984) *Sport and Leisure Participation and Lifestyles in Different Residential Neighbourhoods*. Sports Council/SSRC, London.

Siegenthaler, K.L. (1994) Importance–performance analysis: application to seniors programs evaluation. *Journal of Park and Recreation Administration*, 12(3), 57–70.

Simpson, J.A. (1976) Notes and reflections on animation. In: Haworth, J.T. and Veal, A.J. (eds) *Leisure and the Community*. Conference Papers, Leisure Studies Association, London, pp. 13.1–13.6.

Skates, A. (ed.) (1990) *Where are We Going? Evaluation in Scientific and Cultural Institutions Conference*. Australian Museum, Sydney.

Smith, P. (1975) Comments from a commercial standpoint. In: National Association for the Care and Resettlement of Offenders *Off the Streets: Leisure Amenities and the Prevention of Crime*. NACRO, London, pp. 17–19.

Smith, S.L.J. (1995) *Tourism Analysis*. Longman, Harlow, UK.

Smith, S.L.J. (2000) New developments in measuring tourism as an area of economic activity. In: Gartner, W.C. and Lime, D.W. (eds) *Trends in Outdoor Recreation, Leisure and Tourism*. CAB International, Wallingford, UK, pp. 225–234.

Soper, K. (1981) *On Human Needs: Open and Closed Theories in a Marxist Perspective*. Harvester, Brighton, UK.

Sport England (1997) *England, the Sporting Nation: a Strategy*. Sport England, London.

Sport England (1999) *The Value of Sport*. Sport England, London.

Sport England (2000) *Performance Measurement for Local Authority Sports Halls and Swimming Pools*. Sport England, London.

Sports Council (1968) *Planning for Sport*. Central Council for Physical Recreation, London.

Sports Council (1972) *Provision for Sport: Indoor Swimming Pools, Indoor Sports Centres, Golf Courses*. HMSO, London.

Sports Council (1975) *Indoor Sports Halls: a New Approach to their Dimensions and Use*. Sports Council, London.

Sports Council (1977) Capital grants for sports facilities: a 5-year programme. Duplicated typescript, Sports Council, London.

Sports Council (1978) *Provision for Swimming: a Guide to Swimming Pool Planning*. Sports Council, London.

Sports Council (1982) *Sport in the Community: the Next Ten Years*. Sports Council, London.

Sports Council (1988) *Sport in the Community: Into the 1990s*. Sports Council, London.

Sports Council (1991a) *The Playing Pitch Strategy*. Sports Council, London.

Sports Council (1991b) *District Sport and Recreation Strategies – a Guide*. Sports Council, London.

Sports Council (1993) *Planning and Provision for Sport*. Facilities Factfile 2. Sports Council, London.

Spretnik, C. and Capra, F. (1985) *Green Politics*. Paladin, London.

Springborg, P. (1981) *The Problem of Human Needs and the Critique of Civilization*. Allen & Unwin, London.

Stabler, M. (1996) The emerging new world of leisure quality: does it matter and can it be measured? In: Collins, M. (ed.) *Leisure in Industrial and Post-Industrial Societies*. Leisure Studies Association, Eastbourne, UK, pp. 249–268.

Stankey, G., McCool, S., Clark, R.N. and Brown, P.J. (1999) Institutional and organizational challenges to managing natural resources for recreation: a social learning model. In: Jackson, E.L. and Burton, T.L. (eds) *Leisure Studies: Prospects for the 21st Century*. Venture, State College, Pennsylvania, pp. 435–450.

Stansfield, C.A. and Rickert, J.E. (1970) The recreational business district. *Journal of Leisure Research* 2(4), 213–225.

Stein, T.A. and Sessoms, H.D. (1977) *Recreation and Special Populations*. Holbrook, Boston.

Stevenson, D. (2000) *Art and Organization: Making Australian Cultural Policy*. University of Queensland Press, St Lucia, Queensland.

Stretton, H. (1999) *Economics: a New Introduction*. UNSW Press, Sydney.

Stynes, D.J. (1983) Time series and structural models for forecasting recreation participation. In: Lieber, S.R. and Fesenmaier, D.R. (eds) *Recreation Planning and Management*. E. & F.N. Spon, London, pp. 105–119.

Swain, M.B. (1995) Gender in tourism. *Annals of Tourism Research* 22(1), 247–266.

Sylvester, C. (1999) The Western idea of work and leisure: traditions, transformations, and the future. In: Jackson, E.L. and Burton, T.L. (eds) *Leisure Studies: Prospects for the 21st Century.* Venture, State College, Pennsylvania, pp. 17–33.

Syme, G.J., Shaw, B.J., Fenton, D.M. and Mueller, W.S. (eds) (1989) *The Planning and Evaluation of Hallmark Events.* Avebury, Aldershot, UK.

Tasmanian Gaming Commission (2000) *Australian Gambling Statistics: 1972–1973 to 1998–1999.* Tasmanian Gaming Commission, Hobart.

Taylor, J.N. and Johnson, I.M. (1973) *Public Libraries and Their Use.* HMSO, London.

Taylor, P.W. (1959) 'Need' statements. *Analysis*, 19, 106–111.

Taylor, T. (ed.) (2000) *How You Play the Game: the Contribution of Sport to the Protection of Human Rights, Conference Proceedings.* University of Technology, Sydney.

Theobald, W.F. (1979) *Evaluation of Recreation and Parks Programs.* John Wiley & Sons, New York.

Thompson, P. (1999) Visitors with special needs. In: Dexter Lord, G. and Lord, B. (eds) *The Manual of Museum Planning*, 2nd edn. Stationery Office, London, pp. 69–84.

Throsby, C.D. and O'Shea, M. (1980) *The Regional Economic Impact of the Mildura Arts Centre.* Macquarie University, School of Economic and Social Studies, Sydney.

Throsby, C.D. and Withers, G.A. (1979) *Economics of the Performing Arts.* Edward Arnold, Melbourne.

Tinsley, H.E., Barrett, T.C. and Kass, R.A. (1977) Leisure activities and need satisfaction. *Journal of Leisure Research* 9(2), 110–120.

Tomlinson, A. (ed.) (1990) *Consumption, Identity and Style.* Comedia/Routledge, London.

Toohey, K. and Veal, A.J. (2000) *The Olympic Games: a Social Science Perspective.* CAB International, Wallingford, UK.

Torkildsen, G. (1993) *Torkildsen's Guides to Leisure Management.* Longman, Harlow, UK.

Torkildsen, G. (1999) *Leisure and Recreation Management*, 4th edn, E. & F.N. Spon, London.

Touche Ross (1985) *Michigan: State of the Arts – an Economic Impact Study: Independent Non-Profit Arts Organizations.* Touche Ross, Detroit, Michigan.

Tourism and Recreation Research Unit (1982) *Priority Groups and Access to Leisure Opportunity.* Department of Leisure Services, Lothian Regional Council, Edinburgh.

Tourism Forecasting Council (quarterly) *Forecast.* Office of National Tourism, Canberra.

Tourism New South Wales (1998) *New South Wales Tourism Masterplan to 2010: Action Plan 1998/99 to 2000/01.* Tourism NSW, Sydney.

Tribe, J. (1995) *The Economics of Leisure and Tourism: Environments, Markets and Impacts.* Butterworth-Heinemann, Oxford.

Turley, S.K. (2001) Children and the demand for recreational experiences: the case of zoos. *Leisure Studies* 20(1), 1–18.

Turner, B. (1994) General commentary. In: Turner, B. and Hamilton, P. (eds) *Citizenship: Critical Concepts.* London, Routledge, Vol. I, pp. xv–xxiv.

Turner, B. and Hamilton, P. (eds) (1994) *Citizenship: Critical Concepts.* London, Routledge.

UNESCO (United Nations Educational and Scientific Committee) (1982) UNESCO International Charter of Physical Education and Sport. *International Social Science Journal* 34, 303–306.

Urry, J. (1990) *The Tourist Gaze.* Sage, London.

Van der Stoep, G. (2000) Community tourism development. In: Gartner, W.C. and Lime, D.W. (eds) *Trends in Outdoor Recreation, Leisure and Tourism.* CAB International, Wallingford, UK, pp. 309–321.

Var, T. and Lee, C. (1993) Tourism forecasting: state-of-the-art techniques. In: Khan, M.A., Olsen, M.D. and Var, T. (eds) *VNR's Encyclopedia of Hospitality and Tourism.* Van Nostrand Reinhold, New York, pp. 679–696.

Veal, A.J. (1975) *Recreation Planning in New Communities: a Review of British Experience.* Research Memorandum 46, Centre for Urban and Regional Studies, University of Birmingham, Birmingham.

Veal, A.J. (1979a) *New Swimming Pool for Old.* Study 18, Sports Council, London.

Veal, A.J. (1979b) *Six Low Cost Indoor Sports Facilities.* Study 20, Sports Council, London.

Veal, A.J. (1980) *Trends in Leisure Participation and Problems of Forecasting.* Sports Council/SSRC, London.

Veal, A.J. (1982a) The future of leisure. *International Journal of Tourism Management* 1(1), 42–55.

Veal, A.J. (1982b) *Planning for Leisure: Alternative Approaches.* Papers in Leisure Studies No. 5, Polytechnic of North London, London.

Veal, A.J. (1984) Planning for leisure: alternative approaches. *World Leisure and Recreation* 26(5), 17–24.

Veal, A.J. (1986) Planning for leisure: alternative approaches. *The Planner* 72(6), 9–12.

Veal, A.J. (1987) *Leisure and the Future*. Allen & Unwin, London.

Veal, A.J. (1991) *Australian Leisure Futures*. Publication 13, Centre for Leisure and Tourism Studies, University of Technology, Sydney.

Veal, A.J. (1993a) Lifestyle, leisure and neighbourhood. In: Veal, A.J., Jonson, P. and Cushman, G. (eds) *Leisure and Tourism: Social and Environmental Change, World Leisure and Recreation Association 1991 Congress Proceedings*. Centre for Leisure and Tourism Studies, University of Technology, Sydney, pp. 404–413.

Veal, A.J. (1993b) Planning for leisure: past, present and future. In: Glyptis, S. (ed.) *Leisure and the Environment*. Belhaven, London, pp. 85–95.

Veal, A.J. (1994a) The future of outdoor recreation. In: Mercer, D. (ed.) *Perspectives on Australian Outdoor Recreation*. Hepper-Marriott, Melbourne, pp. 153–159.

Veal, A.J. (1994b) *Leisure Policy and Planning*. Longman, Harlow, UK.

Veal, A.J. (1997) *Research Methods for Leisure and Tourism*. 2nd edn. Financial Times-Pitman, London.

Veal, A.J. (1998) Leisure studies, pluralism and social democracy. *Leisure Studies* 17(4), 249–268.

Veal, A.J. and Lynch, R. (1998) Economics versus leisure in the development of gambling in Australia. *Annals of Leisure Research* 1, 67–84.

Veal, A.J. and Lynch, R. (2001) *Australian Leisure*, 2nd edn. Longman, Sydney.

Veal, A.J. (2002) A brief history of work. In: Haworth, J.T. and Veal, A.J. (eds) *Work and Leisure*. Routledge, London.

Veal, A.J., Jonson, P. and Cushman, G. (eds) (1993) *Leisure and Tourism: Social and Environmental Change, World Leisure and Recreation Association 1991 Congress Proceedings*. Centre for Leisure and Tourism Studies, University of Technology, Sydney.

Vickerman, R. (1983) The contribution of economics to the study of leisure. *Leisure Studies* 2(3), 345–364.

Vickerman, R. (1989) Economic models of leisure and its impact. In: Jackson, E.L. and Burton, T.L. (eds) *Understanding Leisure and Recreation – Mapping the Past, Charting the Future*. Venture, State College, Pennsylvania, pp. 331–357.

Villiers, P. (2001) *Human Rights: a Practical Guide for Managers*. Kogan Page, London.

Voase, R. (1997) The role of flagship cultural projects in urban regeneration: a case-study and commentary. *Managing Leisure* 2(4), 230–241.

Wall, G. (1983) The economic value of cultural facilities: tourism in Toronto. In: Lieber, S.R. and Fesenmaier, D.R. (eds) *Recreation Planning and Management*. E. & F.N. Spon, London, pp. 15–25.

Walzer, N. (ed.) (1996) *Community Strategic Visioning Programs*. Praeger, Westport, Connecticut.

Waters, I. (1989) *Entertainment, Arts and Cultural Services*. Longman, Harlow, UK.

Watkins, G. (1981) Reflections on life. Be in it: still searching for a soul. In: Heine, R. *et al.* (eds) *Consolidation through Integration – Health, Physical Education, Recreation, Sport, Papers from the 13th ACHPER National Biennial Conference, Melbourne, January*. Australian Council for Health, Physical Education and Recreation, Canberra, pp. 113–122.

WCED – see World Commission on Environment and Development

Wearing, B. (1990) Beyond the ideology of motherhood: leisure as resistance. *Australia and New Zealand Journal of Sociology* 26(1), 36–58.

Wearing, B. (1995) Leisure and resistance in an ageing society. *Leisure Studies* 14(4), 263–279.

Wearing, B. (1998) *Leisure and Feminist Theory*. Sage, London.

Wearing, S. and McLean, J. (1997) *Developing Ecotourism: a Community Based Approach*. HM Leisure Planning, Williamstown, Victoria.

Wearing, S. and Neil, J. (1999) *Ecotourism: Impacts, Potential and Possibilities*. Butterworth-Heinemann, Oxford.

Webb, J. (1998) *Junk Male: Reflections on Australian Masculinity*. Harper Collins, Sydney.

Weber, M. (1930) *The Protestant Ethic and the Spirit of Capitalism* (1976 edn). Allen & Unwin, London.

Weir, A. (1999) *Elizabeth the Queen*. Pimlico/Random House, London.

Welch, D. (1991) *The Management of Urban Parks*. Longman, Harlow, UK.

Wheelen, T.L. and Hunger, J.D. (1989) *Strategic Management and Business Policy*. Addison-Wesley, Reading, Massachusetts.

White, G. (2000) Using a community vision to develop integrated plans. *Australian Parks and Leisure* 3(2), 20–25.

Wilkinson, G. and Monkhouse, E. (1994) Strategic planning in public sector organizations. *Executive Development* 7(6), 16–19.

Williams, C. (1998a) Is the SERVQUAL model an appropriate management tool for measuring service delivery quality in the UK leisure industry? *Managing Leisure* 3(2), 98–110.

Williams, C. (1998b) Application of the SERVQUAL model to the UK leisure industry: are they servicing the service rather than servicing the customer? In: Collins, M.F. and Cooper, I.S. (eds) *Leisure Management: Issues and Applications.* CAB International, Wallingford, UK, pp. 225–254.

Williams, E.A., Jenkins, C. and Nevill, A.M. (1988) Social area influences on leisure activity – an exploration of the ACORN classification with reference to sport. *Leisure Studies* 7(1), 81–94.

Williams, S. (1995) *Outdoor Recreation and the Urban Environment.* Routledge, London.

Willis, M. (1968) The provision of sports pitches. *Town Planning Review* 38(2), 293–303.

Wilson, J. (1988) *Politics and Leisure.* Unwin Hyman, London.

Wimbush, E. and Talbot, M. (eds) (1988) *Relative Freedoms: Women and Leisure.* Open University Press, Milton Keynes.

Withers, G. (1981) The great arts funding debate. *Meanjin* 40(4), 442–449.

Witt, S.F. and Witt, C.W. (1992) *Modelling and Forecasting Demand in Tourism.* Academic Press, London.

World Commission on Environment and Development (1990) *Our Common Future – Australian Edition (the Brundtland Report).* Oxford University Press, Melbourne.

World Leisure (2000) *Charter for Leisure.* World Leisure, Okanagan Falls, British Columbia.

World Tourism Organization (1998) *Global Code of Ethics for Tourism,* WTO, Madrid (viewed at: www.world-tourism.org. Jan. 2002).

World Tourism Organization (2001) *Tourism Highlights.* WTO, Madrid, at www.world-tourism.org (viewed January 2002).

World Tourism Organization Business Council (1999) *Changes in Leisure Time: the Impact on Tourism.* WTO, Madrid.

Wortman, M.S. (1979) Strategic management: not-for-profit organizations. In: Schendel, D.E. and Hofer, C.W. (eds) *Strategic Management.* Little, Brown, Boston, Massachusetts, pp. 353–381.

Young, M. and Willmott, P. (1973) *The Symmetrical Family.* Routledge, London.

Young, S. (1980) Children's play in residential settings. In: Mercer, D. and Hamilton-Smith, E. (eds) *Recreation Planning and Social Change in Urban Australia.* Sorrett, Malvern, Victoria, pp. 85–95.

Yule, J. (1997a) Engendered ideologies and leisure policy in the UK. Part 1: gendered ideologies. *Leisure Studies* 16(2), 61–84.

Yule, J. (1997b) Engendered ideologies and leisure policy in the UK. Part 2: professional ideologies. *Leisure Studies* 16(3), 139–154.

Zalatan, A. (1994) *Forecasting Methods in Sports and Recreation.* Thompson Educational Publishing, Toronto.

Zukin, S. (1995) *The Cultures of Cities.* Blackwell, Oxford.

Zuzanek, J. and Veal, A.J. (1999) Trends in time pressure: two ends against the middle? *Loisir et Société* 21(2) 319–326.

Author Index

Subject Index

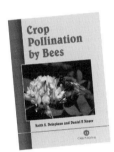
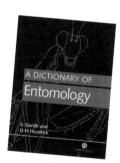
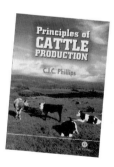